AFRICAN POLITICAL, ECONOMIC AND SECURITY ISSUES

ECONOMIC, POLITICAL AND SOCIAL ISSUES OF AFRICA

AFRICAN POLITICAL, ECONOMIC AND SECURITY ISSUES

Additional books in this series can be found on Nova's website under the Series tab.

Additional E-books in this series can be found on Nova's website under the E-books tab.

AFRICAN POLITICAL, ECONOMIC AND SECURITY ISSUES

ECONOMIC, POLITICAL AND SOCIAL ISSUES OF AFRICA

JEREMY S. MCQUEEN
EDITOR

Nova Science Publishers, Inc.
New York

Library of Congress Cataloging-in-Publication Data

Economic, political, and social issues of Africa / editor, Jeremy S.
McQueen.
p. cm.
Includes index.
ISBN 978-1-61209-957-6 (hardcover)
1. Africa--Politics and government--21st century. 2. Africa--Economic
conditions--21st century. 3. Africa--Social conditions--21st century. I.
McQueen, Jeremy S.
JQ1875.E267 2011
960.3'3--dc22

2011005018

Published by Nova Science Publishers, Inc. †New York

CONTENTS

PREFACE

This new book presents and discusses the current economic, political and social issues of Africa. Topics discussed include current conditions and prospects for a lasting peace in Somalia; the crisis in Darfur and status of the North-South Peace Agreement; conditions and issues in Algeria, Kenya and Tunisia; the Democratic Republic of Congo; piracy off the horn of Africa and international criminal court cases in Africa.

Chapter 1 - Tunisia has a stable, highly authoritarian government led by President Zine ben Ali, who was elected to a fourth term on October 24, 2004 and will run for a fifth term in October 2009. Ben Ali's Constitutional Democratic Rally party controls parliament, state and local governments, and most political activity. There are significant limitations on human rights but marked advancements for women and girls. Tunisia has experienced occasional attacks by Islamist terrorists, and Tunisian expatriates have been arrested in Europe and North America on terrorism- related charges. Tunisia is a non-oil-exporting, middle-class country with a diverse, growing economy, and high unemployment. U.S.-Tunisian relations today largely emphasize cooperation in terrorism, although Tunisia would like greater focus on trade.

Chapter 2 - In February 2006, Ugandans voted in the first multi-party elections in almost 26 years. President Yoweri Museveni and his ruling National Revolutionary Movement (NRM) parliamentary candidates won a decisive victory over opposition candidate Kizza Besigye and the Forum for Democracy Coalition. Nevertheless, poll results showed a notable decline in support for President Museveni from previous elections. International election observers did not condemn the election results, nor did they fully endorse the electoral process. Critics charged the government with intimidating the opposition during the pre-election period, and Besigye spent much of the campaign period in jail. The election followed a controversial move by the Ugandan parliament in July 2005 to remove the constitutional two-term limit on the presidency.

In the north, the government of Uganda has long fought the Lord's Resistance Army (LRA), an armed rebel group backed by the government of Sudan. Through over 20 years of civil war, the brutal insurgency has created a humanitarian crisis that has displaced over 1.5 million and resulted in the abduction of over 20,000 children. In 2006-07, the government of Uganda and the LRA have been actively engaged in an effort to resolve the conflict peacefully. The Government of Southern Sudan (GOSS) has been mediating the talks since June 2006. In August 2006, the government of Uganda and the LRA signed a Cessation of

Hostilities Agreement. In February 2008, the parties agreed on a Permanent Ceasefire, amended the Agreement on Accountability and Reconciliation, and Agreement on Comprehensive Solutions. However, the leader of the LRA, Joseph Kony, failed to show up for the final signing of the agreement on a number of occasions. Kony and his forces are in the Democratic Republic of Congo (DRC).

The cessation of hostilities has allowed an estimated 400,000 displaced people to return to their homes. In June 2007, the parties signed an agreement on Accountability and Reconciliation. In late October, a LRA delegation went to Kampala for the first time and held talks with senior Ugandan officials. In October, Vincent Otti, the Deputy Commander of the LRA, reportedly was killed in Uganda by Joseph Kony, the head of the LRA. Over the past several months, a number of senior LRA commanders have surrendered to authorities in the Democratic Republic of Congo (DRC) and Uganda.

In late October 2007, President Museveni visited Washington, D.C. and met with President Bush and other senior administration officials. President Museveni also met with several Members of Congress. During his visit, President Museveni discussed a wide range of issues, including U.S.- Uganda relations, the crises in Somalia and Darfur, trade, and HIV/AIDS. Uganda deployed an estimated 1,800 peacekeeping troops to Somalia, shortly after Ethiopian forces invaded Mogadishu and installed the Transitional Federal Government (TFG). Ugandan forces have not been a major target of the insurgents in Mogadishu, although a number of Ugandan peacekeepers have been killed over the past several months.

Chapter 3 - Sudan, geographically the largest country in Africa, has been ravaged by civil war intermittently for four decades. More than 2 million people have died in Southern Sudan over the past two decades due to war-related causes and famine, and millions have been displaced from their homes. There were many failed attempts to end the civil war in southern Sudan. In July 2002, the Sudan government and the Sudan People's Liberation Movement (SPLM) signed a peace framework agreement in Kenya. On May 26, 2004, the government of Sudan and the SPLM signed three protocols on Power Sharing, on the Nuba Mountains and Southern Blue Nile, and on the long disputed Abyei area. The signing of these protocols resolved all outstanding issues between the parties. On June 5, 2004, the parties signed "the Nairobi Declaration on the Final Phase of Peace in the Sudan." On January 9, 2005, the government of Sudan and the SPLM signed the final peace agreement at a ceremony held in Nairobi, Kenya.

In October 2007, the government of Southern Sudan suspended the participation of its Ministers, State Ministers, and Presidential Advisors from the Government of National Unity to protest measures taken by the National Congress Party and to demand full implementation of the Comprehensive Peace Agreement (CPA). In response to these demands and unexpected developments, President Bashir reportedly accepted a number of the government of South Sudan (GoSS) demands in late October, except those related to the Abyei issue. In late December 2007, the new ministers were sworn in office. In May 2008, Government forces burned Abyei town and displaced more than 60,000 people. An agreement reached in June 2008 between the Government of South Sudan (GoSS) and the National Congress Party (NCP) on Abyei largely ended the tense situation between the two sides.

The crisis in Darfur began in February 2003, when two rebel groups emerged to challenge the National Congress Party (NCP) government in Darfur. The crisis in Darfur in western Sudan has led to a major humanitarian disaster, with an estimated 2.45 million people displaced, more than 240,000 people forced into neighboring Chad, and an estimated 450,000 people killed. In July 2004, the House and Senate declared the atrocities in Darfur genocide, and the Bush Administration reached the same conclusion in September 2004. On May 4, 2006, the Government of National Unity and the Sudan Liberation Movement/Army (SLM/A) signed the Darfur Peace Agreement (DPA) after almost two years of negotiations.

In July 2007, the U.N. Security Council passed Resolution 1769, authorizing the deployment of a robust peacekeeping force to Darfur. The resolution calls for the deployment of 26,000 peacekeeping troops to Darfur. The resolution authorized the United Nations African Union force in Darfur (UNAMID) to take all necessary measures to protect its personnel and humanitarian workers. As of May 31, 2009, UNAMID deployed a total of 16,402 peacekeeping personnel. In July 2008, International Criminal Court (ICC) Chief Prosecutor Luis Moreno-Ocampo accused President Omar Bashir of Sudan of genocide, crimes against humanity, and war crimes and asked ICC judges to issue an arrest warrant for President Bashir. On March 4, 2009, the ICC Pre-Trial Chamber issued a warrant of arrest for President Bashir for war crimes and crimes against humanity.

Chapter 4 - The situation in Algeria is fluid. Parliament passed a constitutional amendment abolishing term limits, allowing President Abdelaziz Bouteflika to be reelected for a third term in April 2009. The voice of the military, the most significant political force since independence, has been muted. Low voter turnout in the May 2007 parliamentary election may have indicated lack of public faith in the political system, and so the authorities specifically boasted a higher turnout in the 2009 presidential election. Domestic terrorism persists and Algerians continue to be linked to terror abroad. The U.S. State Departments lists the two Algerian groups as Foreign Terrorist Organizations (FTOs). The most notorious is Al Qaeda in the Land of the Islamic Maghreb (AQLIM), which pledged allegiance to Al Qaeda. Terrorism provides a rationale for Algeria's uneven human rights record. Oil and gas revenues have grown markedly, but public investment has yet to remedy the country's many socioeconomic ills. Bouteflika has energized foreign policy and broadened cooperation with the United States. This report will be updated if warranted. See also CRS Report RS20962, *Western Sahara: Status of Settlement Efforts*, by Carol Migdalovitz.

Chapter 5 - Kenya, a nation of about 36.9 million people, has been an important ally of the United States for decades. Kenya moved from a one-party state to a multi-party democracy in 1992. Kenyans voted in record numbers in the country's first multi-party election in almost 26 years. President Daniel arap Moi defeated opposition candidates by a small margin. In 1997, Kenya held its second multiparty elections, at the height of tensions between the opposition and the ruling party. President Moi was re-elected with 40% of the votes cast, while his nearest rival, Mwai Kibaki, won 31%. In the 2002 presidential and parliamentary elections, the opposition National Rainbow Coalition (NARC) defeated the ruling Kenya African National Union (KANU). In the presidential election, NARC leader Kibaki defeated Uhuru Kenyatta, the leader of KANU.

On December 27, 2007, millions of Kenyans went to the polls in Kenya's fourth multi-party elections, with the hope of strengthening the institutions of democracy and, most important in the view of many observers, of bringing change. An estimated 14.2 million (82% of the total eligible voters) Kenyans were registered to vote, while 2,547 Parliamentary candidates were qualified to run in 210 constituencies, according to the Electoral Commission of Kenya (ECK). Nine candidates competed in the presidential election. The opposition reportedly made significant gains in the parliamentary elections. The ECK, however, hastily declared President Kibaki as the winner of the elections. Kibaki was quickly sworn in as president, while international and domestic election observers declared the elections as rigged and deeply flawed.

Following the announcement of the election results, violence erupted in many parts of Kenya. More than 1,000 people have been killed and an estimated 350,000 reportedly displaced. In August 2008, the Kenya National Commission on Human Rights (KNCHR) released a report on the post-election violence. In early February, the opposition and the government began negotiations under the leadership of former U.N. Secretary General Kofi Annan. The two parties agreed to work together to end the violence, improve humanitarian conditions, and to write a new constitution within a year. In late February, the government and the opposition reached a power- sharing arrangement. On March 18, 2008, the Kenya parliament unanimously approved the Agreement. On April 3, 2008, the parties agreed on a 40-member cabinet. But important reforms agreed to by the parties have yet to be implemented.

The initial United States government reaction to the December elections was considered by some international observers as contradictory and seen by some Kenyans as being one-sided in favor of President Kibaki. On December 30, the United States government reportedly congratulated President Kibaki. Senior Bush Administration officials visited Kenya in an effort to resolve the crisis and provided support to Kofi Annan's mediation efforts. In June 2008, Prime Minister Raila Odinga visited Washington and met with senior Bush Administration officials and Members of Congress.

Chapter 6 - Tunisia has a stable, highly authoritarian government led by President Zine ben Ali, who was elected to a fourth term on October 24, 2004 and will run for a fifth term in October 2009. Ben Ali's Constitutional Democratic Rally party controls parliament, state and local governments, and most political activity. There are significant limitations on human rights but marked advancements for women and girls. Tunisia has experienced occasional attacks by Islamist terrorists, and Tunisian expatriates have been arrested in Europe and North America on terrorism- related charges. Tunisia is a non-oil-exporting, middle-class country with a diverse, growing economy, and high unemployment. U.S.-Tunisian relations today largely emphasize cooperation in terrorism, although Tunisia would like greater focus on trade

Chapter 7 - In October 2008, the forces of the National Congress for the Defense of the Congolese People (CNDP), under the command of General Laurent Nkunda, launched a major offensive against the Democratic Republic of Congo Armed Forces (FARDC) in eastern Congo. Within days, the CNDP captured a number of small towns and Congolese forces retreated in large numbers.

Eastern Congo has been in a state of chaos for over a decade. The first rebellion to oust the late President Mobutu Sese Seko began in the city of Goma in the mid-1990s. The second rebellion in the late 1990s began also in eastern Congo. The root causes of the current crisis are the presence of over a dozen militia and extremist groups, both foreign and Congolese, in eastern Congo, and the failure to fully implement peace agreements signed by the parties. Over the past fourteen years, the former Rwandese armed forces and the Interhamwe militia have been given a safe haven in eastern Congo and have carried out many attacks inside Rwanda and against Congolese civilians. A Ugandan rebel group, the Lord's Resistance Army (LRA) is also in Congo, despite an agreement reached between the LRA and the Government of Uganda.

In November 2008, United Nations Secretary General Ban Ki-Moon appointed former Nigerian President Olusegun Obasanjo as his envoy to help broker a peace agreement to end the crisis in eastern Congo. Since his appointment, Obasanjo has met with President Joseph Kabila, General Nkunda, President Paul Kagame, and other officials in the region. The parties have agreed to participate in a U.N.-led peace initiative. The current crisis in eastern Congo has displaced more than 250,000 civilians.

In late 2008, the governments of Rwanda and Congo agreed on a wide range of issues. The two governments agreed to launch a joint military offensive against the National Congress for the Defense of the Congolese People (CNDP) and the FDLR. They also agreed to restore full diplomatic relations and to activate economic cooperation. In January 2009, Rwanda and Congo launched the joint military operation in eastern Congo. In late February Rwandese forces pulled out of Congo as part of an agreement reached with Congo.

The United States has been actively engaged in facilitating the Tripartite Plus talks among the four key players in the Great Lakes region: Rwanda, DRC, Burundi, and Uganda. The Tripartite Plus process has led to a number of agreements over the past several years, including the creation of a Joint Verification Mechanism (JVM) to address cross-border issues. The Bush Administration provided an estimated $205.1 million in FY2008, and an estimated $199.7 million for FY2009. The Obama Administration has requested $177 million for FY2010.

Chapter 8 - Zimbabwe's prospects appeared promising in 1980, as it gained independence after a long liberation war. Rising inflation and unemployment bred discontent in the 1990s and led in 1999 to the formation of the opposition Movement for Democratic Change (MDC). The new party surprised many with its initial success, campaigning against a 2000 referendum that would have legalized the president's continued rule, made government officials immune from prosecution, and allowed the uncompensated seizure of white-owned land for redistribution to black farmers. The referendum failed, and the MDC won nearly half the seats in the 2000 parliamentary election. The government of President Robert Mugabe has since taken numerous, often undemocratic actions to bolster its power.

President Mugabe's government has been seen in the past decade as autocratic and repressive by its critics, and its human rights record is poor. The government has suppressed freedom of speech and assembly, and many contend that the government has restricted access to food, already scarce, in opposition areas. The MDC, divided over how to respond, split into two factions in 2005, hampering its ability to challenge the ruling party. Reports of political violence rose sharply after Zimbabwe's March 2008 elections, when, for the first time since independence, Mugabe's party lost its majority in the National Assembly. Mugabe's re-election as president in the June runoff was viewed as illegitimate by the United States and the United Nations Secretary-General, among others. In September 2008, after several weeks of negotiations, Mugabe and MDC leader Morgan Tsvangirai signed a power-sharing arrangement aimed at resolving the political standoff. As part of the deal, Tsvangirai became Prime Minister of a new coalition government in February 2009, and cabinet positions have been divided among the parties. Many observers are skeptical that the MDC will be able to implement major reforms through the arrangement, although there has been some initial progress. The cost of rebuilding the economy may be as high as $8 billion.

Zimbabwe's economic output has decreased dramatically since 1998. Official inflation rose above 200,000,000% in 2008, and unemployment is estimated at more than 90%. The adult HIV prevalence rate of 15.3% has contributed to a sharp drop in life expectancy, and three-quarters of the population is expected to require food aid in early 2009. The country has yet to contain a cholera outbreak with over 90,000 infections and over 4,000 deaths. Deteriorating conditions have led many to emigrate to neighboring countries, creating a substantial burden on the region.

Robert Mugabe has enjoyed considerable popularity in Africa as a former liberation leader, but some African leaders have viewed his policies as damaging to the continent and have urged democratic reforms. Following controversial elections in 2000 and citing abuses of human rights and the rule of law, the United States and some other former allies of the government became vocal critics. The United States has enforced targeted sanctions against top Zimbabwe officials and associates since 2002. This report provides background on events leading up to the country's most recent elections, in March and June 2008. For further discussion of those elections, the coalition government, and other current events, please see CRS Report RL34509, *Zimbabwe: The Power Sharing Agreement and Implications for U.S. Policy*, by Lauren Ploch.

Chapter 9 - Recent attacks, including those on U.S.-flagged vessels, in the waters off the Horn of Africa have brought new U.S. and international attention to the long-standing problem of piracy in the region. The International Maritime Bureau recorded 111 attacks in the waters off the Horn of Africa in 2008, almost double the number in 2007. As of April 20, 2009, The International Maritime Bureau had counted 84 attacks since January: approximately 300 non-U.S. crew members on 18 hijacked vessels remain in Somali captivity. Previously concentrated in the Gulf of Aden between Yemen and the northern coast of Somalia and along the country's eastern coastline, attacks on merchant ships are now taking place over an area of more than 1 million sq. miles in the Gulf and the west Indian Ocean, posing a significant threat to commercial shipping. Pirate attacks also have threatened relief shipments bound for East Africa and the countries of the Horn, amid a humanitarian crisis in the region that experts are calling the worst since 1984.

The increase in pirate attacks off the Horn of Africa is directly linked to continuing insecurity and the absence of the rule of law in war-torn Somalia. The absence of a functioning government in Somalia remains the single greatest challenge to regional security and provides freedom of action for those engaged in piracy along the Somali coast. Some observers also have alleged that the absence of coastal security authorities in Somalia has allowed illegal international fishing and maritime dumping to occur in Somali waters, which in turn has undermined the economic prospects of some Somalis and may be providing economic or political motivation to some groups engaged in piracy. The apparent motive of many active Somali pirate groups is profit, and piracy has proven to be a lucrative activity for many thus far. Ransoms paid to Somali pirates and their supporters, estimated at over $30 million in 2008, may exacerbate ongoing fighting and further undermine security in the region.

The U.N. Security Council issued four resolutions (1816, 1838, 1846, and 1851) in 2008 to facilitate an international response to piracy off the Horn of Africa. At present, Resolution 1851 has authorized international naval forces to carry out anti-piracy operations in Somali territorial waters and ashore, with the consent of Somalia's Transitional Federal Government (TFG). In January 2009, a multilateral Contact Group on Piracy off the Coast of Somalia (CGPCS) was established to coordinate antipiracy efforts. U.S., NATO, European Union, regional, and other naval forces are currently patrolling waters near Somalia in coordination with a U.S.-led Task Force.

Some members of the 111th Congress have expressed concern about the threat posed by piracy, and President Obama has stated that his Administration is resolved to halt the rise of piracy in the Horn of Africa region. On April 15, the Obama Administration outlined preliminary plans for a more robust policy response to the threat of piracy and pledged to continue working through multilateral coordination and enforcement mechanisms established during the Bush Administration. Most experts believe that the reestablishment of government authority in Somalia is the only guarantee that piracy will not persist or reemerge as a threat. Congress may seek to influence U.S. policy through oversight of U.S. military operations and diplomacy and through foreign assistance appropriations and authorizations. Also see CRS Report RL339 11, Somalia: Current Conditions and Prospects for a Lasting Peace, by Ted Dagne and CRS Report R4008 1, *Ocean Piracy and Its Impact on Insurance,* by Rawle O. King

Chapter 10 - The International Criminal Court (ICC), established in 2002, has to-date initiated investigations exclusively in Sub-Saharan Africa. The ICC Prosecutor has opened cases against 16 individuals for alleged crimes in northern Uganda, the Democratic Republic of Congo, the Central African Republic, and the Darfur region of Sudan. In addition, the Prosecutor is analyzing situations—a preliminary step toward initiating a full investigation—in Kenya, Côte d'Ivoire, and Chad, as well as in Colombia, Afghanistan, and Georgia. Recent congressional interest in the work of the ICC in Africa has arisen from concern over gross human rights violations on the African continent and beyond.

On March 4, 2009, ICC judges issued an arrest warrant for Sudanese President Omar Hassan alBashir for war crimes and crimes against humanity. The case against Bashir represents the first attempt by the ICC to prosecute a sitting head of state. The prosecution has drawn praise from human rights advocates as a step toward ending impunity for serious human rights abuses in Africa. However, it also has raised concerns that ICC actions could endanger peace processes in Darfur and southern Sudan. Additional fears that the ICC could imperil international humanitarian operations in Sudan were heightened when the Sudanese government responded to the warrant by expelling international relief agencies.

Unlike the three other African countries under ICC investigation, Sudan is not a party to the ICC; instead, the ICC was granted jurisdiction over Darfur through a United Nations Security Council resolution in March 2005. The United States, as a member of the Security Council, may influence the ICC's actions. Obama Administration officials have expressed support for the prosecution of perpetrators of atrocities in Darfur and have suggested that Bashir should face the accusations against him. Legislation before the 111th Congress references the ICC warrant against Bashir and, more broadly, U.S. government support for ICC prosecutions.

Four suspects in other ICC investigations are currently in ICC custody, pending trial. Three are alleged leaders of Congolese militias, and the fourth is a former Congolese rebel leader, transitional vice president, and senator and who is accused of overseeing war crimes in neighboring Central African Republic. Additionally, a Darfur rebel leader summoned by ICC judges voluntarily appeared before the Court in May.

This report provides background on ICC investigations in Africa and gives an overview of cases currently before the Court. The report also examines issues raised by the ICC's actions in Africa, including the ICC's possible role in deterring future abuses and the potential impact of international criminal prosecutions on peace processes, ongoing in many countries on the continent. In-depth background on U.S. policy toward the ICC can be found in CRS Report RL31495, U.*S. Policy Regarding the International Criminal Court (ICC),* by Jennifer K. Elsea.

In: Economic, Political and Social Issues of Africa
Editor: Jeremy S. McQueen

ISBN 978-1-61209-957-6

Chapter 1

SOMALIA: CURRENT CONDITIONS AND PROSPECTS FOR A LASTING PEACE*

Ted Dagne

ABSTRACT

In October 2002, the Inter-Governmental Authority for Development (IGAD) launched a peace process designed to end factional fighting in Somalia, led by the government of Kenya. In September 2003, the parties agreed on a Transitional National Charter (TNC). In August 2004, a 275-member Transitional Parliament was inaugurated in Kenya. In October 2004, parliament elected Abdullahi Yusuf Ahmed as the new president of Somalia. In June 2006, the forces of the Islamic Courts Union (ICU) took control of the capital, Mogadishu. During the six-month rule by the ICU, Mogadishu became relatively peaceful, but efforts to bring peace did not lead to a major breakthrough. On December 28, 2006 Ethiopian troops captured Mogadishu with little resistance from the ICU. The Ethiopian intervention led to more chaos and instability in Somalia over the past two years. Humanitarian, political, and security conditions continue to deteriorate across south-central Somalia. In the past two years, more than 15,000 civilians have been killed, an estimated 1.1 million people displaced, and 476,000 Somalis have fled to neighboring countries. In 2008, fighting between insurgent groups and Ethiopian-TFG forces intensified, and by late 2008, the TFG had lost control of most of south-central Somalia to insurgent groups. In November 2008, the Ethiopian government announced that its forces would pull out of Somalia by the end of 2008. In January 2009, Ethiopian forces completed their withdrawal from Somalia. In late December 2008, President Yusuf resigned from office and left for Yemen.

In June 2008, the TFG and the Alliance for the Re-Liberation of Somalia (ARS), a group dominated by members of the ICU, signed an agreement in Djibouti mediated by United Nations Special Envoy Ahmedou Ould-Abdullah. The parties agreed to a cease-fire, the withdrawal of Ethiopian forces, and the deployment of a United Nations peacekeeping force. Several towns are now administered by the ARS,

* This is an edited, reformatted and augmented version of CRS Report RL33911, dated May 21, 2009.

including Jowhar and Beledweyne. A number of other towns, including the third largest town, Kismaayo, are now under the control of the Al-Shabaab, a group opposed to the TFG and the ARS-Dj ibouti faction. The next phase of the Somali conflict is likely to occur between the ARS and the Al-Shabaab. In February 2008, Secretary of State Condoleezza Rice designated Al-Shabaab as a Foreign Terrorist Organization. In January 2009, the Somali Parliament elected the leader of the ARS, Sheikh Sharif Sheikh Ahmad as president. In February 2009, President Ahmad appointed Omar Abdirashid Ali Sharmarke as prime minister.

Meanwhile, Somali pirates have intensified their attacks in the Gulf of Aden, carrying out attacks on over 90 commercial ships, and successfully hijacked over 35 ships in 2008. Currently an estimated 14-18 ships are under the control of the pirates, including a Saudi-owned supertanker, Sirius Star, and a Ukrainian-owned ship, MV Faina, with 33 T-72 tanks and other weapons. In January-February 2009, Somali pirates released a number of the hijacked ships, including the MV Faina. The pirates have earned more than $120 million in ransom payments, and have released a number of the ships and crew members. The United States, Russia, India, and several other countries have deployed warships to tackle piracy in the Horn of Africa region. Some insurgent leaders have warned the pirates to end their illegal activities and to release crew members and ships that they currently control. This report will be updated as circumstances warrant.. According to the International Maritime Bureau (IMB), piracy in the first quarter of 2009 has surpassed that of 2008. According to IMB, "in 2008, there were 111 incidents including 42 vessels hijacked. So far in 2009, there have been 29 successful hijackings from 114 attempted attacks."

Recent Developments

Ongoing Fighting in Mogadishu

In early May 2009, Somali extremist groups backed by foreign fighters, launched a major offensive against the Transitional Federal Government (TFG) of Somalia and the African Union Mission to Somalia (AMISOM). Over the past ten days, more than 150 people have been killed and over 400 wounded. The primary objective of this offensive is to oust the TFG from power and force AMISOM to leave Somalia. Several Al-Shabaab factions, Hizb al-Islam, and foreign fighters have been engaged in a series of battles against government forces. Senior Somali officials, African Union sources, and other regional officials estimate that more than 400 foreign fighters from Afghanistan, Yemen, Pakistan, the United States, Canada, United Kingdom, and Saudi Arabia have been engaged in support of the Al-Shabaab forces over the past week. More than 290 fighters reportedly entered Mogadishu in the past two weeks, while an estimated 50 fighters were in Mogadishu for much longer.

The U.S. State Department issued a press release confirming the presence of foreign fighters in Mogadishu, while France, the United Nations, and the African Union made similar statements. According to senior security sources in Mogadishu and regional officials, an estimated 10 foreigners have taken the lead to command both Somali and foreign fighters in Mogadishu and other parts of Somalia. In May 2009, the spokesman of Al-Shabaab admitted that foreign fighters have joined the fighting. According to Sheik Husayn Fidow, "the Muslim people of Somalia have asked for assistance from other Muslim nations worldwide." In response to these well coordinated attacks, TFG President Sheik Sharif Ahmad stated that "the administration is prepared to preserve until free elections are held. We shall persist to make sure free elections are the only method to bring about the transition of power and not through the barrel of the gun."

In late April 2009, Sheik Sharif Hassan Aweys returned to Mogadishu from Eritrea. Sheik Aweys had remained in Eritrea and formed his own faction after the top leadership of the Alliance for the Re-Liberation of Somalia (ARS) signed an agreement in Djibouti with other Somali parties, which led to the formation of the current government. ARS-Asmara, under the leadership of Aweys, did not garner significant support, although Aweys intensified his support for the extremist groups inside Somalia. ARS-Asmara leaders were not in full agreement with Aweys and his support for the extremist groups inside Somalia. They provided written documentation to a visitor in April 2009. These leaders stated that they have formed their own organization and would disassociate themselves from Aweys [1]. Sheik Aweys came under intense pressure from some of his supporters in recent months to return to Mogadishu. He also came to the conclusion that he was isolated and losing support in Eritrea. Sheik Aweys seemed confused at times and routinely contradicted himself in a recent interview in Asmara, Eritrea [2]. When asked if he was prepared to state publicly his support for a peaceful participation in the current political process, Aweys responded positively.

However, when he was asked whether he would denounce terrorism and call for an end to violence against civilians, Aweys stated that since he considers the American interpretation of terrorism is targeting Islam, he "can not condemn terrorism. Doing so, he asserted, is denouncing his own religion." Aweys believes that he was placed on the U.S. terrorism list because of his religion and beliefs. When asked if he wished to be removed from the list, Aweys stated that he will not seek to be removed because that will be going against his religion. Sheik Aweys asserted that since there are no major differences among Somalis, if left alone, Somalis will find their own solution. When confronted about his role in support of terrorism and violence in Somalia, he characterized these acts as a struggle against the enemies of Somalia. Upon his return to Mogadishu in late April 2009, Sheik Aweys discovered that the clan elders and militia who supported him in the past now wanted him to work with the government and end the violence. The militia group he helped create, Hizb al-Islam, also was split and some have joined Al-Shabaab. Some of the top leaders of the Al-Shabaab also want him to declare an alliance with Osama Bin Laden and cut his ties with Eritrea, measures he has resisted thus far.

Political Developments

In late December 2008, President Yusuf resigned from office and left for Yemen. President Yusuf was opposed to the Djibouti peace process and repeatedly clashed with his prime minister. In January 2009, the Somali Transitional Parliament elected the leader of the ARS, Sheikh Sharif Sheikh Ahmad as president. President Ahmad is seen by many Somalis as a leader with the best chance of bringing peace and stability to Somalia and as someone who can bring those elements outside the peace process to join the new government. In January 2009, President Ahmad went to Ethiopia and took part in the African Union (AU) summit where he was welcomed by member states. In 2006, Ethiopian forces attacked and forced out Ahmad's Islamic Court's Union from power. However, President Ahmad was warmly welcomed by Ethiopian authorities during the AU summit in Ethiopia.

In February 2009, President Ahmad appointed Omar Abdirashid Ali Sharmarke as prime minister. Sharmarke is the son of former President of Somalia, who was killed during the

1969 military coup. Sharmarke received overwhelming support in the Transitional Parliament. The appointment of Sharmarke provided important representation in the new government for the Darod clan. Sharmarke belongs to the same sub-clan, the Majertain, as former president Yusuf. Moreover, the Transitional Parliament was expanded and now includes an additional 149 members from the main opposition group, the ARS. Parliament also extended the mandate of the Transitional Federal Government by another two years. Some observers expressed concern about the size of the new parliament, while others argued that it was a necessary measure to make the parliament more inclusive.

Humanitarian and security conditions continue to deteriorate in south-central Somalia, despite some political progress and a recent peace agreement between the Somali Transitional Federal Government (TFG) and the Alliance for the Re-Liberation of Somalia (ARS), a group formed by former members of the Islamic Courts Union (ICU) and Somalis from different backgrounds. The ouster from power of the ICU by Ethiopian forces in December 2006 created a security vacuum that was soon occupied by the more radical elements of the ICU's military factions. The moderate leadership of the ICU became marginalized, splintered, and weakened over the past year. U.S., TFG, and Ethiopian officials labeled the entire leadership of the ICU as extremist and terrorist in 2006. Eighteen months later, however, the same officials supported the inclusion of some former ICU members in a U.N.-led peace process.

In May-June, 2008, TFG and ARS officials met in Djibouti under the auspices of the United Nations. Officials from the United States, Europe, the African Union, the Arab League, the Organization of Islamic Conference, and regional governments took part as observers during the talks in Djibouti. The parties agreed on a wide range of issues, including cessation of hostilities and a commitment to find a durable peace agreement [3]. The parties agreed to support the deployment of a United Nations peacekeeping force and the phased withdrawal of Ethiopian forces from Somalia. The agreement, however, links the withdrawal of Ethiopian forces with the deployment of a U.N. peacekeeping force, although Ethiopian forces have already withdrawn from some areas. In addition, in November 2008, the Ethiopian government announced that its forces would pull out of Somalia by the end of 2008. In January 2009, Ethiopian forces completed their withdrawal from Somalia. The parties also agreed to provide unhindered humanitarian access to civilians in need and to establish a Joint Security Committee to ensure implementation of security arrangements and create an interim joint security force [4]. The parties established a High Level Committee, chaired by the United Nations, to deal with political, justice, and governance issues.

The Djibouti agreement is complicated and has repeatedly been undermined by in-fighting within the TFG, insecurity, growing influence of insurgent groups, and limited support by the international community. The TFG forces, under the leadership of President Yusuf, were weak, ineffective, and seriously debilitated by defections. Over the past year, an estimated 40% of the police force, trained by the United Nations, left the force due to lack of payment. Some donor governments have withheld funds pledged to the TFG due to lack of transparency and human rights abuses. Infighting within the TFG, especially between then-Prime Minister Nur Adde and then-President Yusuf, weakened the TFG. In November 2007, Prime Minister Nur Adde replaced Ali M. Ghedi, a man seen by many Somalis as ineffective and highly partisan.

Prime Minister Nur Adde, who was seen by many Somalis and Somali observers as a key actor to bridge the gap between the TFG and the opposition, often clashed with President Yusuf. In July 2008, the prime minister dismissed the mayor of Mogadishu and Governor of

Benadir region, Mohamed Dheere, because of mismanagement of funds. In protest, ten pro-Yusuf ministers resigned, triggering a crisis within the TFG. In August 2008, the prime minister and the president met in Ethiopia, and later reached an agreement on a number of issues. In Mid-December 2008, President Yusuf fired Prime Minister Nur and named Mohamed Mohamud Guled as the new prime minister. The prime minister rejected his dismissal arguing that President Yusuf lacked the legal authority to dismiss him and that only Parliament has the power to dismiss the prime minister. On December 15, 2008, a majority of the Somali Parliament voted in support of Prime Minister Nur Adde. The government of Kenya imposed a travel ban and asset freeze against President Yusuf.

Some of the Al-Shabaab leaders have been engaged in talks with some members of the ICU. But most of the leaders of the Al-Shabaab are not well known, with the exception of some. Some of the key commanders and leaders of the Al-Shabaab come from Somaliland. Ahmed Abdi Godane, who is on the U.S. terrorism list, and, who trained and fought in Afghanistan and is a key commander from Somaliland. Mukhtar Robow, who is on the U.S. terrorism list, is the spokesman of the Al-Shabaab. Another key leader is Ibrahim Haji Jama, who is on the U.S. terrorism list, reportedly trained and fought in Afghanistan. In February 2008, Secretary of State Condoleezza Rice designated Al-Shabaab as a Foreign Terrorist Organization and as a Specially Designated Global Terrorist. The TFG was able to win over some Al-Shabaab fighters to join the government side. However, several hundred fighters who recently joined the government forces were sent by the extremist groups to infiltrate the government security forces [5]. In May 2009, at the height of the recent fighting in Mogadishu, most of these fighters went back to rejoin the militia groups they left earlier.

Security Conditions: Background

In 2008, insurgent groups stepped up attacks against Ethiopian and TFG forces in south-central Somalia. In some cases, TFG forces simply withdrew from some areas. As of May 2009, insurgent groups were in control of most of south-central Somalia, including the third largest town, Kismaayo. TFG forces, as well as the African Union Mission to Somalia (AMISOM), do not have control or presence outside Baidoa and Mogadishu. Even in the case of Mogadishu, the insurgents control some parts of Mogadishu and some of their forces are active outside the capital. The Al-Shabaab forces also have expanded their military operations to other parts of Somalia and routinely assassinate opponents and government officials.

Security conditions are likely to deteriorate further in the coming months, despite the peace agreement between the TFG and the ARS. In late October 2008, simultaneous and well-coordinated suicide attacks in Puntland and Somaliland reportedly killed an estimated 20 people and injured many more. The targets of the attacks were the Ethiopian Consulate, the office of the United Nations Development Program (UNDP), and a security office close to the Presidential Palace. The suicide mission was reportedly carried out by members of the Al-Shabaab, although no organization claimed credit for the attacks. One of the suicide bombers was an American- Somali from Minneapolis, who, according to press reports, left the U.S. to take part in the suicide attacks.

Reportedly, over a dozen Somali youth from Minneapolis have left the U.S, and some community leaders believe they went to Somalia to join the insurgency. There is no clear evidence of how many and for what purpose these Somalis left Minneapolis [6].

Over the past decade, many Somalis have returned to Somalia to work as journalists, humanitarian workers, and teachers. A number of these Somalis have been killed in the past two years by insurgents and security forces.

Human Rights and Humanitarian Conditions

In 2008, humanitarian and human rights conditions became worse than in previous years, according to United Nations officials and Somali humanitarian workers. The recent fighting in Mogadishu has added more challenges to already poor conditions on the ground. An estimated 1.1 million people have been displaced and more than 475,000 have fled to neighboring countries in the past two years. Human rights groups and Somali observers estimate more than 22,000 people have been killed over the past two years. Civilians, humanitarian workers, journalists, and human rights advocates have been the primary targets of the insurgents, TFG, and Ethiopian security forces. According to Amnesty International, "rape, killings and looting have become widespread. Entire neighborhoods have been destroyed" [7]. A number of Somali journalists covering the crisis in Somalia have been assassinated by insurgents and security forces over the past eighteen months. Dozens of humanitarian and human rights advocates have been killed, injured, or imprisoned by TFG and Ethiopian security forces. Because of these targeted attacks, many human rights advocates and journalists have fled Somalia to neighboring countries for safety.8 Somalis working for international NGOs and foreign media have also been attacked by insurgents and TFG/Ethiopian security forces. According to the May 2009 Complex Emergency report by the U.S. Agency for International Development (USAID), an estimated 3.2 million people are in need of emergency assistance. In the first two weeks of May 2009, an estimated 27,500 people have been displaced due to the recent fighting in Mogadishu. As of May 2009, the United States has provided $136.6 million in humanitarian assistance to Somalia in FY2009. In FY2008, the United States provided $318 million in assistance to Somalia.

Somali Piracy in the Horn of Africa [9]

Overview

Somali pirates have intensified their attacks in the Gulf of Aden, carrying out attacks on over 111 commercial ships, and successfully hijacked an estimated 40 ships in 2008. As of mid-February 2009, an estimated 11-15 ships were under the control of the pirates, including a Saudi-owned supertanker, Sirius Star, and a Ukrainian-owned ship, MV Faina, which is carrying 33 T-72 tanks and other weapons, according to press reports. In January-February 2009, Somali pirates released several ships, including a Japanese-owned ship, MV *Chemstar*, and the MV *Faina*. The pirates have reportedly earned more than $120 million in ransom payments, and have released a number of ships and crew members. The United States, Russia, India, and several other countries have deployed warships to tackle piracy in the Horn of Africa region. In February 2009, the U.S. Navy arrested 16 suspected Somali pirates. In December 2008, the Indian Navy reportedly arrested 23 Somali and Yemeni pirates. Moreover, the Russian Navy also arrested a number of suspected Somali pirates. According to the International Maritime Bureau (IMB), piracy in the first quarter of 2009 has surpassed that of 2008. According to IMB, "in 2008, there were 111 incidents including 42 vessels hijacked. So far in 2009, there have been 29 successful hijackings from 114 attempted attacks."

In January 2009, the United States and Britain signed legal agreements with the Government of Kenya to extradite suspected pirates to be prosecuted in Kenya. Some insurgent leaders have warned the pirates to end the piracy and to release crew members and ships currently controlled by the pirates. On December 16, 2008, the United Nations Security Council passed a resolution authorizing the use of "all necessary measures" by foreign military forces to stop piracy in Somalia. The resolution authorizes military operations inside Somalia and in its airspace for one year, with the consent of the TFG.

Who Are the Pirates?

The number of Somali pirates is unknown. While there are more pirates now than previous years, the pirates do not seem to have a unified organization with clear command structure. Many of these pirates are reportedly fishermen and former militia members of the Somali warlords. The pirates primarily come from Puntland region of Somalia and are members of different clans. Some press reports have suggested that the pirates are being controlled and directed by the Islamic insurgents in south-central Somalia. There is no evidence, however, to support this assertion, and during the six months the ICU was in power, the leaders took measures to end piracy and other criminal activities. In November 2008, one of the top leaders of the insurgents, Sheik Hassan Aweys, called on the pirates to end their criminal activities, and other insurgent leaders threatened to take military action against the pirates. The pirates, however, are not operating alone, according to a number of Somali and regional sources. Some Somali businessmen and officials in Puntland are reportedly behind the piracy. The pirates are reportedly receiving valuable information about the types of ships, cargo, and timing from Somalis in the Persian Gulf [10]. They also possess sophisticated technology, including Global Position Systems (GPS), Automatic Identification System (AIS), and satellite phones.

The Views from Somalia

Some Somalis view the piracy crisis as a foreign problem with little impact on their daily life. Some argue that the piracy problem will continue as long as the ship-owners are willing to pay the pirates ransom. In the face of difficult economic conditions and growing humanitarian crisis, many Somalis resent the fact that the piracy problem has received a great deal of international attention. Some Somali community leaders contend that some Somalis get involved in criminal activities in order to survive, while many others have made these kinds of criminal activities a lifetime profession. Since the collapse of the Siad Barre government in 1991, Somalis have been principal victims of criminals. Somalis had to pay "taxes" to warlords in order to pass from one neighborhood to another. Humanitarian assistance convoys are routinely targeted by criminal elements, forcing humanitarian agencies to hire gunmen for protection. Many Somalis contend that in the absence of a better alternative, they have come to accept life with all the difficulties they face daily [11].

Somalia: Facts & Statistics

Population: 9.5 million (2008 est.)
Growth rate: 2.85% (2008 est.)
Life expectancy: 49.2 years
Approximate size: slightly smaller than Texas
Capital: Mogadishu
Infant Mortality Rate: 110.97 deaths/1,000 live births (2008 est.)
HIV/AIDS, adult prevalence rate: 1% (2001 est.)
GDP, per capita: $600 (2007 est.)
GDP, real growth rate: 2.6% (2007 est.)
Ethnic groups: Somali, 85%; Bantu & other non-Somali, 15% (including Arabs, 30,000)
Religion: Sunni Muslim
Official language: Somali
Source: CIA Factbook

Some Somalis argue that the fishermen have become pirates because their way of life was destroyed by illegal fishing and toxic waste dumping that has been ignored by foreign governments. In 2005, the United Nations Environment Program (UNEP) released a report documenting the damages resulting from toxic waste dumping on Somalia's shores. According to a UNEP spokesman, "there's uranium radioactive waste, there's lead, there's heavy metals like cadmium and mercury, there's industrial waste, and there's hospital wastes, chemical wastes, you name it." According to the report, the primary reason for toxic dumping in Somalia is cost. The report states that it costs $2.5 per ton to dump toxic waste in Africa compared to $250 per ton to dump waste in Europe [12]. In July 2008, United Nations Special Envoy Ould-Abdallah stated that "because there is no (effective) government, there is so much irregular fishing from European and Asian countries." The Special Envoy argued that it is important to tackle these illegal activities by some countries, and not to solely focus on the problem of piracy [13].

Policy Options in Dealing with Piracy

The international community has responded to the threat of piracy by deploying warships to the Gulf of Aden. The United Nations Security Council has passed resolutions on piracy in the Horn of Africa. Since the deployment of these warships to the region, however, the number of hijacked ships has increased. Somali community leaders and regional analysts argue that the groups most capable and best positioned to handle the piracy problem are the Islamic insurgents and the clan elders. The Islamic Courts dealt with this problem effectively when they were in power, according to senior leaders of the Islamic Courts and independent observers. The Islamic insurgents claim that they are opposed to these kinds of criminal activities for religious reasons. The Islamic leadership sees the piracy problem as a source of concern because they fear that they could erroneously or deliberately linked to the piracy phenomenon and become targets of punitive action by the international community. Another option is to provide quick and robust economic incentives to lure the unemployed away from piracy and other criminal activities. Moreover, the TFG and the Government of Puntland are currently finalizing a proposal on anti-piracy measures.

Policy Options in Dealing with Political and Security Problems

The international community may consider engagement with the Islamic insurgents and clan elders to deal with the political and security problems facing Somalia. According to some observers, it is pivotal to strengthen the moderate elements of the Islamic movements discretely. Most observers believe that the Al-Shabaab can only be contained by another Islamic movement supported by clan elders. Some of the most influential leaders in the Al-Shabaab are on the U.N. and U.S. Terrorism Lists. Some observers argue that removing some of these individuals from the Terrorism List in exchange for some concessions, including an end to the insurgency and acceptance of a negotiated settlement, should be considered as an option. One of the key players in facilitating the Djibouti talks was a Somali man on a United Nations Terrorism List. According to U.N. officials, that man is no longer on the Terrorism List.

Some of the leaders in the Al-Shabaab are determined to continue their military campaign and are not inclined to participate in negotiations. According to some experts, targeted measures, including sanctions and assassination of the most extreme elements of the Al-Shabaab, could pave the way for other moderate leaders to emerge. However, others believe that this option is likely to backfire in the short term and increase anti-western violence. Another option is to refer some of these individuals to the International Criminal Court (ICC) for war crimes. The most effective way of containing the extremists, most observers contend, is to look for a Somali-led solution, both political and military. The TFG, Islamic Courts, Somaliland, Puntland, and other moderate Somali forces could form a coalition to contain the advances of the most extreme elements of the Al-Shabaab politically and militarily. Such a coalition is likely to get the support of the Somali population rather than a peacekeeping force. The coalition can be assisted by neighboring countries. A Somali-led initiative would take away one of the most powerful justifications used by the Al-Shabaab to wage war, the presence of foreign forces. A unified regional approach is pivotal, however. Most believe that Eritrea has leverage over some of the influential Islamic leaders, some of whom are in Eritrea. The ARS was founded in Eritrea, and some of its leaders are now engaged in the U.N.-led negotiation in Djibouti.

The Alliance for the Re-Liberation of Somalia

In September 2007, Somalis from the Diaspora, civil society, opposition groups, and former members of parliament met in Eritrea and formed the Alliance for the Re-Liberation of Somalia (ARC). More than 400 people participated at the founding conference. The Al-Shabaab, the Youth, did not participate, and later condemned the leadership of the Alliance. The Alliance significantly reduced the dominance of the Council of the Islamic Courts and brought into the leadership people from civil society, women's groups, and former members of the TFG. The Alliance also brought into the coalition people from different regions and clans of Somalia.

Table 1. The Leadership of the Executive Council of the ARS before the Split

Name	Title	Affiliation
Sheikh Sharif Sheikh Ahmed	Chairman	Somali Council of the Islamic Courts (SCIC)
General Jama Mohmed Galib	Vice Chairman	Civil Society
Zakaria Hagi Mohamud Abdi	Vice Chairman	Parliament
Prof. Ibrahim Hassan Addou, Ph.D.	Foreign Affairs Advisor	SCIC
Dr. Mohamed Ali Dahir	Administration Consultant	Somali intellectual
Prof. Abdirahman Ibrahim Ibbi	Assistant to the Chairman	Parliament
Ambassador Yusuf H. Ibrahim	Foreign Affairs Secretary	Parliament
Ahmed Abdullahi Sheikh	Information Secretary	Civil Society
Col. Omar Hashi Aden	Interior Secretary	Parliament
Ahmed Abdullahi Sheikh	Information Secretary	Civil Society
Col. Omar Hashi Aden	Interior Secretary	Parliament
Abdifitah Mohamed Ali	Finance Secretary	SCIC
Yusuf Mohamed Siad	Defense Secretary	SCIC
Dr. Mohamed Ahmed Mohamed, MD	Health Secretary	Civil Society
Dr. Mohamed Ali Ibrahim, Ph.D.	Justice Secretary	SCIC
Dr. Mohamud Abdi Ibrahim	Relief and Rehabilitation Secretary	
Mrs. Fowsia Mohmed Sheikh	Human Rights Secretary	Parliament
Mohamud Ahmed Tarzan	Planning & Training Secretary	Diaspora
Abdulkadir Mohmed Dhakane	Education Secretary	Parliament
Mohmed Ibrahim Garyare	Social Affairs Secretary	Diaspora
Ahmed Abdulle Hussain	Reconciliation Secretary	SCIC
Abdullahi Sheikh	Auditing Secretary	SCIC

In addition, individuals, such as Hassan Aweys, considered by the west as extremists or terrorists, were not given leadership positions. According to the Alliance, the main objectives of the coalition are:

- The liberation of Somalia from Ethiopia.
- Somali solutions by Somali-stake-holders through dialogue and peaceful means.

- To establish a National Government "completely devote its utmost care to the welfare of the people, protect its rights, properties and promote its spiritual and material development" [14]
- Fighting crimes and violence targeted against civilian population, such as killing, raping, pillaging, dislodging and displacing.
- Resettlement of displaced people.
- Organize general elections once peace and security is established.

In March 2008, the Chairman of the Alliance in a letter to the President of the Security Council wrote "A peacekeeping mission would be possible only after the departure of the Ethiopian troops. Experience has shown that when peacekeepers are unilaterally imposed by the Security Council, they turn into peace enforcers. To avoid such a situation, the consent of the parties to the conflict is essential." In January 2008, the Alliance leadership informed a congressional delegation that the Alliance will accept a humanitarian cease-fire, zones of tranquility, and negotiations with the TFG and others once Ethiopian forces are replaced by a neutral force. This position led to a split of the Alliance. Many of the top leaders of the Alliance left Eritrea for Djibouti to participate in the U.N.-sponsored negotiations.

BACKGROUND: 2006-2008

On December 24, 2006, Ethiopian and TFG forces launched a military campaign against the forces of the ICU, a group that took over power in Mogadishu, the capital of Somalia, in June 2006. On December 28, 2006 Ethiopian troops captured Mogadishu with little resistance from the ICU. The ICU leadership decided a day before the Mogadishu attack to leave the city in order to avoid bloodshed and the destruction of Mogadishu, according to a senior official of the ICU [15]. On January 1, 2007, the ICU lost its last stronghold, Kismaayo, after its forces withdrew to an area near the Kenyan border, although most of its fighters and leaders either simply melted into society throughout Somalia or fled to neighboring countries. Some of the top leaders of the ICU are in Yemen, Djibouti, Kenya, and Somalia [16]. In late January, the Chairman of the Executive Committee of the Somali Council of Islamic Courts (SCIC), formerly known as ICU, Sharif Sheik Ahmed, traveled to Kenya. On January 24, 2007, the U.S. Ambassador to Kenya, Michael Ranneberger, reportedly met with Sheik Ahmed. Other leaders of the Courts have also been approached by U.S. officials as part of a new strategy to reach out to Court officials and others to participate in proposed negotiations among Somali groups and the TFG.

The Ethiopian military intervention, while it has accomplished its military objective of ousting the Courts from Mogadishu and other areas the Courts controlled, has been criticized by governments and regional organizations. The African Union, the European Commission, the Arab League, and others have called for the deployment of a United Nations peacekeeping force. Ethiopian officials argued that their military action is justified because the Islamic Courts posed a serious threat to Ethiopia and regional stability, and because the Islamic Courts is an extremist, Jihadist group. Ethiopian and U.S. officials also have accused the Courts of being influenced or tied to well known terrorist individuals and Al Qaeda. Islamic Courts officials have repeatedly rejected these allegations and on a number of occasions have offered to work with U.S. officials, according to one senior Courts official. Allegations about the presence of the three suspects involved in the bombings of the U.S. embassies in Tanzania and Kenya in 1998 have been made on many occasions over the years. However, the Islamic Courts did not exist as an organized group when these allegations were made. Those in charge of Mogadishu and other areas in southern Somalia were the warlords who were and in some cases still are ministers in the current Transitional Federal Government.

On January 8, 2007, the United States Air Force, using AC-130 gun ships, attacked several locations in southern Somalia, reportedly to kill the three terror suspects in the 1998 U.S. embassy bombings in Kenya and Tanzania. Reportedly, the United States launched another attack the following day, although U.S. officials deny any further attacks by its forces. The British humanitarian group, Oxfam, stated in a press release that an estimated 70 people were killed in the bombings and vital water resources were destroyed in Afmadow district. A number of governments criticized the U.S. attacks, including officials in Europe and the Government of Djibouti, where U.S. forces are currently stationed. Djiboutian Foreign Minister Mahmoud Ali Yusuf told the BBC that the raid was counterproductive to achieving peace. He also stated that his government had not been informed about the air strikes. According to a New York Times article, the United States actively coordinated with Ethiopian forces in targeting suspected terrorists and Islamic Union forces [17]. U.S. Special Operations troops from Task Force 88 were reportedly deployed to Ethiopia and entered Somalia. Moreover, the United States reportedly shared intelligence with Ethiopian military and used an airstrip in Eastern Ethiopia to launch attacks inside Somalia. A senior Ethiopian government official denied that there was any coordination with U.S. forces.

Ethiopian troops have come under attack, and a number of Ethiopian soldiers have been killed by snipers or in ambushes. Some Somalis and human rights advocates are concerned over what some people refer to as a witch hunt by TFG and Ethiopian security forces. Ethiopian and TFG security forces reportedly have been going house to house arresting Oromos (an Ethiopian ethnic group), supporters of the Islamic Courts, and members of the TFG considered not supportive of the new Somali government and the Ethiopian intervention.

The government of Kenya has deported dozens of Somalis and other nationals to TFG officials and Ethiopian security forces, according to Kenyan sources. In one particular case, Kenyan officials reportedly blindfolded and handcuffed 30 individuals and returned them to Mogadishu, where these detainees were taken by Ethiopian and TFG security personnel to unknown locations, according to Somali sources and government officials in the region. A number of Kenyan Muslims that were in Ethiopian detention were released in 2008.

On January 17, 2007, the Transitional Federal Parliament ousted the Speaker of Parliament, Sharif Hassan Sheik Adan, from his position. The former Speaker, who has been a vocal critic of the Ethiopian intervention and the U.S. air strike, has a strong following in Mogadishu and has been active in reaching out and engaging the Islamic Courts officials when they had control over Mogadishu.

U.S. Assistant Secretary of State for Africa Jendayi Fraser stated in mid-January 2007 that "the no-confidence motion brought against the Parliament Speaker is likely to have a negative impact on this process of dialogue" [18]. In late January, the TFG elected Sheikh Adan Mohamed Nur Madobe, a former warlord and an ally of President Abdullahi Yusuf, as Speaker of Parliament.

Peacekeeping Mission: Background

On December 6, 2006, the United Nations Security Council passed Resolution 1725, "reiterating its commitment to a comprehensive and lasting settlement of the situation in Somalia through the Transitional Federal Charter, and stressing the importance of broad-based and representative institutions and of an inclusive political process, as envisaged in the Transitional Federal Charter." U.N. Security Council Resolution 1725 further called for "all Member States, in particular those in the region, to refrain from any action in contravention of the arms embargo and related measures, and should take all actions necessary to prevent such contravention." Moreover, the Security Council expressed its "willingness to engage with all parties in Somalia who are committed to achieving a political settlement through peaceful and inclusive dialogue, including the Union of Islamic Courts." The Security Council, acting under Chapter VII of the Charter of the United Nations, authorized the Inter-Governmental Authority for Development (IGAD) and the African Union to establish "a protection and training mission in Somalia." U.N. Security Council Resolution 1725 specifically stated that countries bordering Somalia "would not deploy troops to Somalia."

At the African Union Summit in late January 2007, several African countries pledged to contribute troops for a peacekeeping mission in Somalia. Ghana, Nigeria, Burundi, Uganda, and Malawi have pledged troops. The African Union is facing difficulties getting governments to make serious troop contributions for the mission. Observers contend that without a negotiated settlement with groups still outside the TFG, it will be difficult to maintain peace and stability in Somalia. As of November 2008, there were an estimated 3,400 AU peacekeeping troops in Somalia from Uganda and Burundi. The African Union peacekeeping mission is mandated to:

- support dialogue and reconciliation in Somalia, working with all stakeholders,
- provide, as appropriate, protection to the TFIs and their key infrastructure, to enable them carry out their functions,
- assist in the implementation of the National Security and Stabilization Plan of Somalia, particularly the effective reestablishment and training of all inclusive Somali security forces, bearing in mind the programs already being implemented by some of Somalia's bilateral and multilateral partners,
- provide, within capabilities and as appropriate, technical and other support to the disarmament and stabilization efforts,
- monitor, in areas of deployment of its forces, the security situation,
- facilitate, as may be required and within capabilities, humanitarian operations, including the repatriation and reintegration of refugees and the resettlement of IDP s, and
- protect its personnel, installations and equipment, including the right of selfdefense [19]

On February 20, 2007, the U.N. Security Council passed resolution 1744 reiterating its support for the Transitional Federal Institutions and authorizing the African Union to establish a mission in Somalia. Resolution 1744 calls for "a national reconciliation congress involving all stakeholders, including political leaders, clan leaders, religious leaders, and representatives of civil society." The resolution, while it welcomed the withdrawal of Ethiopian troops from Somalia, did not include a provision that restricts the participation of Somalia's immediate neighbors in the peacekeeping operation as resolution 1725 did.

The Security Council unanimously adopted Resolution 1772 on August 20, 2007, authorizing the African Union to maintain its operation in Somalia for an additional six months. The resolution also authorized peacekeeping forces on the ground to take all necessary measures to support and protect those involved in the Reconciliation Congress. Finally, Resolution 1772 called on all Member States, especially those in close proximity to Somalia, to comply with the arms embargo that was established in 1992 by Resolution 733.

THE ISLAMIC COURTS UNION

In early 2006, factional violence in Mogadishu once again erupted, killing hundreds of civilians and displacing many more people. The surge in violence was between militia loyal to the Islamic Courts and a self-proclaimed anti-terrorism coalition backed by powerful local warlords. The fighting in Mogadishu erupted when the forces loyal to a well known warlord and then Minister of National Security of the TFG, Mohamed Qanyare, attacked one of the Courts. The fighting received unusual attention in Somalia and in the region due, in large part, to reports that the warlords were backed by the United States government. The Bush Administration acknowledged that Washington was assisting "responsible individuals" to help bring stability and fight terrorism in Somalia. Assistant Secretary of State for Africa, Jendayi Fraser reportedly stated that the United States "will work with those elements that will help us to root out Al Qaeda and prevent Somalia becoming a safe haven for terrorists" [20]. In late June 2006, Fraser stated that the United States has three major policy goals in Somalia: counter-terrorism efforts, creation of an effective government, and responding to the humanitarian needs of the Somali people.

On February 18, 2006, the Alliance for the Restoration of Peace and Counter-Terrorism (ARPCT) was created. Very little is known about ARPCT, although the founders of the Alliance are known warlords who contributed to numerous armed clashes and instability in Somalia over the past decade. Members of the Alliance reportedly include Bashir Rage, Mohammed Qanyare Afrah, Muse Sudi Yalahow, Omar Finnish, and Abdirashid Shire Ilqyete. These actors were seen by many Somali groups as major obstacles to the creation of central authority in Mogadishu, as agreed to by all major Somali groups under the IGAD peace agreement in 2004. In early June 2006, Prime Minister Ali Mohamed Gedi dismissed four ministers from the Transitional Federal Government belonging to ARPCT.

These ministers include Mohamed Qanyare (National Security Minister), Musa Sudi Yalahow (Commerce Minister), Issa Botan Alin (Rehabilitation Minister), and Omar Finnish (Minister for Religious Affairs). The warlords were dismissed because they reportedly ignored calls by Prime Minister Ghedi's government to stop the fighting in Mogadishu. The Islamic Courts leaders argued then that the TFG did nothing to challenge these warlords and kept them in senior positions in the TFG until the Islamic Courts defeated the warlords in Mogadishu. In late July 2006, members of the TFG parliament complained that the U.S. government bypassed the TFG and provided support to the warlords, the same warlords who obstructed peace in Somalia. A member of the TFG parliament told a U.S. Congressional delegation in August 2006 that "you cannot fight terrorism by supporting warlords" [21].

In early June 2006, the forces of the Islamic Courts captured Mogadishu, forcing ARPCT militia to flee the capital. The chairman of the Islamic Courts, Sharif Shaykh Ahmed, stated that his group would negotiate with the TFG. In response to accusations that the Islamic Courts Union was associated with or had harbored international terrorist elements, Shaykh Ahmed stated that "we are not terrorists and we will not allow anyone to hijack the capital. We have said hundreds of times that America's talk of terrorism in Somalia is fabricated and serves suspicious political purposes" [22].

The forces of the Islamic Courts Union strengthened and expanded areas under their control after the defeat of the warlords in Mogadishu. The Islamic Courts forces captured the towns of Jowhar and Beledweyne in mid-June 2006. Moreover, for the first time in years, Mogadishu became relatively peaceful, and the Islamic Courts received support from the population in areas it controlled. The level of support enjoyed by the Islamic Courts is difficult to measure, although the group had constituencies from multiple sub-clans and had broad support among Somali women. According to Somali sources in Mogadishu and Islamic Courts officials, the people provided crucial support by feeding their forces and working with Islamic Courts officials in bringing peace and stability. During the Mogadishu fighting, women supporters of ICU played important roles. Since the Islamic Courts largely functioned as providers of social services, the Courts did not maintain a large fighting force. The warlords maintained a robust force in different parts of Mogadishu, with heavy weapons and "technicals" (machine-guns mounted on pickup trucks). The Islamic Courts group had only four technicals when the fighting erupted with Qanyare and other warlords, according to a senior Courts official. The ICU success in Mogadishu effectively led to the collapse of the ARPCT and forced the warlords to flee.

Negotiations between the Transitional Federal Government and the Islamic Courts in Sudan did not lead to a major breakthrough, although the talks ended speculation that the Islamic Courts rejected negotiations. The Islamic Courts leaders stated that they would work with the Baidoa-based transitional government, although disagreement on key issues remained. In June 2006, the transitional parliament voted in favor of a foreign peacekeeping force. But this move was rejected by some Islamic Courts leaders as being unnecessary and counter productive. Earlier, in 2005, the African Union had approved a proposal for Uganda and Sudan to deploy a peacekeeping force to Somalia under the auspices of the IGAD. The deployment did not take place in large part because of the refusal of the United Nations Security Council to remove a United Nations arms embargo on Somalia. The Bush Administration did not support the lifting of the arms embargo, although the United Nations Security Council did provide the necessary exemption in December 2006.

In mid-June, an International Somalia Contact Group, consisting of the United States, Norway, United Kingdom, Sweden, Italy, Tanzania, and the European Union, was formed and met to discuss the unfolding Somalia crisis. The United Nations, the African Union, the Arab League, and IGAD were also invited as observers. The Contact Group did not invite Somalia's immediate neighbors, in part due to Somali opposition and international concern that these countries are engaged in activities in support of or against some groups in Somalia. In a press release after its first meeting, the Contact Group stated that "the goal of the International Contact Group will be to encourage positive political developments and engagement with actors inside Somali to support the implementation of the Transitional Federal Charter and Institutions.

The Contact Group will seek to support efforts, within the framework of the Transitional Federal Institutions, to address the humanitarian needs of the Somali people, establish effective governance and stability, and address the international community's concern regarding terrorism." Meanwhile, in early January 2007, the International Contact Group on Somalia issued another communiqué strongly urging that it is "essential that an inclusive process of political dialogue and reconciliation embracing representative clan, religious, business, civil society, women's, and other political groups who reject violence and extremism be launched without delay."

The Islamic Courts, while well received by the people in the areas the Courts controlled, received bad press coverage, especially in the West. The Courts' activities were often characterized as extremist and jihadist. The ICU was accused of shutting down cinemas and prohibiting women from working. Some of these measures were taken by the Courts, although for different reasons and not because of the Courts' alleged jihadist and extremist ideology. For example, movies were banned in the morning in response to requests from parents because Somali children were going to movies in the morning instead of school [23].

The ban on television did not take place, except for restrictions on watching soccer games late at night, according to Islamic Courts officials and Somali residents in Mogadishu. This measure was reportedly taken because of disturbances and fighting late at night. There is no evidence to support the allegation that women were prohibited from working. Islamic Courts officials point out that in the short time they were in power, they did more than restore law and order.

Properties taken by warlords were returned to the rightful owners. For example, the family of President Yusuf reportedly returned to Mogadishu after almost sixteen years when the Courts restored order in the capital, according to an Islamic Courts official. Most important, they argue, they gave hope to the people of Somalia that after over a decade of violence they can live in peace.

The Leadership of the Somali Council of the Islamic Courts

General knowledge of the top leadership of the Somali Council of the Islamic Courts (SCIC) is sketchy. The leadership was often referred to as jihadist, extremist, and at times terrorist by some observers without much evidence to support the allegations. For example, the assessment of the Islamic Courts by U.S. officials was that less than 5 percent of the Islamic Courts leadership can be considered extremist, according to a senior State Department official. In late June 2006, the Courts established a consultative body to function as the legislative (Shura) arm of the Courts. Hassan Dahir Aweys was elected to head the Legislative Council. Aweys was one of the top leaders of the now-defunct Al-Ittihad Al-Islamiya (AIAI—for more see below) and was designated by the Bush Administration as a terrorist. Sharif Sheik Ahmed, the leader of the Courts, was appointed chairman of the Council's Executive Committee to lead the day-to-day affairs of the Courts. Some observers and government officials have erroneously described Aweys as the leader of the Courts.

However, the moderate leader of the Courts, Sharif Sheik Ahmed, was never replaced by Aweys. Some observers argued that referring to Aweys as the leader of the Courts was deliberately designed by some groups and governments to give the Courts a bad image.

The leadership of the Islamic Courts remained largely under the control of religious scholars and academics (see below). The focus by some observers and officials on three individuals, Aweys, Hassan Al-Turki, and Aden Ayro, may have been to show the Islamic Courts as a group controlled and influenced by these individuals. Al-Turki, a man born in the ethnically Somali Ogaden region of Ethiopia, was listed by the Bush administration as a terrorist because of his membership in Al- Ittihad. According to Courts officials, Al-Turki did not even hold a leadership position within the organization. Both Aweys and Al-Turki were placed on the list because of their membership in Al-Ittihad. There is no public record to support that these individuals were engaged in terrorist activities against U.S. or western interests. Ayro's role within the Courts was highly exaggerated since he did not have a leadership position in the organization. Ayro was often referred to as the leader of the Shibaab, the Youth, although there is no evidence to support that he was the leader of that group. Ayro was suspected of killing four aid workers in the breakaway region of Somaliland as well as a Somali scholar in Mogadishu named Abdulqadir Yahya. In May 2008, Ayro was killed in a U.S. air strike. Since the killing of Ayro, the insurgency has intensified its attacks and is now in control of many parts of south-central Somalia.

The Top Leaders of the Courts

The Executive Council

Sheikh Sharif Ahmed. Received a Law Degree from a University in Libya; served as President of Somali Intellectuals Associations; President of the District Court in Jowhar; President of Somali Council of Islamic Courts (SCIC); never been active in politics; married with two children. Now, Chairman of the ARS.

Abdurahman Muhamoud Farah. Vice President of SCIC. Studied in Mogadishu; a longtime advocate of peace and clan unity; never active in politics.

Abdulqadir Ali Omar. Vice President of SCIC. Longtime advocate of clan unity; religious scholar, and advocated against abuses by the warlords.

Ibrahim Hassan Addou. Foreign Secretary and a member of the Shura (Legislative Council) of the SCIC; Ph.D., MA, BA from American University, Washington, D.C.; Worked at American University from 1981 to 1992; held several positions at Benadir University in Mogadishu, including Vice President for Academic Affairs and President; married with three children.

The Legislative Council or Shura

Hassan Dahir Aweys. Speaker of the Shura. Former army officer in the Somali Armed Forces; fought in the Ethiopia-Somalia wars in the 1970s; former senior member of Al-Ittihad; fought against Ethiopia and Abdullahi Yusuf in the mid-1990s.

Omar Imam Abubakar. Number two in the Shura and effectively the most influential and active member of the Shura; received his Ph.D. from a University in Saudi Arabia; lectured in Mauritania and Somalia for many years.

Abdulahi Ali Afrah. Senior leader in the Shura. Holds a BA in Agriculture, longtime civil servant in the Siad Barre government; received an MA from a University in the U.S. and lived in Canada for many years.

Muhamoud Ibrahim Suleh. Senior member of the Shura, son of a well known religious leader.

Leadership of the Transitional Federal Government

Abdullahi Yusuf Ahmed. President of the TFG. A former senior army officer in Somalia; imprisoned by Siad Barre; attempted a coup against Barre in 1978 and later fled Somalia; led one of the first armed groups against Siad Barre with Ethiopian support; imprisoned by Ethiopian military dictator Mengistu Hailemariam in 1985 and released in 1991 after the ouster of the Mengistu regime by the current government; leader of the autonomous northeastern region of Puntland until 2001.

Ali Mohamed Ghedi. Prime Minister of the TFG. Studied in Somalia and Italy; A veterinarian by training; a lecturer and researcher at the Somali National University; no affiliation with warlords or political groups. Ghedi was replaced by Mr. Nur Adde in late 2007.

Sharif Hassan Sheik Adan. Former Speaker of Transitional Federal Parliament. Ousted from his position in January 2007; vocal critic of Ethiopia's intervention; had serious disagreements with President Yusuf; initiated negotiations with Courts leadership; a businessman and an advocate of reconciliation efforts. He joined the ARS in 2007.

Adan Mohamed Nur Madobe. Speaker of Parliament of the TFG. A former warlord and served as the Deputy Chairman of the Rahanweyn Resistance Army (RRA) and as Justice Minister of the TFG.

Hassan Muhammad Nur Shatigadud. Minister of Finance of the TFG; a known warlord and Chairman of the RRA.

Barre Adan Shire Hiiraale. Minister of defense. Served as the Chairman of the Juba Valley Alliance; Studied at West Point and served as army Colonel in the Barre regime; former commander of the Somali National Front (SNF).

Hussein Farah Aideed. Minister of Public Works and Housing. Served as Minister of Interior from 2005 to February 7, 2007; son of former faction leader Mohamed Farah Aideed; studied and lived in the United States; succeeded his father after his death in 1996. He left Somalia in 2007.

Ethiopia-Somalia Relations

For over four decades, relations between successive Ethiopian governments and Somalia have been poor. Somalia invaded Ethiopia twice in the 1960s under Emperor Haile Selassie and in 1976 during the Mengistu Haile Mariam military rule. In the first war, the Ethiopian military commander General Aman Andom defeated Somali forces, but his request to go inside Somalia was rejected by the Emperor, and he was ordered to remain behind the border. The 1976 invasion of Ethiopia by Somali forces and Western Somali Liberation Front (WSLF) initially succeeded, leading to the capture of many Ethiopian towns by Somali forces. Somali forces briefly captured the third largest city, Dire Dawa, in Eastern Ethiopia. However, Ethiopian forces, with the support of Cuban and South Yemeni forces, were able to defeat the Somali forces, although elements of the Somali rebel forces remained in control of remote areas in the largely Somali inhabited areas of Ethiopia.

Both Ethiopian and Somali governments intervened in the internal affairs of the two countries, and successive governments on both sides supported each others' armed opposition groups. The current president of the Transitional Federal Government, President Abdullahi Yusuf, was one of the first to receive Ethiopia's assistance after he fled Somalia in the late 1970s. He was one of the first senior officials to challenge the Siad Barre government. Ethiopia was also the principal backer of the Somali National Movement (SNM), the group that liberated the northwest region of Somalia, currently known as Somaliland. The change of government in Ethiopia did not end Ethiopia's intervention in Somali affairs. The current government of Ethiopia became a key backer of a number of Somali factions and leaders, including the current president of the TFG, Abdullahi Yusuf, Hussein Aideed, and other Somali factions.

The Barre government was also a major sponsor of Ethiopian armed rebel groups. The current ruling party of Ethiopia, the Ethiopian People's Revolutionary Democratic Front (EPRDF), received assistance from Somali authorities and a number of the EPRDF leaders reportedly carried Somali-issued passports. Other rebel groups, including the Ogaden National Liberation Front (ONLF) and the Oromo Liberation Front (OLF), also received assistance from Somalia. The ouster of the Siad Barre government and the absence of a central government in Somalia ended support for Ethiopian armed groups, although some Somali factions continue to support the ONLF. For most of the 1990s, Ethiopia's primary concern was Al-Ittihad in Somalia and its activities in support of the ONLF.

Al-Ittihad and ONLF carried out a number of attacks against Ethiopian targets, and Ethiopian security forces have violently retaliated against these groups and their supporters. The fighting with Al-Ittihad was triggered in the early 1990s when Ethiopian security forces brutally cracked down on the Ogaden National Liberation Front, a member of the first transitional government of Ethiopia. The ONLF joined the transitional government of Ethiopia in part because the Ethiopian Transitional Charter provided nations and nationalities the right to self determination; however, the ONLF push for self determination created tension between the ruling EPRDF and the ONLF.

In the early 1990s, Ethiopian security forces assassinated a number of ONLF leaders, cracked down on the organization, and moved the Ethiopian Somali Region capital from Gode to Jijiga, a central government stronghold. Members of the ONLF fled to Somalia and were embraced by Al- Ittihad, a fairly new group at that time. Hence, some observers view Al-Ittihad as a group largely concerned with domestic issues. Ethiopia's principal interest at that time was to ensure that a united Somalia did not pose a threat to Ethiopia and that the Somali-inhabited-region of Ethiopia remained stable. Ethiopian forces attacked Somalia a number of times over the past decade and often maintained presence inside Somali territory. Ethiopia's relationship with the current president of the TFG was strengthened when Yusuf backed Ethiopia's efforts against Al-Ittihad in the 1990s. The Ethiopian government's animosity towards the ousted Shura leader of the Islamic Courts, Sheik Aweys, is linked to Aweys' role as one of the leaders of Al-Ittihad fighting against Ethiopia and that of Abdullahi Yusuf.

In 2004, the government of Ethiopia released a report, the Federal Democratic Republic of Ethiopia's Foreign Policy, Security Policy and Strategy. The 158-page report covers a wide range of issues, including Ethiopia's assessment of its relations with Somalia. The report states that Somalia attacked Ethiopia twice in pursuit of its Greater Somalia ambition. The report notes that "at this time the Greater Somalia agenda has failed." Moreover, the Greater Somalia agenda no longer poses a serious threat to Ethiopia. The report contends that the factionalization of Somalia has allowed anti-peace and extremists elements to become strong, posing a threat to Ethiopia.

In order to reduce the threat from some parts of Somalia, the Ethiopian government must pursue a policy of engagement and support to Puntland and Somaliland, according to the report. The report also recommends a policy of targeting those armed elements that threaten Ethiopian security.

This report was released two years before the Islamic Courts emerged, although the report gave the same labels of extremist, terrorist, and anti-peace to groups that were dominant at that time.

Somalia: Background (1991-2006)

In 1991, General Mohamed Siad Barre, who came to power through a military coup in 1969, was ousted from power by several Somali armed groups. Following the collapse of central authority in Mogadishu, rival Somali groups engaged in armed struggle for personal political power and prevented food and medicine from reaching innocent civilians suffering from drought and famine. An estimated 500,000 people died from violence, starvation, and disease as Somalia was wracked by continued internal chaos. On November 9, 1992, then-President George H.W. Bush authorized Operation Restore Hope, using the U.S. military, to safeguard non-governmental organizations (NGOs) and their efforts to provide humanitarian assistance to the suffering Somali civilian population.

The U.S.-led United Task Force (UNITAF) successfully subdued the warlords and armed factions and enabled NGOs to safely provide humanitarian relief to Somalis. In May 1993, UNITAF handed over the operation to the United Nations. The U.N. effort was known as United Nations Operation in Somalia (UNOSOM) II. In May 1993, UNOSOM II coalition forces were attacked by one of the factions in Mogadishu. On October 3, 1993, after a seventeen-hour battle between U.S. troops and Somali factions in Mogadishu, in which 18 U.S. Rangers were killed, President Clinton ordered the withdrawal of U.S. troops from Somalia. In March 1994, the United States completely pulled out of Somalia and, one year later, the United Nations pulled out the remaining peacekeepers. Since the withdrawal of United Nations forces in March 1995, Somalia has been without a central government and has been splintered into several regions controlled by clan- based factions.

Peace Processes

There have been 14 Somali reconciliation or peace conferences to bring an end to the fighting in Somalia since the early 1 990s. Some were held under the auspices of or were supported by the United Nations, or governments in the Horn of Africa. These efforts have largely failed to bring about lasting peace in Somalia. Moreover, competing efforts by international actors contributed to the failure of peace efforts in Somalia. In 1996, the Government of Ethiopia convened a peace process in the resort town of Sodere, Ethiopia. Many political actors and armed factions participated, although a few boycotted the peace process. The Sodere process collapsed when the government of Egypt convened another meeting of the Somali groups in Cairo in 1997. Subsequently, the Cairo initiative failed when yet another peace conference was convened by Somali factions in Bosaso, Somalia in 1998.

In February 2000, IGAD approved a peace plan proposed by the government of Djibouti. In May 2000, the Somali Reconciliation Conference opened in Arta, Djibouti in which 400 delegates took part for several months of deliberation. The Arta process was boycotted by several powerful warlords, as well as the governments of Somaliland and Puntland.

On August 13, 2000, participants agreed to the creation of a Transitional National Government (TNG) and a Transitional National Assembly (TNA). On August 26, 2000, participants nominated Abdulqassim Salad Hassan as president of the TNG. In October 2002, the Inter-Governmental Authority for Development launched another peace process, led by the government of Kenya. An estimated 350 delegates from different regions of Somalia participated in the opening session of the conference in the Kenyan town of Eldoret. The Government of Somaliland boycotted the conference. In the first phase of the conference, the parties signed a temporary cease-fire, and agreed to respect and honor the outcome of the conference. The parties further agreed to establish a federal system of government and committed themselves to fight terrorism. In September 2003, the parties agreed on a Transitional National Charter, paving the way for a National Unity government.

In August 2004, a new Transitional Somali Parliament was inaugurated in Kenya. The 275- member parliament consists of the major political factions and seems to represent all the major clans of Somalia. The Transitional Charter allocated 61 seats for the major four clans and 31 seats for the small clans. The Charter also allocated 12% of the seats to women. The Charter accepted Islam as the national religion and agreed that Sharia law would be the basis of national legislation. In fact, previous Somali constitutions had similar provisions. In October 2004, the Somali Transitional Parliament elected Abdullahi Yusuf Ahmed as the new president of Somalia. The swearing in ceremony was attended by 11 heads of government from African countries and representatives from regional organizations and the United Nations.

In November 2004, President Abdullahi Yusuf Ahmed appointed Professor Ali Mohamed Gedi as prime minister. The transitional government, however, was not able to function effectively or move to Mogadishu in large part due to opposition from the warlords in Mogadishu, even though some of these warlords signed the agreement and were ministers in the government. The inability of the transitional government to establish effective control allowed warlords and clan factions to dominate many parts of Somalia until late December 2006. Some observers contend that the defeat of the warlords by the Islamic Courts paved the way for the establishment of central authority in Mogadishu.

National Reconciliation Conference

Somalia's recent peace effort, the National Reconciliation Congress, convened in the Shagaani district of Mogadishu on July 15, 2007 after being postponed twice for logistical and security reasons. The first phase of the conference came to an end on August 30, 2007. Somali Ambassador to Kenya Mohammed Ali Nur spoke optimistically about the results of the first phase of the conference at a news conference in Nairobi, Kenya: "I am happy to announce the declaration of peace agreement between major clans who are participating in the congress has already been signed... The transitional government has done and will continue doing its best to lead the process of reviving Somalia from the ashes of the vicious civil war." Whereas the first phase of the conference focused on the resolution of clan conflicts and disarmament, the second phase focused on issues such as power sharing, governance, sharing of natural resources, sea piracy, welfare, and internally displaced persons. The TFG did not take steps to address these issues since the Congress ended its meeting in late 2007.

SOMALIA: SAFE HAVEN FOR TERRORIST GROUPS?

The United States, Somali neighbors, and some Somali groups have expressed concern over the years about the spread of Islamic fundamentalism in Somalia. In the mid-1990s, Islamic courts began to emerge in parts of the country, especially in the capital of Mogadishu. These courts functioned as local governments and often enforced decisions by using their own Islamic militia. Members of the Al-Ittihad militia (see background below) reportedly provided the bulk of the security forces for these courts in the areas AIAI had a presence. The absence of central authority in Somalia created an environment conducive to the proliferation of armed factions throughout the country. Ethiopian security forces invaded Somalia on a number of occasions to disrupt the activities of Al-Ittihad and its allies or in support of certain armed factions.

Somali factions, including the so-called Islamic groups, often go through realignments or simply disappear from the scene. Very little is known about the leadership or organizational structure of these groups, including Al-Ittihad. There have been three known Islamic groups in Somalia whose prominence has alternately waxed and waned: Al-Ittihad Al-Islamiya (mentioned below), Al-Islah (Reform), and Al-Tabligh (Conveyers of God's Work). In 1995, a group called Jihad al- Islam, led by Sheikh Abbas bin Omar, emerged in Mogadishu, and gave the two main warlords, General Mohamed Farah Aideed and Ali Mahdi, an ultimatum to end their factional fighting. The group claimed at that time that it maintained offices in several countries, including Yemen, Pakistan, Kenya, and Sudan. Not much was heard subsequently from Jihad al-Islam, although a group of Somalis later formed the Sharia (Islamic law) Implementation Club (SIC) in 1996.

SIC's principal objective was to establish Sharia courts throughout the country. Some members of the Mogadishu-based former Transitional National Government (TNG) reportedly were key players in the establishment of these courts. Very little is known about al-Islah, although it is perceived as a group dominated by Hawiye clan businessmen. According to the State Department's 2006 Country Reports on Terrorism, "while numerous Islamist groups engaged in a broad range of activities operate inside Somalia, few of these organizations have any known links to terrorist activities. Movements such as Harakat al-Islah (al-Islah), Ahlu Sunna wal Jamaa (ASWJ), and Majma Ulimadda Islaamka ee Soomaaliya (Majma') sought power by political rather than violent means and pursued political action via missionary or charity work. Missionary Islamists, such as followers of the Tablighi sect and the "New Salafis" generally renounce explicit political activism. Other Islamist organizations became providers of basic health, education, and commercial services, and were perceived by some as pursuing a strategy to take political power."

U.S. officials have long expressed concern about the presence of known terrorist individuals in East Africa. Some observers contend that Somalia is being used as a transit and hiding place by some of these individuals, including Haroon Fazul, the leader of the 1998 and 2002 bombings, Saleh Nabhan, and Talha al-Sudani. But no Somali group has been directly linked to any terrorist attacks against the U.S. or its allies.

Al-Ittihad

Al-Ittihad was perhaps the most active and at one point most successful of all the Islamic groups. Al-Ittihad is an Islamic group whose principal ideology was to establish an Islamic state and to bring law and order by utilizing the Islamic court system. Founded in the late 1980s and early 1990s, Al-Ittihad unsuccessfully sought to replace clan and warlord politics with an Islamic state. In the early 1990s, Al-Ittihad had modest successes; for example, it administered territories under its control in the south. But Al-Ittihad never emerged as a major military or political force in Somalia. The clan-based groups and factions led by warlords in Mogadishu are secular and have been at odds with Al-Ittihad, even though some of these groups maintained tactical alliances from time to time with Al-Ittihad. Al-Ittihad's failure to maintain control over territories and spread its ideology led to a shift in strategy in the mid-1990s. Al-Ittihad abandoned its ambition to spread its ideology through military means and began to concentrate on providing social services to communities through Islamic schools and health care centers.

Al-Ittihad's social activities and religious objectives in Somalia seemed inconsistent with its activities in support of armed groups in the Somali-inhabited region of Ethiopia. In Ethiopia, Al Ittihad was reportedly engaged in military activities in support of ethnic Somalis. Several anti- Ethiopian groups are active in the Somali region and Al-Ittihad cooperated with these groups in carrying out attacks against Ethiopian targets.

In 1999, the Ogaden Islamic Union under the leadership of Muhammad Muallem Omar Abdi, the Somali People's Liberation Front under the leadership of Ahmed Ali Ismail, and the Western Somali Liberation Front under the leadership of Muhammad Haji Ibrahim Hussein formed a coalition called the United Front for the Liberation of Western Somalia, their term for the Somali-inhabited region of Ethiopia [24]. The Ogaden National Liberation Front was engaged in military activities in the region, and in the past formed alliances with other Ethiopian opposition groups.

Many Somali watchers believe that Al-Ittihad's strength was highly exaggerated and that information about its alleged links with international terrorist organizations is unreliable. The State Department's Country Reports on Terrorism stated in 2006 that "in recent years the existence of a coherent entity operating as AIAI (Al-Ittihad) has become difficult to prove."

There is no reliable information or pattern of behavior to suggest that Al-Ittihad had an international agenda as was the case with the National Islamic Front (NIF) government of Sudan. Some observers note that if Al-Ittihad had a clear internationally-oriented agenda, its obvious ally in the region would be the NIF regime in Sudan or the Sudanese-backed Eritrean Islamic Jihad. The Sudanese regime did back regional extremist groups and international terrorist organizations, but there was no apparent relationship between the NIF and Al-Ittihad. Many Somalis often refer to Al-Ittihad's social services and the peace and stability that prevailed in the areas it controlled.

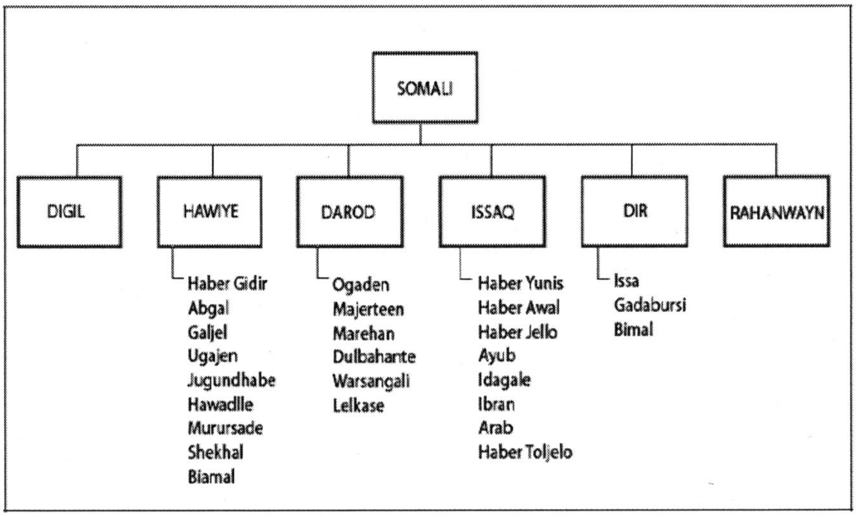

Figure 1. Major Somali Clans and Subclans.

In late September 2001, the Bush Administration added Al-Ittihad to a list of terrorism-related entities whose assets were frozen by an Executive Order. Bush Administration officials accused Al-Ittihad of links with Al Qaeda. The Administration did not publicly offer evidence supporting its allegations, but some officials asserted that links between AIAI and Al Qaeda date back to the U.S. presence in Somalia during Operation Restore Hope (1992-1994). This assertion, however, seems inconsistent with the reality on the ground at that time, according to some observers. Then, the dominant players in Mogadishu were the warlords and not Al-Ittihad. In early November 2001, federal authorities raided several Somali-owned money transfer businesses in the United States operated by Al-Barakaat Companies.

The Bush Administration ordered the assets of Al-Barakaat frozen because of its alleged links to Al Qaeda. U.S. officials, however, later seemed to back off from their earlier assertion that Al-Barakaat and individuals associated with the money transfer business sector are directly linked to Al Qaeda. In September 2002, U.S. officials cleared three Somalis and three Al-Barakaat branches accused of ties with Al Qaeda. The three individuals and businesses were removed from the U.S. Treasury Department list of terrorist supporters and their assets were also unfrozen. Nonetheless, the Bush Administration remains concerned about terrorist activities in Somalia, although no attacks against U.S. interests have been carried out by any known Somali groups. The United States has had no presence in Somalia since Washington pulled out of the peacekeeping operation in 1994. In September 2008, the

European Court of Justice annulled the decision taken by the EU Council to freeze the assets of two Somalis and Al-Barakaat International Foundation of Sweden.

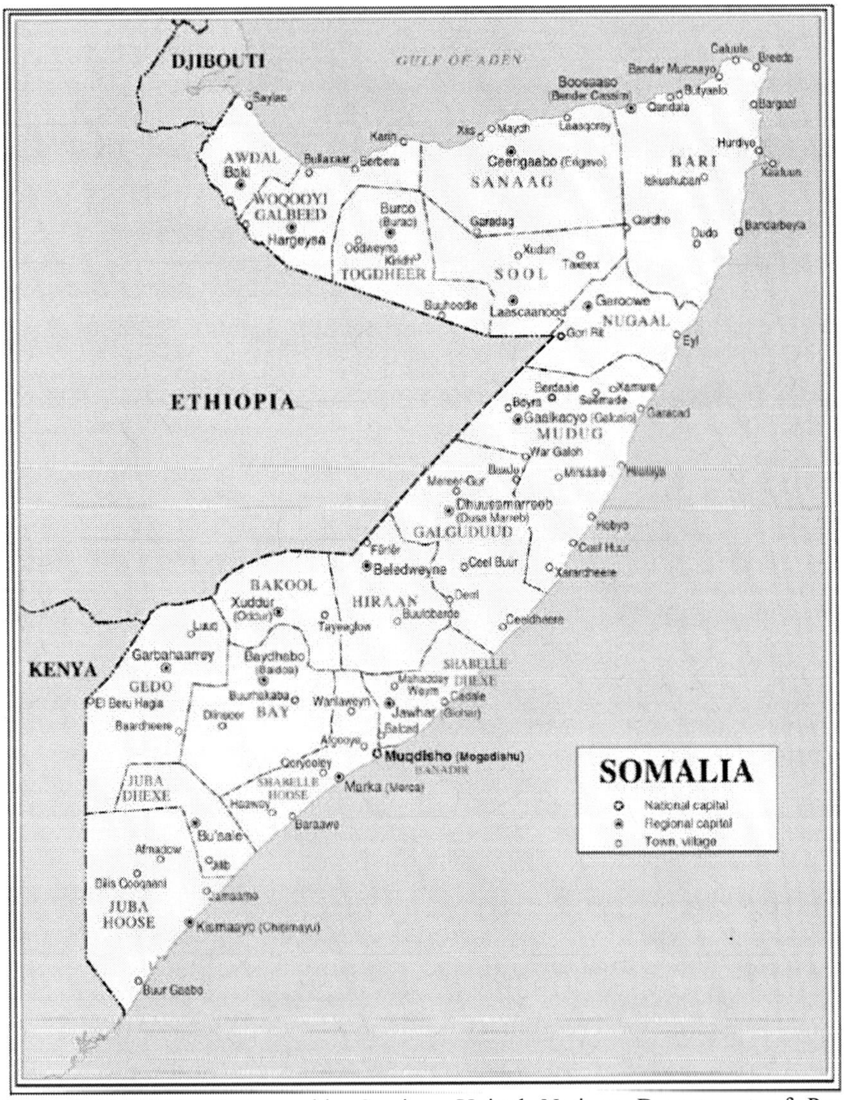

Source: Adapted by CRS. Cartographic Section, United Nations Department of Peacekeeping Operations, Map No. 3690 Rev. 7, January 2007.

Figure 2. Map of Somalia.

REFERENCES

[1] Ted Dagne interviewed ARS-Asmara leaders in Eritrea in April 2009.
[2] Ted Dagne interviewed Sheik Aweys in Eritrea in late April 2009.
[3] CRS interview with senior TFG officials and members of the Somali opposition in Kenya, May and August 2008.
[4] United Nations Political Office for Somalia (UNPOS), August 2008.

[5] CRS interview with senior security and government officials in Mogadishu, April 2009.

[6] "Young Somali Men Missing from Minneapolis," *International Herald Tribune*, November 27, 2008.

[7] "Routinely Targeted Attacks on Civilians in Somalia," *Amnesty International*, May 2008.

[8] CRS interviewed a number of journalists and human rights advocates in Kenya in 2007 and 2008. In November 2008, CRS met with a group of Somali human rights advocates, who fled from Somalia for safety.

[9] For more on piracy in the Horn of Africa, please see CRS Report R40528, *Piracy off the Horn of Africa*, by Lauren Ploch et al.

[10] CRS interviews with Somali officials, opposition leaders, and regional officials.

[11] Ted Dagne interviewed many Somalis in Dadaab refugee camp in Kenya in 2007-2008.

[12] http://new.unep.org/tsunami/reports/TSUNAMI_SOMALIA_LAYOUT.pdf

[13] Ted Dagne interview with U.N. Special Envoy in Kenya, August 2008.

[14] Political program of the Alliance for the Re-Liberation of Somalia.

[15] Author interview with senior ICU official in late December 2006.

[16] Author interview with senior ICU official and regional sources in the Horn of Africa.

[17] Michael Gordon and Mark Mazzetti. "U.S. Used Base in Ethiopia to Hunt Al Qaeda," *New York Times*. February 23, 2007.

[18] http://news.bbc.co.uk/2/hi/africa/6273949.stm

[19] Communiqué of the African Union Peace and Security Council 69th Meeting, January 19, 2007.

[20] Peter Goodspeed, "Somalia Looking Like Pre-Taliban Afghanistan: U.S. Backed Warlords, Al Qaeda-Linked Thugs Kill Dozens" *National Post*, with files from News Services. May 16, 2006.

[21] The author met with several Members of Parliament and the TFG Foreign Minister in Kenya in August 2006.

[22] "Somali Islamic Courts Leader Comments on Domestic Situation, Future Outlook." Al-Ashraq Al-Awsat. June 6, 2006.

[23] The author had over 25 conversations between July 2006 and March 2007 with senior Islamic Courts officials and Somali residents in Mogadishu.

[24] *Foreign Broadcast Information Services (FBIS)*. "Islamists Regroup Their Forces After Ethiopian Preemptive Strike," May 17-23, 1999.

In: Economic, Political and Social Issues of Africa
Editor: Jeremy S. McQueen
ISBN 978-1-61209-957-6

Chapter 2

UGANDA: CURRENT CONDITIONS AND THE CRISIS IN NORTH UGANDA*

Ted Dagne

ABSTRACT

In February 2006, Ugandans voted in the first multi-party elections in almost 26 years. President Yoweri Museveni and his ruling National Revolutionary Movement (NRM) parliamentary candidates won a decisive victory over opposition candidate Kizza Besigye and the Forum for Democracy Coalition. Nevertheless, poll results showed a notable decline in support for President Museveni from previous elections. International election observers did not condemn the election results, nor did they fully endorse the electoral process. Critics charged the government with intimidating the opposition during the pre-election period, and Besigye spent much of the campaign period in jail. The election followed a controversial move by the Ugandan parliament in July 2005 to remove the constitutional two-term limit on the presidency.

In the north, the government of Uganda has long fought the Lord's Resistance Army (LRA), an armed rebel group backed by the government of Sudan. Through over 20 years of civil war, the brutal insurgency has created a humanitarian crisis that has displaced over 1.5 million and resulted in the abduction of over 20,000 children. In 2006-07, the government of Uganda and the LRA have been actively engaged in an effort to resolve the conflict peacefully. The Government of Southern Sudan (GOSS) has been mediating the talks since June 2006. In August 2006, the government of Uganda and the LRA signed a Cessation of Hostilities Agreement. In February 2008, the parties agreed on a Permanent Ceasefire, amended the Agreement on Accountability and Reconciliation, and Agreement on Comprehensive Solutions. However, the leader of the LRA, Joseph Kony, failed to show up for the final signing of the agreement on a number of occasions. Kony and his forces are in the Democratic Republic of Congo (DRC).

The cessation of hostilities has allowed an estimated 400,000 displaced people to return to their homes. In June 2007, the parties signed an agreement on

* This is an edited, reformatted and augmented version of CRS Report RL33701, dated July 31, 2009.

Accountability and Reconciliation. In late October, a LRA delegation went to Kampala for the first time and held talks with senior Ugandan officials. In October, Vincent Otti, the Deputy Commander of the LRA, reportedly was killed in Uganda by Joseph Kony, the head of the LRA. Over the past several months, a number of senior LRA commanders have surrendered to authorities in the Democratic Republic of Congo (DRC) and Uganda.

In late October 2007, President Museveni visited Washington, D.C. and met with President Bush and other senior administration officials. President Museveni also met with several Members of Congress. During his visit, President Museveni discussed a wide range of issues, including U.S.- Uganda relations, the crises in Somalia and Darfur, trade, and HIV/AIDS. Uganda deployed an estimated 1,800 peacekeeping troops to Somalia, shortly after Ethiopian forces invaded Mogadishu and installed the Transitional Federal Government (TFG). Ugandan forces have not been a major target of the insurgents in Mogadishu, although a number of Ugandan peacekeepers have been killed over the past several months.

BACKGROUND

Uganda, a country slightly smaller than Oregon, gained its independence from Britain in 1962. Until the mid-1980s, the East African country was mired in civil war and ethnic strife, and its people suffered under a brutal dictatorship. By the time President Yoweri Museveni's National Resistance Army/Movement (NRA/M) took power in early 1986, the country's economy was in ruins, with an inflation rate of over 240% and an almost non-existent economic infrastructure. President Museveni is credited with bringing relative political and economic stability to Uganda, although he has not been able to end the conflict in northern Uganda.

His strategy in the late 1980s and 1990s was to co-opt his political opponents and, when necessary, to use military means to neutralize rebel groups. Museveni's first government included opposition figures who had served in previous governments and arch critics of the NRM. Despite efforts aimed at achieving national reconciliation, armed opposition to his government continued for much of the 1980s and 1990s.

Uganda at a Glance

Population: 31.3 Million
Population Growth: 3.6% (2008)
Comparative Area: Slightly smaller than Oregon
Infant Mortality Rate: 65.9 deaths/1,000 live births (2007)
Life Expectancy at Birth: 52.34 years
HIV/AIDS Prevalence Rate: 6.7 % (2005)
HIV/AIDS Deaths: 78,000 (2003)
Religions: Roman Catholic 42%, Protestant 42%, Muslim 12%, Indigenous beliefs 4%.
Language: English (official)
GDP (purchasing power parity—PPP): $29 billion (2007)
GDP per capita (PPP): $900 (2007)
Source: CIA—The World Factbook, 2008.

UGANDA: POLITICAL PROFILE

In May 1996, after a long transition period, President Museveni was elected to a five year term in direct presidential elections in what was known until 2005 as a "no-party" system. Museveni won 74.2% of the votes, while his opponent, Paul Ssmogerere, former deputy prime minister and longtime rival of the president, received 23.7%. The elections were declared by international observers to be free and fair. A national referendum on multiparty politics was held in June of 2000. Museveni prevailed, with 90.7% of Ugandans favoring a no-party government system. The President stated that multiparty politics could only be introduced once a no-party system had succeeded in eliminating the threat of a return to sectarian politics. In 2005, Museveni changed his position on this issue (see below). The NRM remains the dominant party, although some of its members openly express their opposition and frustration about NRM's leadership. Some party leaders are also focused on the issue of succession, while new members of parliament challenge the old establishment of the ruling party. Despite some serious challenges facing the leadership, Uganda has made and continues to make important progress on a number of fronts. The East African country is more stable today than a few years back and the prospect of a final agreement with the Lord's Resistance Army (LRA) could lead to lasting peace in Uganda.

The 2001 Presidential Elections

On March 12, 2001, Uganda again held national elections, and President Museveni won 69.3% of the votes cast, [1] while his closest challenger, Kizza Besigye, received 27.8%. Besigye, a doctor and Museveni's one-time ally, was a member of the NRM and Museveni's personal physician during the insurgency in the early 1980s. He ran on an anti-corruption platform, vowing to rid the government of its excesses. He also raised questions about Uganda's military involvement in the Democratic Republic of the Congo (DRC). Election observers, both local and international, declared the elections to be free and fair, although they acknowledged that the electoral process and management had many weaknesses. The results of the elections were rejected by Besigye on the grounds that there were discrepancies and inconsistencies in the electoral process. He filed a petition at the Supreme Court challenging the declaration of Museveni as president-elect and sought to annul the elections. Besigye subsequently lost the petition and said he would respect the Supreme Court verdict. In August 2001, Besigye fled Uganda and later surfaced in South Africa [2]

The Third-Term Debate and Adoption of a Multi-Party System

Uganda was ruled under a "no-party" system after Museveni took power in 1986. In March 2003, President Museveni suggested to his National Executive Committee, the leadership organ of the NRM, that the Movement should consider lifting the ban on a multi-party system. He and his supporters also urged a review of the two-term limit for a president. According to the Ugandan constitution at the time, "A person shall not be elected under this

Constitution to hold office as President for more than two terms as prescribed by this article" [3].

Under this provision, President Museveni's term would have expired in 2006, but many of his supporters argued that without Museveni, Uganda might plunge into another civil war. Critics of the President contended that Museveni did not wish to relinquish power. The President holds most executive powers. In January 2003, President Museveni told a British reporter "we will follow the Constitution because that is what I fought for. The present Constitution says not more than two consecutive terms" [4]

Those ruling party members who criticized the President's third term proposal were removed from power, including Eriya Katagaya, the then-First Deputy Prime Minister and a longtime ally of President Museveni [5]. The Vice President also resigned, reportedly to pursue her academic studies in the United States. In May 2005, the Ugandan parliament voted to approve a referendum on multi-party politics.

On July 28, 2005, Ugandans voted overwhelmingly in favor of a multiparty system, after almost 19 years of a "no party" system. Reportedly, more than 92% of the registered voters said yes to a multi-party system, although the polls were boycotted by the Forum for Democratic Change, an opposition group. In July 2005, the Ugandan parliament voted to remove the two-term limit on the presidency.

The 2006 Multi-Party Elections

In February 2006, Ugandans voted in the first multi-party elections in almost 26 years. President Museveni won 59% of the votes, while the leading opposition candidate, Kizza Besigye, won 37% of the votes. The ruling NRM won 202 seats in parliamentary elections, while the opposition Forum for Democracy Coalition won 40 seats. The election results show a decline in support for President Museveni from his 74% and 69% victories in the 1996 and 2001 elections, respectively. Meanwhile, Besigye's 37% share represented a 10% gain over his 2001 vote share. International election observers did not condemn the election results nor did they fully endorse the electoral process. According to the European Union election monitoring group report, "Uganda's first multi-party presidential and parliamentary elections since 1980 have demonstrated significant improvements in comparison to previous elections." According to the same report,

> "Despite a number of problems experienced by voters on election day, EU Chief Observer Max van den Berg, who spent the day traveling between Kampala, Gulu and Soroti, noted that voters came out in large numbers, knew that they had a choice between change or continuity, and made this choice with calm and dignity."

But the elections were marred by intimidation, counting irregularities, voter name deletions, and show of force by the government. Harassment by authorities and the trial of the opposition candidate, Besigye, were seen as part of the overall strategy to secure victory. Kizza Besigye was charged and imprisoned soon after his return to Uganda to run as a candidate for president. He was charged with rape, terrorism, and treason. He was released from prison in January 2006 and challenged President Museveni in the February 2006 presidential election.

THE SITUATION IN NORTHERN UGANDA

While much of the country has remained stable since the NRM took power in 1986, civil war has ravaged northern Uganda for over 20 years. The situation has been characterized as one of the world's worst humanitarian crises, where civilians, particularly children, are the most affected, according to the United Nations and numerous reports by non-governmental organizations. The conflict and the humanitarian crisis in northern Uganda have killed tens of thousands of civilians due to deliberate targeting of children by the Lord's Resistance Army (LRA) (see below), although the actual number of those killed is unknown.

According to a report by the Civil Society Organizations for Peace in Northern Uganda (CSOPNU), a coalition of 50 Ugandan and international groups, more than two million civilians have been affected. An estimated 90% of the population in the northern region of Acholiland, particularly in the districts of Gulu, Kitigum, and Pader, have been displaced; and some estimate that 80% of the forces in the LRA are the abducted children from these areas. For the past two decades, the victims in this conflict have largely been civilians, although the conflict began as an effort to overthrow the Museveni regime. The victims reportedly were abused routinely by security forces and the government failed to provide adequate protection to civilians, particularly children in northern Uganda, according to several reports.

The LRA: Early Years

In 1985, the Milton Obote regime was ousted in a military coup by General Tito Lutwa Okello and other military officers from northern Uganda. The coup came at a time when the NRM attacks against the Obote regime threatened Obote's hold on power. In 1986, the NRA defeated the Okello regime, forcing the military and their supporters to flee to northern Uganda. Shortly afterward a rebel alliance was formed, the Uganda People's Democratic Army (UPDA). The UPDA began attacks against government military installations primarily in northern Uganda. The same year, Alice Lakwena, an Acholi spiritual healer, emerged as the dominant leader of the rebel alliance. Lakwena's faction, the Holy Spirit Movement, initially dominated the alliance and also began to make its move in Southern Sudan. After a devastating battle with the Ugandan military in Jinja, 60 miles from the capital of Kampala, in which a large number of the rebel alliance members were killed or captured, Lakwena fled to Kenya. By the late 1980s and early

1990s, UPDA was no longer active. One of Lakwena's key members and reportedly a relative, Joseph Kony, then in his early 20s, emerged as the leader of the remaining forces and emerged as the LRA leader. A major military strategy shift took place in the early 1990s with the emergence of Kony. Kony's group began to primarily target civilians in northern Uganda and forged a strong alliance with the government of Sudan.

The LRA abducted more than 20,000 children over the past decade for forced conscription and sexual exploitation [6]. According to the United Nations "the most disturbing aspect of this humanitarian crisis is the fact that this is a war fought by children on children - minors make up almost 90% of the LRA's soldiers. Some recruits are as young as eight and are inducted through raids on villages. They are brutalized and forced to commit atrocities on fellow abductees and even siblings. Those who attempt to escape are killed. For those living in a state of constant fear, violence becomes a way of life and the psychological trauma is incalculable." Although the situation in northern Uganda has improved significantly over the past year since the beginning of the peace talks between the LRA and the Government of Uganda, the U.N. Security Council reported in May 2007 that "the LRA has not released any children, women or non-combatants from its ranks." Similarly, the U.N.S.C. report voiced deep concern over "the absence of any concrete signs regarding the release of children associated with various forces, especially local defense units and LRA." The U.N.S.C. report also stated that government security forces continue to occupy schools in abandoned communities, thereby significantly delaying the reopening of schools.

The overall impact of the crisis in northern Uganda is not clear, although day to day life for many in this region has changed significantly. The economy in northern Uganda has been devastated, especially in light of the fact that much of the population is displaced internally and some have left the region. According to various sources, there are an estimated 1.5-1.7 million internally displaced people in northern Uganda. Children who are not in internally displaced persons camps often leave their homes at night to sleep in hospitals or churches, although over the past year conditions have improved. These children are known as "Night Commuters." Education for many of these children seems out of reach, since many are unable to stay in one place to attend school. According to a World Vision report, *Pawns of Politics*:

> The north has suffered insecurity, manifested by violence against civilians, abductions and displacement. This insecurity has resulted in death, loss of property, and disruption of development activities. Children are losing vital educational opportunities; they are at greater risk for contracting HIV/AIDS and other STDs; and they are forced into child prostitution, child soldiering, and other forms of bondage [7]

As a result of the war and perceived ethnic bias and marginalization, the NRM government is unpopular in northern Uganda. In the 2006 elections, opposition candidate Besigye reportedly won 80% of the votes in Gulu. Over the past year, the Government of Uganda has expanded civilian protection and significantly increased its budget for reconstruction and development in northern Uganda. More than 400,000 displaced persons have also returned to their homes over the past year.

Regional Implications

Under the leadership of Joseph Kony, the LRA has conducted military operations in northern Uganda, the Democratic Republic of Congo (DRC), and Southern Sudan. The regional impact of the northern Uganda crisis has been particularly hard for Southern Sudan, in part because of its geographic proximity and also due to the government of Sudan's support for the LRA rebels. In Southern Sudan, the LRA allied with the government of Sudan to attack the Sudan People's Liberation Army (SPLA), the liberation movement fighting then successive Sudanese governments, according to U.S. and regional officials. Southern Sudanese civilians have been victims of LRA attacks. The LRA was given protection, facilities for training, and supplies by the government of Sudan to wage war in northern

Uganda and Southern Sudan, according to South Sudan, U.S., and regional officials. The LRA targeted civilians in Eastern and Western Equatoria and in the Juba region, the regional capital. The LRA leadership and its troops had a permanent presence in Southern Sudan under the protection of the government of Sudan. In the Juba region, LRA forces used schools and other government facilities to train and house their troops [8]

In late 2005, the LRA intensified its attacks targeting civilians in Southern Sudan, especially in Yei and Juba areas. However, the signing of the Comprehensive Peace Agreement (CPA) in 2005 between the government of Sudan and the SPLM has threatened the survival of the LRA as a force in Southern Sudan. The takeover of the government in Southern Sudan by the SPLM has made LRA activities very difficult. The CPA has a provision in the Security Agreement that all foreign groups must be forced out of Sudan. The late leader of Southern Sudan, Dr. John Garang, had the LRA and foreign terrorist groups in mind when he insisted on this provision [9] In 2005, some LRA units went into DRC, reportedly looking for a new home after the SPLM took power. Military clashes in DRC reportedly led to the killing of 8 Guatemalan United Nations peacekeepers in the DRC. The Congolese government acknowledges the presence of LRA forces in Garamba National Park in 2007. In early November 2007, President Joseph Kabila stated that LRA forces will be forced to leave DRC once a peace agreement is reached between the LRA and the government of Uganda. He also made it clear that the LRA will be expelled from DRC if they failed to reach an agreement [10]

Attempts to End the Conflict

A number of attempts in the past at a negotiated settlement with the LRA failed, in large part due to LRA intransigence and due to the government of Uganda's inconsistent positions. The first serious effort was launched by former Ugandan government minister Betty Bigombe in the early 1990s with the full support of President Museveni. In 1993, Bigombe made contact with the LRA leadership and the LRA initially expressed interest in a negotiated settlement. Prior to this effort, the government of Uganda launched what was known as the Operation North campaign. Operation North campaign was designed to deny the LRA support in the North and to arm the civilian population with bows and arrows, known then as the Arrow Group. The operation failed and created strong animosity between the government and elements in northern Uganda. The Bigombe initiative ended when President Museveni threatened to use force against the LRA and demanded its surrender. Other initiatives, both local and regional, failed to produce tangible results. Bigombe was once again engaged in an effort to bring an end the conflict in northern Uganda. In late 2004-2005, contacts were made with the leadership of the LRA and the LRA also had appointed two senior commanders, Vincent Otti and Sam Kolo, as negotiators in this new initiative. The peace initiative stalled in 2005 when Kolo defected to the government side and the government of Uganda began its military campaign. Resolution of the conflict through military means has not been successful, in part due to ineffective operations against the LRA and an apparent lack of will by the government to end the conflict through a negotiated settlement.

In October 2005, the International Criminal Court (ICC) issued arrest warrants for five top LRA leaders, including Kony. Some observers, while supportive of the ICC prosecution of these leaders, maintain that the ICC action could hinder peace efforts. Other observers argue that despite the ICC process, the parties were able to reach important agreements for the first time in decades. Moreover, many LRA members and leaders have returned to Uganda under a government amnesty program. According to the peace agreement, traditional justice "shall form a central part of the alternative justice and reconciliation framework."

Peace Initiative

After a series of failed peace efforts, the Government of South Sudan appears to have made some significant strides in brokering the conflict. Following months of talks in Juba, Sudan, the two parties signed a formal cessation of hostilities agreement on August 26, 2006. Under the agreement, LRA insurgents were expected to gather at assembly points in southern Sudan. The deadline for assembly was extended after ceasefire observers reported that both sides violated the agreement in October. The Ugandan army has admitted to approaching a rebel safe haven in Sudan, claiming it was escorting journalists and diplomats on a fact-finding mission. Meanwhile, LRA soldiers, claiming they feared attack by the Ugandan forces, violated the agreement by leaving a designated assembly point in southern Sudan. Many observers remain skeptical that all of the remaining LRA insurgents will comply with the terms of the agreement.

President Museveni has offered amnesty if the rebels accept a peace agreement. According to media reports and U.S. officials, there is support among many civilians in northern Uganda for reconciliation rather than revenge against the LRA leaders. Nevertheless, unless the ICC's Chief Prosecutor, Luis Moreno-Ocampo, accepts a local judicial solution, the indicted insurgents would have to accept asylum in a country not bound by the Rome Treaty. The ICC has announced that it will not consider any amnesty proposal until after the successful completion of a peace agreement.

Following speculation that the Ugandan government was going to yield to the LRA's demand that ICC arrest warrants be annulled, President Museveni announced on July 19, 2007, that warrants for the top LRA leaders will remain in place until a peace agreement has been reached: "We are not going to ask the ICC to lift the arrest warrants. If [the LRA leaders] don't conclude the peace talks they could be arrested and taken to the ICC or get killed. If they conclude the peace deal, that is when the government can write to the ICC to say we have found an alternative solution."

In August 2007, he stated that if the parties agreed to resolve their differences peacefully, the issue of accountability could be addressed through local and traditional mechanisms [11]

The Ugandan Government's continued negotiations with the LRA reached the critical question of how Agenda No. 3 (Reconciliation and Accountability), reached in June, 2007, should be concluded. The past year has yielded two other agreements mandating the cessation of hostilities and the withdrawal of LRA forces from northern Uganda. In February 2008, the Government of Uganda and the LRA reached several agreements. The parties agreed on a Permanent Ceasefire, amended the Agreement on Accountability and Reconciliation, and the Agreement on Comprehensive Solutions (see Appendix). The LRA leadership moved into the Garamba National Park in the DRC and has not given indication of signing the agreement since April 2008. In late October, the LRA sent a delegation to Kampala for the first time in almost two decades to meet with senior Ugandan officials. Moreover, the LRA delegation went to northern Uganda to consult with its constituency as the parties get closer to concluding the peace talks.

Operation Lightning Thunder

In late 2008, the governments of the Democratic Republic of Congo, Southern Sudan, and Uganda launched a major military operation against the LRA forces. The operation forced LRA forces to disperse into other parts of DRC but failed to achieve its military objective of defeating the LRA. In retaliation, the LRA killed an estimated 1,000 people in the DRC and Southern Sudan. More that 180,000 people were displaced in the DRC. The joint military operation was the first major coordinated attack against the LRA.

SOCIAL AND ECONOMIC PROFILE

Economic Conditions

Uganda is blessed with fertile soils, regular rainfall, and sizable deposits of copper and cobalt. Its largest sector is agriculture, which employs 78% of the workforce and accounted for about 90% of export earnings and 23.4% of Uganda's Gross Domestic Product (GDP). Coffee exports make up half its export earnings and Uganda is Africa's largest coffee producer. Other major exports include cotton, tea, and to a lesser extent, maize. Crop production has been hampered by security concerns in the northern and western regions of Uganda. To stabilize the economy, Museveni adopted a policy of reducing inflation while simultaneously increasing production and export earnings. Uganda raised producer prices on export crops, increased the prices of imported petroleum products, and boosted civil service wages.

Long periods of forced displacement in northern Uganda have seriously disrupted agricultural productivity in the region, but USAID reports that recent security improvements have allowed a number of farmers to return home and resume normal cultivation. According to USAID officials in Uganda, the restoration of normal farming practices is essential to the recovery process. Throughout FY2007, USAID contributed significant funds to the U.N. Food and Agriculture Organization (FAO) and Catholic Relief Services (CRS) to distribute farm equipment and seeds to Ugandan farmers prior to the Spring 2007 planting season. In 2006-2007, food production was better than expected, in part due to good weather conditions.

The industrial sector has also expanded, with real output growth approaching 10% a year. Industry constituted 20.4% of GDP in 2004/2005. The main industries include the processing of coffee, cotton, tea, sugar, tobacco, edible oils, dairy products, and grain milling as well as brewing. Other ventures include vehicle assembly and the manufacture of textiles and metal products. According to the Economic Intelligence Unit (05/2009):

> As the 2008/09 financial year enters its final quarter, the authorities have lowered the economic growth projection to 6.2% from 8.1% originally forecast in the budget. This is a fall of 3 percentage points compared with growth of 8.9% in 2007/2008.

Obstacles to economic growth remain. Uganda's heavy reliance on coffee exports makes it vulnerable to international commodity price fluctuations and poor weather conditions. Privatization initiatives pose a problem as they are seen by many to be a scramble for previously state-owned property. Another problem plaguing Uganda's economy is corruption. Uganda relies upon international donors for 41% of its national budget. Those donors, in particular Ireland, Norway, Sweden, and the United Kingdom, have become increasingly critical of governance issues and a rise in defense spending.

The late-June discovery of an oil reserve in the fields of western Uganda much larger than initially estimated has many speculating about the potential implications for Uganda's economy. The oil was discovered in an exploratory mission by oil and gas groups Heritage and Tullow. The oil reserve is located in the Albertine Basin, close to Uganda's border with the Democratic Republic of Congo.

HIV/AIDS

In the 1 980s and early 1 990s, Uganda was one of the African countries most devastated by the HIV/AIDS epidemic. Over the past decade, however, Uganda has made significant progress in the fight against HIV/AIDS, and the Museveni government is widely credited for implementing a sweeping reform to address the HIV/AIDS epidemic. According to USAID, the prevalence of HIV has dropped over 50% in the last fifteen years. Today the overall prevalence rate is 6.7%. Moreover, prevalence among pregnant women declined significantly. Despite these impressive declines, HIV/AIDS is still a serious problem in Uganda. An estimated 91,000 Ugandans died in 2005, and there are over one million orphans from the AIDS crisis. Uganda's HIV/AIDS prevention program known as ABC (Abstinence, Be Faithful, or Use Condoms) is credited for the reduction in HIV infections and has been viewed by the U.S. Administration as a model for the rest of sub-Saharan Africa. In 2007, the United States provided $188 million to support Uganda's fight against HIV/AIDS (see table below for a summary of U.S. assistance to Uganda).

Regional Relations

Uganda is a member of the East African Community and enjoys friendly relations with fellow members Kenya and Tanzania. Uganda has at times had tense relations with two of its other neighbors, Rwanda and, more recently, the Democratic Republic of Congo (DRC), resulting from its 1998 troop deployment into eastern Congo. While the Ugandan government claimed the troop presence was aimed at discouraging attacks from Ugandan rebels based in the region, there were widespread allegations of natural resource exploitation, and Uganda eventually removed its troops under international pressure in 2003. In 2005, Museveni threatened to send troops back to the region when LRA forces moved from Sudan to the DRC if Congo failed to deny them sanctuary, although the current peace talks may avert further contention.

UGANDAN TROOPS IN SOMALIA

Approximately 1,800 Ugandan troops have been stationed in Somalia since early 2007 in an effort to increase security and put a stop to the violent conflict in Mogadishu. The Ugandan troops (members of the Uganda People's Defense Forces) are the only AU forces currently serving the African Union Mission in Somalia (AMISOM). Other AU countries (Nigeria, Burundi, Ghana and Malawi) that pledged a combined total of 6,500 troops to AMISOM have attributed their delayed deployment to logistical and financial issues. In January 2008, Burundi deployed an estimated 850 peacekeeping troops to Somalia. The Peace and Security Council of the African Union announced in mid-July that Ugandan troops would remain in Somalia for another six months.

Army Spokesman, Major Felix Kulayigye, announced the extension and argued that it does not make sense to withdraw Ugandan troops simply because the Reconciliation Congress is underway. In mid-September 2 Ugandan peacekeeping troops were killed in Mogadishu, bringing the number of peacekeeping troops killed in Somalia to eight since March 2008.

U.S.-UGANDA RELATIONS

Relations between Washington and Kampala are warm. Over the years, successive American administrations have supported the Museveni government as a reformist regime and a staunch ally of the United States. The Clinton Administration championed the Museveni regime, and President Clinton visited Uganda during his 1998 tour of Africa. Relations cooled, however, when Ugandan troops intervened in the Congo in 1998. Clinton Administration officials were also critical of Uganda and Rwanda when the two former allies clashed in eastern Congo in 1999 and 2000.

The Bush Administration restored good relations with Kampala. Former Secretary of State Colin Powell visited Uganda during his four-nation trip to Africa in 2001. Secretary Powell met with President Museveni and opposition leaders to discuss a wide range of issues, including Sudan and DRC. He praised Museveni for lowering Uganda's HIV-AIDS infection ratc.

In 2001, Uganda withdrew several battalions from the DRC and by May 2003, almost all of Uganda's troops had been withdrawn. President Museveni has also been a leading ally of the United States in the fight against international terrorism and was one of the first African leaders to pledge support in the war against Iraq. Despite the healthy relationship between the United States and Uganda, numerous NGOs and politicians have insisted that the Bush Administration do more.

On June 14, 2007, 44 members of the House and Senate wrote to President Bush urging him to dispatch a special envoy to Juba to facilitate negotiations between the Government of Uganda and the LRA. The letter underscored the many obstacles to the peace process in Uganda, reiterating the importance of U.S. involvement. In October 2007, President Bush assured President Museveni of his commitment to support Uganda on a wide range of issues, including fighting HIV/AIDS and Malaria. The two leaders discussed regional security issues, including the crises in Sudan and Somalia [12]

U.S. Assistance

The United States provides significant humanitarian and development assistance to Uganda. In FY2007, the United States provided $332.1 million to Uganda, and $419 million for FY2008. In FY2009, Uganda is expected to receive $389.3 million. The Obama Administration has requested $428.9 million for FY20 10. In 2007, the Millennium Challenge Corporation approved a $10 million Threshold program to support anti-corruption activities. Moreover, Uganda is eligible for trade benefits, including textile and apparel benefits under the African Growth and Opportunity Act (AGOA).

Approximately half of all U.S. non-food aid in Uganda is directed at ameliorating the crisis in the north. USAID continues its support for the displaced children and orphans in Uganda. The Displaced Children and Orphans Fund (DCOF) assists war-affected children in northern and western Uganda by rebuilding traditional community and family structures and working to fight the spread of HIV/AIDS.

Table 1. U.S. Assistance to Uganda
($ in thousands)

Account	FY2005 Actual	FY2006 Actual	FY2007 Actual	FY2008 Estimate	FY2009 Request
CSH	15,160	20,648	33,960	39,851	31,778
DA	27,967	23,414	28,445	27,600	35,150
FMF	1,984	—	—	—	
GHAI	122,741	145,000	210,660	255,000	255,000
IMET	293	340	283	477	500
NADR-TIP	—	—	150		
INCLE					350
P.L. 480 Title II	64,410		58,770	22,839	23,000

Source: Department of State.

Acronyms. CSH: Child Survival and Health; DA: Development Assistance; FMF: Foreign Military Financing; GHAI: Global Aids Initiative; IMET: International Military Education and Training; NADR-TIP: Nonproliferation, Anti-Terrorism, Demining, and Related programs. INCLE: International Narcotics Control and Law Enforcement.

The DCOF funded programs such as the Community Resilience and Dialogue (CRD), which focused on aiding abducted children between 2002-2005. The CRD rehabilitated 7,000 abducted children and reunified and resettled 5,700 with their families. U.S. funding for northern Uganda is expected to reach $106.3 million in FY2007. The United States provided $87.9 million in 2006 and $77.9 million in 2005. In addition to humanitarian assistance in northern Uganda, the United States has increased development assistance from $18.4 million in 2005 to $51.2 million in 2007. In 2007, USAID opened an office in Gulu, northern Uganda.

APPENDIX. CEASEFIRE AGREEMENT

AGREEMENT ON A PERMANENT CEASEFIRE
JUBA, SUDAN

This Agreement, between the Government of the Republic of Uganda (the Government) and the Lord's Resistance Army/Movement (LRA/M) (herein referred to as the 'Parties') provides as follows:

THE PARTIES:

HAVING BEEN engaged in negotiations in Juba, Southern Sudan, in order to find just, peaceful and lasting solutions to the conflict, and to promote accountability and reconciliation and restore harmony and tranquillity within the affected communities;

HAVING concluded a cessation of hostilities agreement on the 26th of August 2006 and thereafter other agreements;

HAVING resolved to bring to an end all forms of armed conflict;

CONVINCED of the urgent need for a permanent ceasefire to pave way for lasting peace and reconciliation;

RECOGNISING the significance of this agreement in the quest for national unity and development;

NOW THEREFORE AGREE as follows:

1. DEFINITIONS

Unless the context suggests otherwise, the following words and phrases shall have the meaning assigned thereto:

"Buffer zone" refers to the area within the Southern Sudan delineated by a fifteen (15) - kilometres distance from the specified perimeters of the Ri-Kwang-Ba Assembly Area.

"Ceasefire" refers to the permanent cessation of hostilities under this Agreement.

"Child" refers to any person below the age of eighteen (18).

"CHMT" refers to the Cessation of Hostilities Monitoring Team.

"CMT" refers to the Ceasefire Monitoring Team.

"Gender" refers to the two sexes, men and women, within the context of society.

"GoSS" refers to the Government of Southern Sudan.

"GoU" refers to the Government of the Republic of Uganda.

"IDDRS" refers to the Integrated Disarmament, Demobilisation and Reintegration Standards of the United Nations.

"LRA/M" refers to the Lord's Resistance Army/Movement.

"Ri-Kwang-Ba Administrative Headquarters" refers to the area defined by the attached grid reference and map.

"Ri-Kwang-Ba Assembly Area" refers to the area within the Southern Sudan delineated by a ten (10) - kilometres radius from the administrative headquarters of Ri-Kwang-Ba.

"SPLA" refers to the Sudan People's Liberation Army.

"SOP" refers to Standard Operating Procedures.

2(8)

2. DECLARATION AND COMMENCEMENT OF CEASEFIRE

2.1. The Parties hereby declare and shall observe a permanent ceasefire commencing 24 hours after the signature of the Final Peace Agreement.

2.2. Upon the coming into force of the ceasefire the Cessation of Hostilities Agreement shall lapse. This provision supersedes contrary provisions of the Cessation of Hostilities Agreement.

2.3. The LRA/M and the GoU shall ensure that their forces abide by the terms of the ceasefire.

3. ASSEMBLY AND ENCAMPMENT

3.1. All forces of the LRA shall be encamped within Ri-Kwang-Ba Assembly Area.

3.2. The forces of the Parties shall respect the buffer zone around Ri-Kwang-Ba Assembly Area.

3.3. In the preparation of detailed agreements and arrangements for disarmament, demobilisation and reintegration, the implementation of measures necessary to adhere to gender and child specific UN IDDRS standards for encampment shall be given the highest priority.

3.4. Except with the express written permission from the Office of the Chief Mediator, and with notification of the CMT established in Clause 4.1 of this Agreement, nobody shall approach or gain access to the LRA Assembly Area.

4. CEASEFIRE MONITORING

4.1. Upon the coming into force of this Agreement there will be reinforcement of the Cessation of Hostilities Monitoring Team (CHMT) transforming it into the Ceasefire Monitoring Team (CMT) as outlined in Clause 4.3 of this Agreement.

4.2. The CMT shall report to the Chief Mediator.

4.3. The CMT shall be composed of:

(a) The Team Leader who shall be a senior officer in the SPLA.

(b) The Deputy Team Leader who shall be a senior officer in the SPLA.

(c) Five representatives of each of the Parties.

(d) Five members from each of the African Union observer countries to the peace talks.

(e) A five-person liaison team from the United Nations.

4.4. The Chief Mediator may in consultation with the Parties restructure the composition of the CMT.

4.5. The CMT shall be considered constituted when at least the SPLA Team Leader or Deputy Team Leader, at least two (2) members of each of the Parties and two (2) members from each of the African Union observer countries are present.

4.6. The CMT shall receive training on international standards of ceasefire monitoring.

4.7. Upon the coming into force of this Agreement the Standard Operating Procedures (SOP) of the CHMT shall become the Standard Operating Procedures of the CMT.

4.8. The SOP shall whenever necessary, be revised in order to bring it into conformity with this Agreement.

4.9. The CMT shall have free and unhindered access to the Assembly area in carrying out its duties.

4.10. The members of the CMT shall enjoy full protection of both Parties.

4.11. All personnel and equipment of organizations or persons duly authorized to enter or operate in the Assembly Area in support of the Ceasefire Agreement shall be afforded full protection and security.

4.12. The terms of reference for the CMT shall include but not necessarily be limited to:

(a) taking full responsibility for the management of the Assembly Area;

(b) monitoring the implementation of this Agreement;

(c) amicable resolution of any disagreement arising out of the implementation or interpretation of this Agreement;

(d) analyzing and reporting events and trends to the Mediator, who will brief the Parties accordingly;

4(8)

(e) reporting to the mediator violations and cases which the CMT is unable to resolve amicably; and,

(f) monitoring the delivery of basic assistance to the LRA in the Assembly Area.

4.13. The CMT shall carry out its functions consistently with the principles contained in the Final Peace Agreement.

5. CEASEFIRE VIOLATIONS

5.1. The Parties shall refrain from violating the ceasefire.

5.2. The following shall constitute violations of the ceasefire:

(a) Any attacks, threats or acts of violence directed against the other Party and/or civilians and/or any other person or persons by either Party or both Parties.

(b) Harassment, attacks, hostage taking, and arrest of combatants as well as seizure of arms and equipment belonging to the other Party.

(c) Harassment, attacks, abduction, hostage taking or unlawful arrest of civilians and personnel of humanitarian agencies as well as seizure of properties of individuals and organisations.

(d) Obstruction of the activities of the CMT as described in Part 4 of this Agreement and in the CMT Standard Operating Procedures.

(e) All hostile propaganda directed against the other Party, including defamatory, untruthful or derogatory statements.

(f) Violation of the right to life of LRA/M members by either Party or third parties associated with the Parties.

(g) Any presence, movement or other actions of LRA forces outside Ri-Kwang-Ba Assembly Area.

(h) Acquisition, recovery or replenishment of arms, ammunition or other military equipment by the LRA.

(i) Recruitment of forces by the LRA/M.

(j) Any other act that might undermine the ceasefire.

5(8)

6. RESPONSIBILITIES OF THE GOVERNMENT OF SOUTHERN SUDAN

6.1. The GoSS shall ensure that:

(a) a full SPLA battalion is deployed for the protection of the Ri-Kwang-Ba Assembly Area, inclusive of the buffer zone;

(b) in the implementation of this Agreement, international standards and mandates, in particular, relevant mandates in Security Council Resolution 1325 on Women, Peace and Security (2000), and Security Council Resolution 1612 on Children and Armed Conflict (2005) are applied;

(c) adequate security, logistical and service support is provided to the LRA encampment sites in the Assembly Area;

(d) food and other supplies to assembled and encamped LRA forces meet the relevant international standards set by the Integrated Disarmament, Demobilisation and Reintegration Standards (IDDRS) of the United Nations; and,

(e) as far as possible, culturally appropriate food is supplied to the Assembly Area.

6.2. The GoSS and the LRA shall collaborate with relevant Sudanese civil society and international agencies to ensure that the layout, access, services and procedures of LRA encampment sites within the Assembly Area conform to applicable standards and specifications of the UN IDDRS.

7. COMMUNICATION

7.1. The Parties shall ensure that the terms of this Ceasefire Agreement and all orders requiring compliance are communicated to all their forces.

7.2. The terms of this Agreement shall also be communicated to the civilian population via print, electronic and other media.

8. EXTERNAL SUPPORT TO THE CEASEFIRE

8.1. Neighbouring countries, regional and international partners shall respect this Agreement and help ensure its successful implementation.

6(8)

Annexure to the Agreement on Accountability and Reconciliation

This Annexure to the Agreement on Accountability and Reconciliation signed between the Government of the Republic of Uganda (the Government) and the Lord's Resistance Army/Movement (LRA/M) (the Parties) on 29th June 2007 (the Principal Agreement) provides as follows:

THE PARTIES:

HAVING SIGNED the Principal Agreement by which the parties committed themselves to implementing accountability and reconciliation with respect to the conflict;

PURSUANT TO the terms of the Principal Agreement calling for the adoption of mechanisms for implementing accountability and reconciliation;

HAVING CARRIED OUT broad consultations within and outside Uganda, and in particular, with communities that have suffered most as a result of the conflict;

HAVING ESTABLISHED through consultations under Clause 2.4 of the Principal Agreement, that there is national consensus in Uganda that adequate mechanisms exist or can be expeditiously established to try the offences committed during the conflict;

RECALLING their commitment to preventing impunity and promoting redress in accordance with the Constitution and international obligations, and recalling, in this connection, the requirements of the Rome Statute of the International Criminal Court (ICC) and in particular the principle of complementarity;

CONFIDENT that the Principal Agreement embodies the necessary principles by which the conflict can be resolved with justice and reconciliation and consistent with national and international aspirations and standards;

NOW THEREFORE AGREE as follows:

Primacy of the Principal Agreement

1. This Annexure sets out a framework by which accountability and reconciliation are to be implemented pursuant to the Principal Agreement, provided that this Annexure shall not in any way limit the application of that Agreement, whose provisions are to be implemented in full.

2. The Government shall expeditiously prepare and develop the necessary legislation and modalities for implementing the Principal Agreement and this Annexure ('the Agreement').

3. The Government, under clause 2 above, shall take into account any representations from the parties on findings arising from the consultations undertaken by the Parties and any input by the public during the legislative process.

Inquiry into the Past and related matters
(*Principal Agreement: clauses 2.2 & 2.3*)

4. The Government shall by law establish a body to be conferred with all the necessary powers and immunities, whose functions shall include:

   (a) to consider and analyse any relevant matters including the history of the conflict;

   (b) to inquire into the manifestations of the conflict;

   (c) to inquire into human rights violations committed during the conflict, giving particular attention to the experiences of women and children;

   (d) to hold hearings and sessions in public and private;

   (e) to make provision for witness protection, especially for children and women;

   (f) to make special provision for cases involving gender based violence;

   (g) to promote truth-telling in communities and in this respect to liaise with any traditional or other community reconciliation interlocutors;

   (h) to promote and encourage the preservation of the memory of the events and victims of the conflict through memorials, archives, commemorations and other forms of preservation;

   (i) to gather and analyse information on those who have disappeared during the conflict;

(j) to make recommendations for the most appropriate modalities for implementing a regime of reparations, taking into account the principles set out in the Principal Agreement;

(k) to make recommendations for preventing any future outbreak of conflict;

(l) to publish its findings as a public document;

(m) to undertake any other functions relevant to the principles set out in this Agreement.

5. In the fulfilment of its functions, the body shall give precedence to any investigations or formal proceedings instituted pursuant to the terms of this Agreement. Detailed guidelines and working practices shall be established to regulate the relationship between the body and any other adjudicatory body seized of a case relating to this Agreement.

6. The body shall be made up of individuals of high moral character and proven integrity and the necessary expertise for carrying out its functions. In particular, its composition shall reflect a gender balance and the national character.

Legal and Institutional Framework
(Principal Agreement: Part 5)

7. A special division of the High Court of Uganda shall be established to try individuals who are alleged to have committed serious crimes during the conflict.

8. The special division of the High Court shall have a registry dedicated to the work of the division and in particular, shall make arrangements to facilitate the protection and participation of witnesses, victims, women and children.

9. For the proper functioning of the special division of the court in accordance with the agreed principles of accountability and reconciliation, legislation may provide for:

    (a) The constitution of the court;

    (b) The substantive law to be applied;

    (c) Appeals against the decisions of the court;

    (d) Rules of procedure;

(e) The recognition of traditional and community justice processes in proceedings.

Investigations and Prosecutions
(*Principal Agreement: Part 4*)

10. The Government shall establish a unit for carrying out investigations and prosecutions in support of trials and other formal proceedings as envisaged by the Principal Agreement.

11. The unit shall have a multi-disciplinary character.

12. The Director of Public Prosecutions shall have overall control of the criminal investigations of the unit and of the prosecutions before the special division.

13. Investigations shall:

(a) Seek to identify individuals who are alleged to have planned or carried out widespread, systematic, or serious attacks directed against civilians;

(b) Reflect the broad pattern of serious crimes and violations committed during the conflict;

(c) Give particular attention to crimes and violations against women and children committed during the conflict.

14. Prosecutions shall focus on individuals alleged to have planned or carried out widespread, systematic, or serious attacks directed against civilians or who are alleged to have committed grave breaches of the Geneva Conventions.

Cooperation with Investigations and Proceedings
(Principal Agreement: clauses 3.5 & 3.6)

15. Rules and procedures shall regulate the manner in which an individual may cooperate with any investigations and proceedings arising from this Agreement, by disclosure of all relevant information relating to:

(a) His or her own conduct during the conflict;

(b) Details which may assist in establishing the fate of persons missing during the conflict;

(c) The location of land mines or unexploded ordnances or other munitions; and,

(d) any other relevant information.

Provided that a person shall not be compelled to disclose any matter which might incriminate him or her.

Reparations
(Principal Agreement: clauses 6.4 & 9)

16. The Government shall establish the necessary arrangements for making reparations to victims of the conflict in accordance with the terms of the Principal Agreement.

17. Prior to establishing arrangements for reparations, the Government shall review the financial and institutional requirements for reparations, in order to ensure the adoption of the most effective mechanisms for reparations.

18. In reviewing the question of reparations, consideration shall be given to clarifying and determining the procedures for reparations.

Traditional Justice
(Principal Agreement: clause 3.1)

19. Traditional justice shall form a central part of the alternative justice and reconciliation framework identified in the Principal Agreement.

20. The Government shall, in consultation with relevant interlocutors, examine the practices of traditional justice mechanisms in affected areas, with a view to identifying the most appropriate roles for such mechanisms. In particular, it shall consider the role and impact of the processes on women and children.

21. The Traditional Justice Mechanisms referred to include:

i. Mato Oput in Acholi, Kayo Cuk in Lango, Ailuc in Teso, Tonu ci Koka in Madi and Okukaraba in Ankole; and

ii. Communal dispute settlement institutions such as family and clan courts.

22. A person shall not be compelled to undergo any traditional ritual.

Provisions of General Application

23. Subject to clause 4.1 of the Principal Agreement, the Government shall ensure that serious crimes committed during the conflict are addressed by the special Division of the High Court; traditional justice mechanisms; and any other alternative justice mechanism established under the Principal Agreement, but not the military courts.

24. All bodies implementing the Agreement shall establish internal procedures and arrangements for protecting and ensuring the participation of victims, traumatised individuals, women, children, persons with disabilities and victims of sexual violence in proceedings.

25. In the appointment of members and staff of institutions envisaged by the Agreement, overriding consideration shall be given to the competences and skills required for the office, and gender balance shall be ensured.

26. The Mediator shall from time to time receive or make requests for reports on the progress of the implementation of the Agreement.

IMPLEMENTATION PROTOCOL TO THE AGREEMENT ON COMPREHENSIVE SOLUTIONS

This Implementation Protocol (the Protocol) to the Agreement on Comprehensive Solutions (the Principal Agreement) signed between the Government of the Republic of Uganda (the Government) and the Lord's Resistance Army/Movement (LRA/M) (the Parties) provides as follows:

THE PARTIES:

HAVING SIGNED the Principal Agreement by which the Parties agreed to various measures aimed at attaining comprehensive, just and durable solutions to the conflict;

RECALLING the constitutional principles affirmed by the Parties in the terms of the Principal Agreement;

PURSUANT to the commitment in Clause 18 of the Principal Agreement to adopt implementation modalities for the Principal Agreement;

AGREE as follows:

1. This Protocol sets out the framework by which the principles and commitments agreed in the Principal Agreement are to be implemented and shall form an integral part of the Principal Agreement.

Participation in National Politics and Institutions

(Principal Agreement: Part C)

2.

The LRA/M shall nominate at least five (5) persons who shall be appointed by the President as cabinet Ministers in key Ministries within a period of six (6) months from the signing of the Peace Agreement.

The LRA/M shall nominate at least five (5) persons who shall be apponted by the President as ambassadors within a period of six (6) months from the date of the signing of the Peace Agreement.

In other Government Departments, Commissions, and other statutory bodies the LRA/M shall nominate at least twenty (20) qualified persons for appointment to senior positions by the Government through the relevant organs within six (6) months from the signing of the final Agreement.

3. The Government shall actively promote a policy for increasing access to all levels of education and training for people from the conflict affected areas, with a view to enhance their capacity to participate in National Institutions.

4. In furtherance of the above, the Government shall, in each year, in addition to any other scholarships within the District or National budget or the quota systems, fully sponsor 50 students from each of the districts in the conflict affected areas at University level or any other higher institution of learning for the next five years and of the fifty the LRA/M shall nominate five (5) persons per District in the conflict areas per year.

5. The Government shall operationalise the provision of the

Principal Agreement reaffirming the freedom of Ugandans to choose, advocate and promote democratically a system for their governance and the right of any Ugandan or groups of Ugandans to promote any system of governance including fedaralisl through constitutional means.

6. During the implementation of the Final Agreement, the Government will operationalise the Equal Opportunities Commission Act within six (6) months from the date of the signing of the Final Ageement.

7. The LRA/M shall nominate at least two (2) qualified persons as Commissioners under the Act and Government shall effect their appointment.

8. On the operationalisation of the Equal Opportunities Commission Act, the Commission shall immediately review and assess the nature and extent of any regional or ethnic imbalances and disparity in Central Government Institutions.

9. In addition to the above, the issues to be addressed shall include:

10.

11.

(a) analysis of the current composition of state bodies ;

(b) steps to be taken to remedy any anomalies in the composition of state bodies;

(c) time frame in which to implement the recommendations of the Commission;

(d) a requirement to publish the terms of the referral and the final report of the Commission.

12. The Government shall publish its plan for implementing the recommendations of the Commission and shall implement the

recommendations.

13. The Government shall, where necessary, move Parliament to amend the Equal Opportunities Act for the effective implementation of the Final Peace Agreement.

14. The Government shall ensure that Ugandans from the conflict affected areas living abroad are encouraged to return and participate in nation building. The Government will strengthen existing arrangements in the Ministry of Foreign Affairs for this purpose.

15. The Government shall not victimize, arrest, detain or in any way mistreat any Ugandan who returns from abroad under this Peace Agreement.

16. The Government shall facilitate and finance the return of political leaders of LRM and any member of the negotiation team currently living abroad or any other person actively involved in the peace process and shall not victimize, arrest, detain or in any way mistreat such a person on his or her return by virtue of his or her association with the LRA/M.

17. The Government shall ensure the return of the property unlawfully confiscated from the returning persons in relation to the conflict. Where such property has been destroyed, compensation at market rate shall be paid by Government.

18. The Government shall provide a resettlement package to the LRA/M, the amount of which shall be agreed to in the Final Peace Agreement.

19. In addition, Government shall, in consultation with the Mediator, in recognition of all the LRA/M delegates and their efforts in brokering peace, provide a golden handshake in cash and kind to be agreed on in the Final Peace Agreement.

20. The Government shall support business and investment incentives to people in the conflict affected areas by identifying and committing special funds to the implementing agency for that

purpose.

Judiciary and Policing Issues

(*Principal Agreement: Clause 7*)

21. The Government shall strengthen the institutions of justice in the conflict-affected areas through the programmes of the Justice Law and Order Sector and any other relevant body.

22. The Government shall increase and strengthen the deployment of the Uganda Police Force in the conflict-affected areas.

Institutional Arrangements for Security Organs

(*Principal Agreement: Clause 8*)

23. The Government shall take all necessary steps to ensure that the composition of the armed forces and security agencies is based on merit and reflects the national character including regional and gender diversity.

24. In furtherance of Clause 8.2 of the Principal Agreement, the Government shall recognize the current ranks of the LRA combatants. Combatants who wish to join the National armed forces or any other security agencies shall be integrated at their rank. An integrated combatant shall benefit from any further training or promotional programs.

25. Recruitment into the armed forces and other security agencies and promotions shall be based on merit and shall reflect the national character including regional and gender diversity.

26. The Government shall establish and fully finance a specialized school in the conflict area for children of departed LRA combatants and any LRA combatant who would wish to attend such school.

Return, Resettlement and Rehabilitation of Internally Displaced Persons

(*Principal Agreement: Part D*)

Humanitarian Interventions in the Conflict Affected Areas

27. The Government shall develop a strategy for assisting the return of internally displaced persons (IDPs) from the affected areas in accordance with the IDP policy. In implementing the strategy the needs of IDPs who have already returned will be taken into account to ensure equitable support for resettlement.

28. The Government shall promote recovery programmes in the affected areas, and in particular, shall implement the Peace, Recovery and Development Plan (PRDP) expeditiously, and will further ensure that the Plan reflects the principles and commitments of this agreement.

29. The Government shall facilitate the process of the return of internally displaced persons in accordance with the terms of the Internally Displaced Persons policy.

30. The implementation agency, on the advice of the Parties, shall develop a policy for a credible and sustainable conflict affected area-exclusive scheme for re-settlement packages for internally displaced persons. This shall include a clear policy that will define and publish the resettlement packages that the IDPs are entitled to receive and the mechanisms and agencies for their delivery.

Economic and Social Development of North and North Eastern Uganda

(*Principal Agreement: Part E*)

31. The interventions agreed by the parties in Part E of the Principal Agreement shall be developed and delivered by a national, self-accounting body to be established by an Act of Parliament.

32. The Government shall expeditiously prepare and introduce the legislation required for establishing the body, and will ensure that the body commences its work within six months from the signing of the Final Peace Agreement .

33. Half of the members of the above body shall be nominated by the LRA or its designated agent.

34. The Government will promote policies and programmes to address and mitigate any adverse environmental impacts of the conflict.

Strategy for Recovery and Institutional Framework

(*Principal Agreement: Clause10 and 11*)

35. The programmes for recovery of the affected areas shall be implemented through the agency identified in Clause 11 of the Principal Agreement, The implementing body shall be established within a month of the signing of the Agreement.

36. The mechanisms of implementation will ensure easy access to dedicated funds by communities in the affected areas for their resettlement and for the enhancement of productive capacities.

37. The Legislation establishing the agency will provide for the adoption of sound management and accountability controls.

Victims and Vulnerable Groups

(*Principal Agreement: Clause 12*)

38. The Parties agree that the Government shall develop and implement in the affected areas a policy for the support and rehabilitation of the victims of the conflict.

39. The Government shall set up a reparation and compensation fund to be managed by the body mentioned under Part E of the Principal Agreement.

40. For purposes of this Agreement, victims shall be categorized into General and Special victims. General victims are those who suffered generally as a result of the conflict. Special victims are those who suffered personal detriment by way of special injury, loss of loved ones, destruction or loss of property.

41. A victim declared or compensated by any justice mechanism under these agreements shall be compensated from the Reparation Fund.

42. The Government will ensure that the policy for the support of victims and the mechanisms for its implementation are in line with the principles and obligations set out in Clause 8 of the Agreement on Accountability and Reconciliation.

Livestock

(*Principal Agreement: Clause 13*)

43. The Government shall within three months of the commencement of the implementation of the Principal Agreement in accordance with Clause 13 of the Principal Agreement implement the restocking program under the supervision of the implementing agency under Clause 11 of the Principal Agreement or any other body approved by the Parties.

44. In considering individual losses, Government in consultation with the local authorities, shall establish verification committees in the conflict areas to assist in the assessment of individual losses.

Transitional Security Arrangements

(*Principal Agreement: Part F*)

45. The agreement between the Parties on disarmament, demobilisation and reintegration shall specify the arrangements to ensure the safety of members of the LRA including Government's legal steps in handling the ICC warrants.

Stakeholders' Conference and Implementation

(*Principal Agreement: Clause 17*)

46. The full implementation of the Principal Agreement shall commence upon the removal or suspension of the ICC indictments to be followed by the final disarmament of all members of the LRA.

47. The Mediator shall liaise with the Parties on the preparations for the stakeholders' conference provided for in Clause 17 of the Principal Agreement.

Issues Relating to Land

(*Principal Agreement: Clause 14*)

48. Land owners whose lands have been used for settlement of internally displaced persons or establishment of barracks, detaches or any other Government agency , shall be entitled to repossess their land or to receive fair and just compensation.

49. The Government will give priority to strengthening the capacity of the District Land Boards and Tribunals in the affected areas to oversee and adjudicate cases of land ownership and disputes.

50. The implementation agency shall ensure the repossession of land by IDPs or any other rightful owner.

Provisions of General Application

51. After the signing of the Final Peace Agreement, there shall be a pre-implementation period of six (6) months or any other longer period agreed to by the Parties.

52. During the pre-implementatin period, the Parties agree that:

(a) A composite Implementation Schedule will be developed for the Final Peace Agreement (FPA).

(b) Existing Government oversight and monitoring mechanisms for implementation of the FPA will be utilized.

(c) A Pre-implementation Committee for the FPA which is composed of representatives of the two parties shall be established.

53. A dedicated chapter of the Final Peace agreement shall amongst other things, stipulate the composition and functions of the Implementation Committee.

54. In the appointment of members and staff of any implementation bodies envisaged by this Agreement, overriding consideration shall be given to the competences and skills required for the office, sensitivity to the candidate's knowledge of the affected areas, and gender balance.

55. During the pre-implementation period and before the commencement of the Disarmament, Demobilisation and Reintergration Agreement, the Government shall cause the suspension and withdrawal of the warrants issued by International Criminal Court.

56. The Mediator shall receive quarterly reports on the progress of the implementation of the Agreement.

10

References

[1] Ugandan Elections 2001, online at http://www.uganda-elections.com.

[2] Besigye fled into exile a day after he met with visiting U.S. congressional delegation members.

[3] The Constitution of Uganda can be found online at http://www.parliament.go.ug/images/constitution_1995.pdf.

[4] John Kakande. "Museveni Speaks on 3rd Term." *The New Vision*, January 3, 2003.
[5] "President Should Listen to Old Friends, Avoid Disaster (Editorial)." *The Monitor*, May 3, 2002
[6] Uganda Complex Emergency. U.S. Agency for International Development (USAID), July 2003.
[7] *The Pawns of Politics: Children, Conflict and Peace in Northern Uganda.* World Vision, 2004.
[8] The author visited Juba last year and other towns in Southern Sudan over the past decade where LRA has been active.
[9] Ted Dagne interviewed Dr. John Garang on a number of occasions during the Security Arrangement negotiations.
[10] Ted Dagne met with President Kabila and discussed issues related to Uganda and DRC in November 2007
[11] Ted Dagne met with President Museveni in Uganda in August 2007 and discussed a wide range of issues.
[12] http://www.whitehouse.gov/news/releases/2007/10/20071030-1.html. President Bush Meets with President Museveni of Uganda

In: Economic, Political and Social Issues of Africa
Editor: Jeremy S. McQueen

ISBN 978-1-61209-957-6

Chapter 3

SUDAN: THE CRISIS IN DARFUR AND STATUS OF THE NORTH-SOUTH PEACE AGREEMENT*

Ted Dagne

ABSTRACT

Sudan, geographically the largest country in Africa, has been ravaged by civil war intermittently for four decades. More than 2 million people have died in Southern Sudan over the past two decades due to war-related causes and famine, and millions have been displaced from their homes. There were many failed attempts to end the civil war in southern Sudan. In July 2002, the Sudan government and the Sudan People's Liberation Movement (SPLM) signed a peace framework agreement in Kenya. On May 26, 2004, the government of Sudan and the SPLM signed three protocols on Power Sharing, on the Nuba Mountains and Southern Blue Nile, and on the long disputed Abyei area. The signing of these protocols resolved all outstanding issues between the parties. On June 5, 2004, the parties signed "the Nairobi Declaration on the Final Phase of Peace in the Sudan." On January 9, 2005, the government of Sudan and the SPLM signed the final peace agreement at a ceremony held in Nairobi, Kenya.

In October 2007, the government of Southern Sudan suspended the participation of its Ministers, State Ministers, and Presidential Advisors from the Government of National Unity to protest measures taken by the National Congress Party and to demand full implementation of the Comprehensive Peace Agreement (CPA). In response to these demands and unexpected developments, President Bashir reportedly accepted a number of the government of South Sudan (GoSS) demands in late October, except those related to the Abyei issue. In late December 2007, the new ministers were sworn in office. In May 2008, Government forces burned Abyei town and displaced more than 60,000 people. An agreement reached in June 2008 between the Government of South Sudan (GoSS) and the National Congress Party (NCP) on Abyei largely ended the tense situation between the two sides.

The crisis in Darfur began in February 2003, when two rebel groups emerged to challenge the National Congress Party (NCP) government in Darfur. The crisis in

* This is an edited, reformatted and augmented version of CRS Report RL33574, dated July 16, 2009.

Darfur in western Sudan has led to a major humanitarian disaster, with an estimated 2.45 million people displaced, more than 240,000 people forced into neighboring Chad, and an estimated 450,000 people killed. In July 2004, the House and Senate declared the atrocities in Darfur genocide, and the Bush Administration reached the same conclusion in September 2004. On May 4, 2006, the Government of National Unity and the Sudan Liberation Movement/Army (SLM/A) signed the Darfur Peace Agreement (DPA) after almost two years of negotiations.

In July 2007, the U.N. Security Council passed Resolution 1769, authorizing the deployment of a robust peacekeeping force to Darfur. The resolution calls for the deployment of 26,000 peacekeeping troops to Darfur. The resolution authorized the United Nations African Union force in Darfur (UNAMID) to take all necessary measures to protect its personnel and humanitarian workers. As of May 31, 2009, UNAMID deployed a total of 16,402 peacekeeping personnel. In July 2008, International Criminal Court (ICC) Chief Prosecutor Luis Moreno-Ocampo accused President Omar Bashir of Sudan of genocide, crimes against humanity, and war crimes and asked ICC judges to issue an arrest warrant for President Bashir. On March 4, 2009, the ICC Pre-Trial Chamber issued a warrant of arrest for President Bashir for war crimes and crimes against humanity.

Recent Developments

In June 2009, the U.S. Special Envoy to Sudan, Scott Gration, organized a Forum, focused on the Comprehensive Peace Agreement (CPA), with the National Congress Party (NCP) and the Sudan People's Liberation Movement (SPLM). Participants included representatives from regional and international organizations as well as officials from Europe and Africa. The NCP and the SPLM also participated in Trilateral talks to resolve a number of outstanding issues. The second round of the Trilateral talks took place in Khartoum in mid-July 2009.

In Washington, the NCP and the SPLM agreed to implement the decision of the Abyei Arbitration Tribunal as final and binding. The parties, however, failed to agree on a number of other issues, including on the recent census results, representation of Southern Sudan in the civil service, and visiting right of suspected military camps outside the ceasefire zone. There were also disagreements related to the wealth sharing provision of the CPA.

On July 22, 2009, the Abyei Arbitration Tribunal (AAT), seated at the Permanent Court of Arbitration (PCA) in The Hague, will issue its final decision. The decision will clarify whether the Abyei Boundary Commission (ABC) exceeded its mandate. The Abyei issue was referred to the Tribunal in July 2008 because the NCP refused to implement the decision of the Abyei Boundary Commission's decision, which was issued in July 2005.

The International Criminal Court (ICC) and Sudan

On March 4, 2009, the ICC Pre-Trial Chamber issued a warrant of arrest for President Bashir for war crimes and crimes against humanity. This is the first warrant of arrest issued for a sitting head of state. According to the Pre-Trial judges, President Bashir intentionally directed attacks "against an important part of the civilian population of Darfur. President Bashir is accused of five counts of crimes against humanity (murder, rape, torture, extermination, and forceful transfer of civilian population) and two counts of war crimes (killing and pillaging). The Pre-Trial Chamber stated that President Bashir "played a role that went beyond coordinating the implementation of the common plan and was in full control of all branches of the apparatus of the State of Sudan, including the Sudanese Armed Forces and their allied Janjaweed Militia, the Sudanese Police Force, the National Intelligence and Security Services (NISS)" [1]

The Government of Sudan condemned the ICC decision and expelled 13 non-governmental organizations (NGOs) working in Darfur. President Bashir accused these NGOs of collaborating with the ICC. The Government of Sudan and the United Nations agreed to send a Joint Technical mission to assess humanitarian conditions in Darfur. Meanwhile, the National Congress Party (NCP) and the SPLM formed a Crisis Committee to deal with the ICC crisis and other issues. The Obama Administration stated that "the United States is strongly committed to the pursuit of peace in Sudan and believes those who have committed atrocities should be held accountable." The Administration also condemned the expulsions of the NGOs and warned that this measure "seriously threatens the lives and well-being of displaced populations" [2].

In April 2009, U.S. Special Envoy J. Scott Gration reached an agreement with the National Congress Party leaders on the expulsions of the NGOs. The agreement does not call for the return of the expelled NGOs, but provides additional authority to the Government of Sudan to manage and control NGO activities. The agreement states that "expelled NGOs can depart freely, return personal assets, and clearly define future severance pay requirements."

The African Union, the Arab League, China, and a number of other countries called for a deferment of the ICC process against President Bashir. In a press statement, the African Union Peace and Security Council stated that "despite the risks posed by the ongoing ICC process to the search for lasting peace and stability in the Sudan and in the region, the United Nations Security Council has failed to consider with the required attention the request made by the AU to implement the provisions of article 16 of the ICC Statute." The African Union appointed former South African president, Thabo Mbeki, to chair a High-Level Panel to make recommendations on the most effective way to deal with impunity, accountability, and reconciliation in Sudan. In July 2009, the African Union in a resolution stated that member states will not co-operate with the ICC. In a statement, the AU stated that "the AU member states shall not co-operate relating to immunities for the arrest and surrender of Sudanese President Omar al-Bashir to the ICC."

Background

In July 2008, the ICC Chief Prosecutor accused President Bashir of Sudan of genocide, crimes against humanity, and war crimes. The Prosecutor asked ICC judges to issue an arrest warrant for President Bashir. The judges are expected to issue their decision in February 2009. In late September 2008, the U.N. Secretary General, Ban Ki-Moon, the African Union Commission Chairman, Jean Ping, ICC Special Prosecutor, and other government officials met in New York to discuss the status of the ICC case against President Bashir. Special Prosecutor Moreno-Ocampo stated that "We presented a solid case. The evidence shows that crimes against Darfurians continue today. President al-Bashir has complete control of his forces, and they are raping women today, they are promoting conditions in the camps to destroy complete communities and they are still bombing schools." Ocampo added that "the judges will decide. Those sought by the court have to face justice. It is an immense challenge for the political leaders of the world. They have to protect the victims and ensure the respect for the court's decisions" [3].

The government of Sudan condemned the ICC action, while the African Union asked for a deferment of the ICC case against Bashir. However, the then-Chairman of the African Union, President Jakaya Kikwete of Tanzania, stated at the United Nations in September that "when we talk about deferment, we should not in any way be perceived as condoning impunity. Justice is a matter of essence." President Museveni of Uganda stated that "you cannot stand up and say: 'Don't touch Bashir because he is a president.' Suppose he made those mistakes. If you take that position, you will be ignoring the right of the victims" [4]. Other African leaders also expressed similar views concerning the ICC case against Bashir.

The SPLM Position

In 2008, the SPLM issued a press release stating that "the solution to the crisis is for the Government of National Unity to forge an understanding with the international community and to co-operate with ICC on the legal processes." Vice President Salva Kiir was appointed to chair a "Crisis Committee" to deal with the ICC process and other emerging issues. Foreign Minister Deng Alore of Sudan informed President Bashir that he will not defend him at the United Nations or lobby against the ICC case. This led to a decision by Bashir to appoint Vice President Osman Ali Taha to lead a 50-person delegation to the United Nations in September 2008. The Bashir government is currently actively engaged in a lobbying campaign against the ICC. Senior government officials, who in the past ignored or harassed the international press, are now giving the international media unprecedented access.

In early February 2009, the SPLM Political Bureau passed a resolution to respond to the ICC investigation. The SPLM leadership created a Committee on the ICC, whose membership include senior SPLM members, including the Chairman of the SPLM, Salva Kiir, Sudan Foreign Minister, Deng Alore, SPLA Affairs Minister, Nhial Deng, and several other senior SPLM leaders. The Committee is tasked with reaching out to relevant actors in Sudan, the region, and the international community to respond to the on-going crisis in Darfur. The Committee is expected to come up with recommendations on the ICC investigation, the crisis in Darfur, and reconciliation efforts. On the other hand, the SPLM leadership has put in place a contingency plan in case of emergency.

The U.S. Response

The Bush Administration's Special Envoy to Sudan, Richard Williamson, at a briefing before the U.S. Commission on Religious Freedom in late September, stated that "we believe strongly that there should be no impunity for the atrocities committed in Darfur. The people of Darfur have suffered for far too long." He also stated that the United States will veto any resolution for deferment under Article 16 of the Rome Statute. Then-Secretary of State Rice reportedly informed Vice President Taha at a meeting in New York that the U.S. will veto a resolution on deferment.

The Obama Administration is also opposed to a deferral of the ICC case against President Bashir. In early February 2009, U.S. Ambassador to the United Nations Susan Rice told the Washington Post that "it is our view that we support the ICC investigation and the prosecution of war crimes in Sudan, and we see no reason for an article 16 deferral" [5]. Meanwhile, the African Union at its Summit in January 2009, once again, urged deferral of the ICC investigation.

Possible Consequences and New Developments.

The Government of Sudan is reaching out to allies and foes in an effort to defeat the ICC investigation. Senior members of the NCP reportedly are considering a number of options. According to senior Sudanese government officials, the NCP leadership is reportedly pushing for President Bashir to go into exile. They are also considering ousting Bashir from power through a military coup, according to Sudanese sources.

Senior SPLM officials and some regional actors aware of this development have expressed serious concern at the prospect of such an outcome. According to these sources, those planning to oust Bashir and take over power in Khartoum are seen as radical and extremist. They contend that if this group of NCP leaders succeeds in ousting President Bashir, the new leadership will consist of people who have been involved in directing the Darfur atrocities.

Some observers argue the Bashir regime may decided to abandon its commitment to the CPA or any new efforts aimed at resolving the Darfur crisis. Others assert that this development could lead to a possible war between the North and the South. President Bashir and his allies are behind some of these assertions in an effort to defeat the ICC process. A number of the key NCP leaders seem eager to force Bashir into exile and avoid a possible crisis as a result.

Another likely scenario is to ignore the ICC and maintain the status quo. A deferral of the ICC case after the issuance of the ICC arrest warrant is another option some observers are proposing, provided that the Bashir regime takes serious measures to resolve the Darfur crisis and fully implement the CPA. Senior SPLM leaders and some U.S. officials seem open to this proposal.

Security Conditions in Darfur

In January 2009, the forces of the Justice and Equality Movement (JEM) reportedly attacked the town of Muhajeria in South Darfur. The town and the surrounding areas were under the control of another Darfur rebel group, the Sudan Liberation Army (SLA)-Minawi faction. JEM officials initially denied that they attacked the area, claiming that they were responding to attacks by SLA and government forces. The SLA pulled its forces out, while JEM forces took control. In late January and early February, Sudan government forces attacked JEM, forcing JEM to pull out of the town. The Obama Administration condemned the government of Sudan's actions, while United Nations officials rejected the government of Sudan's demand to pull U.N. peacekeepers out of Muhajeria.

In late August 2008, government forces entered the Kalma Internally Displaced Persons (IDP) camp in South Darfur and killed over 30 civilians and wounded many more. Government forces used heavy weapons during the attack. Civilians lost legs, arms, and other body parts, according to photographs of the wounded in the Kalma camp. During the same period, government forces intensified their ground and air attacks against rebel forces, although the casualties were largely civilians. In July 2008, seven United Nations African Union Mission in Darfur (UNAMID) peacekeepers were killed and over a dozen wounded in an attack by heavily armed pro- government militia. Another peacekeeper was killed a few days later, bringing the total casualties to 25.

North-South Developments

In May 2008, government of Sudan forces destroyed the town of Abyei, displaced over 60,000 people, and killed over a dozen. Abyei town was largely burned, according to witnesses. In June 2008, the government of Sudan and the Sudan People's Liberation Movement (SPLM) signed an agreement on "defining and demarcating" the Abyei area. The parties agreed to refer the Abyei dispute for arbitration. Many of the civilians displaced by the attacks in May remain in displaced camps and the town of Abyei was largely empty as of mid-August 2008. However, by January 2009, an estimated 10,000 displaced people had returned, according to U.N. officials. United Nations officials expect the number of returnees will increase in the coming months, although the fighting in Abyei town in December 2008 had slowed the return of the IDPs [6].

An agreement reached in 2008 between the Government of South Sudan (GoSS) and the National Congress Party (NCP) on Abyei largely ended the tense situation between the two sides. The Agreement established an Interim Administration for Abyei, created a Special Fund for development of the region, and provided for the redeployment of government and SPLA forces out of Abyei. The parties agreed to deploy Joint Integrated Units (JIUs) and a police force. An estimated 257 JIU forces have been deployed as of late 2008. In August 2008, the parties appointed the Chairman and Deputy Chairman of the Executive, and in October 2008 members of the Executive Committee and Abyei Council were appointed. In late 2008, the parties presented their oral arguments before the Permanent Court of Arbitration, and a final decision is expected in June 2009.

Current Status of Peace Talks

Since the Darfur crisis erupted in 2003, there have been a number of peace efforts, although without much success. The Darfur Peace Agreement (DPA), signed between the government of Sudan and the SLM in 2006, has contributed to divisions within the rebel ranks and further instability in Darfur. Currently, there are several ongoing peace efforts. One of the peace efforts is led by Qatar. The Qatar peace process has not been able to bring key players to the table, although JEM is currently engaged in talks aimed at crafting a framework agreement between the Government and JEM.

Some observers doubt that this peace process will lead to any final agreement since the two sides have been battling as recently as late January 2009 in South Darfur. The Joint U.N.-A.U. Mediator, Djibril Bassole, also has been engaged in an effort to bring together the various Darfur rebel groups without much success.

The Government of Sudan and various political groups, including the SPLM, have been engaged in the Sudan People's Forum in an effort to respond to the crisis in Darfur. The Forum met in November and established a number of committees to deal with multiple issues, including the crisis in Darfur and reconciliation in general. At the end of 2008, the Government of Sudan declared a unilateral ceasefire, although government forces continued aerial bombardments and attacks against some rebel groups.

Issues of Interest

The Census

In 2006, the National Population Census Council was established by presidential decree, and in September 2006, the GoSS launched the Higher Council for Population Census in South Sudan. After several delays, the census operation began and ended on May 6, 2008. Combining the North-South data began on January 20th and ended on January 29, 2009. The GoSS has expressed concerns about the census. One of the concerns expressed by GoSS officials is the proper counting of Southerners in the North.

Elections

According to the CPA , national elections are expected to take place in July 2009. The SPLM and other political parties have stated that they would participate in the elections. President Bashir is expected to be the candidate of the NCP. Some observers are concerned about the impact of an ICC indictment against President Bashir. Vice President Kiir has not declared that he will contest the elections. However, Sudanese and some observers are concerned that Sudan is not adequately prepared to conduct the elections as scheduled. In April 2009, the National Elections Commission announced a timetable for the elections. Presidential and parliamentary elections are scheduled for February 2010.

United Nations Peacekeeping in Darfur

On July 31, 2007, acting under Chapter VII of the Charter of the United Nations, the United Nations Security Council adopted Resolution 1769. The resolution called for the deployment of a hybrid United Nations-African Union force in Darfur (UNAMID). The U.N. was expected to fully deploy 26,000 peacekeeping troops to Darfur by mid-2008. As of late December 2008, the United Nations deployed 15,351 peacekeeping personnel to Darfur, Sudan. In March 2008, the United States pledged $100 million to train and equip African peacekeepers for deployment under UNAMID. In late 2008, the United States helped transport equipment and personnel to Darfur. The resolution:

1. Reaffirms its commitment to stop the suffering in Darfur, and to work with the government of Sudan toward this end.
2. Commends Sudan's acceptance of a hybrid operation to be deployed in Darfur and the ongoing efforts of the African Union Mission in Sudan, AMIS.
3. Refers to the Addis Ababa Agreement that the hybrid operation be predominantly comprised of African troops
4. Expresses concern about ongoing attacks on civilians in Darfur and the security of humanitarian aid workers in the region.
5. Welcomes the appointment of the AU-UN Joint Special Representative for Darfur, Rodolphe Adada, and Force Commander, Martin Agwai.
6. Calls on all parties to facilitate the full deployment of Light and Heavy Support Packages to AMIS and preparations for UNAMID within 30 days.

7. States that UNAMID shall establish an initial operational capability for its headquarters by October 2007, in addition to the management and control structure of the operation.
8. Decides that by October 2007, UNAMID shall assume command of all Light Support and Heavy Support personnel as may be deployed by October.
9. States that by December 31, 2007 at the latest, UNAMID will have fully implemented all of the elements of its mandate and will assume authority from AMIS.
10. Calls for a unity of command and control provided by the United Nations.
11. Demands an immediate cessation of hostilities in Darfur.
12. States that UNAMID is authorized to take the necessary actions to protect its personnel and humanitarian workers. The resolution also calls for the protection of civilians, "without prejudice to the responsibilities of the government of Sudan."

In late December 2007, UNAMID officially assumed command and control from the African Union peacekeeping force. The United Nations continues to face serious obstacles in force deployment in large part due to restrictions imposed by the Government of National Unity (GoNU). The Government signed the Status of Forces Agreement (SOFA) with the United Nations in February 2008. In January 2008, a UNAMID supply convoy was attacked by Sudanese government forces in West Darfur. The United Nations and the United States condemned the attack [7] In January 2008, President Omer Bashir of Sudan appointed Musa Hilal, a leader of the Janjaweed, as Advisor to the Minister of Federal Affairs. In April 2006, the United Nations Security Council imposed a travel ban and asset freeze on Musa Hilal. Bush Administration officials criticized the appointment of Hilal [8]. President Bashir argued that Hilal is an influential leader in Darfur and that his government does not accept the allegation against Hilal. The appointment of Hilal is seen by observers as another obstacle to peace in the Darfur region.

Executive Branch Sanctions on Sudan

On May 29, 2007, the Bush Administration imposed new economic sanctions on two Sudanese government officials (Ahmad Muhammed Harun, Sudan's State Minister for Humanitarian Affairs and Awad Ibn Auf, head of Sudan's Military Intelligence and Security), a leader of the Justice and Equality Movement (JEM), Khalil Ibrahim, and 31 Sudanese companies. According to Administration officials, "Harun and Auf have acted as liaisons between the Sudanese government and the government-supported Janjaweed militia, which have attacked and brutalized innocent civilians in the region. The two individuals also have provided the Janjaweed with logistical support and directed attacks" [9] Of the 31 companies sanctioned, 30 are either owned or controlled by the government of Sudan and the other, the Azza Air Transport Company, violated the arms embargo in Darfur. These companies are banned from doing business within the U.S. financial system and with U.S. companies, and U.S. citizens are restricted from doing business with these companies.

The Administration's objective in imposing new sanctions is to increase pressure on the government of Sudan to end the violence in Darfur. President Bush also announced plans to consult with U.S. allies on the United Nations Security Council about additional multilateral sanctions to be imposed on the government of Sudan. Some of the proposed sanctions include an expansion of the existing arms embargo, a prohibition of offensive military flights over Darfur, and improved monitoring and reporting of violations. Deputy Secretary of State John Negroponte also urged European allies to impose financial sanctions to match those of the United States [10] On June 25, 2007, at an international conference on Darfur in Paris, Secretary of State Condoleezza Rice asserted that sanctions must be maintained to discourage the Sudanese Government from reneging on its acceptance of a larger peacekeeping force in Darfur. Rice stated that, "We can no longer afford a situation in Darfur where agreements are made and not kept. Until Sudan has actually carried out the commitments it's taken, I think we have to keep the possibility of consequences on the table" [11]

Humanitarian Conditions

Conditions in Darfur continue to deteriorate, according to United Nations officials and nongovernmental organizations. According to the U.N. Secretary General's December 2008 report to the Security Council, "despite the unilateral declaration of a cessation of hostilities by the Government on 12 November, aerial bombings were reportedly conducted in different locations in Northern Darfur, including Kurbia, Um Mahareik, Wadi Fede and Sayah between 12 and 15 November and in Jebel Moon, Kulbus and Silea (Western Darfur) on 17 November" [12] The same report stated that "humanitarian aid organizations continue to struggle to maintain existing programmes and expand operations to recently accessible areas. The critical humanitarian challenges continue to be those of access and protection of civilians. The total number of new displacements this year has reportedly reached nearly 310,000 people." Humanitarian workers have also seen an escalation in violence against NGOs throughout Darfur. More than 400 humanitarian workers have been relocated to other locations on several occasions because of security concerns. Over two dozen trucks have been taken from NGOs and properties damaged. In July 2008, eight UNAMID peacekeepers were killed in an attack by pro-government militia in Darfur. In May 2009, a UNAMID peacekeeper was killed in Darfur.

China and Sudan

Relations between China and Sudan are warm. In the 1 990s, political, economic, and military relations between Sudan and China expanded, and China became a key trading partner, investing billions of dollars in Sudan's oil sector. China reportedly imports an estimated 64% of Sudan's oil and China's National Petroleum Corporation is the largest shareholder (47%) in the two biggest oil consortiums in Sudan, Petrodar and the Greater Nile Petroleum Operating Company (GNPOC). In addition to the oil sector, China is an important player in other sectors of the Sudanese economy. In February 2007, China signed a $1.2 billion agreement to upgrade the railway between Khartoum and Port Sudan. China is also an active participant in power generation, the arms industry, and other major infrastructure projects. China built the 1000-mile oil pipeline used by Sudan to move its oil from the oil fields in South Sudan to Port Sudan.

China is an important supplier of weapons to the Government of Sudan. Sudan also produces significant quantities of weapons itself and is the third largest arms manufacturer in Africa, after South Africa and Egypt. Human rights groups and other observers accuse the Chinese government of being the principal supplier of weapons in violation of a U.N. weapons embargo on Sudan. In 2005, China reportedly sold Sudan $24 million in arms and ammunition and $57 million worth of spare parts for aircraft and helicopters [13]. In July 2008, a BBC Television report presented evidence of Chinese army trucks and several A5 Fantan fighter planes in Darfur. In February 2008, Fantan fighter planes were used to bomb the town of Beybey in Darfur in which a number of civilians were reportedly killed. In June 2008, the BBC acquired satellite photographs of two Fantan fighter planes at Nyala airport in South Darfur [14]

China provides important political and financial support to the Government of Sudan. As a Permanent Member of the Security Council, China has threatened several times to veto U.N. Security Council resolutions or has influenced the Council either to withdraw or amend statements. In July 2008, a British-drafted Presidential Statement was withdrawn because of Chinese opposition. China also has abstained on resolutions 1556, 1591, 1593, and 1706 relating to Darfur. In 2007, China forgave $70 million in debt and provided $13 million in interest-free loan to Sudan to build a new Presidential Palace.

Advocacy groups in the United States and in other parts of the world have engaged in a campaign to highlight Chinese support to the Sudanese government and link that support to the upcoming Beijing Olympics. The advocates refer to the Beijing Olympics as the "Genocide Olympics." These advocates argue that the main purpose of the campaign is to "shame" China into using its influence over Sudan in order to bring an end to the crisis in Darfur. The campaign does not advocate boycotting the Olympics or targeting the athletes, although these groups have called on world leaders to boycott the opening ceremony in Beijing. The pressure on China has yielded some results. The Chinese government appointed a Special Envoy for Sudan and has also deployed an estimated 315 engineers to take part in the U.N. peacekeeping mission in Darfur.

Developments in Southern Sudan

In October 2007, the Government of Southern Sudan suspended the participation of its Ministers, State Ministers, and Presidential Advisors from the Government of National Unity to protest measures taken by the National Congress Party and to demand full implementation of the Comprehensive Peace Agreement (CPA). The Sudan People's Liberation Movement (SPLM) has been complaining and urging the Sudanese government to implement key provisions of the CPA and to consult the First Vice President on key issues. They complained that President Omer Bashir has been taking important decisions with little or no consultation with the First Vice President since the signing of the peace agreement in 2005. On Darfur, President Bashir has been waging war and deliberately sidelining the SPLM on key decisions. For example, the Eastern Sudan Agreement was negotiated and signed between the National Congress Party and the Eastern rebels without serious consultation with the First Vice President. According to the CPA, "the President shall take decisions with the consent of the First Vice President on declaration and termination of state of emergency, declaration of war, appointments that the president is required to make according to the peace agreement, summoning, adjourning, or proroguing the National Assembly." A request by the First Vice President to reshuffle Southern Ministers in the Government of National Unity was held up for several months by President Bashir in large part due to Bashir 's opposition to the proposed change of the Foreign Minister.

In October the SPLM leadership submitted a number of demands to President Bashir. In a letter to President Bashir, First Vice President Salva Kiir wrote: [15]

> "At this critical juncture of the history of our country, the Sudanese people, the region and the international community at large, do follow with concern the evolving situation in our country. In particular, they follow closely with concern what both of us, and the parties we lead, are doing to enhance and consolidate peace in our country. The Comprehensive Peace Agreement (CPA) is the corner stone of that peace. It is with this spirit that I am addressing you today on behalf of the SPLM, and on my own behalf as a partner in peace.
>
> The SPLM was encouraged by the creation of bilateral permanent mechanisms for the resolution of outstanding issues on CPA implementation as well as for the enhancement of cooperation and partnership between our two parties. Despite the progress made on several issue areas, critical flash points remain. Thereby giving rise to the impression that the mechanisms we have created were mere vehicles for public relations exercises and not meant to help the parties in resolving critical differences.
>
> The above impression was reinforced by recent provocative actions emanating from authorities within the Government of National Unity (GONU) of which we are part, indeed the major partner to the NCP. The height of these provocations was the raids in Khartoum on SPLM premises and the Mess of SPLA senior officers in the Joint Defense Board (JDB). The JDB is the highest military organ created by the CPA and INC to oversee the smooth implementation of Security Arrangements. Those indecorous acts were compounded by the unrepentant reaction by their perpetrators to SPLM's protest. The perpetrators include NCP Ministers and officers in the law enforcement agencies who are duty-bound by the INC to steer away of politics. It became clear to us, however, that the provocations reflected a pattern of behavior intended to humiliate the SPLM. The SPLM, therefore, should not be expected to take that behavior lightly. Indeed, the situation called for a pause and a deep reflection on the way and spirit with which we are handling the implementing of CPA.
>
> To that end, the SPLM Interim Political Bureau (IPB) met in Juba from October 4th—11th 2007 to assess and evaluate the status of CPA implementation and draw concrete actions for the way forward. In that evaluation, the IPB identified CPA violations and enumerated unacceptable deliberate actions demeaning to the SPLM and its leadership. I am enclosing herewith copy of the IPB's resolutions encompassing violations to the CPA as well as actions to which the SPLM takes serious exception. In presenting these resolutions, I am confident that you shall address, with wisdom and statesmanship, the serious issues raised therein. Truly, those violations and actions constitute a major challenge to the sustenance of peace and consolidation of unity in our country. On my part, I remain committed to the full implementation of the CPA and I do not wish for a moment to contemplate the collapse of the CPA, let alone take part in that collapse.
>
> Furthermore, the IPB expressed deep concern with Your Excellency's inaction on the reshuffle of SPLM Ministers in GONU which, in the spirit of collegial decision-making, I proposed. In doing that, I was exercising my constitutional rights and prerogatives as the Chairman of the SPLM to effect the recommendations of my Party. In view of the perception that this inaction amounts to an encroachment on the First Vice President's constitutional powers, the IPB recalled all SPLM Presidential Advisors, Ministers and State Ministers in GONU and they have been directed to stay away from their duties till considerable progress is

seen in addressing the issues raised in the attached resolutions. In order not to paralyze the work of GoNU, I am again presenting to your Excellency our new list of ministerial changes in GONU. I am confident that you shall address this matter together with other pressing issues contained in the resolutions of IPB with due regard to the risks inherent in the present stalemate. This stalemate, if left unresolved, may degenerate into a crisis which none of us wants. It is our political duty and national obligation to avert actions that might endanger the CPA. It is also our moral and constitutional responsibility to provide the necessary leadership so that our country is enabled to enjoy peace, stability, democracy and unity based on the free will of its people."

In response to these demands and unexpected developments, President Bashir reportedly accepted a number of the Government of South Sudan (GoSS) demands in late October, except those related to the Abyei issue. According to senior SPLM officials, the acceptance of their demands by President Bashir does not resolve the crisis. They would like to see a timeline and a roadmap for implementation of their demands before they return to government. President Bashir accepted a new list of ministers submitted by the First Vice President, although he deleted the name of one senior official who was appointed as a Presidential Adviser, according to Sudanese sources. In late December 2007, the new ministers were sworn in office. Former Minister of Foreign Affairs, Lam Akol, was replaced by Deng Alore, a senior member of the SPLM.

STATUS OF THE COMPREHENSIVE PEACE AGREEMENT HISTORICAL CONTEXT

In 1956, Sudan became the first independent country in sub-Saharan Africa, having gained independence from Britain and Egypt. For almost four decades, the east African country, with a population of 35 million people, has been the scene of intermittent conflict. An estimated 2 million people died over two decades from war-related causes and famine in Southern Sudan, and millions more were displaced. The sources of the conflict were deeper and more complicated than the claims of most political leaders and some observers. Religion was a major factor because of the Islamic fundamentalist agenda of the current government, dominated by the mostly Muslim/Arab north. Southerners, who are Christian and animist, reject the Islamization of the country and favor a secular arrangement. Social and economic disparities were also major contributing factors to the Sudanese conflict.

Former President Jaafer Nimeri's abrogation in 1983 of the 1972 Addis Ababa agreement, which had ended the first phase of the civil war in the south, is considered a major factor triggering the civil war. The National Islamic Front (NIF) government, which ousted the democratically elected civilian government in 1989, pursued the war in southern Sudan with vigor. Previous governments, both civilian and military, had rejected southern demands for autonomy and equality. Northern political leaders for decades treated southerners as second-class citizens and did not see the south as an integral part of the country.

Southern political leaders argue that under successive civilian and military governments, political elites in the north have made only superficial attempts to address the grievances of the south, reluctant to compromise the north's dominant economic, political, and social status. In recent years, most political leaders in the north, now in opposition to the current government, have said that mistakes were made and that they are prepared to correct them. But the political mood among southerners has sharply shifted in favor of separation from the north.

The North-South Peace Agreement: Background

On January 9, 2005, the government of Sudan and the Sudan People's Liberation Movement (SPLM), after two and half years of negotiations, signed the Sudan Comprehensive Peace Agreement at a ceremony in Nairobi, Kenya. More than a dozen heads of state from Africa attended the signing ceremony. Secretary of State Colin Powell, who led the U.S. delegation, reportedly urged the government of Sudan and the SPLM to end the conflict in Darfur. The signing of this agreement effectively ended the 21-year-old civil war and triggered a six-year Interim Period. At the end of the Interim Period, southerners are to hold a referendum to decide their political future. National, regional, and local elections are to take place during the second half of the Interim Period.

On July 30, 2005, First Vice President and Chairman of the SPLM, Dr. John Garang, was killed in a plane crash in southern Sudan (discussed below). His death triggered violence between government security forces and southerners in Khartoum and Juba. More than 100 people were reported killed. The government of Sudan has established a committee to investigate the violence. The crash was investigated by a team from Sudan, Uganda, Russia, United Nations (UN), and the United States. The final report was issued in April 2006. In early August 2005, the SPLM Leadership Council appointed Salva Kiir as Chairman of the SPLM and First Vice President of Sudan. Salva Kiir had served as Garang's deputy after the SPLM split in 1991. He was officially sworn in as First Vice President in the Government of National Unity (GNU) on August 11, 2005. On August 31, 2005, the National Assembly was inaugurated. According to the CPA, the National Congress Party was allocated 52% of the seats (234), 28% to the SPLM (126), and the remaining 20% for the northern and southern opposition groups.

In September 2005, after weeks of contentious negotiations, the SPLM and the National Congress Party (NCP), formerly known as the National Islamic Front (NIF), agreed on a cabinet. At the core of the dispute was the distribution of key economic ministerial portfolios. The NCP insisted on keeping the Energy and Finance ministries, while the SPLM argued that each party should be given one or the other. The SPLM ultimately gave up its demand and managed to secure eight ministries, including Foreign Affairs, Cabinet Affairs, Labor, Transportation, Health, Education, Humanitarian Affairs, and Trade. Several advisers were also appointed to the Presidency (the Presidency consists of President Bashir, First Vice President Kiir, and Vice President Osman Ali Taha), including two from the SPLM.

Implementation of the CPA

Implementation of the CPA by the Government of National Unity has been selective and at times deliberately slow, according to United Nations officials and Sudan observers. President Bashir, for example, rejected implementation of the Abyei Boundary Commission (ABC) recommendations, and the formation of the Joint Integrated Units has been slow, although in 2008 important progress was made. The ABC was mandated to "define and demarcate" the area known as the nine Ngok Dinka Chiefdoms transferred in 1905 to Kordofan in North Sudan. The ABC was chaired by former U.S. Ambassador to Sudan Donald Peterson, with active international engagement. In July 2005, the ABC submitted its final report to the Presidency. According to the CPA, "upon presentation of the final report, the Presidency shall take necessary action to put the special administration status of Abyei Area into immediate effect."

The CPA faces serious challenges, despite the number of commissions created and decrees issued by the Presidency to address issues related to the agreement. Government force redeployment from Southern Sudan, as called for in the peace agreement, has been slow, especially in the oil field regions of Southern Sudan. The SPLA completed redeployment of its forces from East Sudan in 2006. The government of Sudan redeployed most of its forces as of December 2007, although thousands of Sudanese Armed Forces (SAF) remain in the oil region of South Sudan. SAF has increased its forces in the Nuba Mountains and Southern Blue Nile in violation of the CPA. According to the CPA, forces in these two states were supposed to be at a level of peace time. SPLA forces also had a presence in the Nuba and Southern Blue Nile regions. According to senior SPLM officials, the SPLA will pull out of the area once the SAF reduces its presence and the Joint Integrated Units (JIUs) are fully deployed. In early January 2008, the SPLA withdrew some of its forces from Nuba [16] As of January 2009, an estimated 84.7 percent of the CPA authorized JIU forces have been deployed.

A number of Commissions remain dysfunctional, although many of the Commissions have been created by the government of Sudan. According to the January 2009 CPA Monitor, the National Human Rights Commission, the Electoral Commission, the Land Commission, and several other Commissions have been established. The Assessment and Evaluation Commission (AEC), which was mandated under CPA to monitor implementation of the peace agreement, has created four Working Groups to monitor implementation of the CPA, although the parties to the agreement have not been actively engaged in the process. The parties have made some progress in the implementation of the wealth-sharing and power-sharing provisions of the CPA, although work on the north-south border is behind schedule. Failure to fully resolve the border issue is likely to complicate the redeployment of forces and sharing of oil revenues, since a number of the oil fields are located along the 1956 north-south border. In December, the SPLM and the National Congress Party reached agreement to resolve the north-south border issue and on oil-related issues [17]

The United States and the North-South Peace Agreement

The United States played a key role in the North-South peace process, while pressing for a resolution of the Darfur crisis in Western Sudan. Throughout the Inter-Governmental Authority for Development (IGAD)-sponsored talks, the Bush Administration engaged the parties at the highest levels, reportedly including calls by President Bush to the principals at critical times during the negotiations, and frequent visits to Kenya by senior State Department officials, where the talks were being conducted. President Bush's former Special Envoy, John Danforth, also made several trips to the region to encourage the parties to finalize an agreement. Former Secretary of State Colin Powell was actively engaged in the peace process and traveled to Kenya to encourage the parties, according to U.S. officials and Sudanese sources. U.S. financial support for the peace process and technical assistance during the talks were considered by the parties and the mediators as critical, according to U.S. officials. The United States provided funding for the SPLM delegation for travel and other related expenses. American interventions at critical times during the negotiations helped break a number of stalemates, including during security arrangement talks and the three disputed areas of Nuba, Southern Blue Nile, and Abyei.

Sustained U.S. pressure on the government of Sudan helped secure the Comprehensive Peace Agreement. The Bush Administration, while maintaining U.S. bilateral sanctions, also engaged the Government in critical dialogue and offered the normalization of bilateral relations as an incentive for the resolution of the Darfur crisis and settlement of the North-South conflict, according to U.S. officials and Sudanese sources. U.S. policy toward Sudan is complicated because the same government that signed the peace agreement with the South is also the one implicated in atrocities in Darfur, which the U.S. government has declared is genocide. This reality has led to some criticism of the Bush Administration, although many praise the Administration's sustained engagement in the North-South talks. According to some critics, the Administration did not initially consider the Darfur crisis to be a priority; instead the Administration was largely focused on the talks between the government of Sudan and the SPLM. The first statement on Darfur by the White House, they point out, was issued in early April 2004. The Bush Administration and Congress, however, have been at the forefront in calling for an end to the crisis in Darfur and demanding accountability, especially since mid-2004.

THE DARFUR CONFLICT AND IMPACT ON CHAD AND CAR

The crisis in Darfur continues to affect Chad and the Central African Republic (CAR), in large part due to rebellions supported by the government of Sudan against the governments of Chad and CAR. Indeed, the conflicts in Chad and CAR are largely internal political disputes between the respective governments and a number of armed groups. In Chad, some of the belligerents are armed and given safe havens for training purposes by the government of Sudan. The most affected areas in Chad are towns and villages near the border with Sudan. The government of Sudan accuses the Government of Chad of supporting some of the rebel groups in Darfur. The Sudan Liberation Army (SLA) reportedly benefitted from outside support, including from fellow Zagawa elements in Chad. The Zagawa are dominant in some SLA factions. President Idriss Deby of Chad is a Zagawa and some of the senior officers in the Chadian army come from the Zagawa ethnic group. Successive governments in Sudan have intervened in the internal affairs of Chad by providing support to armed factions.

The current instability in eastern Chad is also due to pro-Sudanese government militia groups and the Janjaweed crossing the border into Chad and attacking civilians. A February 2007 U.N. Secretary General report on Chad and CAR stated that "fighting between the Chadian armed forces and rebel groups, some of which are armed and supported by the Sudan, and attacks by militia on the civilian population have continued to destabilize eastern Chad, leading to widespread insecurity and human rights violations, including continued displacement of civilian populations" [18]. According to international NGOs and the United

Nations, more than 120,000 people have been internally displaced in eastern Chad. Chad has more than 230,000 refugees from Darfur, according to these sources. The incursion by the Janjaweed and the fighting between government forces and Chadian rebel groups have contributed to the suffering of the internally displaced and the refugees in eastern Chad. The internally displaced persons often move to areas closer to the refugee camps because humanitarian assistance to the displaced has been limited. In December 2006, President Deby reached an agreement with one of the rebel groups led by Mahamat Nour. In March 2007, Mr. Nour was appointed as Minister of Defense.

In the Central African Republic, the fighting between rebel groups and government forces has displaced more than 70,000 people in northeastern CAR, according to the United Nations. Over the past several months, the CAR government has recaptured towns taken by rebel groups. The CAR armed forces, supported by French troops and a multinational force from the Central African Economic and Monetary Community (CEMAC) have largely succeeded in containing rebel advances. Meanwhile, negotiations between the government of President Francois Bozize' and several rebel groups have led to some agreements. In February 2007, in negotiations mediated by Libya, two rebel leaders, Abdoulaye Miskine and Andre' Ringui Le Gaillard, signed an agreement with the CAR government. However, the agreement was rejected by the military chief of one of the rebel groups.

The United Nations has been working towards the deployment of a peacekeeping force to Chad and CAR over the past several months, and has concluded two technical assessment missions to Chad and CAR. The mandate of the proposed U.N. multidimensional presence would include the protection of civilians and internally displaced persons, maintenance of law and order, facilitation of the free movement of humanitarian assistance, and coordination with African Union Mission in Sudan (AMIS) and the U.N. Mission in Sudan (UNMIS). The area of operations would be in eastern Chad and northeastern CAR. The U.N. Secretary General recommended to the Security Council the deployment of 10,900 personnel to Chad and CAR. The government of Chad has reportedly expressed reservations about the deployment of an armed force but stated that the government would welcome a police force.

The Crisis in Darfur: Background

The crisis in Darfur began in February 2003, when two rebel groups emerged to challenge the National Congress Party (NCP) government in Darfur. The Sudan Liberation Army (SLA) and the Justice and Equality Movement (JEM) argued that the government of Sudan discriminates against Muslim African ethnic groups in Darfur and has systematically targeted these ethnic groups since the early 1990s. The government of Sudan dismisses the SLA and JEM as terrorists. The conflict primarily pits three African ethnic groups, the Fur, Zaghawa, and Massaleit, against nomadic Arab ethnic groups. Periodic tensions between the largely African-Muslim ethnic groups and the Arab inhabitants of Darfur can be traced to the 1930s and had surfaced again in the 1980s. Most observers note that successive governments in Khartoum have long neglected the African ethnic groups in Darfur and have done little to prevent or contain attacks by Arab militias against non- Arabs in Darfur. Non-Arab groups took up arms against successive central governments in Khartoum, albeit unsuccessfully. In the early 1 990s, the National Islamic Front (NIF) government, which came to power in 1989, began to arm Arab militias and attempted to disarm the largely African ethnic groups.

The conflict in Darfur burgeoned when the government of Sudan and its allied militias began what is widely characterized as a campaign of terror against civilians in an effort to crush the rebellion and to punish the core constituencies of the rebels. At the heart of the current conflict is a struggle for control of political power and resources. The largely nomadic Arab ethnic groups often venture into the traditionally farming communities of Darfur for water and grazing, at times triggering armed conflict between the two groups. Darfur is home to an estimated 7 million people and has more than 30 ethnic groups, which fall into two major categories: African and Arab. Both communities are Muslim, and years of intermarriages have made racial distinctions difficult, if not impossible. Fighting over resources is one of several factors that has led to intense infighting in Darfur over the years. Many observers believe that the NIF government has systematically and deliberately pursued a policy of discrimination and marginalization of the African communities in Darfur, and has given support to Arab militias to suppress non-Arabs, whom it considers a threat to its hold on power. In 2000, after the ouster of the founder of the NIF, Hassan al-Turabi, and after a split within the Islamist Movement, the government imposed a state of emergency and used its new authority to crack down on dissidents in Darfur. By 2002, a little-known self defense force emerged as the SLA, challenging government forces in Darfur.

With the NCP regime internally in turmoil and mounting international pressure to end Sudan's North-South conflict, the SLA and JEM were able to gain the upper hand in the initial phase of the conflict against government forces in early 2003, and appeared well armed and prepared. The rebels also enjoyed the support of the local population, as well as officers and soldiers in the Sudanese army.

A significant number of senior officers and soldiers in the Sudanese armed forces come from Darfur. The SLA reportedly benefitted from outside support, including from fellow Zaghawa elements in Chad and financial support from some Darfur businessmen in the Persian Gulf region. In late 2004, another Darfur armed group, the National Movement for Reform and Development (NMRD) emerged. Initial reports suggested that the NMRD was created by the government of Sudan in order to undermine the SLA and JEM. In December 2004, the NMRD and the government of Sudan signed a ceasefire agreement in Chad and a month later agreed to cooperate in facilitating the return of refugees from Chad to Darfur.

Regional officials and Sudanese opposition figures assert that the NMRD is backed by the government of Chad and that the rebels wear uniforms and carry arms similar to those of the Chadian army. Over the past year, the rebel groups have splintered into different factions and often clashed with each other. In June 2006, another rebel group was formed, the National Redemption Front (NRF), consisting of several rebel faction groups. These include splinter groups from SLM and JEM, as well as the Sudan Federal Democratic Alliance (SFDA).

DARFUR DEVELOPMENTS: ACCOUNTABILITY FOR ATROCITIES

In July 2004, the U.S. House of Representatives and the Senate unanimously passed resolutions (H.Con.Res. 467, S.Con.Res. 133) declaring the crisis in Darfur to be genocide, based on the five criteria for genocide enumerated in Article 2 of the Convention on the Prevention and Punishment of the Crime of Genocide. On September 9, 2004, then Secretary of State Colin Powell, in his testimony before the Senate Foreign Relations Committee, declared the atrocities in Darfur genocide. Secretary Powell stated that, after reviewing evidence collected by the State Department team, "genocide has been committed in Darfur and that the government of Sudan and the Jingaweit bear responsibility—and that genocide may still be occurring." Powell further stated that because the United States is a contracting party to the Geneva Convention, Washington will demand that the United Nations "initiate a full investigation." Shortly after Powell's testimony, a draft U.N. resolution (1564) was adopted.

The resolution requested the Secretary General of the United Nations to "establish an international commission of inquiry in order to immediately investigate reports of violations of international humanitarian law and human rights law in Darfur by all parties, to determine also whether or not acts of genocide have occurred, and to identify the perpetrators of such violations with a view to ensuring that those responsible are held accountable." The declaration of genocide by the Bush Administration did not lead to a major shift in U.S. policy or a threat of intervention to end genocide. Instead, Bush Administration officials continued to support a negotiated settlement between the rebels in Darfur and the government of Sudan. But continued violence in Darfur and the government's failure to disarm the Janjaweed militia further strained relations between Khartoum and Washington.

In January 2005, the International Commission of Inquiry on Darfur submitted its report to Secretary-General Kofi Annan. The 176-page report provided a detailed accounting of atrocities committed by the government of Sudan and its Janjaweed militia allies. The Commission declared that "based on thorough analysis of the information gathered in the course of the investigations, the Commission established that the government of Sudan and the Janjaweed are responsible for serious violations of international human rights and humanitarian law amounting to crimes under international law" [19] The Commission found, however, that "the government of Sudan has not pursued a policy of genocide." The Commission, while acknowledging that government officials and other individuals may have committed genocidal acts, stated that "the crucial element of genocidal intent appears to be missing." The Commission submitted a sealed document listing 51 suspects for prosecution by the International Criminal Court (ICC).

U.S. officials argue that the government of Sudan is responsible for genocide in Darfur, despite the Commission's conclusion of no genocidal intent. Washington initially did not support the Commission's referral of these cases to the ICC. U.S. opposition to the ICC is unrelated to the Darfur case. It is largely driven by concerns about the potential prosecution of U.S. personnel by the ICC, and because of this concern, the United States is not signatory to the ICC. In March 2005, the United States abstained on Security Council Resolution 1593, paving the way for its passage. Resolution 1593 refers the situation in Darfur to the International Criminal Court (ICC). In June 2005, the Special Prosecutor of the ICC formally began an investigation. ICC spokesman Yves Sorokobi indicated that the decision to launch the investigation came after the ICC had finished its analysis of the referral by the UN Security Council. This analysis included, he said, consultations with experts, ensuring that the ICC had met statutory requirements before beginning the investigations. Meanwhile, ICC officials continue to gather information and pursue their investigation, although the ICC has not issued any indictments to date. In July, the ICC Chief Prosecutor charged President Bashir with genocide, crimes against humanity, and war crimes [20].

Since the crisis began in 2003, sources estimate 450,000 people have been killed, more than 2 million displaced, and some 234,000 Sudanese are in refugee camps in neighboring Chad. The security situation continues to deteriorate, especially since the signing of the peace agreement in May 2006 reportedly due to recent troop deployments by the government of Sudan. According to human rights groups, over a dozen humanitarian workers have been killed in Darfur, including an International Rescue Committee nurse on September 1 and an International Committee of the Red Cross driver on August 30, 2006. In 2007, according to reports, tens of thousands of Darfuree civilians have been displaced from their homes by government and Janjaweed attacks. According to a February 2008 United Nations report, "tensions inside camps of internally displaced persons and carjacking incidents continued. One week after the transfer of authority from the African Union Mission in the Sudan (AMIS) to UNAMID, the force faced its first armed attack." [21]

Meanwhile, humanitarian groups have warned that they may not be able to continue to provide assistance to the civilian population because of deteriorating security conditions. In November 2006, the government of Sudan ordered the Norwegian Refugee Council to leave the country, while a German relief organization, Welthungerhilfe, announced it would pull out of Darfur for safety reasons. In October 2006, armed militia attacked a village in Jebel Moon and Seleah in West Darfur, killing over 50 people, including children and elderly. Meanwhile, security conditions inside IDP camps have also deteriorated in recent months, with an increasing number of armed groups in the camps. In his monthly report to the Security Council in November 2006, Secretary General Kofi Annan stated that "the insecurity, banditry and fighting which have characterized the reporting period continued to prevent access to populations in need of humanitarian assistance" [22] According to the same report "In Northern Darfur alone, the World Food Program (WFP) reported that 355,000 people went without food aid during July and August."

In early August 2006, the government of Sudan submitted a letter to the United Nations Security Council outlining the government's decision to deploy significant new security forces and implement other measures in Darfur. According to the government of Sudan, "the National Plan embodies several priority themes for the restoration of normal life in Darfur." The government of Sudan began to deploy more than 26,500 troops and 7,050 police personnel in order to address "threats imposed by the non-signatories of the Darfur Peace Agreement and getting control of the security situation and restoration of peace in Darfur." Human rights groups, U.N. Secretary General Kofi Annan, and U.S. officials have criticized the deployment of these troops and stated that this action violates the peace agreement. Meanwhile, senior commanders of the SLM, the only group that signed the peace agreement, have stated that continued government attacks in Darfur and continued rejection of a U.N. force could lead to the collapse of the peace agreement.

The Janjaweed: Background

Since the crisis in the Darfur region began in 2003, the name Janjaweed (also spelled as Janjawid, Janjawad, Jingaweit, Jinjaweed) has become a very familiar name to many in the international community. The Janjaweed and the government of Sudan have been accused of committing genocide against civilians in Darfur by the United States government in 2004 and accused of war crimes and crimes against humanity by the United Nations and other governments.

The existence of the Janjaweed goes back over a decade. In the mid-1980s, the government of Sudan began to arm Arab militias in order to prevent African Darfuris from joining the Southern Sudanese rebellion against the government. In 1983, the Sudan People's Liberation Movement/Army (SPLM/A) began its armed struggle against the government of Sudan. Attacks against Darfuri African tribes and Nubans increased in intensity for most of the 1980s.

In 1991 - 1992, an SPLM commander from Darfur led a force into Darfur in support of the Darfuris, who were being targeted by the government of Sudan and pro-government Arab militia. Those targeted were the Fur, Massaliet, and Zagawa peoples. More than 200 villages were attacked and later occupied by pro-government Arab militia in the Garsilla District, now know as the Wadi-Saleh Province. These attacks were carried out by a group now known as the Janjaweed.

Daoud Yahya Bolad, who was a senior member of the National Islamic Front (NIF) in Darfur before the 1989 coup, was the leading figure in the SPLM-led rebellion against the Sudanese government in Darfur in the early 1 990s. In 1 976, Bolad, an ethnic Fur, was Chairman of the student union of the University of Khartoum. He was sent by the NIF leadership to Darfur in the late 1970s to recruit members for the NIF. He left the NIF due to a major disagreement with the leader of the NIF, Hassan al-Turabi. Turabi and other NIF leaders recruited Arab youth to go to Libya and other places for training purposes and began other activities without consultation with Bolad and other Darfuri leaders.

The traditional leaders in Darfur described the Janjaweed then as men who own a horse and a G-3 rifle and who commit crimes against civilians. Darfuri leaders link the Janjaweed to a manifesto called the Quresh. The principal objective of the Quresh, they argued, was to create a region called Dar-el-Arab, Land of the Arabs. The architects of the manifesto and those who signed it are senior members of the National Islamic Front government, currently known as the National Congress Party.

The 1991-1992 rebellion against the NIF regime failed in large part due to lack of preparation inside Darfur and major Janjaweed and government operations against the small SPLA force in the region. The commander of the SPLA force decided to withdraw his troops after the government and Arab militia forces discovered the location of the SPLA force before final preparation for operations.

Elements within the government intensified their campaign to bring Bolad back into the NIF for talks with pledges to change policies and address the concerns of the Darfuris. Bolad decided to return to engage NIF officials against the advice of the SPLA leadership and the force commander, believing that since he knew some of the leaders in the government and the NIF he might be able to make a deal. Upon his return he was captured, tortured, and executed, according to Sudanese sources.

For many Darfuris, the war between the various groups started well before 2003. Darfuris who experienced the atrocities in the mid-1980s, in large part, are the ones currently fighting the Janjaweed and the government of Sudan. The groups that were targeted in the mid-1980s are the same ones currently being attacked by the Janjaweed and the government of Sudan: the Fur, Massaliet, and Zagawa.

In the current crisis in Darfur, the Janjaweed are armed and protected by the government, and their attacks against civilians are coordinated with the Sudan Armed Forces, the Popular Defense Force, and other government-supported militia groups. Senior Sudanese government officials and leaders of the Janjaweed admit this collaboration between the Janjaweed and the government. As was the case in the mid-1980s, one of the main objectives of the Janjaweed is to push out African Darfuris in order to take control of areas belonging to non-Arabs.

Human rights groups, foreign governments, and Sudanese groups have documented the atrocities committed by the Janjaweed against Darfur civilians, humanitarian workers, and African Union peacekeepers. Human Rights Watch in its report "Darfur Destroyed," [23] provides detailed accounts of Janjaweed atrocities as well as those committed by government forces. Janjaweed leaders and government officials claim that they are fighting rebels and violent militia. But the victims of these atrocities have been reported as the civilians in Darfur, mainly the Zagawa, Fur, and Massaliet. The Janjaweed, like the Interhamwe in Rwanda and the Lord's Resistance Army in Uganda, are reported to principally target civilians and terrorize the civilian population.

The Darfur Peace Agreement and Status of Implementation

On May 5, 2006, the Government of National Unity and the Sudan Liberation Movement (SLM) signed the Darfur Peace Agreement (DPA) after almost two years of negotiations. The agreement was rejected by two other Darfur groups: the Justice and Equality Movement (JEM) and a splinter group from the SLM. The agreement calls for the integration of 4,000 SLA troops into the Sudan Armed Forces, provides $300 million initially and $200 million each in 2007 and 2008 from government funds for reconstruction and development purposes for Darfur, and establishes the Transitional Darfur Regional Authority (TDRA), a new entity mandated under the DPA to administer Darfur. The agreement provides seats for the SLM in the national and regional parliaments and several top positions, including the chairmanship of the TDRA and Senior Assistant to the President.

On August 7, 2006, the leader of the SLM, Mini Minawi, was sworn in as Assistant to the President. The agreement also calls for the disarmament and demobilization of the Janjaweed. Since the signing of the agreement, the DPA has failed to win popular support in Darfur. The faction that signed the agreement is also accusing the government of violating the agreement. In mid-May 2006, violent demonstrations in IDP camps led to a number of deaths and injuries. AMIS personnel have also been targeted, forcing African Mission in Sudan to reduce its presence in IDP camps. Meanwhile, implementation of the agreement is also moving slowly. According to the United Nations DPA Monitor report, "the parties continued to miss critical DPA implementation deadlines" [24] The Preparatory Committee, tasked to organize the Darfur-Darfur Dialogue, was not fully functional, although in late September a chairman was appointed to head the Committee. On October 16, 2006, a day-long forum on pre-Darfur to Darfur Dialogue Consultation took place in Khartoum.

U.S. Humanitarian Funding

The United States continues to provide significant humanitarian assistance to Darfur and to Darfur refugees in Chad. The United States has provided more than $5 billion in humanitarian and development assistance to Sudan since 2005. As of May 2009, the United States had provided $531.

The African Union and the Crisis in Darfur

The African Union (AU) was slow in responding to the crisis in Darfur. The AU became actively engaged during the cease-fire negotiation in Chad in 2004 and subsequently assumed a central role in monitoring the cease-fire agreement and facilitating political dialogue between the government of Sudan and SLA/JEM.

Table 1. U.S. Bilateral Assistance to Sudan ($ in thousands)

	FY2008 Actual	FY2009 Estimate	FY2010 Request
Total	906,396	460,451	433,000
Development Assistance	127,721	25,550	
Economic Support Fund	145,876	253,550	296,034
Global Health and Child Survival (State)	3,245	6,327	7,036
Global Health & Childe Survival (USAID)	17,488	23,185	29,730
International Military Education and Training	349	400	300
Int. Narcotics Control and Law Enforcement	23,578	15,400	24,000
Non-proliferation, Anti-terrorism, Demining and Related Programs	4,400	4,000	3,900
Peacekeeping Operations	70,822	38,000	42,000
PL 480	512,917	94,039	30,000

Source: State Department FY2010 International Affairs Budget Request.

In March 2004, the AU sent a team led by Ambassador Sam Ibok, Director of the AU's Peace and Security Department, to participate in talks in Chad. In the April Cease-Fire Agreement, the AU was tasked to take the lead in the creation of a Cease-Fire Commission. The Commission was tasked to define the routes for the movement of the respective forces, assist with demining operations, and collect information about cease-fire violations. The Commission reports to a Joint Commission composed of the parties to the agreement, Chad, and members of the international community.

In January 2006, the African Union stated that transforming AMIS into a United Nations force is acceptable to the AU in principle. In March, the AU agreed to accept a United Nations peacekeeping mission for Darfur. Meanwhile, the Security Council requested that authorities in the U.N. provide options for a U.N. peacekeeping operation. On September 20,

2006, AU officials extended the AMIS peacekeeping operation until the end of December 2006, and in December the AU extended the AMIS operation for another six months.

United Nations officials and many observers of Sudan argue that failure to resolve U.N. peacekeeping deployment is likely to lead to the collapse of the DPA and a major humanitarian crisis. In addition to its peacekeeping responsibilities, AMIS is a key player in the implementation of key provisions of the DPA. The Ceasefire Commission and the Joint Commission are chaired by AMIS, while it is also tasked to establish and play a key role in the Joint Humanitarian Facilitation and Monitoring Unit. Security in IDP camps, creation of Demilitarized Zones, verification of disengagement and demobilization are also the responsibility of AMIS.

Possible Policy Options Concerning Darfur

There are a number of unilateral and multilateral policy options available to consider in facing the Darfur crisis. These options are complicated by a number of factors. Members of the international community are divided over Sudan, and some governments are allies of the regime in Khartoum. Since the late 1 990s, the European Union has adopted a policy of engagement, instead of containment, while the United States pursued a policy of isolation and containment of the government of Sudan.

Sudan's neighbors are also divided. Relations between Eritrea and Sudan were poor, although in recent years relations have improved, while relations with Chad are poor. For some of the options outlined below to be successful, close cooperation and coordination between the United States and the international community, especially the Security Council and Sudan's neighbors, is pivotal. Some of the other options are not dependent on close cooperation with the international community.

Engagement

One option is engagement with the government of Sudan. The government of Sudan is eager to appease the international community as long as it can avoid punitive sanctions and ensure its own political survival. In this scenario, engaging the government might yield some positive results, short of full cooperation and accountability by the government. Past engagement with the current government, however, has not succeeded in changing its behavior. The government of Sudan signs peace agreements or shows flexibility when it feels that it is in its interest to do so.

Sanctions

Many observers assert that the current regime only responds to real pressure. The Clinton Administration imposed comprehensive economic and trade sanctions in 1997; the impacts of these sanctions are mixed. Over the past decade, a number of punitive measures have been imposed on the government of Sudan. The government of Southern Sudan is exempted from these sanctions. But the government of Sudan has survived years of sanctions imposed by the United States. Moreover, some countries oppose sanctions against the government of Sudan, especially those countries with business interests in Sudan's oil sector. Multilateral targeted sanctions, including oil embargo, travel ban, and asset freeze, might have serious impact, especially if enforced by the international community. Another option is prohibiting foreign businesses from raising capital or trading their securities in the United States if they are engaged in business activities in Sudan.

Regime Change

Some observers and Sudan opposition leaders argue that the regime is incapable of change. They argue that since the National Congress Party government came to power in 1989, it has committed war crimes in south Sudan, the Nuba Mountains, and now in Darfur. They also maintain the regime has ties to international terrorist and extremist groups. A regime change in Khartoum, they argue, could bring a swift end to the crisis in Darfur, and help implement the North-South agreement. But opposition groups are not strong or united enough to pose a serious threat to the regime. Moreover, 21 years of war with the SPLA and other armed groups did not lead to the collapse of the regime in Khartoum. For this option to be viable, the opposition would have to be united and assisted. Nonetheless, the only force capable of countering the regime in Khartoum is the SPLA. Proponents of the regime change concept argue that strengthening the SPLA militarily, unifying the Darfur factions, and assisting other opposition elements in the North could pose a threat to the regime in Khartoum.

International Intervention

Another option involves military intervention by the international community. The international community could disarm the Janjaweed, enforce a no-fly zone, and provide protection to civilians in Darfur by deploying large numbers of peacekeepers with a Chapter VII mandate. The government of Sudan has rejected the deployment of a United Nations peacekeeping force after the Security Council passed resolution 1706. Deployment without government consent is an option, although there seems to be no strong support for such a forceful measure.

Bilateral Targeted Military Measures

Another force-based option is the targeting of certain military assets of the Sudanese government. These targets might include the Sudanese air force, military airfields, intelligence and military headquarters, and training facilities for the Janjaweed and the Sudanese armed forces. In 2005, 138 Members of Congress cosponsored H.R. 1424, which would have given the President authority to take similar measures.

Appendix A. Executive Order: Blocking Property of and Prohibiting Transactions with the Government of Sudan

By the authority vested in me as President by the Constitution and the laws of the United States of America, including the International Emergency Economic Powers Act (50 U.S.C. 1701 et seq.)(IEEPA), the National Emergencies Act (50 U.S.C. 1601 et seq.)(NEA), and section 301 of title 3, United States Code, and taking appropriate account of the Darfur Peace and Accountability Act of 2006 (the “Act”),

I, GEORGE W. BUSH, President of the United States of America, find that, due to the continuation of the threat to the national security and foreign policy of the United States created by certain policies and actions of the government of Sudan that violate human rights, in particular with respect to the conflict in Darfur, where the government of Sudan exercises administrative and legal authority and pervasive practical influence, and due to the threat to the national security and foreign policy of the United States posed by the pervasive role played by the government of Sudan in the petroleum and petrochemical industries in Sudan, it is in the interests of the United States to take additional steps with respect to the national emergency declared in Executive Order 13067 of November 3, 1997. Accordingly, I hereby order:

Sec. 1. Except to the extent provided in section 203(b) of IEEPA (50 U.S.C. 1702(b)) or in regulations, orders, directives, or licenses that may be issued pursuant to this order, all property and interests in property of the government of Sudan that are in the United States, that hereafter come within the United States, or that are or hereafter come within the possession or control of United States persons, including their overseas branches, are blocked and may not be transferred, paid, exported, withdrawn, or otherwise dealt in.

Sec. 2. Except to the extent provided in section 203(b) of IEEPA (50 U.S.C. 1702(b)) or in regulations, orders, directives, or licenses that may be issued pursuant to this order, and notwithstanding any contract entered into or any license or permit granted prior to the effective date of this order, all transactions by United States persons relating to the petroleum or petrochemical industries in Sudan, including, but not limited to, oilfield services and oil or gas pipelines, are prohibited.

Sec. 3. (a) Any transaction by a United States person or within the United States that evades or avoids, has the purpose of evading or avoiding, or attempts to violate any of the prohibitions set forth in this order is prohibited.

(b) Any conspiracy formed to violate any of the prohibitions set forth in this order is prohibited.

Sec. 4. (a) Subject to paragraph (b) of this section, restrictions imposed by this order shall be in addition to, and do not derogate from, restrictions imposed in and under Executive Order 13067.

(b)(I) None of the prohibitions in section 2 of Executive Order 13067 shall apply to activities or related transactions with respect to Southern Sudan, Southern Kordofan/Nuba Mountains State, Blue Nile State, Abyei, Darfur, or marginalized areas in and around Khartoum, provided that the activities or transactions do not involve any property or interests in property of the government of Sudan.

(ii) The Secretary of State, after consultation with the Secretary of the Treasury, may define the term "Southern Sudan, Southern Kordofan/Nuba Mountains State, Blue Nile State, Abyei, Darfur, or marginalized areas in and around Khartoum" for the purposes of this order.

(c) The function of the President under subsection 6(c)(1) of the Comprehensive Peace in Sudan Act of 2004 (P.L. 108-497), as amended by section 5(a)(3) of the act, is assigned to the Secretary of the Treasury as appropriate in the performance of such function.

(d) The functions of the President under subsection 6(c)(2) and the last sentence of 6(d) of the Comprehensive Peace in Sudan Act of 2004 (P.L. 108-497), as amended by subsections 5(a)(3) and (b), respectively, of the act, are assigned to the Secretary of State, except that the function of denial of entry is assigned to the Secretary of Homeland Security.

(e) The functions of the President under sections 7 and 8 of the act are assigned to the Secretary of State.

Sec. 5. Nothing in this order shall prohibit:

(a) transactions for the conduct of the official business of the Federal Government or the United Nations by employees thereof; or

(b) transactions in Sudan for journalistic activity by persons regularly employed in such capacity by a news gathering organization.

Sec. 6. For the purposes of this order:

(a) the term "person" means an individual or entity;

the term "entity" means a partnership, association, trust, joint venture, corporation, group, subgroup, or other organization;

(b) the term "United States person" means any United States citizen, permanent resident alien, entity organized under the laws of the United States or any jurisdiction within the United States (including foreign branches), or any person in the United States; and

(c) the term "government of Sudan" includes the government of Sudan, its agencies, instrumentalities, and controlled entities, and the Central Bank of Sudan, but does not include the regional government of Southern Sudan.

Sec. 7. For those persons whose property and interests in property are blocked pursuant to section 1 of this order who might have a constitutional presence in the United States, I find that, because of the ability to transfer funds or other assets instantaneously, prior notice to such persons of measures to be taken pursuant to this order would render these measures ineffectual. I therefore determine that for these measures to be effective in addressing the national emergency declared in Executive Order 13067 there need be no prior notice of a determination made pursuant to section 1 of this order.

Sec. 8. The Secretary of the Treasury, after consultation with the Secretary of State, is hereby authorized to take such actions, including the promulgation of rules and regulations, and to employ all powers granted to the President by IEEPA as may be necessary to carry out the purposes of this order. The Secretary of the Treasury may delegate any of these functions to other officers and agencies of the United States Government, consistent with applicable law. All executive agencies of the United States Government are hereby directed to take all appropriate measures within their authority to carry out the provisions of this order and, where appropriate, to advise the Secretary of the Treasury in a timely manner of the measures taken. The Secretary of the Treasury shall ensure compliance with those provisions of section 401 of the NEA (50 U.S.C. 1641) applicable to the Department of the Treasury in relation to this order.

Sec. 9. This order is not intended to, and does not, create any right, benefit, or privilege, substantive or procedural, enforceable at law or in equity by any party against the United States, its departments, agencies, instrumentalities, or entities, its officers or employees, or any other person.

Sec. 10. This order shall take effect upon the enactment of the Darfur Peace and Accountability Act of 2006.

GEORGE W. BUSH
THE WHITE HOUSE,
October 13, 2006.

APPENDIX B. EXECUTIVE ORDER: BLOCKING PROPERTY OF PERSONS IN CONNECTION WITH THE CONFLICT IN SUDAN'S DARFUR REGION

By the authority vested in me as President by the Constitution and the laws of the United States of America, including the International Emergency Economic Powers Act (50 U.S.C. 1701 et seq.)(IEEPA), the National Emergencies Act (50 U.S.C. 1601 et seq.)(NEA), section 5 of the United Nations Participation Act, as amended (22 U.S.C. 287c)(UNPA), and section 301 of title 3, United States Code,

I, GEORGE W. BUSH, President of the United States of America, find that an unusual and extraordinary threat to the national security and foreign policy of the United States is posed by the persistence of violence in Sudan's Darfur region, particularly against civilians and including sexual violence against women and girls, and by the deterioration of the security situation and its negative impact on humanitarian assistance efforts, as noted by the United Nations Security Council in Resolution 1591 of March 29, 2005, and, to deal with that threat, hereby expand the scope of the national emergency declared in Executive Order 13067 of November 3, 1997, with respect to the policies and actions of the government of Sudan, and hereby order:

Sec. 1. (a) Except to the extent that sections 203(b) (1), (3), and (4) of IEEPA (50 U.S.C. 1702(b)(1), (3), and (4)) may apply, or to the extent provided in regulations, orders, directives, or licenses that may be issued pursuant to this order, and notwithstanding any contract entered into or any license or permit granted prior to the effective date of this order, all property and interests in property of the following persons, that are in the United States, that hereafter come within the United States, or that are or hereafter come within the possession or control of any United States person, including any overseas branch, are blocked and may not be transferred, paid, exported, withdrawn, or otherwise dealt in:

(I) the persons listed in the Annex to this order; and

(ii) any person determined by the Secretary of the Treasury, after consultation with the Secretary of State:

(A) to have constituted a threat to the peace process in Darfur;

(B) to have constituted a threat to stability in Darfur and the region;

(C) to be responsible for conduct related to the conflict in Darfur that violates international law;

(D) to be responsible for heinous conduct with respect to human life or limb related to the conflict in Darfur;

(E) to have directly or indirectly supplied, sold, or transferred arms or any related materiel, or any assistance, advice, or training related to military activities to:

(1) the government of Sudan;

(2) the Sudan Liberation Movement/Army;

(3) the Justice and Equality Movement;

(4) the Janjaweed; or

(5) any person (other than a person listed in subparagraph (E)(1) through (E)(4) above) operating in the states of North Darfur, South Darfur, or West Darfur that is a belligerent, a nongovernmental entity, or an individual;

(F) to be responsible for offensive military overflights in and over the Darfur region;

(G) to have materially assisted, sponsored, or provided financial, materiel, or technological support for, or goods or services in support of, the activities described in paragraph (a)(ii)(A) through (F) of this section or any person listed in or designated pursuant to this order; or

(H) to be owned or controlled by, or acting or purporting to act for or on behalf of, directly or indirectly, any person listed in or designated pursuant to this order.

(b) I hereby determine that, to the extent section 203(b)(2) of IEEPA (50 U.S.C. 1702(b)(2)) may apply, the making of donations of the type of articles specified in such section by, to, or for the benefit of any person listed in or designated pursuant to this order would seriously impair my ability to deal with the national emergency declared in Executive Order 13067 and expanded in this order, and I hereby prohibit such donations as provided by paragraph (a) of this section.

(c) The prohibitions of paragraph (a) of this section include, but are not limited to, (I) the making of any contribution or provision of funds, goods, or services by, to, or for the benefit of any person listed in or designated pursuant to this order, and (ii) the receipt of any contribution or provision of funds, goods, or services from any such person.

Sec. 2. (a) Any transaction by a United States person or within the United States that evades or avoids, has the purpose of evading or avoiding, or attempts to violate any of the prohibitions set forth in this order is prohibited.

(b) Any conspiracy formed to violate any of the prohibitions set forth in this order is prohibited. Sec. 3. For the purposes of this order:

(a) the term "person" means an individual or entity;

(b) the term "entity" means a partnership, association, trust, joint venture, corporation, group, subgroup, or other organization;

(c) the term "United States person" means any United States citizen, permanent resident alien, entity organized under the laws of the United States or any jurisdiction within the United States (including foreign branches), or any person in the United States; and

(d) the term "arms or any related materiel" means arms or related materiel of all types, military aircraft, and equipment, but excludes:

(I) supplies and technical assistance, including training, intended solely for use in authorized monitoring, verification, or peace support operations, including such operations led by regional organizations;

(ii) supplies of non-lethal military equipment intended solely for humanitarian use, human rights monitoring use, or protective use, and related technical assistance, including training;

(iii) supplies of protective clothing, including flak jackets and military helmets, for use by United Nations personnel, representatives of the media, and humanitarian and development workers and associated personnel, for their personal use only;

(iv) assistance and supplies provided in support of implementation of the Comprehensive Peace Agreement signed January 9, 2005, by the government of Sudan and the People's Liberation Movement/Army; and

(v) other movements of military equipment and supplies into the Darfur region by the United States or that are permitted by a rule or decision of the Secretary of State, after consultation with the Secretary of the Treasury.

Sec. 4. For those persons listed in or designated pursuant to this order who might have a constitutional presence in the United States, I find that because of the ability to transfer funds or other assets instantaneously, prior notice to such persons of measures to be taken pursuant to this order would render these measures ineffectual. I therefore determine that, for these measures to be effective in addressing the national emergency declared in Executive Order 13067 and expanded by this order, there need be no prior notice of a listing or determination made pursuant to section 1 of this order.

Sec. 5. The Secretary of the Treasury, after consultation with the Secretary of State, is hereby authorized to take such actions, including the promulgation of rules and regulations, and to employ all powers granted to the President by IEEPA and UNPA as may be necessary to carry out the purposes of this order. The Secretary of the Treasury may delegate any of these functions to other officers and agencies of the United States Government, consistent with applicable law. All agencies of the United States Government are hereby directed to take all appropriate measures within their authority to carry out the provisions of this order and, where appropriate, to advise the Secretary of the Treasury in a timely manner of the measures taken. The Secretary of the Treasury shall ensure compliance with those provisions of section 401 of the NEA (50 U.S.C. 1641) applicable to the Department of the Treasury in relation to this order.

Sec. 6. The Secretary of the Treasury, after consultation with the Secretary of State, is hereby authorized to submit the recurring and final reports to the Congress on the national emergency expanded by this order, consistent with section 401(c) of the NEA (50 U.S.C. 1641(c)) and section 204(c) of the IEEPA (50 U.S.C. 1703(c)).

Sec. 7. The Secretary of the Treasury, after consultation with the Secretary of State, is hereby authorized to determine, subsequent to the issuance of this order, that circumstances no longer warrant the inclusion of a person in the Annex to this order and that the property and interests in property of that person are therefore no longer blocked pursuant to section 1 of this order.

Sec. 8. This order is not intended to, and does not, create any right, benefit, or privilege, substantive or procedural, enforceable at law or in equity by any party against the United States, its departments, agencies, instrumentalities, or entities, its officers or employees, or any other person.

Sec. 9. This order is effective at 12:0 1 a.m. eastern daylight time on April 27, 2006.

GEORGE W. BUSH
THE WHITE HOUSE,
April 26, 2006

ANNEX

Individuals

1. Gabril Abdul Kareem Badri [Colonel for the National Movement for Reform and Development (NMRD), born circa 1961]
2. Gaffar Mohmed El Hassan [Major General for the Sudan Armed Forces, born June 24, 1952]
3. Musa Hilal [Sheikh and Paramount Chief of the Jalul Tribe in North Darfur, born circa 1960]

4. Adam Yacub Shant [Commander for the Sudan Liberation Army (SLA), born circa 1976]

REFERENCES

[1] http://www.icc-cpi.int
[2] Department of State Press Release, March 4, 2009.
[3] United Nations News Wire, September 22, 2008.
[4] The Sudan Tribune. *Ugandan President Does Not Condemn the ICC*, August 3, 2008.
[5] The Washington Post. *Sudan Retains Clout While Charges Loom*, February 9, 2009.
[6] Ted Dagne visited Abyei in May 2008 at the height of the conflict and took video and photographs of the destruction of Abyei
[7] http://www.state.gov/r/pa/prs/ps/2008/jan/98954.htm
[8] http://afp.google.com/article/ALeqM5gvhevbfJOD4I9EAeZ5OxHyHtkPUw
[9] http://www.treasury.gov/press/releases/hp426.htm
[10] http://www.state.gov/s/d/2007/85716.htm
[11] http://www.usatoday.com/news/world/2007-06-25-darfur_N.htm
[12] http://www.UN.org/docs
[13] Amnesty International. *Sudan: Arms Continuing to Fuel Serious Human Rights Violations in Darfur*, May 2007.
[14] BBC News. *China is Fueling War in Darfur*, July 13, 2008. Ted Dagne spoke with the reporter on a number of occasions, in preparation for the BBC Television report, which was aired on July 14, 2008.
[15] Government of Sudan source.
[16] Ted Dagne met with senior SPLA commanders in January 2008 in Juba, South Sudan.
[17] Ted Dagne interview of President Salva Kiir in Juba, South Sudan.
[18] Report of the Secretary General on Chad and the Central African Republic, February 23, 2007, at http://www.un.org/ Docs/sc/sgrep07.htm
[19] Report of the International Commission of Inquiry on Darfur to the United Nations Secretary General. January 25, 2005.
[20] For recent developments on the ICC and Sudan, please see the ICC and Sudan Section.
[21] CBC News. Darfur heading for disaster unless U.N. troops are allowed: Annan, September 13, 2006, at http://www.cbc.ca/world/story/2006/09/13.
[22] Monthly report of the Secretary General on Darfur, November 8, 2006.
[23] Human Rights Watch. Darfur Destroyed: Ethnic Cleansing by Government Forces and Militia. May 2004, at http://hrw.org/reports/2004/sudan0504/sudan0504simple.pdf.
[24] Report on the Implementation of the Darfur Peace Agreement, at http://www.unmis.org/english/dpaMonitor.htm.
[25] http://www.usaid.gov/our_work/humanitarian_assistance/disaster_assistance/countries/sudan/template/fs_sr/ sudan_ce_sr02_12-20-2007.pdf

In: Economic, Political and Social Issues of Africa
Editor: Jeremy S. McQueen
ISBN 978-1-61209-957-6

Chapter 4

ALGERIA: CURRENT ISSUES*

Carol Migdalovitz

ABSTRACT

The situation in Algeria is fluid. Parliament passed a constitutional amendment abolishing term limits, allowing President Abdelaziz Bouteflika to be reelected for a third term in April 2009. The voice of the military, the most significant political force since independence, has been muted. Low voter turnout in the May 2007 parliamentary election may have indicated lack of public faith in the political system, and so the authorities specifically boasted a higher turnout in the 2009 presidential election. Domestic terrorism persists and Algerians continue to be linked to terror abroad. The U.S. State Departments lists the two Algerian groups as Foreign Terrorist Organizations (FTOs). The most notorious is Al Qaeda in the Land of the Islamic Maghreb (AQLIM), which pledged allegiance to Al Qaeda. Terrorism provides a rationale for Algeria's uneven human rights record. Oil and gas revenues have grown markedly, but public investment has yet to remedy the country's many socioeconomic ills. Bouteflika has energized foreign policy and broadened cooperation with the United States. This report will be updated if warranted. See also CRS Report RS20962, *Western Sahara: Status of Settlement Efforts*, by Carol Migdalovitz.

GOVERNMENT AND POLITICS

After a 1965 coup, the military became the most significant political force in Algeria. In 1992, it carried out another coup to prevent the Islamic Salvation Front (FIS) from coming to power, leading to a decade of war between security forces and Islamist terrorists. In 1999, former Foreign Minister Abdelaziz Bouteflika, a civilian with military backing, won the presidential election after all other candidates withdrew, charging fraud. In April 2004, he was reelected with 83.5% of the vote in a multiparty contest; the military was officially

* This is an edited, reformatted and augmented version of CRS Report RS21532, dated April 16, 2009.

neutral. International observers hailed that election as progress toward democratization even though the bureaucracy and judiciary had manipulated the political process to favor Bouteflika in the pre-election period. Many saw Bouteflika's victory as an accurate reflection of the popular will and an endorsement of his effort to decrease violence and for continued political stability [1]. There have been persistent rumors about the 71-year-old president's health since 2005, but no apparent concern that he lacks a clear successor. Bouteflika selected most of the current military high command, which probably will play a role in the choice of his replacement.

In November 2008, a joint session of parliament adopted constitutional amendments that, among other provisions, abolished presidential term limits and allowed Bouteflika to run for a third term. Perhaps related to the amendments' passage by 500 out of 529 cast was a huge salary increase for legislators passed in September. Some critics had argued that the constitutional changes should have required a national referendum, but the Constitutional Court did not agree. Hence, on April 9, 2009, Bouteflika as expected won another term as president with more than 90.24% of the vote over five challengers, none of whom were seen as having a remote chance of ending his leadership. The Interior Ministry claimed a 74% voter turnout. Once again, the President's rivals alleged fraud and that the authorities had inflated turnout figures.

The President heads the Council of Ministers (cabinet) and the High Security Council, and appoints the prime minister. On June 23, 2008, Bouteflika named National Democratic Assemblage (RND) leader Ahmed Ouyahia, who had served as prime minister from 1995 to 1999 and from 2003 to 2006 and who is known to be close to the military, to the post again. Ouyahia replaced National Liberation Front (FLN) Secretary General Abdelaziz Belkhadem, who remains a presidential advisor.

The bicameral, multiparty parliament is weak. The 380-seat National People's Assembly was last elected on May 17, 2007, with a voter turnout of 36.5% – the lowest ever, reflecting lack of popular faith in the political system. Parties in the governing coalition placed at the top: the FLN won 23% of the vote and 136 seats; the RND 10.3%, 61 seats; and the moderately Islamist Movement for a Peaceful Society (MSP) 9.6%, 51 seats; 18 other parties and 33 independents also won seats. The Council of Nations has 144 seats, one-third appointed by the president and two-thirds selected by indirect vote. FLN has 29 seats, RND 12, MSP 3; independents and presidential appointees also are represented.

TERRORISM

Up to 200,000 lives were lost to terrorism and related violence between 1992 and 2000. Two Algerian groups are U.S.-designated Foreign Terrorist Organizations (FTOs). The Armed Islamic Group (GIA) was most active from 1991 to 2001 and last attacked in 2006. The Salafist Group for Preaching and Combat (GSPC) split from GIA in 1998, declared its allegiance to Al Qaeda in 2003, and, after Abdelmalik Droukdel (aka Abu Musab Abdulwadood) became "emir" or leader, united with it officially on September 11, 2006, taking the name Al Qaeda in the Land of the Islamic Maghreb (AQLIM or AQIM). AQLIM seeks to replace the current Algerian regime with an Islamic state and calls for jihad against the United States and France. The practical meaning of the union with Al Qaeda is uncertain.

Moreover, the group's cohesiveness has been questioned as it may operate in relatively autonomous cells and has experienced defections.

After Droukdel became leader, AQLIM increased attacks against the government, security forces, and foreigner workers. In 2007, it shifted tactics to more frequent, "Iraqi style," suicide attacks, with simultaneous bombings of the Government Palace (the prime and interior ministries) and a suburban police station on April 11, 2007 and of the Constitutional Council and the U.N. headquarters on December 11, among other attacks. In addition, an AQLIM suicide bomber unsuccessfully attempted to assassinate President Bouteflika on September 6, 2007. All of these bombings resulted in many civilian casualties. After a relative lull, terrorist attacks escalated in July and August 2008, as security forces became frequent targets. In August, suicide bombers perpetrated a particularly bloody attack at a police academy, resulting in more than 40 deaths.

AQLIM raises funds by kidnapping for ransoms and by smuggling arms, vehicles, and drugs. It also gets small-scale funding from cells in Europe [2]. AQLIM communicates via internet with sophisticated videos. The group appears to have focused on the Berber region of the Kabyle, where the security force presence was reduced after civil unrest in 2001. AQLIM also operates in the Sahel and has carried out attacks in Mauritania in line with its regional pretensions, but it has had limited success outside of Algeria [3]

Algeria is a major source of international terrorists and was the fourth largest supplier of anti- coalition fighters to Iraq [4]. Some Algerians captured in Afghanistan are being held at the U.S. Naval Base at Guantanamo Bay, Cuba; others have been repatriated and others are still fighting in Afghanistan. Both the Bush and Obama Administrations have sought to repatriate more of the Algerian detainees, but seek assurances from Algiers that they would not pose a future danger and be treated fairly. Several have disappeared after their return amid fears that Algeria has secret detention facilities. Algerians have been arrested on suspicion of belonging to or supporting AQLIM in France, Spain, Italy, Germany, and Britain.

Several international terrorist plots involved Algerians. In December 1999, Ahmed Ressam, an Algerian who had trained in Afghanistan, was arrested after attempting to enter the United States from Canada; he was convicted for the so-called Millennium Plot to carry out bomb attacks in Los Angeles. His associates and other Algerians in Canada were linked to the GIA and Al Qaeda. In January 2003, six Algerians were arrested in a London apartment with traces of ricin, a deadly poison with no known antidote.

In September 1999, a national referendum approved the "Civil Concord," an amnesty for those who had fought the government. In September 2005, another referendum approved the Charter for Peace and National Reconciliation, including an amnesty for all except murderers, rapists, and bombers, exemption for security forces from prosecution for crimes of the 1990s, and compensation for families of victims of violence and the disappeared. Critics charge that it has resulted in the freeing of recidivist terrorists or that it failed to provide accountability for the disappeared and for truth-telling about the role of the security forces. A presidential commission determined that excesses of unsupervised security forces were responsible for the disappearances of 6,146 civilians from 1992 to 2000 and recommended compensation. Organizations representing victims' families claim up to 20,000 disappeared. The government has extended the amnesty period indefinitely and has controversially extended it to some former GSPC leaders.

HUMAN RIGHTS

A state of emergency declared in 1992 remains in effect. According to the U.S. State Department Country Report on Human Rights Practices-2008, human rights problems include restrictions on freedom of association which significantly limit citizens' ability to change the government through elections, failure to account for persons who disappeared in detention in the 1 990s, reports of torture and abuse, official impunity, abuses of pretrial detention, poor prison conditions, limited judicial independence, and restrictions on freedom of speech, press, and assembly. There also have been increased limitations on religious freedom and problems with security-based restrictions on movement, corruption and lack of government transparency, discrimination and violence against women, and restrictions on workers rights [5]. The Department's International Religious Freedoms Report, 2008, noted that U.S. officials had raised concerns with Algerian interlocutors about religious discrimination, government orders to close some churches (which had been operating without official permits that have been required since 2006), and the treatment of Muslims who wish to convert to other religions [6]. Proselytism as espoused by evangelical churches is a crime. The State Department categorizes Algeria as a Tier 3 worst offender with regard to human trafficking because its government does not fully comply with the minimum standards for the elimination of trafficking in persons and is not making significant efforts to do so [7]

Berbers, who are the natives of North Africa from before the 7th century Arab Muslim invasions, seek language and cultural rights and an end to government discrimination and neglect. In April 2001 ("black spring"), the death of a Berber youth in custody sparked riots in which security forces killed 126 people. The government agreed to compensate the victims and recognize Tamazight, the Berber language, as a national but not an official language (as Berber activists want but President Bouteflika opposes).

The government engaged in a dialogue with Berber representatives known as the *Arouch*. In January 2005, the government agreed to rehabilitate protesters and remove security forces from Berber areas, and established a joint committee to follow up.

ECONOMY

Algeria has the eighth largest natural gas reserves and is the second largest gas exporter in the world. It ranks 15th for oil reserves. Hydrocarbons are the engine of the economy, providing about 60% of the budget revenues, 30% of the gross domestic product (GDP), and 97% of export earnings.8 High oil prices have boosted foreign monetary reserves and economic growth, fueled a construction boom, and produced some decline in unemployment and early repayment of foreign debt.

A 2005- hydrocarbon law diminished the monopoly of SONATRACH, the state energy company, opening the sector for private and foreign investment. A 2006 law, however, requires international companies to give SONATRACH a 51% stake in new oil, gas, and related transport projects. In 2008, Algeria's Energy Minister Chakib Khelil assumed the rotating presidency of the Organization of Petroleum Exporting Countries (OPEC); at the time, he blamed the weak dollar, speculators, and geopolitical tensions for rising oil prices, not the market.9 Khelil seeks formation of a "gas OPEC" to protect exporters.

Algeria Basic Facts

Population: 34.18 million (2009 est.)
GDP growth rate: 3% (2008 est.)
GDP per capita: $7,000 (2008 est.)
Inflation rate: 3.6% (2008 est.)
Unemployment: 12.9% (2008 est.)
Exports: petroleum, gas, petroleum products
Export Partners: United States, Italy, Spain, Canada, France (2007)
Imports: capital goods, food, consumer goods
Import Partners: France, China, Italy, Spain , United States (2007)
Source: CIA, World Factbook, April 9, 2008.

Central control of the economy is easing very slowly, with a only a selective privatization program and tight conditions on foreign investment that the government argues are intended to encourage domestic companies. Despite considerable oil and gas income, there are chronic socioeconomic problems: high unemployment and underemployment; inadequate housing, health services, and education; decaying infrastructure; great inequality of income distribution; and government corruption.10 The government is directing some of its energy resource revenues for development. A $140 billion, five-year plan ending in 2009 invested in infrastructure, highways, ports, airports, and water resources. When its term is completed, another five-year plan for $100 billion to $150 billion will follow. These public investment plans are generating non-carbon growth which is seen as essential to remedy socioeconomic ills. Algeria has applied to join the World Trade Organization, but has many problems to overcome first.

In October 2008, Finance Minister Karim Djoudi asserted that the global financial crisis would not affect Algeria because it is not present in international banking, has sharply reduced its national debt, relies increasingly on domestic financing to fund development, and rejected total convertibility of the dinar (the national currency). Officials also boast of $135 billion in foreign reserves. Critics, however, point to the absence of a modern financial market, an undeveloped stock exchange, an underdeveloped banking system, and a failure to integrate in the world economy as weaknesses [11]. Others point to a continuing tide of illegal young Algerian immigrants to Europe as evidence of the failure of the economy to serve the poor and middle class.

Foreign Affairs

After independence in 1962, Algeria was in the forefront of Third World politics, especially the Non-Aligned Movement, and very active in the Arab world and Africa. It was considerably less active in the 1990s, when it was preoccupied by domestic violence. Since Bouteflika became President, Algeria has reemerged as a regional actor, especially in Africa.

Algeria's relations with neighboring Morocco are strained because Algeria supports and hosts the Popular Front for the Liberation of Saqiat al-Hamra and Rio de Oro (POLISARIO), which seeks the independence of the former Spanish Sahara, known as the Western Sahara. Morocco also claims and largely occupies the region. Algeria considers the problem one of decolonization to be resolved by the U.N. and maintains that it is not a party to the conflict. It views with favor the direct, unconditional talks between the POLISARIO and Morocco that began in June 2007 in response to a U.N. Security Council call, but no progress has been reported thus far. Algeria says that it would like to improve bilateral relations with Morocco by excluding the Western Sahara issue from that equation. Yet, Algiers has not reopened the border, which it closed 14 years ago in retaliation for Moroccan accusations that Algerians were involved in terror attacks in Marrakesh. Algiers now maintains that smuggling, drug-trafficking, and illegal immigration need to be dealt with before the border is opened [12].

Algeria and France, its former colonizer, have complex relations. France is Algeria's major trading partner. More than two million Algerians and individuals of Algerian descent live in France, but France has decreased visas for Algerians out of fear of terrorism and absorption difficulties. With France's support, Algeria signed an association agreement with the European Union (EU) in 2001 and has participated in the Europe-Mediterranean Partnership (MEDA) since 1995. Under Bouteflika, French-Algerian relations have warmed considerably. However, a planned treaty of friendship fizzled when France rejected Algeria's demand for an apology for the crimes of colonization. President Nicolas Sarkozy refuses to apologize, but acknowledges that colonialism was "profoundly unjust." He seeks to deepen bilateral business and trade ties, advance civilian nuclear energy cooperation, and promote the EU Union for the Mediterranean (UfM), a community of states bordering the Sea. However, Algerians appear to be hostile to the UfM.

RELATIONS WITH THE UNITED STATES

U.S.-Algerian ties date from a Treaty of Peace and Friendship in 1775. Algerians have fond memories of President Kennedy's support for their independence from France. Relations suffered later due to Cold War ideological differences; Algeria was a socialist republic with close ties to the Soviet Union. They were energized in recent years, as Bouteflika and President Bush met several times. Bouteflika attended the June 2004 G-8 summit of industrialized states and Russia in Sea Island, Georgia.

U.S. policy has tried to balance appreciation for Algeria's cooperation in counter-terrorism with encouragement of democratization. U.S. officials have urged Algiers to lift the state of emergency and described the April 2004 presidential election as an important phase in a democratic process. Algerian authorities have shared information regarding terrorists of Algerian origin with U.S. counterparts. High-level U.S. officials visit Algeria to discuss cooperation in the fight against terror. Algeria receives limited U.S. aid. In 2008, it is receiving an estimated $198,000 for International Narcotics Control and Law Enforcement (INCLE) and $666,000 for International Military Education and Training (IMET). For FY2009, the Administration requested $800,000 for IMET and $965,000 in Development Assistance (DA).

In 2005, the United States and Algeria launched a Joint Military Dialogue to foster exchanges, training and joint exercises. Algeria participates in the U.S. multi-country Trans-Sahara Counter Terrorism Partnership (TSCTP), but prefers bilateral activities with the United States that recognize its regional importance. As part of TSCTP, U.S. Special Forces train, equip, and aid national forces in fighting the AQLIM in southern Algeria and the Sahel

[13]. U.S. intelligence also is shared [14]. Algeria participates in the NATO-Mediterranean dialogue and in NATO naval exercises. Algerian officials have expressed perplexity about the U.S. Africa Command (AFRICOM), and oppose hosting U.S. bases. To support Algeria's efforts to combat terrorism, the U.S. Treasury Office of Foreign Assets Control (OFAC) has listed leaders of AQLIM, including Droukdel, as Specially Designated Global Terrorists.

The United States was first to invest in the hydrocarbon sector after the 2005 liberalization law opened it to foreigners. Economic ties have broadened beyond the energy sector, where most U.S. investment has been made, to financial services, pharmaceuticals, and other industries, although U.S. investors confront many bureaucratic and policy obstacles. Algeria receives duty-free treatment under the Generalized System of Preferences (GSP). In June 2007, Algeria and the United States signed an agreement to cooperate in the peaceful use of nuclear energy, but other countries have and will build reactors for Algeria.

Despite improving ties, Washington and Algiers strongly disagree about some U.S. Middle East policies. Bouteflika condemned the use of force against Iraq and called for the early withdrawal of foreign troops. He criticized U.S. charges against Syria, but Algeria only abstained from voting on a U.N. Security Council resolution calling on Syria to withdraw from Lebanon. Algeria supports the Arab Peace Initiative, which promises full normalization of relations with Israel after it withdraws from Arab lands. It roundly criticized Israel's military operation against Hamas in the Gaza Strip in December 2008-January 2009. Algeria considers the situation in the Darfur region of Sudan to be the result of ethnic conflict and poverty and not a genocide and is concerned about its regional implications. In particular, Algeria objects to the International Criminal Court's warrant for the arrest of Sudanese President Omar al Bashir because it finds unacceptable a trial of a head of state by an international court and because the warrant impedes a political solution to the Darfur situation.

REFERENCES

[1] Marwane Ben Yahmed, "Les Raisons D'Un Plebiscite," *Jeune Afrique Intelligent*, No. 2258, 18-14 April 2004.

[2] See also, Michael Jonson and Christian Nils Larson, "Illegal Tender: Funding Al-Qaeda in the Islamic Maghreb," *Janes Intelligence Review*, October 2008.

[3] See also, U.S. Department of State, *Country Reports on Terrorism*, 2007, released April 30, 2008, available online at http://www.state.gov

[4] Combating Terrorism Center at West Point, Harmony Project, "Al-Qaida's Foreign Fighters in Iraq: A First Look at the Sinjar Records," January 2008.

[5] U.S. Department of State, *Country Reports on Human Rights Practices - 2008, Algeria*, February 25, 2009, 2008, online at http://www.state.gov.

[6] U.S. State Department, *International Religious Freedom Report* – 2008, online at http://www.state.gov.

[7] U.S. State Department, *Trafficking in Persons Report*, June 4, 2008, online at http://www.state.gov

[8] U.S. Department of State, Bureau of Near Eastern Affairs, *Background Note: Algeria*, October 2007, online at http://www.state.gov.

[9] Randah Taqiy-al-Din, "'OPEC' Decides to Maintain its Current Production," *Al-Hayat*, March 6, 2008, BBC Monitoring Middle East.

[10] Algeria ranks 99 out of 179 countries on Transparency International's 2007 *Corruption Perceptions Index*, online at http://www.transparency.org

[11] William Maclean, "Algerian Shielded from Financial Turmoil," Reuters, October 5, 2009.

[12] "Zerhouni Responds to Call by Rabat, Algeria not in Hurry to Open Border," *El-Khabar*, March 23, 2008, BBC Monitoring Middle East.

[13] "Desert Shadows," *Africa Confidential*, Vol. 45, No. 4, February 10, 2004, p. 8.

[14] Brian Whitmore, "US Pushes Antiterror Alliance for North African Nations," *Boston Globe*, April 11, 2004.

In: Economic, Political and Social Issues of Africa
Editor: Jeremy S. McQueen

ISBN 978-1-61209-957-6

Chapter 5

KENYA: CURRENT CONDITIONS AND THE CHALLENGES AHEAD*

Ted Dagne

ABSTRACT

Kenya, a nation of about 36.9 million people, has been an important ally of the United States for decades. Kenya moved from a one-party state to a multi-party democracy in 1992. Kenyans voted in record numbers in the country's first multi-party election in almost 26 years. President Daniel arap Moi defeated opposition candidates by a small margin. In 1997, Kenya held its second multiparty elections, at the height of tensions between the opposition and the ruling party. President Moi was re-elected with 40% of the votes cast, while his nearest rival, Mwai Kibaki, won 31%. In the 2002 presidential and parliamentary elections, the opposition National Rainbow Coalition (NARC) defeated the ruling Kenya African National Union (KANU). In the presidential election, NARC leader Kibaki defeated Uhuru Kenyatta, the leader of KANU.

On December 27, 2007, millions of Kenyans went to the polls in Kenya's fourth multi-party elections, with the hope of strengthening the institutions of democracy and, most important in the view of many observers, of bringing change. An estimated 14.2 million (82% of the total eligible voters) Kenyans were registered to vote, while 2,547 Parliamentary candidates were qualified to run in 210 constituencies, according to the Electoral Commission of Kenya (ECK). Nine candidates competed in the presidential election. The opposition reportedly made significant gains in the parliamentary elections. The ECK, however, hastily declared President Kibaki as the winner of the elections. Kibaki was quickly sworn in as president, while international and domestic election observers declared the elections as rigged and deeply flawed.

Following the announcement of the election results, violence erupted in many parts of Kenya. More than 1,000 people have been killed and an estimated 350,000 reportedly displaced. In August 2008, the Kenya National Commission on Human Rights (KNCHR) released a report on the post-election violence. In early February, the opposition and the government began negotiations under the leadership of former

* This is an edited, reformatted and augmented version of CRS Report RL34378, dated May 14, 2009.

U.N. Secretary General Kofi Annan. The two parties agreed to work together to end the violence, improve humanitarian conditions, and to write a new constitution within a year. In late February, the government and the opposition reached a power-sharing arrangement. On March 18, 2008, the Kenya parliament unanimously approved the Agreement. On April 3, 2008, the parties agreed on a 40-member cabinet. But important reforms agreed to by the parties have yet to be implemented.

The initial United States government reaction to the December elections was considered by some international observers as contradictory and seen by some Kenyans as being one-sided in favor of President Kibaki. On December 30, the United States government reportedly congratulated President Kibaki. Senior Bush Administration officials visited Kenya in an effort to resolve the crisis and provided support to Kofi Annan's mediation efforts. In June 2008, Prime Minister Raila Odinga visited Washington and met with senior Bush Administration officials and Members of Congress.

Recent Developments

The coalition government in Kenya is currently experience serious problems since President Kibaki's and Prime Minister Odinga's parties reached a power-sharing agreement in April 2008. In March 2009, two human rights advocates, Mr.Kamau King'ara and Mr. John Paul Oulu, were assassinated by unknown gunmen. The Government of Kenya has yet to address some of the important reforms agreed to by the parties in 2008. According to Kenyan observers and officials, the constitutional review process is stalled, while serious disagreement remains over the Special Tribunal. The Government has not taken measures to fight corruption. In May 2009, a new electoral commission, the Interim Independent Electoral Commission (IIEC) was formed. The previous Electoral Commission of Kenya was disbanded in December 2008.

In August 2008, Kenyan authorities came close to arresting the mastermind in the bombings of the U.S. embassies in Kenya and Tanzania, Fazul A. Mohammed. According to press reports, Kenyan authorities raided a house that was being used by Fazul and took into custody passports allegedly used by Fazul and a computer hard disk. Several people were arrested, allegedly for giving Fazul a safe haven. Fazul was in the Indian Ocean resort of Malindi.

In August 2008, United Nations officials informed a congressional delegation [1] that the Dadaab refugee camp for Somalis and Ethiopians is full of refugees and that they have no space for new refugees. Kenyan authorities have suggested that perhaps some of the refugees can be moved to another camp.

In August 2008, the Kenya National Commission on Human Rights released a report on the post-election violence. The Commission accused five cabinet members, 13 Members of Parliament, some members of the security force, and a number of individuals of financing and fueling the violence. The 300-page report was reportedly submitted to President Kibaki and Prime Minister Odinga.

In June 2008, Prime Minister Raila Odinga visited Washington and met with senior Bush Administration officials and Members of Congress. Odinga stated that, although the post-election crisis is largely over, many challenges remain [2] Hundreds of thousands of people are still indeed of assistance. Unknown number of Kenyans accused of taking part in the post-election violence remain in prison, and some have called for amnesty, while others continue to demand justice and accountability.

In June 2008, Kenya held by-elections for five parliamentary seats. The opposition Orange Democratic Party (ODM) won three seats, while the Party for National Unity (PNU) won two seats.

In late February, the Kibaki government and the opposition reached a power sharing agreement, after weeks of negotiations. The agreement calls for the creation of a prime minister and two deputy prime ministers positions. The agreement known as the National Accord and Reconciliation Act of 2008 calls for a new coalition government. On March 18, 2008, the Kenya parliament unanimously approved the Agreement. On April 3, 2008, the parties agreed on a 40- member cabinet. Key provisions of the agreement are as follows: [3]

- There will be a Prime Minister of the Government of Kenya, with authority to coordinate and supervise the execution of the functions and affairs of the Government of Kenya.
- The Prime Minister will be an elected member of the National Assemble and the parliamentary leader of the largest party in the National Assembly, or a coalition, if the largest party does not command a majority.
- Each member of the coalition shall nominate one person from the National Assembly to be appointed a Deputy Prime Minister.
- The Cabinet will consist of the President, the Vice President, the Prime Minister, the Deputy Prime Ministers and the other Ministers. The removal of any Minister of the coalition will be subject to consultation and concurrence in writing by the leaders.
- The Prime Minister and the Deputy Prime Ministers can only be removed if the National Assembly passes a motion of no confidence with a majority vote.
- The composition of the coalition government will at all times take into account the principle of portfolio balance and will reflect their relative parliamentary strength.
- The coalition will be dissolved if the Tenth Parliament is dissolved; or if the parties agree in writing; or if one coalition partner withdraws from the coalition.
- The National Accord and Reconciliation Act shall be entrenched in the Constitution.

The December 2007 Elections

On December 27, 2007, millions of Kenyans went to the polls in Kenya's fourth multi party elections, with the hope of strengthening the institutions of democracy and, most important in the view of many observers, of bringing change. Several months before the December elections, a number of polls indicted that the incumbent President trailed behind opposition candidate Raila Odinga. Many observers, including key President Mwai Kibaki advisors, acknowledged that President Kibaki and his party would lose in December.4 An estimated 14.2 million (82% of the total eligible voters) Kenyans were registered to vote, while 2,547 Parliamentary candidates were qualified to run in 210 constituencies, according to the Electoral Commission of Kenya (ECK). A total of 15,331 candidates were approved to compete in the 2,498 local wards. Nine candidates competed in the presidential election. According to the European Union Election Observation Mission preliminary report, the ECK deployed an estimated 245,000 staff to 27,555 polling stations. These polling station staff members were reportedly well trained.

The elections were administered by the ECK, a government body established by the Kenyan Constitution. The ECK has 22 Commissioners, 19 of the Commissioners were appointed by President Kibaki last year, consistent with the authority provided under the Kenyan Constitution. However, the appointment of the new Commissioners was reportedly done without proper consultation with opposition parties, according to the EU and Kenyan observers. The appointments also violated the Inter-Parliamentary Parties Group (IPPG) Agreement of 1997 that calls for consultation with opposition parties. Moreover, the newly appointed Commissioners reportedly lacked experience in effectively carrying out their electoral administrative responsibilities, according to Kenyan sources and EU officials.

State media coverage of the elections was reportedly one-sided, with the President's party, the PNU, getting significantly more attention than the opposition. According to the EU Electoral Observation Mission (EU EOM) report, the government-controlled Kenya Broadcasting Corporation (KBC) Radio coverage gave the PNU 76% share of coverage, compared to the opposition ODM 13% and ODM-Kenya 5%. The KBC-TV gave PNU 71% of the share of coverage, ODM 11%, and ODM-Kenya, a splinter party that broke from ODM, 5%. Private media provided a larger share of coverage to opposition groups, although the PNU received more coverage than the opposition parties, according to the EU EOM. The December 2007 elections were monitored by international and local election observers, according to press reports and Kenyan officials.

Table 1. Electoral Commission of Kenya: Official National Results

Other Names	First Name	Votes	Party Abrev	Party
Mwai	Kibaki	4,578,034	PNU	Party of National Unity
Raila Amolo	Odinga	4,352,860	ODM	Orange Democratic Movement
Stephen Kalonzo	Musyoka	879,899	ODM-K	Orange Democratic Movement - Kenya
Joseph Ngacha	Karani	21,168	KPTP	Kenya Patriotic Trust Party
Pius Muiru	Mwangi	9,665	KPP	Kenya People's Party
Nazlin Omar Fazaldin	Raj put	8,624	WCP	Workers Congress Party of Kenya
Kenneth Stanley Njindo	Matiba	8,049	SSA	Saba Saba Asili
David Waweru	Ngethe	5,976	CCU	Chama Cha Uma Party
Nixon Jeremiah	Kukubo	5,926	RPK	Republican Party of Kenya

The opposition reportedly made significant gains in the parliamentary elections and early election results showed Odinga ahead of Kibaki. The Electoral Commission of Kenya, however, hastily declared President Kibaki as the winner of the elections. President Kibaki was quickly sworn in as president, while international and domestic election observers declared the elections as rigged and deeply flawed. Several members of the ECK openly declared shortly after the election results were announced that they did not agree with the decision to declare Kibaki as the winner of the election and that there were serious problems in vote tallying, according to press reports. The Chairman of the Commission also admitted that he was under intense political pressure from powerful political leaders and the ruling party. According to current and former Kenyan government officials, even before the Electoral Commission announced the results, the spouses of senior government officials were preparing for the swearing-in ceremony. The Kenya Electoral Commission Chairman, Samuel M. Kivuitu, was quoted in a press report that the day he went to deliver the certificate declaring Kibaki the winner, he saw the Chief Justice already at State House reportedly waiting to swear in Kibaki. The swearing-in ceremony was said to be so rushed that the organizers forgot to include the National Anthem in the program [5].

Table 2. Electoral Commission of Kenya: Official Parliamentary Results

Party	Name	Symbol	Seats
ODM	Orange Democratic Movement	Orange	99
PNU	Party of National Unity	Two Torches with Flames	43
ODM-K	Orange Democratic Movement - Kenya	Oranges	16
KANU	Kenya African National Union	Cockerel	14
SAFINA	Safina Party	Safina	5
NARC KENYA	Narc Kenya	Flower	4
NARC	National Rainbow Coalition	Traditional African Torch(Mwenge)	3
FORD-P	Forum for the Restoration of Democracy for the People	Pen	3
NFK	New Ford Kenya	Cup	2
PICK	Party of Independent Candidates of Kenya	Child	2
CCU	Chama Cha Uzalendo	Whistle	2
SKSPK	Sisi Kwa Sisi Party of Kenya	Train	2
DP	Democratic Party of Kenya	Lantern	2
PDP	Peoples Democratic Party	Traditional African Banjo	1
MGPK	Mazingira Greens Party of Kenya	Tree	1
PPK	Peoples Party of Kenya	Trumpet	1
NLP	National Labour Party	Bull (Ndume)	1
KADDU	Kenya African Democratic Development Union	Fruit Basket (Mavuno)	1
KENDA	Kenya National Democratic Alliance	Bell	1
KADU-ASILI	Kenya African Democratic Union Asili	Coconut Tree	1
FORD-K	Forum for the Restoration of Democracy - Kenya	Lion	1
UDM	United Democratic Movement	Milk Can	1
FORD-A	Forum for the Restoration of Democracy - Asili	Two Fingers Raised	1

Source: Electoral Commission of Kenya.

According to a report by EU observers, "a lack of adequate transparency and security measures in the process of relaying the results from local to national level questioned the integrity of the final results" [7]. The EU report concluded that "the 2007 General Elections have fallen short of key international and regional standards for democratic elections. Most significantly, they were marred by a lack of transparency in the processing and tallying of presidential results, which raises concerns about the accuracy of the final results of this election." Election observers from the East African Community also raised serious concerns about the December 2007 elections.

The initial United States government reaction to the December elections was considered by some international observers as contradictory and seen by some Kenyans as being one-sided in favor of President Kibaki. On December 30, the United States government reportedly congratulated President Kibaki. Shortly after the election results were announced, an official statement from the U.S. declared that "those alleging vote tampering may pursue legal remedies and should be able, consistent with respect for freedom of speech, to make their case publicly." [8]. This was a position supported by President Kibaki, but rejected by the opposition and seen by many Kenyans as a mechanism that has failed to resolve past political disputes. The judiciary is seen by the opposition as an institution controlled by Kibaki loyalists. President Kibaki appointed a number of senior judges just before the elections last year. In addition, Kenyans point out that President Kibaki announced his new cabinet shortly after he concluded a meeting with the U.S. Assistant Secretary of State for African Affairs Jendayi Frazer. The U.S. position shifted somewhat by January, as the Assistant Secretary declared that "serious flaws in the vote tallying process damaged the credibility of the process" [9].

Post-Election Violence

Shortly after the election results were announced, supporters of the opposition took to the streets in what many observers described as spontaneous demonstrations of anger and engaged in violent attacks targeting pro-government districts and properties. More that 1,000 people have been killed since late December and an estimated 350,000 have been displaced, including 80,000 children under five years of age, according to U.N. and Kenyan sources. Many protestors were reportedly shot and killed by police, while many others died in mob violence, according to Kenyan sources and international observers. Protestors also burned houses and properties, especially in Eldoret, Kisumu, Naivasha, and Nairobi, as well as in other parts of Kenya. Thousands of Kenyans, mostly children and elderly were displaced in Nairobi and many of them sought refugee in Jamhuri Show ground. In Jamhuri, Kenyans from different backgrounds, including church leaders, individuals, the Red Cross Society of Kenya, and others came together to help thousands of displaced people. More than 500 volunteers offered their help, while Kenyans donated food, money, toys, and blankets [10]. The number of registered adults and children in Jamhuri fluctuates, although in early January there were 6,000 registered people from Kibera, the poorest neighborhood in Kenya, with an estimated 1.5 million people.

The Kenyan military did not engage in riot control functions for most of January, while the Kenyan police and security were given authority to use lethal force, according to press reports and Kenyan sources. According to some reports, Kenyan security forces targeted opposition supporters, provided assistance to pro-government gangs, and failed to protect the civilian population in some places. Two opposition Members of Parliament were killed in late January, one reportedly by a police officer. The police officer reportedly killed the MP and his girlfriend, who was in the same car, according to press reports. Moreover, opposition leaders accuse the security forces and pro-government gangs of targeting their supporters and family members [11]. The government also initiated a number of media restrictions and banned demonstrations, although opposition supporters launched another three-day protest in mid-January. On January 16, the opposition took to the streets in over a dozen locations throughout Kenya. Several people were killed and many more injured. Opposition supporters have also engaged in targeted attacks against government supporters. In a number of communities in Kenya, people have been burned to death and hacked by machetes.

Some observers have described the violence as a tribal conflict between the President's Kikuyu ethnic group and the Luo and Kalenjin ethnic groups. Indeed, Kikuyus were principal targets in some areas, although the Luo and other ethnic groups were also targeted by the security forces and by Kikuyu groups. Kenyan civil society and human rights advocates argue that it is a mistake to simply describe the current violence as a tribal conflict, since the trigger and the reason behind the violence for many Kenyans is the rigged elections and what they fear is a return to dictatorship. Opposition leaders and their supporters strongly believe that the election was stolen from them, and they consider reversing the current trend in Kenya as necessary in order to ensure that the gains made in democracy over the past decade would not be lost. Some Kenyans view the violence in some places as driven by economic factors rather than ethnic or political. The victims of some of the violent attacks have been wealthy or middle class Kenyans from diverse ethnic backgrounds. The last major ethnic violence before an election was in 1992. In that particular case, the violence was triggered over land dispute between the Kalenjin and the Luo.

Mediation Efforts

International efforts to bring a negotiated settlement failed in the initial phase of the crisis. The African Union, the Kenyans, and the European Union all encouraged a power-sharing arrangement between Odinga and President Kibaki. Odinga, while willing to negotiate with Kibaki, was reluctant to agree to a deal without international guarantee. Kibaki was elected president in 2002 largely due to strong support from Odinga and current opposition leaders. As part of the coalition agreement, Odinga was to become prime minister in the Kibaki government, although Kibaki reportedly reneged in that agreement (see background section for more on this issue).

Initial efforts by African Union president, President John Kufuor of Ghana, failed to bring the two parties to engage in negotiations. Since the failed AU initiative, former United Nations Secretary General Kofi Annan began to actively engage in mediation efforts since mid-January. He succeeded in getting Kibaki and Odinga to meet for the first time since the crisis erupted in late December. In late January, both sides agreed to start negotiations and later appointed their respective negotiation team members. In early February, the parties also agreed to work together to end the violence, although reportedly more than 70 people were killed a day after the agreement was signed.

In mid-January, the Kenyan Parliament met and elected a new Speaker. The opposition candidate won with 105 votes, while the president's candidate, former Speaker Francis Kaparo, lost. Opposition leader Odinga called for a negotiated agreement with President Kibaki. He supported the creation of a transitional coalition government, with a mandate to draft a new Constitution, new electoral law, and establish a new independent Electoral Commission [12]. The opposition initially called for an investigation of the election results by an independent body and a re-run of the presidential election within two years. In February, the government and the opposition agreed on a wide range of issues, including a power-sharing arrangement and an independent investigation of the December 2007 election disputes.

Kenya at a Glance

Population: 39 million
Comparative Area: Slightly more than twice the size of Nevada
Ethnic Divisions: Kikuyu 22%, Luhya 14%, Luo 13%, Kalenjin 12%, Kamba 11%, Kisii 6%, Meru 6%, other African 15%, Asian, European, and Arab 1%
Religions: Protestant 45%, Roman Catholic 33%, indigenous beliefs 10%, Muslim 10%, other 2%
Languages: English (official), Swahili (official), numerous indigenous languages.
GDP (purchasing power parity) $61.8 billion (est. 2008)
GDP Per Capita (purchasing power parity): $1,600 (est. 2008)
Source: The CIA World Factbook 2009

Background

Kenya, a nation of about 36.9 million people, became independent in December 1963 after a prolonged and bloody uprising against Britain, with over 13,000 casualties. Kenya resisted the Marxist-Leninist ideological tide that swept much of Africa in the 1960s and 1970s and maintained a fairly stable political system in a region marred by civil strife and political violence. Although it was governed under one-party rule until 1992, Kenya had a relatively open political system. Kenya's first president was Jomo Kenyatta, an independence advocate from Kenya's largest ethnic group, the Kikuyu. Kenyatta's successor as president was Vice President Daniel arap Moi, who took over as president upon Kenyatta's death in 1978. Moi, a teacher before entering politics, is a Kalenj in—traditionally a pastoral people based in the western portion of the Kenya highlands. Many non-Kikuyu initially hoped that his presidency would redistribute the benefits that they felt had unfairly accrued to the Kikuyu under Kenyatta. In 1991, President Moi reluctantly and under pressure agreed to move to multi-party politics, eight years after his government had amended the constitution to legalize one-party rule. The move to a multi-party state came after two years of an anti-government political campaign by opposition groups and persistent pressure by donor governments, including the United States.

In 1992, Kenyans voted in record numbers in the country's first multiparty election in almost 26 years. President Moi defeated opposition candidates by a small margin. His party, the Kenya African National Union (KANU), also won a majority in the 210-seat parliament, despite the defeat of several senior KANU officials by little-known opposition candidates. The three major opposition parties, the Forum for Restoration of Democracy-Kenya (FORD-Kenya), FORD-Asili, and the Democratic Party (DP), each received substantial votes, but fell short of expectations. In 1997, Kenya held its second multi-party elections, at the height of tensions between the opposition and the ruling party. President Moi was re-elected with 40% of the votes cast, while his nearest rival, Mwai Kibaki, won 31%. The ruling party, KANU, won 107 seats in the 222- member parliament (12 seats out of the 222 are appointed by the president), while the opposition secured the remaining 103 seats. International and Kenyan election observers said that while there were some irregularities, the results of the elections reflected the wishes of most Kenyans. The victory by Moi was largely due to divisions within the opposition and the inability of the opposition to back a single candidate against Moi.

The opposition learned from its mistakes, and in 2002 it succeeded in forming and holding together a coalition, known as NARC (National Rainbow Coalition), that ousted KANU from power by wide margins. NARC won 132 seats in parliament, compared with KANU's 67, while Kibaki defeated Uhuru Kenyatta, son of Jomo Kenyatta, for the presidency with a 62% majority. Moi had designated Kenyatta as the KANU candidate for president in October 2002, prompting Raila Odinga, who had sought the nomination, to leave KANU and, with other defectors, form the Liberal Democratic Party. Kibaki's National Alliance of Kenya (NAK) courted these KANU defectors, and in November 2002, NAK and the LDP agreed to create NARC. NAK is itself a coalition, including Kibaki's Democratic Party and 12 other parties which typically have an ethnic or regional base. President Kibaki announced his cabinet on January 3, 2003, consisting of longtime opposition figures and also senior members of KANU. President Kibaki had to take several factors into consideration in the selection of his cabinet members, including ethnic balance, technical skills, and government experience, as well as rewarding old and new political allies.

The Challenges Ahead

The 24-year rule of President Moi kept Kenya united, but left the East African country in serious economic and political trouble. The most immediate political challenge to President Kibaki is how to deal with the post election challenges and jointly govern with his coalition partners.

Another challenge is the economy, which was stagnant in the 1990s, but has shown solid growth in recent years. The GDP grew by an estimated 5.4% in 2006 and 7% in 2007. According to the Economic Intelligence Unit (EIU) June 2008 report, "real GDP is expected to subside to 4.1% in 2008, owing to post-election disruption." Read GDP growth in 2009 is expected at 4.2%. The IMF sent a mission in January 2006 to review progress. In April 2007, the IMF resumed lending to Kenya, after a second review of the Poverty Reduction and Growth Facility (PRGF). The IMF also agreed to extend the PRGF until November 2007. The World Bank also began assistance to Kenya, with an estimated $800 million assistance package for projects through June 2008. Meanwhile, inflation rates reached an average 14.5% in 2006, in part due to 12-20% pay raises for civil servants and teachers. In 2008, inflation rates are estimated at 23% and 7% in 2009. Unemployment is high and corruption is still a serious problem, although the Kibaki government has taken a number of measures to deal with this problem.

Tackling corruption is another serious challenge facing a new government in Kenya. Rooting out official corruption may require removing senior members of the government from power and prosecution of former senior government officials. Several ministers were forced to resign in 2006, and the Kibaki administration faced serious allegations of corruption. The resignation of the Finance Minister in February 2006 for alleged corruption was seen by some as an important step in fighting official corruption in Kenya. However, the clearing of the Energy Minister from corruption charges raised serious doubt about the government's resolve to fight corruption. In early 2005, the government's anti-corruption chief resigned from his position, arguing that the Kibaki government is not serious about fighting corruption and accusing a number of senior officials of corruption [13]. The United States, Britain, and other donor governments have also made similar accusations [14]. In October 2006, Attorney General Amos Wako declared that he will not prosecute suspects in the corruption case against Anglo-Leasing, a British firm. According to Wako, successful prosecution will not be possible because of "a number of material and significant gaps."

Constitutional reform had been the rallying cry for opposition groups prior to the 2002 elections. As part of a pre-election agreement reached among the key players within NARC, a proposed new constitution would create a position of prime minister with executive powers. Reportedly, leaders from the main opposition groups agreed that this position would go to Raila Odinga, one of the major political figures within NARC. The constitutional drafting process was marred by delays, changes, and serious disagreement within NARC. President Kibaki and his supporters managed to get a draft approved in a process seen by some senior members of NARC as undemocratic. These members campaigned against the draft constitution, arguing that the agreement reached earlier was violated, and in November 2005, Kenyans defeated the draft constitution in a national referendum [15]. In late 2005, a number of senior officials left NARC and formed the Orange Democratic Party (ODM).The defeat of the 2005 draft constitution signaled that President Kibaki had lost the support of many Kenyans who once gave strong support to NARC. President Kibaki's credibility was further shaken in February 2006 by the resignation of three ministers on corruption allegations. Following these events, some observers asserted that President Kibaki would struggle to complete his term. However, the formation of a new party, NARC-Kenya, appears to have altered the Kenyan political landscape. NARC-Kenya, formally launched in June 2006, replaced NARC, and demonstrated its political strength by winning three of the five parliamentary seats in the July 24, 2006 by-elections. In September 2007, President Kibaki announced the formation of a new coalition, the Party of National Unity. The PNU includes KANU, NARC-Kenya, FORD-Kenya, FORD-People, and the Democratic Party.

Despite the enormous challenges facing Kenya, the Kibaki victory in 2002 had a positive impact in Kenya as well as in Africa generally. The smooth transfer of power and the transparency in the conduct of the elections indicated that democracy can flourish in Africa. For example, the power of incumbency and the entrenched clout of a ruling party did not stop an opposition victory in Kenya. The lessons learned from the 2002 Kenyan elections are many and could strengthen democracy movements elsewhere in Africa. Kenya is also a key player in regional affairs, having hosted negotiations on Sudan and Somalia. Kenya is home to many refugees from Uganda, Sudan, and Somalia. In recent months, Kenya has come under criticism from the United Nations and human rights groups for barring additional Somali refugees. The government of Kenya handed over more than 40 Somalis to the Transitional Federal Government of Somalia (TFG) and the Ethiopian government. Human rights groups are concerned that some of these individuals would be tortured or killed. In addition, Kenyan Muslim leaders accuse the Kibaki government of handing over Kenyan Muslims to Ethiopian and Somali security services.

U.S.-Kenya Relations: Issues

Kenya has been a valuable U.S. ally since independence, providing the United States with access to its military facilities and political support in the United Nations. Washington once considered Kenya a model developing country with shared democratic values in a continent where civil wars raged and military and authoritarian governments reigned. In the early 1 990s, relations between Kenya and the United States became strained due to deteriorating human rights conditions and the government's resistance to a multi-party system, though relations improved slightly after the 1992 multi-party elections. Relations have improved significantly in the past several years; however, the United States remains concerned about corruption and human rights conditions. The most recent edition of the State Department Country Reports on Human Rights Practices, issued in March 2008, stated that The government in many areas respected the human rights of its citizens or attempted to institute reforms to address deficiencies; however, serious problems remained. The following human rights problems were reported: unlawful killings, torture, and use of excessive force by police; vigilante justice; police impunity; harsh and life-threatening prison conditions; arbitrary arrest and detention; arbitrary interference with the home; prolonged pretrial detention; executive influence on the judiciary; disrespect for freedom of speech and of the press; internally displaced persons, refugees, and stateless persons; government corruption; abuse of, and discrimination against, women; female genital mutilation (FGM); child prostitution and labor; trafficking in persons; interethnic violence; and lack of enforcement of workers' rights.

Kenya has been an important ally in the war against terrorism, especially since the U.S. embassy bombings in Kenya and Tanzania in 1998. As many as 5,000 people were injured in the Nairobi blast, and 86 people in Dar es Salaam. Kenya became a target again, when on November 28, 2002, near simultaneous terrorist attacks struck targets in Mombasa, Kenya. Suicide bombers drove a truck packed with explosives into the Israeli-owned Paradise Hotel in Mombasa, killing 10 Kenyans and three Israelis. Minutes earlier, terrorists fired two shoulder-fired missiles that missed an Israeli passenger plane taking off from the Mombasa airport. The State Department's 2006 Country Report on Terrorism stated that " Important Kenyan officials spoke out publicly about the dangers of terrorism and key elements of the Kenyan security apparatus took concrete steps to increase counter-terrorism efforts, including the formation of an interagency Coastal Security Steering Committee. At the same time, however, political and bureaucratic resistance remained to the formation of an interagency Kenyan Joint Terrorism Task Force (JTTF)."

Table 3. Kenya: U.S. Assistance ($ in thousands)

Account	FY2005 Actual	FY2006 Actual	FY2007 Actual	FY2008 Estimate	FY2009 Request
CSH	14,600	17,840	18,950	38,492	18,361
DA	15,782	21,615	23,327	32,125	42,750
ESF	7,678	6,420	5,066		
FMF				198	100
GHAI	116,495	175,950	337,918	501,879	501,879
IMET	139		45	524	750
NADR-ATA	3,484	3,168	4,565	5,777	5,500
NADR-CTF	700	100	600		
NADR-EXBS	75	100	500		
NADR-TIP	285		300		
INCLE					100
P.L. 480	45,056	85,700	47,303	6,951	
Peace Corps	3,150	3,264	3,190		

Source: Department of State. CSH: Child Survival and Health; DA: Development Assistance; ESF: Economic Support Fund; FMF: Foreign Military Financing; GHAI: Global Aids Initiative; IMET: International Military Education and Training; NADR-TIP: Nonproliferation, Anti-Terrorism, Demining, and Related programs; NADRCTF: Counter Terrorism Financing; NADR-ATA: Anti-Terrorism Assistance; NADR-EXBS:Export Control and Related Border Security Assistance; P.L. 480: food assistance; International Narcotics Control and Law Enforcement (INCLE).

U.S. Assistance

Kenya has been one of the major recipients of U.S. foreign assistance in Sub-Saharan Africa for decades, and is an important trading partner with the United States. Despite Kenya's years of poor economic performance and serious corruption problems, the United States maintained a robust development assistance program focused on good governance, economic development, education, health care, and rural area development efforts in income generation and the effective use of natural resources. In regard to the promotion of good governance, the U.S. Agency for International Development (USAID) "continues to promote transparent and accountable governance by improving the balance of power among the various branches of government" [16] U.S. support for health care is largely focused on the fight against HIV/AIDS. Kenya is one of the major focus countries of the President's Emergency Plan for AIDS Relief (PEPFAR) and a major recipient of the Global HIV/AIDS Initiative funding. Security co-operation and support is another area in which Kenya and the United States work closely. In October 2006, the Bush Administration removed restrictions on IMET funding for Kenya. The restrictions were imposed because of Kenya's refusal to sign an agreement with the United States to provide immunity to U.S. personnel from prosecution by the International Criminal Court (ICC). In response to the humanitarian crisis in Kenya, the United States has provided, as of late September 2008, $126.6 million in humanitarian assistance in FY2008.

REFERENCES

[1] Congressman Donald Payne led a delegation in August 2008 to Kenya.

[2] Ted Dagne interview with Prime Minister Odinga in May in Kenya and June in Washington.

[3] The National Accord and Reconciliation Act of 2008.

[4] Ted Dagne interviewed a senior Kibaki campaign advisor in August 2007 in Kenya.

[5] Ted Dagne interview with several Kenyan opposition and government officials. January 2008 in Nairobi, Kenya.

[6] Shashank, Bengali. *How Kenya's Election Was Rigged*, the McClatchy Newspapers. January 31, 2008.

[7] European Union Election Observation Mission. Kenya General Election Preliminary Statement.

[8] Press Release issued on December 31, 2007 by the U.S. Embassy in Kenya.

[9] BBC News. USA Urges Political Settlement to Kenya's Post-Electoral Crisis. January 13, 2008.

[10] In January 2008, Congressman Donald Payne led a delegation to Kenya. As a member of that delegation, Ted Dagne visited the Jamhuri Showground and Kibera.

[11] Ted Dagne interviewed a number of opposition leaders and human rights advocates in Kenya

[12] Ted Dagne spoke to Raila Odinga in late January 2008.

[13] "*An Exile Sees Graft as a Piece of Kenya's Social Puzzle*." The New York Times, March 18, 2006.

[14] "*Corruption haunts Kenya's leader*." BBC News Online, February 2005.

[15] The author interviewed opposition leaders and government officials in Kenya in 2005 and 2006.

[16] USAID' s Strategy in Kenya. http://www.usaid.gov.

In: Economic, Political and Social Issues of Africa
Editor: Jeremy S. McQueen
ISBN 978-1-61209-957-6

Chapter 6

TUNISIA: CURRENT ISSUES*

Carol Migdalovitz

ABSTRACT

Tunisia has a stable, highly authoritarian government led by President Zine ben Ali, who was elected to a fourth term on October 24, 2004 and will run for a fifth term in October 2009. Ben Ali's Constitutional Democratic Rally party controls parliament, state and local governments, and most political activity. There are significant limitations on human rights but marked advancements for women and girls. Tunisia has experienced occasional attacks by Islamist terrorists, and Tunisian expatriates have been arrested in Europe and North America on terrorism- related charges. Tunisia is a non-oil-exporting, middle-class country with a diverse, growing economy, and high unemployment. U.S.-Tunisian relations today largely emphasize cooperation in terrorism, although Tunisia would like greater focus on trade.

GOVERNMENT

Tunisia has a stable, highly authoritarian government that places a higher priority on economic growth than on political liberalization. It has had only two leaders since gaining independence from France in 1956: the late Habib Bourguiba and Zine el-Abidine ben Ali, a former Minister of National Security, Minister of the Interior, and Prime Minister, who has been president since 1987. Constitutional amendments approved in May 2002 lifted term limits for the presidency and raised the age allowed for a candidate to 75. The 68-year-old Ben Ali easily won a fourth five-year term with 94.49% of the vote and a 91% voter turnout on October 24, 2004. He will run for a fifth term in October 2009. Three small "official" opposition parties also fielded candidates in 2004; other opposition parties endorsed Ben Ali. ("Official" opposition parties are those which the government allows to hold seats in parliament.) The powerful president appoints the prime minister, the cabinet, and 24 regional

* This is an edited, reformatted and augmented version of CRS Report RS21666, dated June 29, 2009.

governors. There is no vice president or designated successor to Ben Ali. Mohammed Ghannouchi has been prime minister since 1999.

RCD controls the Chamber of Deputies or lower house of parliament with 152 out of 189 seats [1]. Five weak, official opposition parties share the remaining, reserved 37 seats. Two others are not represented in parliament. One of these, the Democratic Progressive Party (PDP), withdrew its candidates from the parliamentary elections, charging official "harassment," including the rejection of candidate lists and the banning of its election manifesto, which criticized the regime and the President. There are 43 women in parliament mainly due to Ben Ali's decision to reserve 25% of the slots on the RCD parliamentary list for women. A referendum in 2002 created a Chamber of Advisors (upper house) of 126 members: 85 elected by municipal councils, professional associations, and trade unions and 41 appointed by the president. Parliament does not originate legislation and passes government bills with minor or no changes.

Commenting on the 2004 election, the U.S. State Department noted, "The ruling party's domination of state institutions and political activity precluded credible and competitive electoral challenges from unsanctioned actors." Some analysts believe that the 2009 election may result in the same conclusion.

TERRORISM

The Tunisian government is focused on the possibility of an Islamist threat at home, while Tunisians have been implicated in terrorism abroad. The government harshly suppressed An Nahdah (Renaissance), which it considered to be a violent, domestic Islamist terrorist group, after unearthing an alleged conspiracy in 1991. An Nahdah denied the accusation, but, in 1992, Tunisian military courts convicted 265 An Nahdah members on charges of plotting a coup. Some analysts consider Rashid Ghannouchi, An Nahdah's leader in exile, to be a moderate seeking to accommodate Islam with democracy [2].

In November 2008, authorities released all 21 remaining imprisoned An Nahdah members. However, a former leader of the group, Mohammed Sadiq Chourou, was rearrested three weeks later after demanding that the movement be rehabilitated and allowed to resume its political activities; he was sentenced to one year in jail, which was later extended by one year.

In 2002, the U.S. State Department labeled the Tunisian Combatant Group (TCG), a group of concern and froze its assets [3]. It was a terrorist group that sought to establish an Islamic state in Tunisia, and was considered to be a radical offshoot of An Nahdah. The TCG was suspected of plotting, but not carrying out, attacks on U.S., Algerian, and Tunisian embassies in Rome in December 2001. The Algerian Salafist Group for Preaching and Combat (GSPC), now known as Al Qaeda in the Islamic Maghreb (AQIM), actively recruits Tunisians and reportedly had ties with the TCG [4]. In January 2007, in somewhat mysterious circumstances, Tunisian security forces claimed to have engaged in gun battles with terrorists linked to GSPC who had infiltrated from Algeria and possessed homemade explosives, satellite maps of foreign embassies, and documents identifying foreign envoys. Some 30 Tunisians were convicted later in the year of plotting to target U.S. and British interests in Tunisia. AQIM later claimed responsibility for kidnapping two Austrian tourists in Tunisia in

February 2008. Algerian and Tunisian authorities have arrested Tunisians along their border, going in both directions.

Tunisians have fought with Al Qaeda in Iraq. In December 2006, Turkish authorities arrested a Tunisian suspected of helping Al Qaeda insurgents infiltrate into Iraq. On April 24, 2009, General David Petraeus, Commander of the Central Command, told a House Appropriations Committee subcommittee that the perpetrators of suicide bombings in Iraq that month may have been part of a network based in Tunisia [5].

Some Tunisian terrorists have operated elsewhere abroad. In 2002, Tunisian authorities convicted 34 persons (31 in absentia) of belonging to another alleged terrorist group linked to Al Qaeda— Al Jamaa wal Sunnah (idiomatically, the Followers of Tradition)—and recruiting Europe-based expatriate Tunisians to fight in Chechnya, Bosnia, and Afghanistan [6]. Tunisians, mainly residents of Italy, are on a U.N. Security Council Al Qaeda watch list. A Tunisian-Canadian who allegedly plotted acts against the United States was on U.S. alert lists issued in 2003 and 2004. In August 2005, Syria extradited to Tunisia 21 suspected Islamist extremists it had detained following clashes with security forces in June. In 2007, Tunisians were with the Al Qaeda-inspired, and perhaps linked, Fatah al Islam organization that fought and fell to the Lebanese army in the Nahr al Barid Palestinian refugee camp in Lebanon.

Tunisian expatriates suspected of ties to Al Qaeda have been arrested in Afghanistan, Pakistan, Iraq, Western Europe, and the United States. Some are detained at the U.S. Naval Base in Guantanamo Bay, Cuba, and their possible return to Tunisia has proven to be somewhat controversial [7]

Al Qaeda deputy leader Ayman al Zawahiri appeared to acknowledge an Al Qaeda presence in Tunisia in a taped message broadcast in October 2002, when he seemed to claim responsibility for the bombing of a synagogue on the Tunisian island of Djerba, noted for its Jewish minority, in April 2002. In all, 21, including 14 German tourists, 5 Tunisians, and 2 French citizens, were killed in the attack [8]. France, Spain, Italy, and Germany arrested expatriate Tunisians for alleged involvement in the attack. In January 2009, French authorities put two alleged culprits on trial.

In December 2003, the Tunisian parliament passed a sweeping anti-terrorism law. The U.S. State Department called it "a comprehensive law to 'support the international effort to combat terrorism and money laundering.'" [9]. Since passage of the law, approximately 1,000 Tunisians have been detained, charged, and/or convicted on terrorism related charges. Critics claim that the law "makes the exercise of fundamental freedoms ... an expression of terrorism" [10]. In June 2008, an Amnesty International report, In the Name of Security: Routine Abuses in Tunisia, detailed concerns "regarding serious human rights violations being committed in connection with the government's security and counterterrorism policies."

HUMAN RIGHTS

The Ben Ali regime uses the fear of an Islamist threat and the example of Islamist-fueled civil conflict in neighboring Algeria to justify its poor human rights record and failure to carry out political reforms. Ben Ali maintains that he is ushering in democratic reforms in a "measured way" so that religious extremists cannot take advantages of freedoms [11]. Yet, most observers fail to see evidence of even a gradual reform program.

Year after year, the U.S. State Department Country Report on Human Rights Practices in Tunisia has used almost the same language to describe and criticize unchanging human rights abuses in Tunisia. It observes significant limitations on citizens' right to change their government and notes that local and international nongovernmental organizations (NGOs) have reported that security forces torture and physically abuse prisoners and detainees and arbitrarily arrest and detain individuals. The security forces act with impunity sanctioned by high-ranking officials. Lengthy pretrial and incommunicado detention remain serious problems. The government infringes on citizens' privacy rights and imposes severe restrictions on freedoms of speech, press, assembly, and association. It remains intolerant of public criticism and uses intimidation, criminal investigations, the court system, arbitrary arrests, residential restrictions, and travel controls to discourage human rights and opposition activists [12].

The Tunisian government tries to squelch criticism of its human rights practices made outside of the country. In September 2008, the Committee to Protect Journalists (CPJ) stated that Tunisian "authorities aggressively counter criticism at international forums by recruiting 'spoilers,'" and described how one such group tried to dominate discussion at a Johns Hopkins University event featuring Tunisian journalist and human rights activist Sihem Bensedrine, who has been jailed and physically abused in Tunisia [13]. The same tactic was deployed at a May 2009 National Democratic Institute event with Ahmed Najib Chebbi, head of opposition Democratic Progressive Party (PDP) [14]. CPJ also describes the government's use of charges against journalists unrelated to journalism as a way to protect itself from international scrutiny.

Reporters Without Borders (RSF) lists President Ben Ali among the world's worst press freedom predators; its website is inaccessible in Tunisia. International human rights organizations claim that Tunisia's internet policies are among the world's most repressive: all internet cafes are state- controlled; authorities aggressively filter internet websites; President Ben Ali's family and friends control local internet service providers; and independent bloggers have been jailed.

In November 2005, Tunisia hosted the U.N. World Summit on the Information Society in an effort to burnish its image, but its conduct had the opposite effect. Before the summit, local authorities closed the Association of Judges, which had called for a more independent judiciary, and prevented conferences of journalists and the League of Human Rights. They also beat a French correspondent who had reported on clashes between police and supporters of Tunisian hunger strikers. During the conclave, the European Union complained after plainclothes policemen physically prevented international non-governmental organizations from meeting and then stopped the German ambassador from meeting with their representatives. The Swiss government protested after its delegation head's speech that referred to these events was censored. After the summit, Tunis banned the International Federation of Journalists' website.

On a positive note in human rights practices, Tunisia has long been in the forefront of Arab countries guaranteeing women rights and affording them educational and career opportunities. It is the only Arab Muslim country that bans polygamy. Women serve in the military and in many professions and constitute more than 50% of university students; the first woman governor was appointed in May 2004. In 2006, the government banned the headscarf from public places, claiming that it was protecting women's rights and preventing religious extremism. Critics charged that it was violating individual rights.

ECONOMY

Tunisia has almost completed a transition from a socialist to a market economy. It is considered a middle-class country, and one of the best-performing non-oil exporting Arab countries. Widespread home and car ownership support that characterization. Ben Ali's 2004 election manifesto called for diversification, that is, ending reliance on textiles, which have been a primary engine of economic growth, due to increased competition from China; modernization by providing investment incentives to foreign businesses and passing legal reforms; liberalization with the coming free-trade zone with the EU; and privatization. The textile sector has since shifted to higher quality goods. The tourism sector also has been emphasized; it is a major employer and earns some 20% of the country's hard currency receipts. Unemployment remains a major problem, however; the official rate is high and the unofficial rate is believed to be even higher.

Basic Facts

Population: 10.4 million (2009 est.)
Gross Domestic Product Growth Rate: 6.3% (2007 est.)
GDP per capita: $7,900 (2008 est.)
Inflation rate: 5% (2008 est.)
Unemployment rate: 14% (2008 est.)
Exports: clothing, semi-finished goods, agricultural products.
Imports: textiles, machinery and equipment, hydrocarbons
Trading Partners: France, Italy, Germany, Spain, Libya
Source: CIA, The World Factbook, April 30, 2009.

In 2008, there was social unrest in the impoverished mining region of Gafsa, where unemployment is particularly high. The government sent in the army to aid the police, who were unable to contain the demonstrations. Some 38 people were sentenced to prison in connection with the protests.

RELATIONS WITH THE UNITED STATES

The United States and Tunisia have enjoyed continuous relations since 1797. The Bush Administration considered Tunisia to be an important ally, a moderate Arab, Muslim state, and a partner in the global war on terror. However, Tunisia did not support the 1991 Gulf War or the 2003 war against Iraq and, when the 2003 war began, Ben Ali expressed regret and fear that the conflict might destabilize the Middle East [15]. Tunisian officials' criticism was not voiced directly at the United States and was circumspect, and their stance did not harm bilateral relations. U.S. - Tunisian relations today largely emphasize cooperation in counterterrorism, although Tunisia would like greater focus on increasing trade.

Table 1. U.S. Aid to Tunisia

	FY2008 Actual	FY2009 Estimated	FY2010 Request
FMF	$8.3 million	$12 million	$15 million
ESF	$1.2 million	$800,000	0
IMET	$1.7 million	$1.7 million	$2.3 million
INCLE	$198,000	0	0
NADR	$100,000	$425,000	$300,000
1206	$9.8 million	$8.8 million	unavailable

Notes: FMF: Foreign Military Financing; ESF: Economic Support Funds, IMET: International Military Education and Training funds, INCLE: International Narcotics Control and Law Enforcement Funds, NADR: Nonproliferation, Anti-Terrorism, Demining, and Related Programs funds. P.L. 109-163, the National Defense Authorization Act, FY2006, Section 1206 authorizes the Secretary of Defense to train and equip foreign military and foreign maritime security forces. Section 1206 funding for Tunisia has supported counterterrorism programs. For more information, see CRS Report RS22855, Section 1206 of the National Defense Authorization Act for FY2006: A Fact Sheet on Department of Defense Authority to Train and Equip Foreign Military Forces, by Nina M. Serafino.

In an explanatory statement on H.R. 1105, the Omnibus Appropriations Act, 2009, Chairman of the House Appropriations Committee David Obey, regarding the $12 million in FMF, said that "restrictions on political freedom, the use of torture, imprisonment of dissidents, and persecution of journalists and human rights defenders are of concern and progress on these issues is necessary for the partnership between the United States and Tunisia to further strengthen" [16]. This language is not in P.L. 111-8, the Omnibus Appropriations Act, 2009, signed into law on March 11, 2009.

A U.S.-Tunisian Joint Military Commission meets annually and joint exercises are held regularly. Tunisia agreed to exempt U.S. military personnel from the jurisdiction of the International Criminal Court. Tunisia is part of the U.S. Trans-Saharan Counterterrorism Partnership (TSCTP), helping countries in the region better control their territory and strengthen their counterterrorism capabilities, cooperates in NATO's Operation Active Endeavor which provides counterterrorism surveillance in the Mediterranean, participates in NATO's Mediterranean Dialogue, and allows NATO ships to make port calls at Tunis.

The U.S. State Department's Middle East Partnership Initiative (MEPI) has a regional office, responsible for Algeria, Egypt, Lebanon, and Morocco as well as Tunisia, which opened in Tunis in August 2004. MEPI has run very few bilateral programs in Tunisia. Given the Bush Administration's emphasis on building democracy in the Middle East, critics suggested that it might have been sending mixed signals to Tunisia by aiding the military while not strongly supporting democratizing elements. During President Ben Ali's visit to Washington in February 2004, Secretary of State Colin Powell expressed U.S. interest "in (Tunisia's) carrying on political reforms, media openness, and other issues," and President Bush publicly said that he would discuss with Ben Ali "the need to have a press corps that is vibrant and free, as well as an open political process." At the time, Ben Ali claimed to share the U.S. desire for "the establishment of states on the basis of democracy...," but preferred to emphasize the "strategic dimension" of the bilateral relationship [17]. During a February

2006 visit to Tunisia, Secretary of Defense Donald Rumsfeld avoided human rights issues and praised the country as "a moderate Muslim nation that has been and is today providing very constructive leadership in the world.... The leadership here ... certainly in the presidency and in the other senior ministries are all people who have the courage to stand up and speak on behalf of moderation and against violence and against extremism" [18].

U.S.-Tunisian trade is relatively low in volume because Tunisia is a small country and conducts most of its trade with Europe. In 2008, the United States imported $643.4 million in goods from Tunisia and exported $495.1 million in goods to Tunisia [19]. Tunisia is eligible for special trade preferences, that is, duty-free entry for listed products, under the Generalized System of Preferences (GSP) Program. The United States and Tunisia have a trade investment framework agreement (TIFA) and a bilateral investment treaty. TIFAs can be the first step toward a free-trade agreement (FTA). The Tunisian government has expressed interest in concluding an FTA with the United States, but it has not made the reforms needed to proceed toward one.

Other Foreign Policy Issues

Tunisia sympathizes with the Palestinians; it hosted the Palestine Liberation Organization (PLO) headquarters in exile from 1982-1993 and still hosts some PLO offices today. Tunisia had an interests office in Israel until the outbreak of the first Palestinian intifadah, or uprising against the Israeli occupation of the West Bank and Gaza Strip, in 2000. Israelis of Tunisian descent are allowed to travel to Tunisia on Israeli passports, and the Israeli and Tunisian foreign ministers sometimes meet. In September 2005, President Ben Ali sent a personal letter to then Israeli Prime Minister Ariel Sharon, praising his "courageous" withdrawal from the Gaza Strip. The then Israeli Foreign Minister, who was born in Tunisia, and Communications Minister attended the World Summit on the Information Society in Tunisia in 2005. (Prime Minister Sharon was invited along with leaders of all U.N. member states; his invitation provoked demonstrations in Tunisia.)

Tunisia and the EU have cemented a close relationship by means of an Association Agreement, aid, and loans. In 1996, Tunisia entered into an Association Agreement with the EU to remove all tariff and other trade barriers on most goods by 2008. As part of the agreement, the EU is assisting Tunisian businesses to prepare for global competition. More than 80% of Tunisia's trade is conducted with Europe. Tunisia receives aid from the EU's Euro Mediterranean Partnership (MEDA) program and soft loans from the European Investment Bank, the financing arm of the EU. The Europeans hope that their aid will help Tunisia to progress economically, and thereby eliminate some causes of illegal immigration and Islamic fundamentalism. The EU and Tunisia have discussed additional cooperation to control illegal immigration and manage legal immigration flows, a subject that probably is of greater interest to Europe than to Tunisia. Aspiring for closer ties, Prime Minister Ghannouchi has said that Tunisia would like to secure an intermediate status between association and membership in the EU, and to seek a "more solid, more diversified, and more fruitful partnership" [20].

References

[1] The RCD is the current incarnation of the Neo-Destour Party, which was formed in 1934 and led the movement for independence.

[2] Azzam S. Tamimi, *Rachid Ghannouchi: A Democrat within Islamism*, New York: Oxford University Press, 2001.

[3] U.S. State Department, *Country Reports on Terrorism, 2006*, released April 30, 2007.

[4] Craig S. Smith, "Tunisia is Feared as New Islamist Base...," *International Herald Tribune*, February 20, 2007. Note, GSPC renamed itself Al Qaeda in the Islamic Maghreb in January 2007.

[5] Mark Lander, Clinton Makes Surprise Visit to Reassure Iraqis, *Boston Globe*, April 26, 2009.

[6] "Assets of Tunisia Group Are Frozen," *New York Times*, October 11, 2002.

[7] An editorial in the *Orange Country Register* on November 16, 2008 stated, "In 2006, the U.S. sent two prisoners (from Guantanamo) to Tunisia with the explicit understanding that they would not be tortured or mistreated. The Tunisian government broke its promise and inflicted cruel treatment and kangaroo-court trials." In May 2009, the United States asked Italy to receive two Tunisian detainees who objected to their return to Tunisia for fear that they would be subjected to torture. On May 26, 2009, the Tunisian Minister of Justice said that his government was prepared to receive another 10 Guantanamo detainees. "Tunisia asks US to Hand Over two Guantanamo Detainees," Al-Jazeera TV, May 29, 2009.

[8] "Al-Qaeda Deputy Leader Signals Involvement in Attacks," *Financial Times*, October 10, 2002.

[9] U.S. State Department, *Patterns of Global Terrorism, 2003*, released April 29, 2004.

[10] Jeremy Landor, "Washington's Partner," *Middle East International*, March 5, 2004, pp. 23-24.

[11] "Tunisian President Says He Wants to Share Experience in Handling Islamic Extremism with Bush," Associated Press, February 13, 2004.

[12] U.S. State Department, Bureau of Democracy, Human Rights, and Labor, *Country Reports on Human Rights Practices, Tunisia*, released February 25, 2009.

[13] Committee to Protect Journalists, Special Report on Tunisia, September 23, 2008.

[14] A CRS analyst was present at this discussion.

[15] "Ben Ali Expresses 'Deep Regret' at Start of War Against Iraq," *Tunis Infotunisie*, March 20, 2003, Foreign Broadcast Information Service (FBIS) Document AFP2003 0320000266.

[16] *Congressional Record*, February 23, 2009, p. H2417.

[17] Remarks by President Bush, President of Tunisia before Meeting, U.S. Newswire, February 18, 2004.

[18] Secretary Rumsfeld's Press Availability in Tunisia, February 11, 2006.

[19] U.S. International Trade Commission, http://dataweb.usitc.gov.

[20] "Tunisia Wants Special Status with European Union: Prime Minister," *Agence France-Presse*, April 1, 2003.

In: Economic, Political and Social Issues of Africa
Editor: Jeremy S. McQueen
ISBN 978-1-61209-957-6

Chapter 7

THE DEMOCRATIC REPUBLIC OF CONGO: BACKGROUND AND CURRENT DEVELOPMENTS*

Ted Dagne

ABSTRACT

In October 2008, the forces of the National Congress for the Defense of the Congolese People (CNDP), under the command of General Laurent Nkunda, launched a major offensive against the Democratic Republic of Congo Armed Forces (FARDC) in eastern Congo. Within days, the CNDP captured a number of small towns and Congolese forces retreated in large numbers.

Eastern Congo has been in a state of chaos for over a decade. The first rebellion to oust the late President Mobutu Sese Seko began in the city of Goma in the mid-1990s. The second rebellion in the late 1990s began also in eastern Congo. The root causes of the current crisis are the presence of over a dozen militia and extremist groups, both foreign and Congolese, in eastern Congo, and the failure to fully implement peace agreements signed by the parties. Over the past fourteen years, the former Rwandese armed forces and the Interhamwe militia have been given a safe haven in eastern Congo and have carried out many attacks inside Rwanda and against Congolese civilians. A Ugandan rebel group, the Lord's Resistance Army (LRA) is also in Congo, despite an agreement reached between the LRA and the Government of Uganda.

In November 2008, United Nations Secretary General Ban Ki-Moon appointed former Nigerian President Olusegun Obasanjo as his envoy to help broker a peace agreement to end the crisis in eastern Congo. Since his appointment, Obasanjo has met with President Joseph Kabila, General Nkunda, President Paul Kagame, and other officials in the region. The parties have agreed to participate in a U.N.-led peace initiative. The current crisis in eastern Congo has displaced more than 250,000 civilians.

In late 2008, the governments of Rwanda and Congo agreed on a wide range of issues. The two governments agreed to launch a joint military offensive against the National Congress for the Defense of the Congolese People (CNDP) and the FDLR.

---

* This is an edited, reformatted and augmented version of CRS Report R40108, dated July 16, 2009.

They also agreed to restore full diplomatic relations and to activate economic cooperation. In January 2009, Rwanda and Congo launched the joint military operation in eastern Congo. In late February Rwandese forces pulled out of Congo as part of an agreement reached with Congo.

The United States has been actively engaged in facilitating the Tripartite Plus talks among the four key players in the Great Lakes region: Rwanda, DRC, Burundi, and Uganda. The Tripartite Plus process has led to a number of agreements over the past several years, including the creation of a Joint Verification Mechanism (JVM) to address cross-border issues. The Bush Administration provided an estimated $205.1 million in FY2008, and an estimated $199.7 million for FY2009. The Obama Administration has requested $177 million for FY2010.

RECENT DEVELOPMENTS

In late 2008, the governments of Rwanda and Congo agreed on a wide range of issues. The two governments agreed to launch a joint military offensive against the National Congress for the Defense of the Congolese People (CNDP) and the FDLR. They also agreed to restore full diplomatic relations and to activate economic cooperation. In January 2009, Rwanda and Congo launched the joint military operation in eastern Congo. The military operation dislodged and seriously weakened the CNDP forces. In January, the leader of the CNDP, General Laurent Nkunda, was arrested inside Rwanda, after he fled eastern Congo. The FDLR forces were also dislodged from their stronghold in north Kivu and forced to retreat. More than 2,000 Rwandese refugees returned home in January-February, as well as some FDLR militia members.

In late February 2009, Rwandese troops pulled out of Congo as part of the agreement with the Kabila government. The DRC government has requested the extradition of General Nkunda. Nkunda remained under arrest in Rwanda as of early May 2009. In May 2009, the DRC Parliament passed a bill granting amnesty to militias, although the bill excludes amnesty for those accused of war crimes like General Nkunda. Meanwhile, remnants of the FDLR continue to target Congolese civilians. In late April 2009, United Nations officials accused the FDLR of committing serious atrocities against civilians in Luofu, a town north of Goma.

According to the June 2009 U.N. Secretary General report "the overall situation in the Democratic Republic of Congo continued to pose many challenges. In eastern part of the country, despite an improved political environment and expanded State presence, the security situation remained very volatile and the humanitarian situation deteriorated." Foreign armed groups continue to terrorize the civilian population in DRC. More than 1,000 women are raped each month in Eastern Congo, according to U.N. officials and international observers.

Rwanda, CNDP, and General Nkunda

Nkunda still remains under arrest in Rwanda as of mid-March 2009. Congolese forces continue to go after the remaining CNDP and FDLR forces. As part of an earlier agreement, those CNDP forces willing to joint the Congolese army are being integrated. Rwanda is also welcoming FDLR forces willing to return home.

In October 2008, the forces of the National Congress for the Defense of the Congolese People (CNDP), under the command of General Laurent Nkunda, launched a major offensive against the Democratic Republic of Congo Armed Forces (FARDC) in eastern Congo. Within days, the CNDP captured a number of small towns, and Congolese forces retreated in large numbers. The U.N. Mission in Congo (MONUC) also withdrew from some areas and pulled most of its forces into Goma. In late October, General Nkunda declared a unilateral cease-fire and ordered his forces to remain outside Goma. The cease-fire has been violated in recent weeks by both sides, although fighting has not spread to other parts of Congo. On November 19, 2008, the CNDP withdrew from two areas in eastern Congo in order to create humanitarian corridors.

The DRC government initially accused Rwanda of supporting General Nkunda, although a few days later in a meeting in Rwanda, Congolese officials did not bring this issue up with senior Rwandese officials. Rwanda has consistently argued that its forces, while deployed along the Rwanda-DRC border, have not crossed into Congolese territory, a position supported by U.S. and United Nations officials [1]. Congolese officials, however, argue that Rwandese soldiers were captured inside Congo [2]. Congolese officials have provided photographs of alleged Rwandan soldiers to foreign governments in November 2008. In late October, at the height of the crisis, the Congolese Foreign Minister Alexis Thambwe Mwamba paid a visit to Kigali and met with President Paul Kagame and other Rwandese leaders. At that meeting, the minister did not raise the issue of Rwanda's alleged involvement in support of Nkunda [3] A few days later, the Rwandese Foreign Minister, Rosemary K. Museminari, visited Kinshasa and met with Congolese officials as well as other foreign leaders.

In recent weeks, a number of foreign officials visited the Great Lakes region in an effort to find a peaceful solution to the crisis in eastern Congo. Then U.S. Assistant Secretary of State for African Affairs Jendayi Frazer met with the leadership of Congo and Rwanda in November. The foreign ministers of France and Britain visited Congo in early November in an effort to broker a peace agreement. United Nations Secretary General Ban Ki-Moon went to Kenya in early November to take part in a regional summit on the crisis in eastern Congo. Several heads of state participated in the Kenya meeting, including President Kabila and Rwandan President Paul Kagame. General Nkunda was not invited to participate in the Kenyan meeting. The meeting in Kenya did not secure an agreement.

In November 2008, Secretary General Ban Ki-Moon appointed former Nigerian President Olusegun Obasanjo as his envoy to help broker a peace agreement to end the crisis in eastern Congo. The appointment of Obasanjo was welcomed by regional leaders. President Kagame told reporters that Obasanjo is the "right person" to help secure a peace agreement to resolve the crisis in eastern Congo. Since his appointment, Obasanjo has met with President Kabila, General Nkunda, President Kagame, and other officials in the region. He secured an agreement from President Kabila and General Nkunda to take part in U.N.-led peace talks. President Kabila had previously rejected direct talks with Nkunda.

The Role of MONUC in the Current Crisis

The United Nations has been actively engaged in mediation efforts, although MONUC has come under criticism for failing to carry out its mandate to protect civilians [4] Congolese sources and foreign observers have reported that MONUC forces did not provide sufficient protection to civilians who have been the primary target of government forces and militia groups. MONUC has a robust U.N. Security Council-authorized mandate to protect civilians under eminent physical threat. United Nations officials argue that MONUC has done what it could under difficult circumstances and that Congo is a large territory to effectively manage. These officials contend that it is the primary responsibility of the Kabila government to protect its citizens, of which over 250,000 were displaced as a result of the military clashes in eastern Congo. According to United Nations officials, abuses by government forces and militia groups have been carried out against civilians. There is no reliable estimate of the number of people killed since the current crisis erupted.

The Failure of the Congolese Army

The Congolese army has not been able to contain rebel force advances or provide protection to the civilian population. At the height of the crisis, the Congolese army simply retreated and later engaged in looting and attacking civilians, according to United Nations officials and press reports. United Nations officials and longtime Congo observers argue that the Congolese army was ignored and abandoned by the central government in Kinshasa. According to U.N. and Congolese officials, the central government often failed to provide necessary support or pay the salary of the Congolese army in eastern Congo. Moreover, the military leadership is weak, according to many observers in the region.

The fact that the Congolese army did not exist in its current structure until recently also contributed to the problem within the armed forces in recent years. A number of the units in the Congolese army are forces integrated from rebel forces. In November 2008, President Kabila ousted his military chief of staff and named General Didier Etumba Longomba as his new military chief. Donor governments have provided funding to train Congolese forces and local police.

MONUC has also provided support and protection to Congolese forces over the years. General Nkunda has criticized MONUC's cooperation with the Congolese forces on a number of occasions.

Root Causes

At the core of the crisis in eastern Congo is the presence of over a dozen militia and extremist groups, both foreign and Congolese, and the failure to fully implement peace agreements signed by the parties. Over the past 14 years, the former Rwandese armed forces and the Interhamwe have been given a safe haven in eastern Congo and have carried out many attacks inside Rwanda and against Congolese civilians. These well-armed forces are now known as the Democratic Forces for the Liberation of Rwanda (FDLR). Analysts estimate their number between 6,000 and 8,000, and now led by the most extremist leaders of the FDLR. The FDLR reportedly receives assistance from Congolese forces and often coordinates military operations with the Congolese army, according to United Nations and Rwandan officials.

The FDLR also receives assistance and guidance from Rwandese in Europe and the United States. The Government of Rwanda submitted a list of FDLR, Interhamwe and other militia leaders in early 2008 to U.S. and other government officials. On November 4, 2008, German authorities released the Secretary General of the FDLR, Callixte Mbarushimana, who was arrested in Frankfurt in July 2008.

The State Department criticized the release of the FDLR official and blamed the group as the "root cause of instability in eastern Congo" [5]. A week after the release of the FDLR official, German authorities arrested a senior Rwandese government official, Rose Kibuye. Rose Kibuye is a senior Rwandan government official, a liberation fighter with the Rwandan Patriotic Front (RPF), the group that ended the 1994 genocide, and served in different government positions over the past decade, including as Mayor of Kigali and Personal Secretary of President Kagame.

The Government of Rwanda condemned her arrest and later expelled the German ambassador to Rwanda. German authorities did not detain Kabuye in April 2008 when she traveled with President Kagame to Germany because of diplomatic immunity. Rwandan officials contend that Kibuye went to Germany as an advance team member to prepare for President Kagame's visit to Germany. She traveled on her diplomatic passport and the Germany embassy in Rwanda was informed about the purpose of her visit to Germany. On November 19, Kibuye was transferred to France to stand trial.

In addition to the FDLR and other negative forces in DRC, the forces and leadership of the Lord's Resistance Movement (LRA), a Ugandan rebel movement, are also in DRC, even though the LRA agreed to a peace agreement mediated by the Government of South Sudan. Moreover, there are over a dozen militia groups active in eastern Congo, some of which support and coordinate their actions with the Congolese government.

BACKGROUND: THE CRISIS IN DRC

The Democratic Republic of Congo (DRC), formerly Zaire, has been in political turmoil for years. In May 1997, the Alliance of the Democratic Forces for the Liberation of Congo-Zaire (AFDL), with the support of Rwanda and Uganda, marched into Kinshasa and ousted longtime dictator Mobutu Sese Seko. Within one year, tensions between President Laurent Kabila and his Rwandan and Ugandan allies began to mount. By August 1998, open conflict erupted between Kabila and Congolese forces supported by Rwanda. Angola, Namibia, and Zimbabwe joined the fighting in support of Kabila.

DRC at a Glance

- Population: 68.6 million
- Independence: 1960 from Belgium
- Area: Slightly less than one-fourth the size of the United States
- Ethnicity: Over 200 ethnic groups, majority Bantu
- Religions: 50% Catholic, 20% Protestant, 10% Kimbanguist (Syncretic), 10% Muslim, 10% other/indigenous
- Languages: French (official)

- GDP (purchasing power parity): $21 billion
- GDP per capita: $300 (2008)

CIA World Factbook, 2009

In July 1999, at a summit in Lusaka, Zambia, the leaders of Uganda, Rwanda, Congo, Zimbabwe, Namibia, and Angola signed a peace agreement. The agreement called for a cease-fire within 24 hours of the signing of the agreement. Nonetheless, both sides to the conflict consistently violated the cease-fire agreement. The Lusaka Accords established a joint military commission (JMC) to investigate cease-fire violations and to disarm militia groups. The withdrawal of foreign forces from Congo was one of the key elements of the Lusaka Accords.

The Accords also called for political dialogue among Congolese political and armed groups to settle their differences peacefully and to map out a new political chapter for Congo. The former President of Botswana, Sir Ketumile Masire, was appointed to facilitate the talks. The Accords called for the deployment of U.N. military observers.

MONUC: Overview

MONUC Status of Forces and Mandate

In August 1999, the United Nations Security Council authorized the deployment of 90 United Nations military liaison personnel to the DRC. In November 1999, Security Council Resolution 1279 affirmed that the previously authorized United Nations personnel would constitute the United Nations Organization Mission in the DRC (MONUC). The operation is authorized under Chapter VII of the United Nations Charter, which allows peacekeepers to use force, if necessary, to carry out their mandate. As of May 31, 2009, MONUC had 18,381 total uniformed personnel, including 16,626 troops, 681 military observers, 1,074 police, 969 international civilian personnel, 2,154 local civilian staff and 606 United Nations Volunteers [6] MONUC is currently the largest U.N. peacekeeping operation in the world. In late November, the United Nations agreed to send an additional 3,000 peacekeeping troops to DRC.

Over the past eight years, the Security Council passed a number of resolutions to strengthen MONUC's force and its mandate. Resolution 1291, passed in 2000, authorized MONUC to carry out a number of important tasks, including implementation of the cease-fire agreement, verification of disengagement and redeployment of forces, and support humanitarian work and human rights monitoring. The resolution provided MONUC the mandate, under Chapter VII, to protect its personnel, facilities, and civilians under eminent threat of physical violence. Resolution 1565, adopted in 2004, increased MONUC personnel, with a primary objective of MONUC deployment to eastern Congo to ensure civilian protection, seize or collect arms, as called for in U.N. resolution 1493. The resolution also authorized MONUC to temporarily provide protection to the National Unity Government institutions and government officials. Resolution 1493, authorized MONUC to assist the DRC government to disarm foreign combatants and repatriate to their home country. The resolution, under Chapter VII, authorized MONUC to use "all means necessary" to carry out its mandate [7]

MONUC: Human Rights Concerns

MONUC's record has been marred by persistent allegations that it has not been able to halt gross human rights violations of civilians by local groups in the Ituri and Kivu regions and charges of incompetence since its deployment in 1999. In late February 2005, nine Bangladeshi peacekeepers were killed by militia members in the Ituri region. Then-U.N. Secretary General Kofi Annan condemned the killings and called on the then- Transitional Government to "hold accountable those responsible for this reprehensible and criminal attack." The United Nations has increased the number of troops to help bring stability and security, especially in the Kivus and Ituri regions.

MONUC also was the focus of allegations of sexual exploitation and abuse of women and children. In December 2004, in his report to the Security Council, then-Secretary General Annan stated that "between June and September 2004, an Office of Internal Oversight Services investigation into sexual misconduct in Bunia revealed that 8 of some 72 allegations could be corroborated." The report revealed that the majority of these allegations involved "soliciting the services of prostitutes." This kind of behavior by U.N. peacekeeping troops, the report contends, is a violation of the United Nations "Code of Conduct" for peacekeeping troops.

In November 2004, a team from the United Nations Department of Peacekeeping Operations was sent to investigate allegations of sexual exploitation by several United Nations civilian personnel in other parts of DRC. Another U.N. team was sent to DRC to investigate allegations against MONUC personnel. In January 2005, a report by the United Nations Office of Internal Oversight Services (OIOS) issued its findings about sexual exploitation and abuse by MONUC personnel in DRC. The OIOS made a number of recommendations, which it claimed have been accepted by the United Nations Department of Peacekeeping Operations. Still, between January and September 2008, 23 sexual exploitation and abuse allegations were made against MONUC personnel.

POLITICAL DEVELOPMENTS

Some progress has been made over the past several years in moving the DRC from political instability and civil war to relative stability and democratic rule, although Eastern Congo remains a region marred by civil strife. The international community has been actively engaged in support of the transitional process and the elections. On July 30, 2006, the DRC held its first presidential and parliamentary multi-party elections in almost four decades. Regional, local, and international observers monitored the elections. More than 19 million Congolese were registered to vote in the 2006 elections, including 2.9 million in Kinshasa, the capital.

In the presidential elections, there were 33 presidential candidates, while an estimated 9,707 candidates ran for the 500-seat parliament. There were an estimated 50,000 polling stations for the 25.6 million registered eligible voters. According to Congolese and international observers, the elections were largely peaceful and well managed, considering the logistical and other challenges, although post-election conditions were not properly managed in some areas [8] In parliament, no party emerged with a majority, while none of the candidates in the presidential elections secured the necessary 50% of the vote. In October 2006, President Joseph Kabila defeated Jean-Pierre Bemba in the second round of presidential elections. On December 6, 2006, President Kabila was sworn in as president.

The DRC faces serious challenges, despite progress in some areas and relative stability in most regions of the country. Relations between the DRC and its neighbors have improved over the past two years, largely due to facilitation by the United States of the Tripartite Plus process, a policy initiative aimed at regional stability and cooperation. The four key regional participants in the process are DRC, Uganda, Rwanda, and Burundi. Despite progress in regional security, insecurity in parts of the DRC, especially in the east of the country, continues to pose a serious threat to political stability in the Great Lakes region. Relations between DRC and Burundi are warm. Uganda is expected to upgrade its diplomatic presence to ambassadorial level soon, according to Congolese officials.

The presence of armed groups in parts of Congo is a major source of instability. The Special Representative of the Secretary General of the U.N. stated that, while there are many challenges facing Congo, conditions have improved in some parts of eastern Congo since the handover of two militia leaders to the International Criminal Court (ICC) for trial. In October 2007, the DRC government transferred former Ituri militia leader, Germain Katanga, to the ICC in the Hague. In February 2008, Congolese authorities arrested and later transfer to ICC custody Mathieu Ngudj olo Chui, former chief of staff of the Front for National Integration (FNI).

In March 2006, Thomas Lubanga Dyilo, the leader of the Union of the Congolese Patriots (UPC), was handed over to the ICC. In July 2008, U.N. Secretary General Ban Ki-Moon stated that "the creation of a professional, capable and accountable FARDC remains a critically important goal for establishing security, stability and legitimate State authority in the eastern DRC." [9]

The presence of the Lord's Resistance Army militia, a Ugandan rebel force, in the Garamba National Park in eastern Congo, has been a source of tension between Uganda and DRC over the past several years. In September 2007, Uganda and DRC signed an agreement in Arusha, Tanzania to cooperate on a wide range of issues, including removing the LRA from eastern Congo. In October 2007, the third high ranking LRA official, Opio Makasi, surrendered to MONUC and was later transferred to Congolese authorities. In November 2007, Congolese and MONUC officials handed over Makasi to Ugandan authorities. Ugandan authorities reportedly provided amnesty to Makasi. President Kabila has stated on a number of occasions that his government will force the LRA out of DRC [10]

In March 2007, the Congolese army and Bemba's militia clashed in Kinshasa, forcing Bemba to flee to the South African embassy. In April, Bemba was allowed to leave for Portugal with his family. Bemba's departure may have resolved the crisis in the short term, although his supporters and militia could become a source of instability. Bemba demanded that he be allowed to return to Congo in order to participate in the political process where his party controls 20 percent of the seats in the National Assembly. Bemba saw his forced exile as a sign that Congo might be returning to a one man rule [11]. In May 2008, Bemba was arrested in Belgium for alleged war crimes committed by his group in the Central African Republic and was handed over to the ICC.

U.S. ASSISTANCE TO DRC

One of the major objectives of the U.S. Agency for International Development (USAID) program in the DRC is to support the country's transition to democracy and to strengthen its healthcare and education systems. Special attention is being paid to the HIV/AIDS epidemic, with $4 million of funding designated to AIDS treatment and prevention programs. In FY2007, Economic Support Funds (ESF) were targeted on strengthening the Judiciary, the National Assembly, and other political institutions. International Military Education and Training (IMET) funds are intended to focus on training Congolese officers on military justice, human rights and joint operations. The United States also provides significant humanitarian assistance to DRC. In FY2007, the United States provided $114.3 million, and $205.1 million in FY2008. The DRC is expected to receive an estimated $199.7 for FY2009. The Obama Administration has requested $177 million for FY20 10. In addition, the United States provided $9.1 million in Section 120712 assistance in support of peace efforts and local governments in eastern Congo. In fiscal year 2009 to date, the United States provided $120.4 in humanitarian assistance to DRC [13]

HUMAN RIGHTS CONDITIONS

Human rights abuses continued to plague the DRC despite movement toward democratic rule and an end to the civil war. Government security forces and armed rebel groups committed serious abuses against civilians. Security forces were responsible for the arbitrary arrest, abduction, and torture of civilians despite the country's law prohibiting torture, according to human rights groups and the State Department's Country Reports on Human Rights Practices. According to the State Department's 2008 report, "In all areas of the country the government's human rights record remained poor, and security forces continued to act with impunity throughout the year, committing many serious abuses including unlawful killings, disappearances, torture, and rape. Security forces also engaged in arbitrary arrests and detention. Harsh and life-threatening conditions in prison and detention facilities, prolonged pretrial detention, lack of an independent and effective judiciary, and arbitrary interference with privacy, family, and home also remained serious problems. Security forces retained child soldiers and compelled forced labor by civilians. Members of the security forces also continued to abuse and threaten journalists, contributing to a decline in freedom of the press" [14].

There were no confirmed reports that abductions were politically motivated, although some of the abductees were journalists. Government security forces also raped civilians, according to the same report. On a positive note, professionalism among police forces appears to be increasing, while government security forces, however, remained corrupt and ineffective. Prison conditions remained inadequate due to overcrowding and lack of funds. The judicial system remained ineffective and highly corrupt, and civil courts are rarely used by the public. According to the State Department's annual report, the government restricted freedom of speech, although Congolese law provides these rights. Security forces were responsible for arresting, detaining, and harassing individuals for criticizing the president and the transitional government. On a number of occasions, radio and television stations were temporarily closed for violating a media code of conduct.

As the internal conflict in the east continued, according to reports, security forces and rebel groups killed, abducted, tortured, and raped civilians in addition to burning or destroying their homes and villages. Mass rape and sexual violence were used as weapons of war, and FARDC soldiers committed sexual violence against young girls, especially in eastern Congo. Gang rapes also occurred and were frequently committed in front of the victims' families. The trafficking of women and children also remained common in the east. Humanitarian aid workers and NGOs reported being threatened and harassed by armed groups, especially in eastern DRC. The transitional government did not provide adequate protection or assistance to Internally Displaced Persons (IDPs), and armed groups restricted humanitarian access to IDPs, preventing the delivery of supplies, according to the State Department's human rights report.

In Katanga province, Mai Mai militia groups continued to abuse civilians. On May 12, 2006, a Mai Mai militia leader, Kyungu Mutanga Gedeon, surrendered to MONUC forces, with 150 rebel fighters. The Kabila government reportedly offered to integrate Mutanga's forces into the regular armed forces. Gedeon and his forces are accused of serious atrocities against civilians. According to the State Department's annual report, "militias in the Ituri District of Orientale Province, notably the Front for National Integration (FNI), the Congolese Revolutionary Movement (MRC), and the Front for Patriotic Resistance in Ituri (FPRI) continued to commit abuses against civilians, including killings, abductions, rapes, and child soldier recruitment" [15]

ECONOMIC CONDITIONS

Large sums have been invested in the DRC's transition process by both bilateral and multilateral donors. The World Bank has, as of October 2008, 14 active projects in DRC, totaling $2.2 billion. The International Monetary Fund (IMF) is requiring the DRC to implement reforms in macroeconomic stability before it will begin negotiations for a poverty reduction and growth facility program. A tight fiscal policy will be necessary for the DRC to improve economic conditions. The DRC's fiscal policy is primarily concerned with increasing domestic revenue and shifting state expenditures toward infrastructure and the social sectors.

The Central Bank of the DRC appears committed to maintaining price stability and tight control of the country's money supply, according to the most recent Economist Intelligence Unit (EIU) report. Real GDP growth is expected at 6% in 2008-2009, according to the EIU.

Although agriculture is the dominant sector of the economy (accounting for approximately half of GDP and employing 75% of the labor force), development and productivity rates are nearly impossible to gauge due to a lack of reliable statistics. The mining sector is likely to be the country's primary vehicle for growth as foreign direct investment increases. Mining output should also increase the DRC's export earnings and should compensate for falling commodity prices in the international market. Financing the country's external debt was projected to cost nearly $600 million in 2007, which underscores the need for debt relief under the IMF-World Bank's HIPC (heavily indebted poor countries) initiative and the multilateral debt relief initiative.

The Kabila government's budget expenditure plans are very cautious and somewhat vague, a fact government officials attribute to the need for pragmatism to address DRC's large external debt. In recent years, China has expanded its trade and economic activities with DRC. In 2008, China signed a major mining and construction agreement with the DRC government. The mining agreement is a source of contention in Congo.

Regional Issues: Background and Recent Agreements

The 2002 Pretoria Agreement between Rwanda and DRC led to significant improvement in border security in the Great Lakes region. The agreement called for a cessation of hostilities, an inter-Congolese dialogue, withdrawal of foreign forces, and disarmament of the "negative forces". The parties have implemented all of these agreements and a number of the armed groups have been demobilized.

On September 22, 2004, the governments of DRC and Rwanda signed the terms of reference for a Joint Verification Mechanism (JVM), an agreement designed to address cross-border issues, specifically to deal with the threats of the Interhamwe and ex-FAR (former Rwandese Armed Forces), groups responsible for the 1994 genocide in Rwanda.

The Mechanism consists of a Joint Verification Team of experts from the parties, representatives from MONUC and the African Union. In October 2004, the group had its first meeting, and in late November the parties adopted operational procedures for the Joint Verification Teams. In addition, the United States has been facilitating Tripartite Plus talks among the three key regional players: DRC, Rwanda, Uganda, and Burundi. The parties agreed that the most serious threat to regional stability is the presence of the negative forces in DRC. In order to deal with this threat, the parties established a Tripartite Joint Commission and agreed to disarm, demobilize, and repatriate foreign armed groups.

The governments of Rwanda and DRC cooperate on a wide range of issues, including on security matters. Rwanda helped facilitate dialogue between the Kabila government and some political groups in DRC on issues related to the 2006 elections. Moreover, Rwanda agreed to help find a political solution with General Nkunda, as requested by President Kabila. But the process did not go far because the Kabila government launched a campaign against General Nkunda. Kagame stated in August that he remains very concerned about the activities of the remnants of the Interhamwe and FDLR forces. He asserted that these forces are currently reorganizing in eastern Congo [16] In November 2007, the governments of the DRC and Rwanda signed an agreement in Kenya "on a common approach to end the threat posed to peace and stability" in the Great Lakes region.

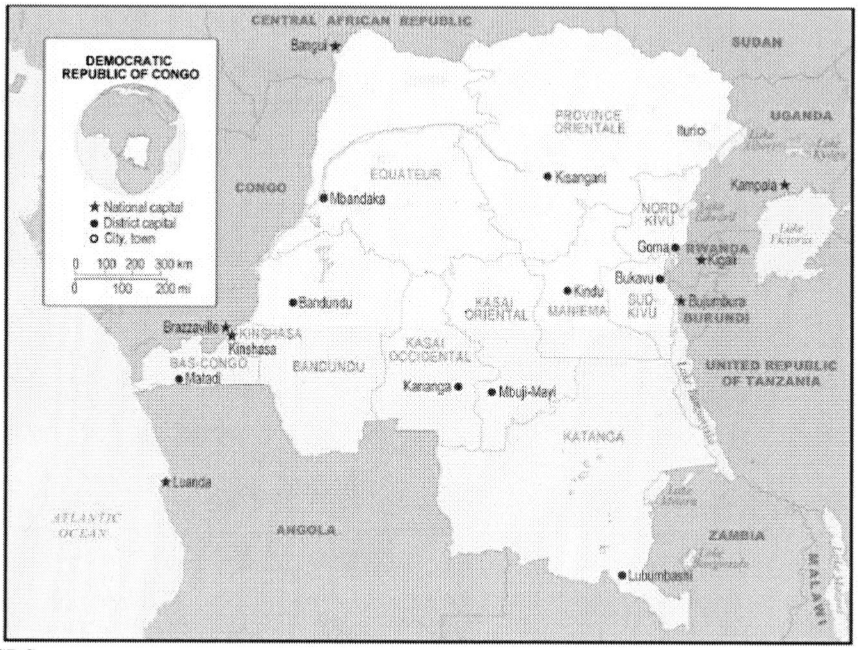

Source: CRS.

Figure 1. Congo.

The parties agreed to end political and material support to armed groups in the region. The government of the DRC agreed to disarm the ex-FAR and Interhamwe militia and to hand over those individuals wanted by the government of Rwanda and International Criminal Tribunal for Rwanda (ICTR). According to the agreement, those who do not wish to return to Rwanda will be placed in a camp away from the border until a solution is found. In January 2007, several dozen rebel groups and the DRC government signed the Goma Accord, primarily focused on ending the violence in Eastern Congo. Since the signing of the agreement, while progress has been made, there have been a number of reports of ceasefire violations and sexual violence against civilians.

References

[1] CRS interview with MONUC, Rwandese, and U.S. officials in August and November 2008.

[2] CRS interview with Congolese ambassador to the United States, November 19, 2008.

[3] CRS interview in late October 2008 with a senior Rwandese official in Kigali by phone.

[4] Tom Maliti, "African Leaders Chide Peacekeepers," Chicago Tribune, November 9, 2008.

[5] State Department Press Release, November 13, 2008.

[6] MONUC Mission website available at http://www.un.org/Depts/dpko/missions/monuc/

[7] http://www.monuc.org

[8] Ted Dagne met with a number of Congolese officials and election observers in DRC in 2006.

[9] Secretary General report to the Security Council, July 2008. S2008/433.
[10] Ted Dagne interview with President Kabila in 2006 and 2007 in Washington and DRC.
[11] Ted Dagne interview of Bemba, August and October 2007.
[12] For more information about Section 1207 programs, see CRS report by Nina Serafino, "Department of Defense Section 1207: Security and Stabilization Assistance: *A Fact Sheet,"* May 7, 2008.
[13] http://www.usaid.gov
[14] http://www.state.gov/g/drl/rls/hrrpt/
[15] http://www.state.gov/g/drl/rls/hrrpt/
[16] Ted Dagne's interview with President Kagame, August 2007.

In: Economic, Political and Social Issues of Africa
Editor: Jeremy S. McQueen
ISBN 978-1-61209-957-6

Chapter 8

ZIMBABWE*

Lauren Ploch

ABSTRACT

Zimbabwe's prospects appeared promising in 1980, as it gained independence after a long liberation war. Rising inflation and unemployment bred discontent in the 1990s and led in 1999 to the formation of the opposition Movement for Democratic Change (MDC). The new party surprised many with its initial success, campaigning against a 2000 referendum that would have legalized the president's continued rule, made government officials immune from prosecution, and allowed the uncompensated seizure of white-owned land for redistribution to black farmers. The referendum failed, and the MDC won nearly half the seats in the 2000 parliamentary election. The government of President Robert Mugabe has since taken numerous, often undemocratic actions to bolster its power.

President Mugabe's government has been seen in the past decade as autocratic and repressive by its critics, and its human rights record is poor. The government has suppressed freedom of speech and assembly, and many contend that the government has restricted access to food, already scarce, in opposition areas. The MDC, divided over how to respond, split into two factions in 2005, hampering its ability to challenge the ruling party. Reports of political violence rose sharply after Zimbabwe's March 2008 elections, when, for the first time since independence, Mugabe's party lost its majority in the National Assembly. Mugabe's re-election as president in the June runoff was viewed as illegitimate by the United States and the United Nations Secretary-General, among others. In September 2008, after several weeks of negotiations, Mugabe and MDC leader Morgan Tsvangirai signed a power-sharing arrangement aimed at resolving the political standoff. As part of the deal, Tsvangirai became Prime Minister of a new coalition government in February 2009, and cabinet positions have been divided among the parties. Many observers are skeptical that the MDC will be able to implement major reforms through the arrangement, although there has been some initial progress. The cost of rebuilding the economy may be as high as $8 billion.

---

* This is an edited, reformatted and augmented version of CRS Report RL32723, dated April 1, 2009.

Zimbabwe's economic output has decreased dramatically since 1998. Official inflation rose above 200,000,000% in 2008, and unemployment is estimated at more than 90%. The adult HIV prevalence rate of 15.3% has contributed to a sharp drop in life expectancy, and three-quarters of the population is expected to require food aid in early 2009. The country has yet to contain a cholera outbreak with over 90,000 infections and over 4,000 deaths. Deteriorating conditions have led many to emigrate to neighboring countries, creating a substantial burden on the region.

Robert Mugabe has enjoyed considerable popularity in Africa as a former liberation leader, but some African leaders have viewed his policies as damaging to the continent and have urged democratic reforms. Following controversial elections in 2000 and citing abuses of human rights and the rule of law, the United States and some other former allies of the government became vocal critics. The United States has enforced targeted sanctions against top Zimbabwe officials and associates since 2002. This report provides background on events leading up to the country's most recent elections, in March and June 2008. For further discussion of those elections, the coalition government, and other current events, please see CRS Report RL34509, *Zimbabwe: The Power Sharing Agreement and Implications for U.S. Policy*, by Lauren Ploch.

Developments Surrounding the 2008 Elections [1]

With official inflation having risen to a level at which prices doubled in less than 24 hours, Zimbabwe's economy continued its collapse in early 2009, and the outlook for its people remained grave. A regional mediation effort between the Zimbabwe government and the opposition in the wake of a 2007 assault by police on government critics had resulted in some changes to laws regarded by many as repressive prior to the country's first harmonized elections, which were held on March 29, 2008. Human rights activists argue that the changes were cosmetic and that the talks failed to create a level playing field prior to the elections [2] Significant reports of political violence followed the elections, and a presidential runoff election, held in June, failed to alleviate the country's political crisis. Subsequent negotiations in South Africa resulted in a power sharing agreement in September 2008, but the agreement was not implemented until February 2009, when a new coalition government was formed. Initial economic reforms by the new government appear to have stemmed Zimbabwe's runaway inflation rate, but significant challenges to the country's recovery remain.

March 2007 Arrests

Zimbabwe received international media attention for the March 2007 crackdown on opposition and civil society activists, during which one opposition supporter was shot and killed by police (see "Opposition Defiance Against a Ban on Protests and Rallies" section below). Morgan Tsvangirai (CHAHN-gih-R-EYE), leader of the Movement of Democratic Change (MDC) party, and several others reportedly received severe beatings by police following their arrest. They were accused of violating a three-month ban on public protests [3]. Tsvangirai was detained again, with other party members, in late March in a police raid on the opposition headquarters.

South African Mediation

International criticism of the situation in Zimbabwe grew after the arrests, even among former allies on the continent. In one of the most critical statements from African leaders, Zambia's President Levy Mwanawasa compared the country to "a sinking Titanic whose passengers are jumping out to save their lives" [4] One of South Africa's Deputy Foreign Ministers told the South African parliament, "the South African government wishes to express its concern, disappointment, and disapproval of the measures undertaken by the security forces in dealing with the political protests," blaming the current situation on an "absence of open political dialogue."5 Southern African Development Community (SADC) leaders convened an emergency summit on March 28, 2007.

Given the strong statements made by some southern African leaders, many observers expected the SADC heads of state to increase pressure on Mugabe to make reforms. Reports suggest that in private the leaders may have been tough on the Zimbabwean president, who was in attendance, but their public response was deemed disappointing by human rights activists and critics of the regime [6]. During the summit, the SADC leaders resolved to promote dialogue within the country, at the same time suggesting that western countries should drop their sanctions against the Mugabe government and that Britain should provide funding to assist in land reform efforts. South African President Thabo Mbeki was appointed to mediate between the Zimbabwean government and the opposition. Mbeki, who opposed calls for regime change, pushed instead for democratic elections, saying "you might question whether these elections are genuinely free and fair but we have to get the Zimbabweans talking so we do have elections that are free and fair" [7]. Talks between the Mugabe Administration and the MDC factions began in Pretoria in June 2007.

According to human rights activists and the U.S. Department of State, political violence against opposition leaders and supporters continued in spite of the negotiations.8 The Mugabe Administration accused the opposition of being responsible for a series of bombings targeting shops, trains, and police stations, although some observers suggest the attacks were an attempt to frame the opposition.9 Harassment of university students by police also reportedly increased. On November 22, 2007, 22 members of the National Constitutional Assembly, a pro-democracy civil society organization, reportedly sustained severe beatings during a peaceful protest set to coincide with a visit by President Mbeki to Harare [10].

Although the South Africa negotiations resulted in several agreements between the parties, leading to the amendment of some laws seen to restrict press freedom and political activity, the talks were abandoned after Mugabe announced that elections would be held on March 29, 2008. Despite President Mbeki's report to SADC leaders that his mediation had achieved "commendable achievements," Morgan Tsvangirai announced in February 2008 that "nothing has changed changes in the law, negotiated by President Mbeki, have not changed the behavior of the dictatorship" [11].

March 2008 Elections

The two factions of the main opposition party, the MDC, which split in 2005, remained divided prior to the elections. Despite rumors of dissatisfaction with Mugabe's continued rule from within his own party, the party's central committee nominated Mugabe to be their presidential candidate in March 2007. The committee also supported a resolution to hold all elections (presidential, parliamentary, and local council) at the same time, and to reduce the terms for all public offices from six to five years. In addition, they voted to back efforts to increase the number of parliamentarians from 150 to 210 and the number of senators from 66 to 84 [12]. Critics contend that these proposals were an effort to manipulate the electoral process through gerrymandering, with the new constituencies created in rural areas where the ruling party had stronger support [13]. The ruling Zimbabwe African National Union - Patriotic Front party (ZANU-PF) also proposed to allow the parliament to select a new president if the sitting president resigns, is incapacitated, or dies in office [14] Analysts suggest that Mugabe may not have intended to serve an entire term if reelected, instead planning to resign mid-term and use parliament to hand-pick his successor [15]. The proposals were included in a controversial Constitutional Amendment Bill, which, to the surprise of many observers, was passed by the parliament in September 2007 with the support of MDC Members of Parliament (MPs). The final version of the legislation, did, however, include some changes seen as concessions to the opposition, and reports suggest that the MDC supported the legislation because of progress in the South Africa negotiations.

In February 2008, a senior member of ZANU-PF, Simba Makoni, announced his intention to run against President Mugabe in the upcoming elections. He was subsequently expelled from the party and ran as an independent, although he was rumored to have the support of several unnamed senior party officials. Makoni, 57, served as Finance Minister from 2000 to 2002 and was reportedly dismissed after criticizing the administration's economic policies. Makoni also previously served as the executive secretary of SADC. Opposition leader Tsvangirai dismissed Makoni as "old wine in a new bottle," but rival MDC leader Arthur Mutambara withdrew as a presidential candidate and expressed his support for Makoni.

In the pre-election period, civic activists reported significant pre-election irregularities. The Zimbabwean government invited election observers from over 40 countries and regional organizations, including SADC, but allegedly barred observers from countries considered to be critical of its policies [16]. Western media organizations and journalists were also reportedly denied permission to cover the elections [17]

Zimbabwe's first "harmonized" elections were held on March 29, 2008 [18]. The Zimbabwe Electoral Commission (ZEC), widely criticized for its delayed release of the electoral results, announced the National Assembly results four days after the election. For the first time since independence, ZANU-PF lost its majority in the National Assembly. The MDC factions, which reunited on April 28, won 109 seats in the 220-seat National Assembly, over ZANU-PF's 97. After a month of rising tensions, the results of the presidential race were belatedly announced on May 2. They indicated that opposition leader Morgan Tsvangirai had received more votes than the incumbent, President Robert Mugabe, but had failed to garner the 50% needed to avoid a runoff [19].

Although the opposition accused the government of manipulating the results and initially objected to participating in a runoff, Morgan Tsvangirai agreed to stand against President Mugabe in a second round of voting. While electoral law requires the government to hold a runoff election within 21 days of announcing the initial results, the ZEC declared that the runoff would not be held until June 27, three months after the first round. During the following weeks, reports of political violence increased dramatically, in what many critics contend was a government- orchestrated attempt to punish opposition supporters and ensure a

Mugabe victory in the runoff. Several of the country's security service chiefs, including the heads of the army and the police, publicly announced that they would not recognize an electoral victory by anyone other that Mugabe [20]. Citing the high number of attacks against MDC supporters and the lack of a level playing field, Tsvangirai withdrew from the race days before the election. Despite public comments from African observer missions and a presidential statement from the United Nations Security Council arguing that conditions for a free and fair election did not exist, the government held the runoff as scheduled. Mugabe was declared the winner with over 85% of the vote and inaugurated on June 29, 2008. His electoral victory in the runoff election was declared illegitimate by several countries, including the United States.

President Mugabe delayed the swearing in of the new parliament and the naming of a new cabinet as President Mbeki and other international leaders pressed for talks between the parties. When the parliament was sworn in on August 25, 2008, Lovemore Moyo, an MP from the MDC Tsvangirai faction, was elected as Speaker. He received 110 votes, beating MDC-M MP Paul ThembaNyathi, who had received 98 votes, including those of most ZANU-PF members of parliament. Two MDC-T MPs were arrested when they arrived for the swearing in, but were later released.

Power Sharing Agreement

On September 15, after several weeks of negotiations overseen by Mbeki, Mugabe and Tsvangirai signed a power-sharing arrangement aimed at resolving the political standoff. The agreement, known as the Global Political Agreement (GPA), outlined a time frame for the drafting and adoption of a new constitution. As part of the deal, Tsvangirai would become Prime Minister in a new unity government. Cabinet positions would be divided among the parties, with 16 ministerial positions for the MDC factions, three of which come from MDC-M, and 15 positions for ZANUPF. Early reports suggested that Tsvangirai would gain control of the police force, while Mugabe, who remains head of state under the agreement, would retain control of the armed forces. The text of the agreement, however, left oversight of the police, which falls under the Ministry of Home Affairs, undetermined, and debate over which party would control the Ministry delayed the agreement's implementation for over four months. As head of state, Mugabe would continue to lead the cabinet, but reports suggest that Tsvangirai, who now chairs a Council of Ministers, will be responsible for the day-to-day management of government affairs [21].

Amid concern that the parties would abandon compromises made in the power sharing agreement, SADC renewed pressure for the agreement to be implemented in January 2009. Tsvangirai agreed to join a coalition government on January 31, and, after Zimbabwe's parliament amended the constitution to allow its creation, Tsvangirai and new MDC ministers were sworn in as members of the new government in early February. Despite the MDC's new role in government, several political activists remain in detention and the eviction of white farmers continues. Many observers remain skeptical that the parties will be able to work together effectively to implement reforms deemed necessary by international donors, and, without an influx of foreign funds, economic and social indicators are expected to continue their downward slide. The coalition government faces considerable challenges in prioritizing humanitarian needs and making the reforms necessary for economic recovery. For further discussion of the coalition government and other current events, please see CRS Report RL34509, *Zimbabwe: The Power Sharing Agreement and Implications for U.S. Policy*, which is updated regularly.

BACKGROUND

After years of economic sanctions by the international community and a decades-long civil war that resulted in more than 30,000 dead, the white minority rule government of Southern Rhodesia concluded a series of agreements with the black majority in 1979 that resulted in the establishment of the government of the Republic of Zimbabwe. Among the greatest challenges facing the new government was the demand by the majority for greater equity in land distribution. At independence, the white minority, who composed less than 5% of the population, owned the vast majority of arable land. Many observers considered the country's white-owned commercial farms crucial to the country's economy, although there was a general recognition that land reform was necessary. Britain initially funded a "willing buyer, willing seller" program to redistribute commercial farmland, offering compensation to white farmers amenable to leaving their lands.

Dissatisfaction with the pace of land reform grew and led in the 1 990s to spontaneous and often violent farm invasions. At the same time, the country's labor movement and a segment of its urban middle class were becoming increasingly critical of the government's economic performance. Facing rising political and economic challenges, the government of Zimbabwe began to implement aggressive land expropriation policies, leading Britain and other donors to begin withdrawing financial support for resettlement.

In 2000, the government held a referendum to approve changes to the constitution that would allow land seizures without compensation, a responsibility that in its view lay with Britain. The referendum was rejected by 55% of voters and was seen as a victory for a new opposition party, the Movement for Democratic Change (MDC). Within days of the vote war veterans and ruling party supporters moved onto an estimated 1,000 white-owned farms, and, months later, the President invoked emergency powers to take land without compensation. During this time there were numerous attacks against white farmers and their employees, as well as against supporters of the MDC; more than 30 people were killed.

Since then, the country's problems have deepened. Substantial political violence and human rights violations have accompanied elections since 2000. The broad scale of such abuses in the wake of the 2008 elections brought international condemnation, but little consensus on how best to stop the violence. Reports of government-orchestrated human rights abuses continued for months afterward. Zimbabwe's political difficulties have been accompanied by a sharp decline in living standards, with more than 80% of the population living on less than $1 per day [22]. Once touted as a potential "breadbasket of Africa," much of Zimbabwe's population is now dependent on food aid. More than 15% of adults are infected by the HIV/AIDS virus, and life expectancy fell from an estimated 56 years in 1990 to 44 in 2008 [23] Foreign Policy magazine has ranked Zimbabwe third in its index of failed states, behind Somalia and Sudan [24]. Observers are concerned that the difficulties confronting Zimbabwe are affecting neighboring countries and deterring investors from the region.

POLITICAL SITUATION

Zimbabwe at a Glance
Population: 11.35 million
Approximate size: Slightly larger than Montana
Population growth rate: -0.787%
Life expectancy at birth: 44.28 years
Ethnic groups: African 98% (Shona 82%, Ndebele 14%, other 2%), Mixed and Asian 1%, White less than 1%
Languages: English (official), Shona, Sindebele and a number of tribal dialects.
Literacy: Total Population: 90.7%; Male: 94.2%; Female: 87.2%
GDP real growth rate: -6.2%; GDP Per Capita: $200
HIV Prevalence Rate: 15.3% (adults, aged 15-49) Unemployment: 94%
Sources: CIA World Factbook; Economist Intelligence Unit; UNAIDS

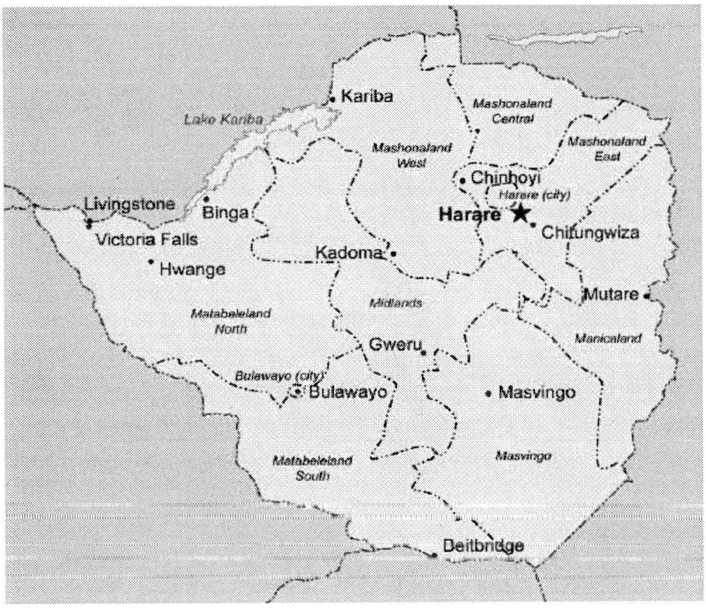

Source: Map Resources. Adapted by CRS.

Figure 1. Map of Zimbabwe.

Zimbabwe has been ruled since independence by ZANU-PF, which has come under increasing scrutiny from human rights activists, both at home and abroad. Critics cite high levels of corruption, political violence, and strictly enforced laws restricting basic freedoms. The government contends its detractors have engaged in a "propaganda war" backed by Britain and the United States, using democracy and human rights as a cover to push for regime change [25]. Many domestic and international observers have judged elections since 2000 to be "far from free and fair." The country's main opposition party, the Movement for Democratic Change (MDC), split over tactical issues in 2005, and despite attempts at reconciliation, the party remained divided until after the March 2008 elections. ZANU-PF has also suffered internal competition, and some observers suggest that opposition to President Mugabe himself has grown within the party.

Parliamentary Elections 2005

Zimbabwe held legislative elections in 2005. The elections, like those before them in 2000 and 2002, were controversial, with the opposition disputing the results and alleging government efforts to deny a fair race. ZANU-PF retained control of the 150-member parliament, taking 108 seats (of these, 30 are appointed by the President rather than elected). The MDC won 41 seats, and one seat went to an independent [26]

The MDC's representation in parliament had declined since 2000, when it won 57 seats in its first elections. Some observers argue that the MDC did not do as well in the 2005 election because it delayed a decision to participate until December 2004, leaving little time to campaign. Violence against MDC voters in past elections, the alleged use of food distributions by the ruling party to secure votes, and a general climate of intimidation may have also discouraged MDC support. Government supporters suggest voters simply lost faith in MDC promises. Opposition access to the state-run media was severely limited, according to Reporters Without Borders, a Paris-based organization that supports press freedom [27]. The MDC was rarely covered on television or in the *Herald,* the government newspaper, and the stories that did appear were typically disparaging.

Election-Related Violence

Although most observers agree that the level of political violence surrounding the 2005 elections was significantly less than that which preceded the 2000 and 2002 elections, many argue the election was not "free and fair," and that there were some incidents of violence. Critics suggest that state harassment of civil society and the political opposition, combined with limitations on press and other political freedoms, left little need for violent repression. Nevertheless, the Zimbabwe Human Rights NGO Forum, a coalition of 17 human rights organizations, reported more than 300 assaults in the pre-election period [28].

Charges of Election Rigging

Many analysts argue that the Zimbabwean political system is undemocratic because elections are administered by institutions and under laws that many consider biased in favor of ZANU-PF. In response to democratic protocols established by the Southern African Development Community (SADC), the government passed the Zimbabwe Electoral Commission (ZEC) Act and the Electoral Act prior to the 2005 elections. However, the new "independent" ZEC, appointed by the president, was only established two months before the election, leaving many of the preparations to the old Electoral Commission, which many considered discredited by its past performance. According to the U.S.-based democracy advocacy group Freedom House, "despite some improvements, the Electoral Act granted the ZEC powers to employ security forces, retained biased residency requirements for voters, denied most expatriates the right to vote, and created an Electoral Court staffed by a deeply compromised judiciary." [29]

The Mugabe government employed other legal tactics seen by critics as designed to intimidate the opposition and produce a political landscape favorable to ZANU-PF. The 2004 gerrymandering of constituencies, which the government attributed to population shifts arising from its land reform program, resulted in the redistricting of three urban seats held by the MDC into three new rural constituencies, which ZANU-PF candidates won in 2005. The International Council of Barristers and Advocates described extensive efforts by ZANU-PF to gain control over the legal system in a 2004 report, suggesting the ruling party had interfered in judicial appointments and forced the removal of impartial judges "through a combination of psychological and physical intimidation and threats of violence" [30]

The MDC challenged the results of numerous 2005 races in court [31]. Their allegations focused on several largely rural districts in which the ZEC announced voter turnout totals before the vote results were reported. Once the results came in, the ZANU-PF candidate won in each case, but the vote for the two candidates added together exceeded the initial ZEC-reported turnout total. This created a suspicion that additional votes had been given to the ZANU-PF candidates during the tabulation phase [32]. According to the ZEC, they had initially released early totals coming in to provide an indication of voter turnout, and the discrepancies between those initial figures and the final tallies were due to poor communications from rural areas. Other allegations focused on large numbers of voters in contested areas reportedly turned away due to registration problems.

Election Observers

Many domestic election observers, such as the Zimbabwe Lawyers for Human Rights (ZLHR) and the Zimbabwe Election Support Network (ZESN), were critical of the 2005 elections. During the pre-election period, they cited a lack of transparency surrounding voter registration as a "significant and serious threat to the overall credibility of the electoral process." Their reports cited no incidents of overt political violence, but noted that the pre-election period was marked by intimidation, "politicization of food distribution," and a lack of media access by the opposition. The observers contended that they were restricted access to the vote counting process at many polling stations, and that in some cases the total voter tally did not coincide with the total number of votes cast for the candidates [33]. Both groups reported the use of POSA, MOA, and AIPPA against opposition supporters. The ZLHR report concluded, "Zimbabwean authorities have failed, on most accounts, to ensure a free and fair electoral process" [34]

The Mugabe government placed limits on foreign observers for the election. No U.S. observers were invited, and Russia was the only European country asked to send a team. Leading the Southern African Development Community (SADC) delegation, South African Deputy President Mlambo-Ngcuka congratulated Zimbabwe on "the holding of a peaceful, credible, well managed and transparent election. The people of Zimbabwe have expressed their will in an impressively instructive manner that will go a long way in contributing to the consolidation of democracy and political stability not only in Zimbabwe, but also in the region as a whole" [35]. The head of South Africa's parliamentary observer mission was quoted saying that the delegation had "unanimously agreed that the elections were credible, legitimate, free and fair." [36] Both statements received substantial criticism in the international press. The SADC Parliamentary Forum, which consists of legislators from the region and had issued a report critical of the 2002 election, was not invited to observe the vote.

Western governments condemned the elections. Based on reports from domestic observers and U.S. Embassy staff who were allowed to observe the election, U.S. Secretary of State Condoleezza Rice issued the following statement:

> Although the campaign and election day itself was generally peaceful, the election process was not free and fair. The electoral playing field was heavily tilted in the government's favor. The independent press was muzzled; freedom of assembly was constrained; food was used as a weapon to sway hungry voters; and millions of Zimbabweans who have been forced by the nation's economic collapse to emigrate were disenfranchised [37].

U.N. Secretary-General Kofi Annan commended the election's lack of violence but noted concern that "the electoral process has not countered the sense of disadvantage felt by opposition political parties who consider the conditions were unfair" [38].

Restrictions on Political Freedoms

Legislative actions in the ZANU-PF-dominated parliament raised concerns about human rights in Zimbabwe. Laws that critics contend have been used to quiet dissent and influence political developments include the following:

- *The Access to Information and Protection of Privacy Act (AIPPA).* This 2002 Act requires that all media services be licensed, and that all journalists, including foreign correspondents, be officially accredited. The government, citing AIPPA, closed The Daily News, the only remaining independent daily, in 2003. In 2005, three Zimbabwean correspondents for the Associated Press, Bloomberg News, and the Times of London, fled Zimbabwe after police raided their office. The Media Institute of Southern Africa (MISA) has stated that AIPPA is "one of the most effective legal instruments of state control over the media and civil society communication anywhere in the world" [39] The government has countered that AIPPA encourages responsible journalism.
- The Public Order and Security Act (POSA), the Criminal Law (Codification and Reform) Act ("Criminal Law Code"), and the Miscellaneous Offences Act (MOA). POSA, also enacted in 2002, prohibits statements deemed to be "abusive, indecent, obscene, or false" about the president or considered to "undermin(e) public confidence" in the security forces, and prohibits false statements prejudicial to the state [40]. The measure has been used in the arrest of thousands of political opponents and in police action to break up public meetings and demonstrations. Zimbabweans overheard criticizing the President in a public place have also been jailed. The MOA criminalized "conduct likely to cause a breach of the peace," and was often used with POSA against activists. Police and "persons assisting the police" may use "all necessary force" to stop unlawful gatherings [41]. In 2006 many offences under POSA and MOA were transferred to the new Criminal Law Code.
- *The Private Voluntary Organizations (PVO) Act.* Critics suggest that the government has used the PVO Act, enacted in 2002, to limit the activities of domestic NGOs.

They are required to register with the government, and a "probe team" of intelligence officers has wide powers to investigate groups and demand documents related to activities and funding. The African Commission on Human and Peoples' Rights has recommended that it be repealed.

The opposition had limited success in preventing ZANU-PF from passing other legislation that it contended would restrict freedoms. The Interception of Communications Bill, which would allow the government to monitor all Internet, email, and telephone communications for threats to national security, was stalled by the Parliamentary Legal Committee (chaired by an MDC MP), but was later revised and approved in June 2007. Critics suggest the revisions were cosmetic.

In the 2005 elections ZANU-PF won over two-thirds of the seats in the House of Assembly, giving the party the power to amend the constitution. The parliament subsequently passed several controversial constitutional amendments which some analysts contend breach international human rights standards. The 2005 Constitution of Zimbabwe Amendment Act (No. 17) allowed the government to limit the right to freedom of movement when it is in "the public interest" or in "the economic interests of the State" and restricts the right to leave Zimbabwe. Journalists, MDC officials, and union leaders have had their passports revoked under the act; the government charged that they planned to lobby abroad for sanctions or military intervention against the country [42].

The act also prevents land owners from challenging the acquisition of agricultural land by the state. It paved the way for the passage of Gazetted Land (Consequential Provisions) Act in late 2006, making it illegal for former farm owners to occupy nationalized land and allowing the government to evict farmers and resettle the land without compensation. The constitutional amendment also revived the upper house of the parliament, the Senate.

The South Africa-led SADC negotiations led in January 2008 to amendments to both AIPPA and POSA. Critics suggest the amendments did not adequately address human rights concerns and were not implemented [43] They cite, for example, a January 2008 MDC "freedom march" that was blocked by police despite prior notification of the event, in accordance with the changes to POSA.

Supporters who defied a police ban were reportedly tear-gassed and beaten with batons. Numerous MDC rallies were likewise blocked in the period preceding the 2008 runoff, despite court orders allowing the events. The Media Institute of Southern Africa dismissed the AIPPA amendments as "dwelling on inconsequential issues which will not advance basic freedoms" [44]

2005 Senate Elections

Elections to the new 66-seat Senate were held in September 2005, and were marked by record low voter turnout. Of 26 MDC candidates who ran, seven were elected; ZANU-PF gained the overwhelming majority of seats. Observers suggest one of the reasons for the low turnout may have been a lack of solidarity on the part of the opposition, which split prior to the election over whether to boycott the vote.

Internal ZANU-PF Struggles

In view of President Mugabe's advanced age, presidential succession has been a matter of intense interest to observers for several years. Prior to the 2008 elections, some analysts expressed concern that if the elections did not lead to a democratic transfer of power, Zimbabwe could experience a violent succession struggle or a possible military coup. Under the constitution, the president may designate one of the country's two vice presidents to serve as acting president until the next election, should he leave office, but Mugabe has never done so. One of the vice presidential posts was vacant prior to the 2004 ZANU-PF party conference, setting off a power struggle that transformed the political scene by revealing internal party divisions. Despite having turned 85 in 2009, President Mugabe is reportedly in good health and in no rush to relinquish his post. Many observers suggest he has used the country's anti-corruption authority to check the political ambitions of his party members. Mugabe endorsed a 2007 proposal to extend the next presidential elections to 2010, but it was defeated by his party's central committee.

Prior to the December 2004 party conference, Emmerson Mnangagwa, then speaker of the parliament and a political veteran long touted as Mugabe's heir, campaigned actively for the position of ZANU-PF's second vice president. His selection to that position would likely have assured his appointment as national vice president, but Mnangagwa was caught off guard when Mugabe decided that the country should have a woman in the post. Mugabe's choice for the position, Joice Mujuru, was inevitably elected, and she was sworn into office as Zimbabwe's second vice president. Mujuru, a veteran of the liberation war and a women's movement leader, had been serving as Minister of Water Resources and Infrastructure.

The outcome of any succession struggle within ZANU-PF may be affected by the country's ethnic and clan divisions. Mugabe and many key party officials are from the Zezuru clan of the Shona people, who are dominant in a wide area encircling the capital, Harare. Retired General Solomon "Rex" Mujuru, a Zezuru and husband of Joice Mujuru, has been one of Mugabe's closest advisors and was once regarded as a king-maker. Mnangagwa is seen as a representative of the large Karanga clan, which has reportedly felt that its turn to control the reins of power has come. Mnangagwa's viability as a presidential contender has been hampered by accusations that he led the purge of alleged regime opponents in provinces of Matabeleland in the 1980s, which is believed to have resulted in the deaths of 20,000 Ndebele civilians. The events of the 1980s help to explain why Bulawayo has long been regarded as a center of opposition to the government, although Mugabe has sought to gain support by elevating Ndebele to party and government posts.

Mnangagwa's power was reduced following the events of 2004, as was that of a number of his backers, including the former minister of information, Jonathan Moyo. Moyo was fired in early 2005 for his sharp-tongued defenses of the regime and for fights with others in leadership. He is reported to have angered Mugabe by holding an unsanctioned meeting of Mnangagwa supporters before the 2004 party convention, allegedly to strategize ways to derail the Mujuru candidacy. Moyo left the party and ran as an independent in 2005. He retained his seat in the 2008 elections.

According to reports, neither the Mnangagwa nor Mujuru camps initially supported Mugabe's proposed term extension. Once a strong Mugabe ally, Solomon Mujuru has been vocal in his disapproval and is rumored to have been pivotal in blocking the proposal at the party's national conference. Some have suggested that Mujuru covertly backed another

ZANU-PF official, Simba Makoni, over his wife as a potential successor to Mugabe. Makoni, a technocrat, was considered by some analysts to be a compromise candidate, untainted by the corruption scandals that have plagued others. Mugabe's own choice for his successor is unknown. Mnangagwa appears to have reconciled with Mugabe, leading the party's 2008 election efforts and taking a central role in guiding the country's security forces. He leads the Ministry of Defense in the new government.

The Movement for Democratic Change (MDC)

Origins of the MDC

The MDC party rose from the Zimbabwe labor movement. As poverty deepened in Zimbabwe in the late 1990s, and allegations of corruption against regime leaders became more frequent, the Zimbabwe Congress of Trade Unions (ZCTU) organized a number of strikes and protests. In September 1999, the MDC was formed on this trade union base with support from many in Zimbabwe's churches and in urban areas. In February 2000, MDC members elected the ZCTU secretary general, Morgan Tsvangirai, born in 1952, as MDC president, and union president Gibson Sibanda as MDC vice president.

The MDC proved formidable in the 2000 referendum and in the 2000 parliamentary election; some contend their success may have prompted a range of repressive actions against the party and its supporters. Among the retaliatory measures alleged, several leaders of the MDC, including Tsvangirai himself, were arrested and charged with treason two weeks before the MDC leader ran against Mugabe in the 2002 presidential elections.

Treason Charges

In October 2004, Tsvangirai was acquitted of a treason charge based on a video recorded in Canada, which the government claimed showed him calling for the "elimination" of Mugabe. The verdict surprised many observers in view of the regime's perceived influence over the courts. The judge stated that the evidence had been unconvincing, with the witnesses produced by the state "suspect" and the video unreliable. The government can appeal the verdict, and Tsvangirai may be tried again because the law does not prohibit double jeopardy. In August 2005, the government dropped a second treason charge that had been based on claims that he urged violence to bring down the government in 2004.

Division in the Opposition

In late 2004, the MDC became increasingly divided in its strategy to defeat the ZANU-PF government. MDC officials initially decided that the party would not participate in the 2005 parliamentary race, unless the government took steps to assure a free and fair election. Several members questioned this stance on grounds that non-participation would deprive the MDC of any influence in the next parliament. Some reportedly felt that a refusal to participate would hand control of parliament to Mugabe on a "silver platter." Tsvangirai supported a boycott, arguing that the elections should be postponed until substantial electoral reforms could be implemented. The party did eventually participate "under protest," but did not do as well as in previous polls.

In the months prior to the 2005 Senate elections, the MDC was once again divided on whether to participate. Supported by some civil society groups who suggested the elections were "meaningless" and "a waste of time and resources," Tsvangirai argued that participating in the Senate would legitimize previous "rigged" elections, and vowed instead to lead the opposition through mass action. He was opposed by a group of MDC politicians led by the party's secretary- general, Welshman Ncube, who had also been accused by the government of treason in 2003 (the charges were subsequently dropped), and Gibson Sibanda. In October, the party's national council voted 33-31 to participate in the election, but Tsvangirai overruled the vote and, reportedly in violation of the party's constitution, expelled 26 senior officials from the party. He announced the boycott, touring the country to encourage voters to stay home. The Ncube faction refused to accept their expulsion and fielded candidates in the Senate race but only gained only seven seats.

Both factions held party conferences in early 2006; Tsvangirai was confirmed as the leader of one faction, while Ncube ceded control of the "pro-senate" faction to Arthur Mutambara, a noted student leader in the 1980s. The two factions attacked each other in the press, and there were allegations that the Tsvangirai faction was behind a violent July 2006 assault on Member of Parliament (MP) Trudy Stevenson and several other Mutambara supporters. Stevenson identified the youths who attacked her as known followers of the former labor leader, but Tsvangirai denied the charges and denounced the beatings. Although his faction was reported to have the larger support base and the backing of the ZCTU, some observers suggested neither faction would be effective unless they could resolve their differences and reunite.

Opposition Defiance Against a Ban on Protests and Rallies

On February 22, 2007, the Zimbabwean government announced a three-month ban on political rallies and public demonstrations in Harare "due to the volatile situation in the country" [45] The MDC filed an appeal with the High Court to lift the ban, which coincided with an increase in public activity by the opposition and civic groups. On February 18, despite a High Court decision allowing Morgan Tsvangirai to launch his presidential campaign at a rally in Harare, police reportedly used batons and water cannons to break up the event. A rally planned by the Mutambara faction in Bulawayo was similarly dispersed, and numerous opposition supporters were arrested. The ban was announced three days later, and police subsequently arrested several hundred civic activists, according to press reports.

On March 11, 2007, police broke up a Save Zimbabwe Campaign prayer meeting attended by both Tsvangirai and Mutambara, arresting an estimated 50 members of the opposition and civil society, including both MDC leaders. Police shot and killed one opposition supporter after MDC youth reportedly began throwing stones at police. The following day, police arrested an estimated 240 opposition supporters during a demonstration protesting the March 11 crackdown. Media and human rights reports suggest that Tsvangirai was severely beaten while in custody, and he appeared in court on March 13 showing signs of head trauma [46]. Other opposition and civic leaders also reportedly sustained injuries after their arrest. The protestors were released into the custody of their lawyers on March 14 after prosecutors reportedly failed to appear at their court hearing. The Zimbabwean government contended that the MDC incited violence and was responsible for attacks on several civilian targets and a Harare police station [47]

The March 11 incident spurred international media attention and drew considerable criticism from many world leaders. U.S. Secretary of State Condoleezza Rice issued a strong statement, saying, "The world community again has been shown that the regime of Robert Mugabe is ruthless and repressive and creates only suffering for the people of Zimbabwe" [48] U.N. Secretary- General Ban Ki-moon also condemned the "reported beating of those leaders in police custody" and criticized the ban, noting that "such actions violate the basic democratic right of citizens to engage in peaceful assembly" [49]. Several of Zimbabwe's neighbors, including South Africa and Zambia, issued statements of concern regarding the incident, and Ghanaian President John Kufuor, then chairman of the AU, called the event "very embarrassing" [50]

Political Violence

Human rights groups have documented numerous accounts of political violence in recent years. According to Freedom House, in 2006 "Zimbabwe's descent into the ranks of the world's most repressive states continued unabated" [51]. In 2007, the State Department reported that Zimbabwe's government has "engaged in the pervasive and systematic abuse of human rights, which increased significantly during the year"and contended that "state-sanctioned use of excessive force increased, and security forces tortured members of the opposition, student leaders, and civil society activists" [52] Amnesty International has been similarly critical [53].

President Mugabe has publicly condoned police and military brutality against Zimbabwean citizens. In 2006, during Heroes' Day, a holiday honoring war veterans, Mugabe warned that his security forces "will pull the trigger" against protesters [54]. A month later, in an incident caught on video, Zimbabwean police conducted a particularly violent crackdown against leaders of the Zimbabwe Congress of Trade Unions (ZCTU), who had planned a civic protest to highlight the impact of inflation on the country's citizenry. Mugabe sanctioned the police action, saying, "Some people are now crying foul that they were assaulted, yes you get a beating ... when the police say move, move, if you don't move, you invite the police to use force" [55]. Subsequent mass ZCTU protests were not held.

Mugabe received international attention for his statement; the U.N. Country Team (UNCT) in Zimbabwe announced "a profound sense of dismay" over comments that "might be interpreted as condoning the use of force and torture to deal with peaceful demonstrations by its citizens." [56] The U.N. Special Rapporteur on Torture [57] has repeatedly requested an invitation from Zimbabwe to investigate, and the Harare magistrate who heard the case against the ZCTU leaders ordered an independent investigation into the allegations of police brutality.

The Zimbabwe Human Rights NGO Forum reports that there were 723 incidents of torture in 2008, 1913 incidents of assault, and 137 incidents of politically motivated abduction/kidnapping. These figures suggest a marked increase in political violence from 2007, during which there were 586 incidents of torture, 855 incidents of assault, and 19 incidents of abduction [58].

The group also reported 107 politically motivated murders in 2008. Human rights activists suggest that abductions and beatings of opposition supporters became "more systematic and widespread" after the events of March 2007 [59]Despite provisions in the new Electoral Laws Amendment Act banning such acts and assurances by security officials that the government would take a "zero tolerance" approach to violence, reports of attacks on opposition supporters rose dramatically after the March 2008 elections [60]. Reports suggest that violent political repression has decreased in early 2009, with no reported incidents of torture or abduction, although acts of political discrimination and unlawful detention continue [61].

Reports suggest that the police have played a significant role in political violence. The Geneva- based International Commission of Jurists, which investigated the May 2007 detention and beating of lawyers, expressed shock at the role police played in the attacks and at the "cavalier response of Zimbabwean authorities" [62].

HUMANITARIAN SITUATION

Operation Murambatsvina

In May 2005, the Government of Zimbabwe initiated Operation Murambatsvina (variously translated as "Restore Order" or "Clean Out the Filth"), a massive demolition program aimed at destroying allegedly illegal urban structures, such as informal housing and markets. By early July 2005, an estimated 700,000 urban Zimbabweans had been rendered homeless or unemployed by the operation, and an estimated 2.1 million (in total, almost 20% of the population) were indirectly affected by the demolitions [63]. These are considered "low-end estimates," and some reports suggest the numbers of those affected was much higher [64]. According to some sources, 70% of the country's urban population may have lost shelter, while approximately 76% lost their source of income [65]. Police and military who carried out the event reportedly arrested forty thousand for allegedly illegal activities and told those whose homes were destroyed to "return to their rural origins," although many had no rural home to which they could return [66].

Operation Murambatsvina had a severe impact on the nation's economy and on the livelihood of its citizens. For many, this was not the first time they had been forcibly removed from their homes. As a result of the 2000 land reform program, an estimated 400,000 black laborers on commercial farms lost their livelihoods and/or homes, and many fled to urban areas to find work. Political violence surrounding the 2002 elections also forced many from their homes, reportedly displacing more than 100,000 [67]. In 2004, under a new phase of land resettlement, an estimated 500,000 who settled on farms during the 2000 invasions were evicted [68]. Many of these displaced inhabited the urban "slums" prior to the demolitions, making their living from trading on the black market. Given the collapse of the formal economy, 40% of the labor force was estimated to be informally employed prior to Murambatsvina, while 44% worked in the communal sector (including the agriculture industry), and 16% worked in the formal sector [69]. Of those living in towns and cities, an estimated 70% were involved in informal trading prior to the demolitions.

Political Motivations?

The government described Murambatsvina as a program designed to restore the capital city to its former image as "the Sunshine City," ridding the country's urban areas of illegal structures that foster criminal activity and stemming the black market trade in foreign currency [70]. Launched shortly after the disputed 2005 parliamentary elections, many contend the demolitions were a political move aimed either at preventing mass protests over the growing economic crisis or at punishing the reputed urban support base of the MDC. The Harare Commission that initiated the campaign was established in order to contravene the authority of the elected City Council, of which the MDC held the majority. The mayor of Harare, an MDC politician who was elected by 80% of the vote, was fired in April 2004, along with 19 MDC-allied city councillors, after having been arrested in 2003 under POSA for holding a public meeting without prior state approval.

The legality of the Harare Commission, which was appointed by the Minister of Local Government, was challenged in a high court ruling that found the Commission did not have the authority to fire the mayor. A new election was supposed to be held within 90 days, according to law, but when no election occurred, the Commission was reappointed. The remaining MDC councillors resigned in protest. With the exception of Harare, the local authorities of the other areas (many of which were MDC-controlled) affected by Murambatsvina reported that they were not informed of the demolitions prior to the event. The implications of this breakdown in governance are reflected in findings of the United Nations, which noted that Murambatsvina "was implemented in a highly polarized political climate characterized by mistrust, fear and a lack of dialogue between Government and local authorities, and between the former and civil society" [71]

The International Response

International reaction to Murambatsvina was highly critical. U.N. Secretary-General Kofi Annan named Tanzanian-born Anna Tibaijuka, Executive Director of UN-HABITAT, as the U.N. Special Envoy on Human Settlements Issues in Zimbabwe to investigate the humanitarian impact of the demolitions. Following a fact-finding mission to the country, she issued a comprehensive report, which concluded:

> Operation Restore Order, while purporting to target illegal dwellings and structures and to clamp down on alleged illicit activities, was carried out in an indiscriminate and unjustified manner, with indifference to human suffering and, in repeated cases, with disregard to several provisions of national and international legal frameworks [72]

The report also described police preventing civil society and humanitarian organizations from assisting those affected by the demolitions, and suggested that the groups were operating in a "climate of fear" and practicing "'self-censorship' to avoid being closed down or evicted" [73] The Chairman of the African Union sent his own envoy, but he was prevented from conducting an assessment (see "International Perspectives," below). The presentation of the U.N. envoy's report to the U.N. Security Council stirred controversy as China, Algeria, Benin, and Russia objected to debate on the report. The majority of Security Council members voted to allow its discussion, albeit in a closed session. Secretary-General Annan also issued a strong statement condemning Murambatsvina, calling on the government of Zimbabwe to stop the evictions and allow unimpeded access for humanitarian assistance:

> "Operation Murambatsvina" has done a catastrophic injustice to as many as 700,000 of Zimbabwe's poorest citizens, through indiscriminate actions, carried out with disquieting

> indifference to human suffering. I call on the Government to stop these forced evictions and demolitions immediately, and to ensure that those who orchestrated this ill-advised policy are held fully accountable for their actions ... the Government must recognize the virtual state of emergency that now exists, allow unhindered access for humanitarian operations, and create conditions for sustainable relief and reconstruction [74]

Continued Evictions and Operation Garikai

Many observers suggest the Zimbabwean government did little to respond to the U.N. envoy's recommendations [75]. Reports indicate that forced evictions continued, despite government declarations to the contrary [76]. As was the case during the initial evictions, several thousand of those made homeless were taken, in some cases reportedly against their will, to police-run "transit camps" in late 2006. Conditions in these camps were described as dire, often lacking shelter, water, or basic latrine facilities [77]. In keeping with the findings of the U.N. report, Amnesty International alleged that the government repeatedly prohibited aid organizations, including the United Nations, from providing the displaced with temporary shelters, such as tents. Secretary- General Annan expressed his concern in October 2005 over the government's rejection of U.N. assistance to "tens of thousands," noting "there is no clear evidence that subsequent Government efforts have significantly benefitted these groups." [78]. The United Nations was subsequently permitted to erect approximately 2,300 shelters, a fraction of their target of 40,000. [79]

In response to international criticism of Murambatsvina, the government announced a new housing scheme, Operation Garikai, in June 2005. Under Garakai, also known as "Hlalani Kuhle" (Live Well), new housing for those rendered homeless was to be built with public funds. The ambitious reconstruction program would allegedly create tens of thousands of new homes, but given the shortage of building materials and the government's budgetary problems, it is highly unlikely the original target of 5,275 homes has been met. Reports suggest that few houses were actually completed, and, instead of going to victims of Murambatsvina, the newly built houses were more likely to be occupied by soldiers, police, and members of the ruling party [80]. The government denied these allegations.

Violations of Domestic and International Law

Human rights organizations have raised questions about how Zimbabwe and the international community should respond to what some have termed "crimes against humanity," [81] as defined by Article 7 of the Rome Statute of the International Criminal Court (ICC), [82] and whether there is a "responsibility to protect" [83] those affected by Murambatsvina, or by subsequent government actions. Among the U.N. report recommendations, the envoy suggested:

> Although a case for crime against humanity under Article 7 of the Rome Statute might be difficult to sustain, the Government of Zimbabwe clearly caused large sections of its population serious suffering that must now be redressed with the assistance of the United Nations and the international community. The international community should encourage the Government to prosecute all those who orchestrated this catastrophe and those who may have caused criminal negligence leading to alleged deaths, if so confirmed by an independent internal inquiry/inquest. The international community should then continue to be engaged with human rights concerns in Zimbabwe in consensus building political forums such as the

UN Commission on Human Rights, or its successor, the African Union Peer Review Mechanism, and in the Southern African Development Community.

The report included a legal analysis of Murambatsvina through international and regional, and national legal frameworks. Several domestic and international organizations, including the International Bar Association (IBA), have called for the Zimbabwean government to be brought before the ICC, not only for violations related to the demolitions, but also for the government's alleged support of political violence against its critics. Responding to President Mugabe's comments supporting the beating of trade union leaders in 2006, the Executive Director of the IBA made the following statement:

> Mugabe's statements add to the weight of evidence that torture and other serious violations of international law are sanctioned at the highest level in Zimbabwe. This underscores the urgent need for international and regional action to hold the Zimbabwean Government to account ... the torture of the trade union activists is not an isolated incident, but part of a dangerous and illegal system of repression which constitutes crimes against humanity in international law. Decisive action is required by both the United Nations and the African Union to end impunity and violence in Zimbabwe [84]

Because Zimbabwe is not a signatory of the Rome Statute, a U.N. Security Council resolution would be needed for any referral to the ICC. Given the objections of some Security Council members to the envoy's report itself, which as stated above suggested an ICC case would be "difficult to sustain," it is unlikely such a referral would be made. The U.N. Envoy found that "The Government of Zimbabwe is collectively responsible for what has happened," but cautioned that "it appears there was no collective decision-making with respect to both the conception and implementation. Evidence suggests it was based on improper advice by a few architects of the operation"[85].

According to one media source, though, Zimbabwe's State Security Minister has claimed, "All the decisions to do with the operation emanated from the politburo [ZANU-PF 's inner cabinet] and were sent through me to the government" [86]

The government of Zimbabwe has yet to prosecute those who might be responsible for crimes related to Operation Murambatsvina or the subsequent evictions. The victims, in most cases, lack the financial resources to seek redress in the courts, although Zimbabwean human rights lawyers have represented groups of victims on several occasions. In one such case, in November 2005, residents of a Harare suburb were given a temporary stay of eviction by the High Court, but police ignored the court order and forcibly moved the group to a transit camp. The inability of the country's judicial system to protect its citizens or their property, or to provide due process to those seeking remedy or compensation, suggests a fundamental crisis in Zimbabwe's rule of law.

Zimbabwe's Food Crisis

Several Southern African countries have suffered from chronic food insecurity in recent years, stemming from a combination of weather-related and man-made factors, including prolonged drought, floods, poor economic performance, and the impact of HIV/AIDS [87].

Zimbabwe has been particularly hard hit. Grain silos across the country that once held strategic grain reserves three times the population's annual food needs now stand empty. Experts attribute this food insecurity to unexpectedly severe crop failure, [88] but some suggest Murambatsvina and other government policies significantly limited the population's ability to feed itself, particularly in urban areas [89]. Aid organizations predict that over nine million Zimbabweans, more than three-quarters of the country's population, will need food assistance in early 2009.

Although drought is partly to blame for the country's food shortages, analysts believe that disruptions to the farming sector resulting from Mugabe's land seizure program are the main reason for reduced food production [90] Nearly all of the country's 4,500 commercial farms have now been taken over; the government's land redistribution program is reportedly plagued by inefficiencies, with large portions of redistributed land not being actively farmed. Tractors and other inputs to production are reportedly in short supply. Thousands of experienced farm workers were reportedly forced to flee seized commercial farms, and many of those who now hold farmland have no agricultural expertise. The government's introduction of price controls in 2007 may have further restricted production—the country's seed and fertilizer producers reported that the controls created "unrealistic prices," which in turn caused supply shortages [91]

Operation Taguta

In late 2005, the Zimbabwean government established Operation Taguta (or "Eat Well"), a move seen by many as an acknowledgment that the government's farm resettlement policies had failed to meet the country's agricultural production needs. With food distribution already under the control of the Grain Marketing Board, reportedly led by military officers, the government established a command agriculture system, in which the military would be responsible for not only the distribution, but also the production of food. Since the program's inception, there have been numerous reports of the illegal seizure of farm equipment, the destruction of the fruit, vegetable, and other cash crops small-scale farmers grow to sell at market to support their families, and even army brutality against farmers. Some critics of the government suggest Operation Taguta was used by the government as an excuse to deploy military forces throughout the country to control the population [92]. A Zimbabwe journalist was jailed in March 2009 for reporting on allegations of corruption within the Grain Marketing Board.

Food as a Political Weapon?

The ZANU-PF government's stance on food aid led many observers to suspect that food has been used as a political weapon, a charge the government denied [93]. Despite assessments by multiple international donor agencies suggesting the need for food assistance, President Mugabe confounded observers in recent years by repeatedly declaring the country was running a maize surplus and would not need food aid [94]. In 2004, the government stopped a U.N. food needs assessment and later halted general food aid distribution by donors (targeted food aid to vulnerable groups continued), despite independent estimates that suggested 4.8 million would require assistance [95]. In March 2005, the government finally acknowledged serious food shortages, but delayed in signing agreement to allow the World Food Program (WFP) and its implementing partners to provide assistance until December of that year [96]. Reports suggested that the government maintained tight control of food distributions, until its ban on the distribution of aid by NGOs prior to the 2008 runoff [97]. The government has accused aid agencies of using food to turn Zimbabweans away from ZANU-PF.

Critics like Pius Ncube, former Catholic Archbishop of Bulawayo, have accused the government of distributing food only in areas where people would agree to vote for ZANU-PF. During past elections, civil rights groups and the opposition have reported instances of ZANU-PF holding campaign rallies in conjunction with government food distributions. In some areas, government officials distributing food required those in line to show a party card—and MDC supporters were reportedly turned away. Two 2005 court rulings supported these claims, finding that ZANU-PF candidates politicized food distribution and used violence against the opposition [98].

HIV/AIDS

In the midst of its political and economic crisis, Zimbabwe is being ravaged by HIV/AIDS. The country's HIV prevalence rate is the world's fifth highest. The United Nations Children's Fund (UNICEF) estimates that almost one quarter of Zimbabwe's children are orphans (primarily attributable to AIDS), the highest percentage globally [99]. The epidemic is also causing a severe strain on the country's healthcare system; reports suggest that 75% of hospital admissions in recent years have been AIDS-related, leaving few beds or resources for other patients. To compound this problem, the economic crisis has resulted in the exodus of many of the country's medical professionals. Of those who remain, many are infected with HIV themselves, leaving Zimbabwe to rely upon assistance from others. The AIDS epidemic is having a crippling effect on the economy- the inability of infected agricultural workers to adequately contribute to food production further hamstrings the struggling industry.

Although its infection rate remains high, Zimbabwe is the only country in Sub-Saharan Africa in which HIV prevalence and incidence rates have declined. While reports suggest evidence of changes in sexual behavior, [100] the country's high mortality rates also play a role in the decreased prevalence rate [101]. Zimbabwe's government claims significant resolve to fight the disease. The country was the first to introduce a tax to finance HIV/AIDS programs (3% on taxable income). President Mugabe announced in Zimbabwe's commitment to universal access to antiretroviral therapy (ART) by 2010. Despite this commitment, access to ART is relatively low, with only 40,000 of 1.3 million HIV positive Zimbabweans on ART in 2008 [102].

For those who are able to access treatment, the country's economic crisis is limiting its impact. Patients taking ART must maintain healthy diets for the treatment to be effective, but with malnutrition rates high, few are able to benefit. Murambatsvina reportedly displaced an estimated 80,000 infected with HIV/AIDS, leaving many not only food insecure but also without access to ART. Experts suggest disruptions in ART may lead to increased resistance in HIV-positive patients to the most common medication, Nevirapine [103]. The displacement and separation of families may also lead to an increase in unsafe sexual behavior, which could reverse the country's decreasing prevalence rate.

Cholera and the Healthcare System Collapse

As of mid-March 2009, over 90,000 suspected cases of cholera, including over 4,000 deaths, have been reported, according to the U.N. World Health Organization (WHO). Neighboring countries have reported confirmed cases in border areas. Cholera, an acute diarrhoeal infection, is spread by contaminated food and water. In Zimbabwe, the reported case fatality rate (CFR) reached almost 6% at its peak in January 2009, much higher than the normal 1% CFR rate for cholera cases globally. The country's CFR decreased to 2.3% in March, and health officials report that the number of cases reported weekly, while still high, is dropping [104].

Many health experts attribute the severity of Zimbabwe's cholera outbreak to the collapse of the country's healthcare, water, and sanitation systems [105] According to reports, water treatment and delivery have dramatically declined in recent years, and the decline of many other basic social services, such as trash collection, pose significant health risks. Public healthcare providers often lack basic medications, supplies and functioning medical equipment. Many health workers have migrated to neighboring countries in search of work, and the cost of transport to and from work for those who remain reportedly outweighs the salary they might receive. Many public hospitals and clinics have closed due to understaffing.

THE ECONOMY

The turmoil in Zimbabwe has led to a severe economic contraction, a sharp drop in living standards for the rural and urban poor, and a massive exodus of Zimbabweans in search of work. According to the Solidarity Peace Trust, founded by clergy from Zimbabwe and South Africa, well over three million Zimbabweans were living outside the country by 2004. The Trust calculated that this amounted to 25%-30% of the total population, or 60%-70% of productive adults [106]. Given the continued economic decline in recent years, many more are believed to have fled Zimbabwe since then. Those who leave the country because of economic hardship often face difficult conditions in their host country. Many of those who remain behind now reportedly rely on remittances from family abroad.

The IMF and the World Bank

Dubbed "the world's fastest shrinking economy," Zimbabwe's Gross Domestic Product (GDP) has declined over 50% since 1998 [107]. World Bank and International Monetary Fund (IMF) lending has been suspended since 2000 due to nonpayment of arrears, and foreign currency for essential imports, particularly fuel, is in short supply. Zimbabweans have faced steep rises in the prices of food and non-food items in recent years. The IMF suggests that the inflation rate will not reverse without significant changes in government spending, although the coalition government's "dollarization" of the economy appears to have stabilized prices [108]

In December 2003, Mugabe selected Gideon Gono, credited with turning around a troubled commercial bank, as governor of the Reserve Bank of Zimbabwe (RBZ). The move was welcomed by some, since Gono was regarded as a successful technocrat. However, critics maintain that his measures to fight corruption and discover illegally held foreign exchange have been used to damage government opponents and further the interests of ZANU-PF [109]. Regardless of Gono's efforts, international assessments of Zimbabwe's economic prospects remain bleak in the near term. Ignoring the advice of the IMF, the government refused to devalue the official exchange rate. Instead, in June 2006, Gono devalued the country's currency, the Zimbabwe dollar, removing three zeros in an effort to mitigate inflation.

Under "Operation Sunrise," the government printed new "rebased" currency, known as "little heroes," in an effort to combat corruption and money laundering, according to the government [110]. Zimbabweans were given only 21 days to exchange their old currency. Individuals were restricted from exchanging more than Z$ 100 million (USD$ 1000) of the old notes without clearance from tax authorities (companies were allowed to exchange Z$5 billion). Police arrested more than 3,000 at roadblocks for holding currency over the individual limit and seized a reported $40 million [111] Analysts suggest the devaluation did little to reverse the foreign exchange rate shortages [112]. More recently, in February 2009, Gono devalued the currency again, removing 12 zeros from the Zimbabwe dollar.

In late September 2008, Zimbabwe began officially trading in foreign currency in an attempt to lower prices, and in February 2009, under the direction of new Finance Minister Tendai Biti of the MDC, the government began issuing government salaries in vouchers good for $100 U.S. dollars. Biti and Prime Minister Tsvangirai have pledged to pay salaries in foreign currency in an effort to get Zimbabweans to return to work. Zimbabwe government officials warn that without a significant influx of foreign currency, they may be unable to maintain these salaries.

Zimbabwe is currently restricted from borrowing from the IMF, to which the country still owes $89 million. The government paid $120 million in 2005 and $9 million in 2006 to settle other outstanding arrears with the Fund and to avoid compulsory withdrawal from the IMF. The source of the funds used to pay the IMF debt has been a source of considerable speculation in the media [113]. Mugabe has dubbed the IMF a "political instrument" and "monster" for regime change [114]. Zimbabwe also owes an estimated $600 million to the World Bank and $460 million to the African Development Bank. In response to the September 2008 power sharing agreement, the IMF 's Managing Director encouraged the Zimbabwe government discuss policy reforms with the Fund and to "take steps to show clear commitment to a new policy direction" [115]. Following a consultation visit to the country in March 2009, the IMF noted positive steps toward fiscal discipline and offered to provide further policy advice, but warned that IMF funding would not be renewed until Zimbabwe begins to repay its debts and establishes "a track record of sound policy implementation [and] donor support" [116].

Attempts to Revive Agriculture Industry

In addition to the ZANU-PF government's attempts to revive its flagging agriculture industry through the introduction of a command agriculture system (see "Zimbabwe's Food Crisis" section, above), the Mugabe administration introduced long-term leases to provide security of tenure for farmers willing to cultivate land nationalized in the 2005 constitutional amendment. One of the unintended side effects of Mugabe's 2000 land reform strategy, which resulted in the abolition of land tenure, was that farmers were unable to use their land as collateral to obtain bank loans to invest in their farms. As a result, few commercial farmers were able to find the capital to maintain productivity. The government began to distribute 99-year leases in November 2006, and among the initial recipients were 19 white farmers, which came as a shock to many after Mugabe declared in July 2005 that his land reform program would be complete only when there was "not a single white on the farms" [117]. Some suggest financial institutions have been reluctant to accept the new leases as collateral, given that the government reserves the right to cancel the lease if it deems the farm unproductive. There are reportedly less than 400 white farmers left in Zimbabwe, and recent evictions in early 2009 have further reduced their number.

The government announced in 2007 its intention to ration electricity to households across the country in order to divert its dwindling supplies for irrigation of Zimbabwe's winter wheat crop [118]. More recent electricity shortages, caused by supply cuts from Mozambique, South Africa, and Zambia, have compounded Zimbabwe's economic woes, cutting the production capacity of the manufacturing and mining sectors by as much 50%, according to some reports [119]. The new MDC Minister for Energy and Power Development asserts that country's power infrastructure is in disrepair and up to $1 billion will be needed to fix the crumbling energy sector [120].

The Mining Industry

While the country's agriculture industry founders, its mining industry has continued to bring much-needed income into Zimbabwe. Mining accounts for almost half of Zimbabwe's total foreign currency revenues. Zimbabwe has the world's second largest reserves of platinum, behind South Africa [121]. In early 2006, the government announced plans to take a 51% share of all foreign-owned mines for local black investors; 25% of that share would be acquired at no cost to the government, and mines that refused to part with their shares would be expropriated. After industry officials cautioned that the plan would deter foreign investment, the proposal was modified, allowing firms that invested in community projects to keep their majority share. They voted to approve similar plans to take a majority share in all foreign-owned businesses in September 2007; the legislation became law in March 2008. The government has insisted that it will not expropriate foreign-owned companies and that the law will not be applied to every company, but rather "on the basis of capital (investment) and employment levels" [122]. Critics argue the law further deters much-needed foreign investment.

The new coalition government has begun to take measures to encourage investment in the mining sector. Under the previous administration, gold miners were required to sell their product to the Reserve Bank of Zimbabwe. As the Bank's foreign currency reserves dwindled, it reportedly ceased to pay miners for the gold, and many of the country's gold mines closed. With current gold prices strong, the new government is now allowing the mines to market their own gold and accept payment in foreign currency. It has also cut the tax on gold export revenues.

Illegal Mining

The Zimbabwe government has taken steps to crackdown on illegal mining, although some suggest that members of ZANU-PF may be complicit. Police arrested an estimated 20,000 illegal miners in late 2006, including several hundred reportedly legal small-scale miners, confiscating gold, diamonds, emeralds, and gold ore. Since the collapse of the formal economy, many of the country's unemployed have resorted to illegal mining, selling their goods on the black market. According to reports, most of the miners were released after paying fines.

"Blood Diamonds"?

The World Diamond Council (WDC), a diamond industry organization that aims to prevent the trade of conflict diamonds, raised concerns in December 2008 that rough diamonds from Zimbabwe were being exported illegally, rather than through the Kimberly Process (KP), an international government certification scheme designed to prevent the "blood diamond" trade. According to civil society reports, Zimbabwean soldiers in the Marange diamond fields are forcing villagers to labor in the mines and then smuggling the stones from the country [123].

Rough stones from Zimbabwe have reportedly been confiscated in India and Dubai. The European Union pressed for an investigation into Zimbabwe's compliance with its Kimberly obligations in early 2008, and a high level KP delegation visited Zimbabwe in March to express the group's concern with reports of violence and smuggling from the Marange area. The KP Secretariat refrained from suspending Zimbabwe from the certification scheme, however [124].

The Kimberly Process had previously investigated allegations that "blood diamonds" from the Democratic Republic of Congo (DRC) were being smuggled along with rough stones from Zimbabwe into South Africa for export. The Mugabe government dismissed those claims as a western attempt to promote regime change. Zimbabwe has been previously linked to conflict diamonds; senior officials were named in a 2003 U.N. report for profiting from illicit trade during Zimbabwe's military operations in the DRC [125]

"Look East" Policy

Blaming the United States, the United Kingdom, and other western governments for the country's economic crisis, President Mugabe has sought to engender investment and trade opportunities with Asia, particularly China. Dubbed the "Look East" policy, Mugabe's efforts have been criticized by his own party as insufficient to address the economy's slide.

In December 2006, the Parliamentary Portfolio Committee on Budget, Finance, and Economic Development, chaired by a ZANU-PF MP, accused the central bank governor of exacerbating inflation with "quasi-fiscal activities" and warned the administration that "the Far East destinations be viewed as a market in its infancy and that the traditional market of the West should not be neglected as the nation moves toward regularizing relations with the international community" [126]

The Military and the Economy

Critics contend that President Mugabe has bought the continued loyalty of the country's security forces through patronage and bribery [127]. Some observers suggest that loyalty of the security forces may have come at a heavy cost to the economy. In 2006, the government reportedly spent more than $20 million to purchase new cars for police, military and intelligence officers. The security forces and civil service also reportedly received an almost 300% pay raise to counter record desertion rates. Observers continue to speculate on how the government has paid for its military purchases from China, including a reported $240 million in fighter jets.

In addition to allegations of land and housing handouts to security personnel, critics of the government highlight a significant number of current and former military officers who have been appointed to civilian government positions. Mugabe previously placed current or former military officers in control of the Ministries of Energy and Industry, the Zimbabwe Revenue Authority (in charge of tax collection), the electoral commission, the state railway, the Grain Marketing Board, and the parks authority, and several have served in the Senate and ambassadorial posts abroad. Several of these individuals still hold these offices.

As the economy continues to collapse, there have been signs that the government may be running out of funds to maintain its security forces. During a parliamentary hearing in mid-2007, the Defense Secretary reportedly suggested that soldiers were dissatisfied with their low salaries and that the forces were running out of food and might have to suspend training if new funds were not released [128]. Later that month, Zimbabwean intelligence officials reportedly uncovered a coup plot led by several senior military officials. Unconfirmed reports suggest that as many as 400 members of the army, air force, and police may have been involved in the plan, which allegedly aimed to remove Mugabe and to install Emmerson Mnangagwa as president. Mnangagwa, who has reportedly long sought to succeed Mugabe, denied any knowledge of the plot. Other sources suggest Vice President Joice Mujuru and her husband were behind the coup attempt and used Mnangagwa's name to discredit him. Neither Mnangagwa nor the Mujurus were officially accused of involvement, although some reports suggest Solomon Mujuru may have been placed under house arrest for a limited time [129]. More recently, in November 2008, soldiers looted Harare stores after they were unable to access their paychecks.

International Perspectives

The international community has been divided on how to respond to Zimbabwe's persistent crises. In general, Western nations and institutions have expressed opposition to Robert Mugabe's methods of rule, and have pursued policies intended to pressure the Zimbabwe government for reforms. In contrast, Mugabe has enjoyed some sympathy in Africa, where he is viewed as an elder statesman and a leader of the anti-colonial struggle, and among the Non-Aligned nations generally. This has changed to an extent in recent years, however, with some African leaders concluding that the Zimbabwe situation is damaging to Africa's interests and that political and economic reforms are needed. Nevertheless, African countries supported Zimbabwe in its successful bid to chair the United Nations Commission on Sustainable Development in 2007, allegedly to show African solidarity against Western opposition. AU member states were unable to come to a conclusion on how to address Zimbabwe's political situation at the 2008 AU Summit in Egypt, despite election observer reports from the AU, SADC, and the Pan-African Parliament finding that the June runoff was not free or fair.

The international donor community has generally expressed support for the new coalition government, but has predicated significant assistance on improvement in the following areas:

the immediate release of all political prisoners;
the end of farm disruptions;
the cessation of politically motivated violence;
the establishment of a credible and transparent Reserve Bank team;
an end to harassment and intimidation of the media;
and a commitment of all stakeholders to holding credible elections in a timely manner [130]

U.S. Policy

The United States has been critical of the ZANU-PF government for its poor human rights record and lack of respect for the rule of law. Key elements of U.S. policy toward Zimbabwe have included targeted sanctions against high-ranking ZANU-PF members and their affiliates, support for South Africa to spearhead an African effort to restore democracy, and assistance intended to help the country's poor and strengthen civil society. Former Secretary of State Condoleezza Rice told the Senate Foreign Relations Committee during her 2005 confirmation hearing, that Zimbabwe was one of six "outposts of tyranny" worldwide and that the United States stood with the oppressed people there [131]. These remarks provoked an angry personal response from Mugabe [132]. Another State Department official was similarly critical, suggesting that Zimbabwe "has now become a textbook case of bad and illegitimate government" [133] Prior to the formation of the unity government, the new Secretary of State, Hillary Rodham Clinton, told the Senate in January 2009 that "the suffering inflicted on the Zimbabwean people by the illegitimate government of Robert Mugabe is appalling." Under her leadership, the State Department has cautiously welcomed the new government but warned, "we will not consider providing additional development assistance or even easing sanctions until we see effective governance" [134]

Sanctions

The Mugabe administration has routinely blamed its economic crisis on sanctions from the west. The United States does not currently have trade sanctions against Zimbabwe, with the exception of a ban on transfers of defense items and services to the country. The U.S. government has, however, frozen all non-humanitarian government-to-government aid [135]. Zimbabwe is not eligible for trade benefits under the African Growth and Opportunity Act (AGOA) because and its poor record of economic management and human rights abuses.

The White House has annually renewed U.S. sanctions against ZANU-PF leaders. The sanctions are intended to punish those responsible for Zimbabwe's difficulties without harming the Zimbabwe population at large. The initial sanctions, imposed in 2003, ban travel to the United States by "senior members of the government of Robert Mugabe and others ... who formulate, implement, or benefit from policies that undermine or injure Zimbabwe's democratic institutions or impede the transition to a multi-party democracy." Persons who benefit financially from business dealings with such individuals are also banned, as are the spouses of people in either group. In 2003, President Bush issued an executive order freezing assets held in the United States by 75 high-ranking Zimbabwe officials and Mugabe's wife, Grace [136]. Nine firms and farms were added in 2004, and the list was further expanded in November 2005 to block the assets of 128 individuals and 33 entities. The executive order also allows the Secretary of the Treasury, in consultation with the Secretary of State, to go beyond previous authority and block the property of additional persons who "have engaged in actions or policies to undermine Zimbabwe's democratic processes or institutions," their immediate family members, and any persons assisting them [137]. President Bush added additional names to the list in December 2007 and November 2008. President Obama renewed the sanctions in March 2009.

Congressional Response

Congress made clear its opposition to Robert Mugabe's policies in the Zimbabwe Democracy and Economic Recovery Act of 2001 (P.L. 107-99), which criticized "economic mismanagement" and "undemocratic practices" in Zimbabwe. This legislation called for consultations with allies on economic sanctions and a travel ban. In the 109th Congress, the U.S. House of Representatives passed H.Res. 409 in December 2005, condemning Operation Murambatsvina, which the resolution termed a "humanitarian disaster that has compounded the country's humanitarian food and economic crises." The resolution also called on the U.N. and African regional bodies to investigate the impact of the demolitions and requested that the Administration use its influence to advocate further action by the IMF against the Zimbabwean government. Senator Russ Feingold (D-WI) introduced S.Amdt. 1254, which was included in the final version of the FY2006 foreign operations appropriations bill (P.L. 109-102). This amendment provided \$4 million for democracy and governance activities in Zimbabwe. The Senate Foreign Relations Subcommittee on African Affairs held a hearing on Zimbabwe's political and economic crisis in June 2001. The Senate Foreign Relations Committee held its most recent hearing on Zimbabwe in July 2008. The House Foreign Affairs Subcommittee on Africa has likewise held hearings on challenges to democracy in Zimbabwe: in June 2000, February 2002, and April 2005.

The 110th Congress was active on Zimbabwe. On April 17, 2007, the House of Representatives passed H.Con.Res. 100, sponsored by Representative Tom Lantos, condemning the Zimbabwean government's recent actions against opposition and civil society activists. In June 2007, the Senate passed parallel legislation, S.Con.Res. 25, introduced by then-Senator Barack Obama. Former Senator Hillary Rodham Clinton introduced S. 1500, the Support for Democracy and Human Rights in Zimbabwe Act of 2007, which would have authorized up to \$10 million to support democracy and human rights programs in the country.

Several Members of Congress issued statements highly critical of the Mugabe Administration surrounding the 2008 elections and the ongoing political violence. Some wrote letters to Bush Administration officials or African leaders. On April 25, the Senate passed S.Res. 533, introduced by Senator John Kerry, calling for the immediate release of the presidential results, an end to the political violence and intimidation, and a peaceful transition to democratic rule. The resolution also supported calls for an international arms embargo and other targeted sanctions against the Mugabe regime, and encouraged the creation of a comprehensive political and economic recovery package in the event a democratic government is installed. The House passed H.Res. 1230, sponsored by Representative Donald Payne and all the House Members of the Congressional Black Caucus, among others, condemning the violence and calling for a peaceful resolution to the political crisis. H.Res. 1270, sponsored by Representative Ileana Ros-Lehtinen, was also passed, calling for an international arms embargo, urging the United Nations to deploy a special envoy to Zimbabwe and encouraging the parties to discuss the creation of a government of national unity. Prior to the June runoff, Representative Adam Schiff introduced legislation calling on the Zimbabwe government to postpone the election. Representative Tom Tancredo also introduced legislation, H.Con.Res. 387, calling for the United States to sever diplomatic ties with Zimbabwe. In the 111th Congress, Representative Ros-Lehtinen has introduced H.Res. 238, declaring the economic and humanitarian crisis in Zimbabwe to be a threat to international security.

U.S. Support for African Diplomacy

During President Bush's visit to South Africa in 2003, he praised the work of Thabo Mbeki as the "point man" in seeking a Zimbabwe solution. The statement suggested to some that the United States was stepping back from a lead role on the Zimbabwe issue and would accede to Mbeki's "quiet diplomacy" (see "South Africa" section, below) as the best means of achieving reform in Zimbabwe [138].

Mbeki reportedly assured President Bush at that time that he would be able to bring about talks between ZANU-PF and the MDC, which did not occur until 2007. In 2004, former U.S. Assistant Secretary of State for Africa Jendayi Frazer, who was Ambassador to South Africa at the time, called for the formation of a "coalition of the willing" to deal with Zimbabwe. Frazer reiterated South Africa's position of leverage, and insisted more needed to be done by African states to return Zimbabwe to democracy [139]

U.S. Assistance

The United States remains the leader in humanitarian relief aid to the Zimbabwean people, supplying over $1 billion in assistance since 2002. That includes over $260 million in food aid and disaster assistance since October 2007. The U.S. government has provided over $7.3 million in FY2009 specifically to address the cholera outbreak. In addition to disaster aid, the United States provided $23.2 million in bilateral assistance for Zimbabwe in FY2007 and an estimated $22.9 million in FY2008. The State Department requested $45.4 million for FY2009. The Department's FY2008 Congressional Budget Justification (CBJ) noted that supplemental assistance would be requested if elections were held that resulted in the election of a "reform- minded" government [140]. Similar language was used in the FY2009 request, which states,

> If elections do not occur in 2008, or if elections continue the status quo, FY 2009 programming... will be reassessed to determine the most promising course to assist the democratic opposition to survive and to deepen its voice, thereby maintaining pressure on the GOZ to reform. Additionally, under a no-change scenario, the United States will promote a

continuing dialogue with domestic and regional audiences on economic mismanagement, political manipulation, and human rights abuses.

The Obama Administration has welcomed the establishment of the new coalition government, but has indicated that non-humanitarian assistance to the government would be predicated on progress toward political and economic reforms. Zimbabwe is not among the countries eligible to participate in the Millennium Challenge Account program, nor is it a focus country for the President's Emergency Plan for AIDS Relief. USAID has supported local democracy advocates in Zimbabwe through a variety of programs aimed at ensuring media freedom and strengthening civil society and the legislative process. USAID partners were reportedly instrumental in documenting the demolitions and human rights violations during Operation Murambatsvina and assisting in relief efforts. Legal restrictions continue to limit the ability of journalists and independent newspapers to provide alternative source for news, and the Zimbabwean government controls all domestic radio and television broadcasting stations. USAID provides funding for Voice of America to broadcast Studio 7, a daily program on shortwave and AM radio that USAID describes as "the principal source of independent electronic media in the country." Studio 7, along with UK-based Shortwave (SW) Radio Africa and the Dutch-funded Voice of the People (VOP) have had their broadcasts periodically interrupted by the ZANU-PF government using Chinese jamming equipment. The U.S. State Department warns that travelers suspected of having a "bias" against the government may be refused entry to Zimbabwe [141]. In 2006, a delegation of the U.S. Coalition of Black Trade Unionists (CBTU), led by AFL-CIO Vice President William Lucy, was expelled from the country. Then-U.S. Ambassador Christopher Dell said,

> Clearly, the Zimbabwe government's decision not to honor the delegation's visas is the result of the events of 13 September, when security forces brutally suppressed planned peaceful demonstrations by the Zimbabwe Congress of Trade Unions.... This transparent attempt to deflect international attention from the vicious beatings is itself an example of the Zimbabwean government's repression and of its fear of the truth.... There is increasing acknowledgment that a man who was regarded as a liberator of his people is an oppressor [142]

Other International Perspectives

United Kingdom

In 2002, in conjunction with the United States and the European Union, the British Parliament imposed targeted sanctions on leading members and affiliates of the ZANU-PF regime, as well an arms embargo and an asset freeze. The UK has imposed travel bans on over 100 members of the ZANU-PF and close affiliates of the party. Britain continues to provide humanitarian aid in Zimbabwe. Concurrently, the UK has maintained its willingness to release funds to Zimbabwe to pay for parts of an orderly land redistribution program if Mugabe retires and the rule of law is returned. With Mugabe remaining in office under the September 2008 power sharing agreement, it is unclear whether Britain will concede to release such funds. Mugabe was extremely hostile toward former British Prime Minister Tony Blair, a persistent critic. Speaking at his 81st birthday celebration, Mugabe said the upcoming election would "kill once and for all the machinations of that man in Number 10 Downing Street, who for some reason thinks he has the divine power to rule Zimbabwe and Britain. On March 31, we must dig a grave not just six feet but 12 feet and bury Mr. Blair and the Union Jack" [143]. Current Prime Minister Gordon Brown has maintained his predecessor's position, boycotting the December 2007 EU-Africa Summit to protest Mugabe's attendance. In an April 2008 speech to the House of Commons, British Prime Minister Gordon Brown called for an international arms embargo against Zimbabwe, accusing the government of rigging the March elections and calling the political situation "completely unacceptable." Britain's Queen Elizabeth stripped Mugabe of an honorable Knighthood he received in 1994.

European Union

The European Union was among the first to take action against Mugabe's government. The EU imposed targeted sanctions on 19 members of Zimbabwe's elite and their spouses after pulling the EU election observer team out of Zimbabwe in February 2002. These "light" sanctions were upgraded by the EU to target 35 Zimbabwean leaders, and have been renewed yearly, with new names added in January 2009. Current EU sanctions include a travel ban on over 160 members and beneficiaries of the ZANU-PF, an arms embargo, and an asset freeze. Mugabe defied the travel ban in 2005 to attend the funeral of Pope John Paul II. The EU continues to provide humanitarian assistance to benefit Zimbabwe's poor.

Commonwealth

The Commonwealth of Nations sent a team of observers to the March 2002 presidential election in Zimbabwe, and the group found "that the conditions in Zimbabwe did not adequately allow for the free expression of the will of the electors" [144]. Consequently, a special committee appointed to monitor and respond to the vote, consisting of Australia, South Africa and Nigeria, determined that Zimbabwe would be suspended from the Commonwealth for one year. The suspension was the first public action against Mugabe by a body that included influential African countries. In December 2003, the Commonwealth, including 19 other African members, voted to suspend Zimbabwe indefinitely. On this occasion, the decision was strongly criticized by South Africa's President Mbeki, who had by then committed to his policy of quiet diplomacy, and by other governments in southern Africa. Mugabe responded by withdrawing Zimbabwe from the Commonwealth and ruling out any further discussions or a possible return.145 Some speculated, as a result, that the Commonwealth's action had backfired by placing Zimbabwe fully outside the bounds of its influence. Others argued that indefinite suspension by a body including many African members had important symbolic value in Africa and worldwide.

China and Iran

While many western governments moved to isolate the ZANU-PF government in the last decade, China and Iran strengthened ties and deepened their involvement in Zimbabwe's economy. China, which became active on the continent in the 1950s and 1960s to gain global influence, now looks to Africa for natural resources to meet the needs of its growing population. A longtime ally of ZANU-PF, which it backed during the liberation struggle, China is reported to be Zimbabwe's second largest trading partner and its largest investor.146 Many observers see Zimbabwe's platinum concessions as a major draw for Beijing, and

Chinese firms are playing roles in the cell phone industry, as well as in television, radio, and power generation. China holds controlling interest in the country's only electricity generator.

Some critics worry China's investment in Zimbabwe comes without the "strings attached" that Western governments might require, such as commitments to human rights, accountability, and anti-corruption. Arms agreements between China and Zimbabwe have attracted considerable attention in recent years, as most Western governments continue to enforce an arms embargo against the country. Zimbabwe's $240 million purchase of twelve Chinese fighter jets has drawn questions from analysts as to why a country that faces no immediate external threat from its neighbors would need such an air force [147]. Reports indicate that Zimbabwe also ordered riot gear, water cannons, armored vehicles, and AK-47 rifles from China. How impoverished Zimbabwe could pay for arms from China is a subject of much speculation; Defense Ministry officials have admitted to being in arrears for the 2005 arms purchases. Some observers suspect that the acquisitions are covered in some way by China's growing economic role in Zimbabwe [148]

In the face of Western condemnation and isolation, Zimbabwe also found an ally in Iran. During a 2006 visit to Tehran, President Mugabe reportedly secured commitments from Iran for direct aid and Iranian assistance to its energy, agriculture, and mining industries. Reports indicate that Iran or one of the Gulf countries may also provide technical assistance to Zimbabwe to revive the country's only oil refinery, built 40 years ago to process Iranian crude. Most of Zimbabwe's fuel comes by road from South Africa; the country has insufficient foreign currency to import fuel in bulk through a pipeline from the nearest port, Beira, Mozambique to Zimbabwe.

In spite of Mugabe's assurances of Iranian assistance, some observers suggest Iran may not have met his expectations. Despite an agreement signed by the two countries in 2005, little financial assistance appears to have been provided. As one economic advisor points out, "At the end of the day, whether its China or Iran, investors want one thing: a return on their investment and they do not seem to believe they can get that return (from Zimbabwe)."149 Likewise, Mugabe, traveling to Beijing in 2005 to request assistance to deal with the country's foreign exchange shortfall and fuel shortage, received only $6 million for grain imports reportedly because Zimbabwe was deemed unworthy of significant investment [150]. Although Mugabe did secure a $200 million buyer credit loan from China to promote agricultural production (reportedly the largest loan to Zimbabwe since western donors ceased lending), China dismissed reports that the countries were negotiating a much larger $2 billion loan to revive the country's flagging economy [151]

In addition to investment and economic assistance, Zimbabwe's Asian partners have offered diplomatic support. A Chinese official visiting in 2004 said that his government "appreciates the reasons for the land issue" and was opposed to any interference by foreign governments [152]. China played a lead role in trying to quiet U.N. efforts to condemn Zimbabwe for Murambatsvina, and has vetoed proposed sanctions against the Mugabe Administration by the Security Council. Iranian President Mahmoud Ahmadinejad expressed support during Mugabe's visit, saying "We believe Zimbabweans have every right to defend their sovereignty and land. We are happy that Zimbabwe has once again taken control over its resources and we support the land redistribution programme ... We strongly condemn the bullying tactics of a number of (Western) governments against Zimbabwe" [153]

Nigeria

Although an observer team from Nigeria endorsed the 2002 presidential election in Zimbabwe, Nigeria's former president, Olusegun Obasanjo, attempted to mediate the country's crisis. He was reportedly concerned about the consequences of the Zimbabwe situation for the credibility of the New Partnership for Africa's Development (NEPAD). NEPAD is an initiative aimed at demonstrating Africa's capabilities for resolving its own problems in exchange for increased aid, trade, and investment [154]. Obasanjo supported Zimbabwe's suspension from the Commonwealth, and in 2004, he held a long discussion with Tsvangirai and an MDC delegation in the Nigerian capital. The Nigerian leader then took the Zimbabwe visitors on a personal tour of his farm—an unusual privilege [155]. After the 2005 elections, Obasanjo met again with Tsvangirai, and the government-owned Herald newspaper accused the Nigerian president of funding the MDC [156]. The country's new president, Umaru Yar'Adua, expressed his own concern with the situation in Zimbabwe, telling journalists at a German-African summit in October 2007 that developments in the country were "not in conformity with the rule of law" [157]

South Africa

Former President Thabo Mbeki's "quiet diplomacy" toward Zimbabwe drew criticism from some for its slow pace, although both sides credit Mbeki with playing a critical role in the September 2008 power sharing agreement. Some analysts point out that his reluctance to openly confront or condemn President Mugabe is understandable on a number of grounds. Mugabe lent aid and shelter to the African National Congress (ANC), now the ruling party in South Africa, during its long struggle against white minority rule, creating a bond of gratitude. Mugabe has enjoyed considerable popularity around Africa and in South Africa itself, not least because of his moves to seize lands owned by comparatively wealthy white farmers.

Nonetheless, many have been dissatisfied that South Africa, which is immensely more powerful than neighboring Zimbabwe, and which has extensive control over Zimbabwe's transport links to the outside world, as well as over its electricity supplies, has not been able to improve the Zimbabwe situation more quickly. As Zimbabwe's largest trading partner, many consider South Africa in a position to exert substantial leverage. At the same time, South Africa must weigh the unintended effects of such leverage—state collapse across its northern border could produce a sharp increase in illegal migration and have a substantial impact on South Africa. Some estimate that over three million Zimbabweans have fled into the country [158] In May 2008, Zimbabwean and other African immigrants became targets of xenophobic violence throughout South Africa. At least 60 were killed.

Through his policy of engagement, President Mbeki repeatedly brought the Zimbabwean government and the MDC together to discuss Zimbabwe's future. Mbeki's offer of economic incentives and an exit strategy for Mugabe in exchange for negotiations with the opposition and a commitment to free and fair elections have been unsuccessful until recently. In 2005, as the IMF threatened to expel Zimbabwe from the Fund for debt payment arrears, the country requested a loan from South Africa for fuel, food, and electricity, as well as to address the IMF payments. Amid rumors that the South African government would make any loan conditional on economic and political reforms, the negotiations stalled and Mugabe found another source from which to repay the IMF dues [159]. In early 2006 speech, Mugabe warned Mbeki that he should "keep away" from interference in Zimbabwe's affairs.

Mbeki's Zimbabwe policies drew criticism from within his country; former President Nelson Mandela, Nobel laureate Archbishop Desmond Tutu, former opposition leader Tony Leon, and even the ANC's ally, the Congress of South African Trade Unions (COSATU), have been vocal detractors. COSATU, South Africa's powerful labor confederation, strongly opposed the quiet diplomacy policy. A certain sympathy on the part of COSATU toward the MDC may be inevitable, since the MDC has its roots in the union movement. COSATU delegations have been forcibly expelled from Zimbabwe twice, first in 2004 and more recently in late 2006, when COSATU members traveled to Harare to express their support for the ZCTU after the incidents of police violence. One COSATU leader remarked, "we are not quiet diplomats," and "we will not keep mum when freedom does not lead to respect for workers and human rights" [160]. When the Mbeki government issued a terse initial statement following the March 2007 arrest of MDC and civil society activists, COSATU criticized the government for a "disgraceful" response, "in the face of such massive attacks on democracy and human rights, especially coming from those who owed so much to international solidarity when South Africans were fighting for democracy and human rights against the apartheid regime." [161].

Defenders of Mbeki's approach have argued that he is the only leader with the influence and prestige needed to sway Mugabe [162]. Some observers expressed hope for Mbeki's mediation role when the President and Morgan Tsvangirai met in October 2004, after Tsvangirai's acquittal. Tsvangirai, who had been critical of quiet diplomacy in the past, said after the meeting that he welcomed President Mbeki's efforts to mediate [163]. But Mbeki stunned the MDC and many supporters of democracy in Zimbabwe in March 2005, when he told a press conference that he had "no reason to think that anyone in Zimbabwe will militate in a way so that the elections will not be free and fair." He insisted that "there will be a free and fair election in Zimbabwe" and that "things like access to the public media, things like violence-free election have been addressed" [164]. Earlier, he had termed Secretary Rice's description of Zimbabwe as an outpost of tyranny as "an exaggeratio." [165]. These remarks left critics questioning the substance behind Mbeki's diplomacy.

The future of South Africa's policy toward Zimbabwe may be determined by Mbeki's successor, should the power sharing agreement falter. Mbeki, who resigned in late September 2008, has been temporarily succeeded by ANC Deputy President Kgalema Motlanthe. Former Deputy President Jacob Zuma, among the possible candidates to represent the ANC in the next elections, was elected as president of the ANC in December 2007 [166]. Zuma has referred to the Zimbabwean president as "a monster," and although he did not call for Mbeki to step down as mediator after the 2008 elections, he did encourage African leaders to "assist" Mbeki, "given the gravity of the situation" [167]. The Congress of the People (COPE) party, which emerged in late 2008 as a possible rival to the ANC's electoral dominance in the 2009 elections, has encouraged strong action on Zimbabwe. Prior to the coalition government's formation, COPE's leadership took the position that Zimbabwe's neighbors should withhold commodities to encourage reforms in the country [168]

The African Union

The African Union (AU) and its predecessor, the Organization of African Unity (OAU), have been supportive of Mugabe in the past. In 2002, an OAU observer team labeled Mugabe's election victory legitimate, free, and fair. In 2004, when the AU allowed a report critical of the Mugabe government to be circulated at its annual summit, some believed the regional body might be indicating a change in its approach. The 114-page report, prepared by a delegation from the African Commission for Human and People's Rights (ACHPR) that visited Zimbabwe in 2002, reportedly criticized the Zimbabwe government for police abuses, press censorship, and compromising the judiciary [169]. The AU tabled the report at the summit, however, and declared it would keep its contents secret until Zimbabwe has had a chance to respond in detail. According to some media reports, the Zimbabwean government used procedural regulations and technicalities to prevent its release [170]. The ACHPR passed a resolution in 2005 calling on the "government of Zimbabwe to respect the fundamental rights and freedoms of expression" and to allow a second fact-finding mission to enter the country. The ACHPR resolution was hailed by human rights advocates, who suggested, "This will exert a lot of pressure on Zimbabwe - this is the first time such a significant body, so close to African heads of state, observes and condemns such defiance of human rights compliance" [171] But like the previous report, the second mission's findings were rejected by the AU's Council of Ministers because of "irregularities and procedural flaws." [172].

Some observers and international human rights organizations such as the International Press Institute (IPI), suggest that the AU's repeated rejection of ACHPR resolutions on Zimbabwe tarnished the integrity of the body. As one AU official warned, "If we continue to throw out every human rights report that comes before us, people out there will stop taking us seriously" [173]. IPI also suggests that refusal of the AU to act on the ACHPR resolutions or to condemn human rights abuses in Zimbabwe damages the credibility of the African Peer Review Mechanism (APRM) initiative, a vital part of the New Partnership for Africa's Development (NEPAD) [174]

Should ZANU-PF fail to abide by the terms of the power sharing agreement, criticism from the AU may have little effect, unless it is accompanied by more substantial policy changes toward Mugabe's administration. The government has routinely ignored its detractors and has frequently denied those who might be critical of the regime access to the country. In 2005, AU Commission Chairman Alpha Konare sent Tom Nyanduga, Special Rapporteur on Refugees, Internally Displaced Persons, and Asylum Seekers in Africa, as his envoy to investigate Operation Murambatsvina. The Zimbabwean government prevented Nyanduga from conducting his assessment and deported him, accusing the envoy of "western collusion and agenda adoption" [175]. More recently, in November 2008, the government reportedly rejected the visa applications of several members of the Elders, a group of senior world leaders, including Kofi Annan and former U.S. President Jimmy Carter.

SADC

Many of the 14 members of the Southern African Development Community (SADC) are linked to Zimbabwe by a common historical experience, as well as cultural and economic ties, and the organization has been seen as disinclined to condemn the actions of President Mugabe's government. At its August 2004 summit in Mauritius, SADC approved new electoral principles and guidelines for all its member nations.176 Analysts were hopeful that these rules might motivate meaningful democratic reforms in Zimbabwe, particularly since they laid out detailed guidelines for SADC observer missions [177]. The signatory countries, including Zimbabwe, are pledged to allow SADC observers freedom of movement and access. As noted above, the SADC observer delegation's favorable report for Zimbabwe's 2005 elections was considered by critics of the Mugabe administration to be disappointing.

Although Mugabe's neighboring leaders have not singled him out for criticism, with the exception of Botswana, they have been increasingly concerned with the impact of Zimbabwe's crisis on their own countries. Southern African leaders blamed Zimbabwe and Swaziland for undermining economic growth in the region at a SADC Summit in Lesotho in 2006. Botswana has spoken out in the past on regional problems attributed to Mugabe's policies, including the burden placed on the country by Zimbabwe's refugees. In March 2007, following the arrest of Tsvangirai and other opposition members, Tanzanian President Jakaya Kikwete traveled to Harare to discuss the incident, and after the SADC summit, President Mbeki was nominated as mediator. SADC's election observer mission to the June 2008 runoff found that the election "did not represent the will of the people of Zimbabwe," and called for dialogue among all political stakeholders toward a negotiated solution [178]. Botswana refused to recognize Mugabe as President after the June 2008 runoff.

Pressure from SADC does appear to have brought the Zimbabwe parties to join together in the new coalition government, but it remains unclear to what extent they might be willing to enforce the deal if the parties cannot work together. At a regional summit in late March 2009, SADC approved an $8 billion plan for Zimbabwe's economic recovery, including $2 billion for short- term recovery projects. Member states are still determining what portion of that assistance they might provide, but many expect the regional body to appeal to foreign donors for much of the total. South Africa will reportedly provide the Zimbabwe government with credit lines.

Prospects for the Future

Despite hopes that the new coalition government may bring change to Zimbabwe, life for many of the country's people remains a daily struggle. The cost of living remains high, and access to foreign currency is extremely limited. In the near term, the country's agriculture industry shows little sign of recovery. The issues of property rights and land reform will be among the most difficult for the government to address. Prospects for Zimbabwe's youngest generation remain poor. Primary school attendance has reportedly dropped dramatically since 2000, and the cost of school fees has risen exponentially. The provision of salary vouchers has brought many teachers back to work, but enticing the thousands who have left the country to return will be a major challenge. Many families are unable to afford basic food items, not to mention medicines or doctors. Analysts have cited a number of reasons for Zimbabwe's economic problems, including recurrent drought, difficulties encountered in implementing economic reforms, and industrial competition from comparatively cheap South African imports [179]. At the same time, analysts place considerable responsibility for Zimbabwe's problems on the policies adopted and actions taken by the government since 1997.

Zimbabwe is now at a critical juncture. Prior to the power sharing agreement, the government took some fiscal measures to reverse the economic downturn, but as hyperinflation continued to rise, they were largely ineffective. Although the MDC has taken control of the Ministry of Finance in the unity government, it remains unclear how effective the new Ministry's economic policies will be in reversing the downturn if foreign donors continue to withhold assistance for its recovery plans, estimated to require $5-8 billion. Many donor governments and institutions are reluctant to release such funds until they can determine whether the coalition government's establishment will result in changes to the policies which brought about sanctions in the first place. The MDC and ZANU-PF, longstanding political foes, must now demonstrate their willingness to work together to put the country's economy on the path toward recovery.

REFERENCES

[1] For further discussion of the 2008 elections, please see CRS Report RL34509, *Zimbabwe: The Power Sharing Agreement and Implications for U.S. Policy*, by Lauren Ploch.

[2] See, for example, Human Rights Watch, *All Over Again: Human Rights Abuses and Flawed Electoral Conditions in Zimbabwe's Coming General Elections,* Vol. 20, No. 2(A), March 2008, and International Crisis Group, "Zimbabwe: Prospects from a Flawed Election," *Africa Report No. 138*, March 20, 2008.

[3] The opposition officials were released into the custody of their lawyers days after the arrest. Two opposition officials who were arrested were later allowed to go to South Africa to receive medical treatment for their injuries. According to media reports, police initially refused to allow their departure, and another opposition official, Nelson Chamisa, was allegedly beaten at the airport when he tried to leave.

[4] "Zimbabwe 'A Sinking Titanic,'" *Financial Times,* March 22, 2007.

[5] "RSA Parliamentarians Urge Stronger Action Against Zimbabwe," *South African Press Association,* March 28, 2007.

[6] "Zimbabwe Crisis Deepens," *Voice of America*, April 6, 2007.

[7] "Mbeki Rejects Regime Change," *Financial Times,* April 2, 2007.

[8] See, for example, Solidarity Peace Trust, *Destructive Engagement: Violence, Mediation, and Politics in Zimbabwe*, Johannesburg, July 10, 2007.

[9] The government's allegations are outlined in reports produced by the Zimbabwe Republic Police, *Opposition Forces in Zimbabwe: A Trail of Violence* and *Opposition Forces in Zimbabwe: The Naked Truth, Volume 2,*available at http://www.moha.gov.zw/. The Zimbabwe Human Rights NGO Forum has refuted the government's claims in *At Best a Falsehood, At Worst, A Lie*, August 2007, available at http://www.hrforumzim.com.

[10] Press Statement of U.S. Department of State Spokesman Sean McCormack, "Zimbabwe: Civil Society Organization Beatings During President Mbeki's Visit," November 26, 2007.

[11] Barry Bearak, "Zimbabwe Opponent Criticizes Mbeki," *New York Times*, February 14, 2008.

[12] Text of report on Zimbabwean Radio, "Zimbabwe Ruling Party Endorses Mugabe Candidacy for 2008 Elections," *BBC Monitoring,* April 1, 2007.

[13] "Zimbabwe Ruling Party Accused of Manipulating Electoral Process," *Voice of America*, April 18, 2007.

[14] "Mugabe Said Planning to Amend Constitution Over Possible Mid-Term Resignation," *Financial Gazette,* April 13, 2007.

[15] Dumisani Muleya, "Mugabe's Latest Survival Strategy," *Zimbabwe Independent,* April 6, 2007.

[16] See "First Poll Observers in Zimbabwe," *BBC*, March 11, 2008.

[17] "CNN Denied Permission to Cover Elections in Zimbabwe," *CNN*, March 25, 2008.

[18] The 2008 "harmonized" elections were held for all levels of government (local, National Assembly, Senate, and presidential) simultaneously.

[19] The ZEC declared that Tsvangirai had received 47.9% of the votes, while Mugabe received 43.2% and Makoni 8.3%.

[20] "Zim Prisons Chief Orders Officers to Vote Mugabe," *Reuters,* February 29, 2008.

[21] "Zimbabwe Rivals Sign Power-Sharing Deal," *Reuters*, September 15, 2008.

[22] Oxfam International, "Humanitarian Crisis in Zimbabwe," January 2009.

[23] UNAIDS, *Report on the Global AIDS Epidemic 2006*, and CIA, *CIA World Factbook.*

[24] The Washington-based Foreign Policy magazine uses 12 economic, social, political, and military indicators to rank countries in order of their "vulnerability to violent internal conflict and social dysfunction." Zimbabwe's ranking on the index dropped 14 points from 2005 to 2006, and two points since then, suggesting that the country's situation had deteriorated. For more information, see "The Failed States Index," *Foreign Policy*, July August 2008.

[25] "Imperialists Can't Preach Human Rights," *The Herald,* January 19, 2007.

[26] Jonathan Moyo, former Information Minister, left ZANU-PF and was elected as an independent candidate.

[27] *Reporters Without Borders*, "No Letup in Abusive Media Tactics Three Weeks Before Legislative Elections," March 8, 2005.

[28] Zimbabwe Human Rights NGO Forum, *Political Violence Report, March 2005.* The forum produces monthly reports on the human rights situation in Zimbabwe and assists victims of violence. See http://www.hrforumzim.com.

[29] Freedom House, "Country Report: Zimbabwe," *Freedom in the World 2006.*

[30] International Council of Barristers and Advocates, *The State of Justice in Zimbabwe*, December 2004. The Council sent an investigative team to Zimbabwe which included Chairmans of the Bar of England and Wales and the Irish Bar, and Vice Chairman of the South African Bar.

[31] Although none of the 2005 results were overturned, a 2006 Zimbabwean supreme court decision gave the opposition further legal recourse. Against the arguments of the chief justice, the attorney-general, and the justice minister, the court ruled that the judicial appointment of commissioners to the electoral court was unconstitutional and violated the principle of separation of powers. "Zimbabwe Court Rules 2005 Electoral Legislation 'Inconsistent' with Constitution," The Financial Gazette, July 27, 2006.

[32] The ZEC eventually halted the release of turnout totals, so it is unknown if there were discrepancies in other districts.

[33] ZESN, *Report on Zimbabwe's 2005 General Election,* April 2005. The ZESN, a coalition of 35 human rights and civic groups based in Zimbabwe, deployed 260 long-term observers and 6000 observers for the election itself.

[34] The report of the ZLHR,a local human rights organization that deployed 44 observers for the election, is available at http://www.zlhr.org.zw

[35] "Zimbabwe's Enabler; South Africa Falls Short as Monitor of Democracy," *Washington Post,* April 4, 2005.

[36] "The Real Fraud in Zimbabwe," *Washington Times*, April 6, 2005.
[37] The statement of Secretary Rice, made on April 1, 2005, is available online at http://www.state.gov/secretary/rm/ 2005/44141.htm.
[38] Secretary-General Annan's statement is available at http://www.un.org/ News/ossg/.
[39] MISA, *Annual Report, April 2003-March 2004*; "Media Institute Says Press Restrictions in Zimbabwe Rule Out Fair Elections," *Voice Of America (VOA)*, April 5, 2004.
[40] For the text of the POSA, see http://www.kubatana.net/docs/legisl/posa060203.doc.
[41] Solidarity Peace Trust, *Policing the State*, December 2006.
[42] "Title Deeds to 4,000 Farms Nullified," *The Herald,* September 23, 2005.
[43] Human Rights Watch, *All Over Again: Human Rights Abuses and Flawed Electoral Conditions in Zimbabwe's Coming Elections,* Vol. 20, No. 2(A), March 2008.
[44] Media Institute of Southern Africa, "AIPPA, POSA, BSA Amendments Signed into Law," *Media Alert Update*, January 12, 2008.
[45] "Rally Ban a Fatal Govt Assault on Social Contract," *Zimbabwe Independent,* March 2, 2007. The ban was lifted on June 29, 2007.
[46] "Zimbabwe Opposition Leader Taken to Hospital From Court," *CNN,* March 13, 2007, and "Mugabe Foes Vow to Intensify Action," *Washington Post,* March 13, 2007.
[47] "Zimbabwean Police 'Fire-Bombed,'" *BBC*, March 15, 2007.
[48] Statement of U.S. Secretary of State Condoleezza Rice, "Call for Immediate Release of Zimbabwean Opposition Leaders," on March 13, 2007.
[49] Statement issued by the Spokesman of the U.N. Secretary General on March 12, 2007.
[50] "Zimbabwe Leader Faces Growing Condemnation," *Associated Press,* March 15, 2007.
[51] Freedom House, "Country Report: Zimbabwe," *Freedom in the World 2006: The Annual Survey of Political Rights and Civil Liberties*.
[52] DOS, "Zimbabwe," *Country Reports on Human Rights Practices 2007*.
[53] See, for example, Amnesty International (AI), "Zimbabwe," *Annual Report 2007* and *Annual Report 2008*.
[54] "Threat by Mugabe," New York Times, August 16, 2006.
[55] See Mugabe's statement in an article from the government-owned newspaper, *The Herald* at "Zimbabwe Press Review for 25 Sep 06", *BBC Monitoring Africa,* September 25, 2006.
[56] "U.N. Slams President Mugabe," *Zimbabwe Independent,* September 29, 2006.
[57] The post of Rapporteur was created by the U.N. Commission on Human Rights in 1985 to investigate questions relating to torture. For information on the Rapporteur's mandate, see http://www2.ohchr.org/english/issues/torture/ rapporteur/index.htm.
[58] Zimbabwe Human Rights NGO Forum, *Political Violence Report,* December 2008.
[59] "Zimbabwe Leaders Accused of Abducting Opponents," *New York Times,* March 29, 2007.
[60] Human Rights Watch, *All Over Again: Human Rights Abuses and Flawed Electoral Conditions in Zimbabwe's Coming General Elections,* Vol. 20, No. 2(A), March 2008.
[61] Zimbabwe Human Rights NGO Forum, Political Violence Report, February 2009.
[62] For more information, see the Mission's report at http://www.icj.org

[63] The U.N. Special Envoy on Human Settlements Issues in Zimbabwe Anna Kajumulo Tibaijuka, *Report of the Fact- Finding Mission to Zimbabwe to Assess The Scope and Impact of Operation Murambatsvina,* July 2005.

[64] A survey by ActionAid International, a Netherlands-based international development agency, found that 840,000 were directly affected and 1.2 million indirectly affected, while a survey by the independent research firm Afrobarometer reported that an estimated 2.7 million were directly affected.

[65] ActionAid International, *The Impact of Operation Murambatsvina/Restore Order in Zimbabwe,* August 2005.

[66] Tibaijuka, 13.

[67] U.S. Committee for Refugees and Immigrants, "World Refugee Survey, Zimbabwe Country Report," 2003.

[68] DOS, "Zimbabwe," *Country Reports on Human Rights Practices 2005.*

[69] Tibaijuka, 34.

[70] "Clean Up Commendable," The Herald, May 23, 2005

[71] Ibid., 7.

[72] Ibid., 7.

[73] Ibid., 54.

[74] The Secretary-General's statement, made on July 22, 2005, is available online at http://www.un.org/apps/sg/ sgstats.asp?nid=1589.

[75] See, for example, Zimbabwe Human Rights NGO Forum , "Political Repression Disguised as Civic Mindedness: Operation Murambatsvina One Year Later," November 2006 and *Political Violence Report, October 2007.*

[76] U.N., *United Nations Consolidated Appeals Process (CAP) 2007,* July 2007.

[77] AI, "Zimbabwe: No Justice for the Victims of Forced Evictions," September 2006.

[78] The October 31, 2005 statement is available at http://www.un.org/ News/ossg/.

[79] AI, "Zimbabwe," *Annual Report 2007.*

[80] See the AI report; Solidarity Peace Trust, *Meltdown: Murambatsvina One Year On,* August 30, 2006.

[81] Institute of War and Peace Reporting, "Prosecution of Mugabe Urged," January 20, 2006.

[82] The United States is not party to the Rome Statute. For more information, see CRS Report RL31495, *U.S. Policy Regarding the International Criminal Court*, by Jennifer K. Elsea.

[83] For more information on the "Responsibility to Protect," see the *Report on the International Commission on Intervention and State Sovereignty*, which aims to "reconcil[e] the international community's responsibility to act in the face of massive violations of humanitarian norms while respecting the sovereign rights of states." The report is available at http://www.iciss.ca/report-en.asp.

[84] The IBA is comprised of Bar Associations and Law Societies around the world. The comments of its Executive Director can be found at http://www.ibanet.org/ iba/article.cfm?article=95.

[85] Tibaijuka, 76.

[86] See an excerpt from South-Africa based website ZimOnline in "Ex-Ethiopian Leader Said Behind Zimbabwe's Cleanup Operation," *BBC Monitoring Africa*, February 20, 2006.
[87] For more information on the region's food crisis, see CRS Report RS21301, *The Food Crisis in Southern Africa: Background and Issues*, by Charles E. Hanrahan.
[88] United Nations, *2006 CAP Mid-Year Review*, June 2006.
[89] ActionAid International, *The Impact of Operation Murambatsvina/Restore Order in Zimbabwe,* August 2005. This study suggests up to 54% of the country may have become food insecure as a result of Murambatsvina. A more recent USAID study also concluded that Murambatsvina and "more recent evictions " increased vulnerability, according to its "Zimbabwe—Drought and Complex Emergency Situation Report #2," Fiscal Year 2007.
[90] On the land takeovers in Zimbabwe, see AI, *Zimbabwe: Power and Hunger—Violations of the Right to Food*, October 15, 2004.
[91] "Zimbabwe: The Mother of All Farming Seasons," *IRIN*, October 25, 2007.
[92] Solidarity Peace Trust, *Operation Taguta/Sisuthi*, April 2006.
[93] AI, *Zimbabwe: Power and Hunger.*
[94] "Mugabe Word for Word," *Sky News*, May 24, 2004.
[95] AI, *Zimbabwe: Power and Hunger,* and USAID, *2004 Annual Report for the Office of Foreign Disaster Assistance (OFDA).*
[96] "ZANU-PF Admits Food Crisis," Institute for War and Peace Reporting (London), March 7, 2005; "10 More Die of Hunger in Bulawayo," Zimbabwe Standard, March 7, 2005; "14 More Die of Hunger in Bulawayo," *Zimbabwe Standard,* February 15, 2005.
[97] "Govt Delays Stall WFP Food Distribution," *Financial Gazette*, December 13, 2006.
[98] Reference to the rulings, made by Judges Nicholas Ndou and Rita Makarau, can be found in DOS, "Zimbabwe," *Country Reports on Human Rights Practices 2005.*
[99] "Zimbabwe Has Highest Percentage of Orphans in the World," *Associated Press*, December 6, 2006.
[100] UNAIDS, *AIDS Epidemic Update,* December 2007.
[101] Dr. Peter Piot, "Launch of the 2005 AIDS Epidemic Update," UNAIDS, November 21, 2005.
[102] ART figures are available at the website of the President's Emergency Plan for AIDS Relief (PEPFAR), http://www.pepfar.gov.
[103] Tibaijuka, 40.
[104] World Health Organization, "Cholera in Zimbabwe- Update 3," March 23, 2009.
[105] See, for example, Physicians for Human Rights, *Health in Ruins: A Man Made Disaster in Zimbabwe*, January, 2009.
[106] Solidarity Peace Trust, *An Account of the Exodus of a Nation's People*, November 2004.
[107] See, for example, Simon Robinson, "Great Leap Backwards," Time, May 29, 2005, and the World Bank's "Country Brief" on Zimbabwe, available at http://www.worldbank.org.
[108] IMF, *Regional Economic Outlook: Sub-Saharan Africa,* September 2006.
[109] "Gono's Mission Is to Save ZANU-PF, Not the Economy," *LiquidAfrica*, December 3, 2004.

[110] "Country is Committed to Uprooting All Forms of Corruption," *The Herald*, August 24, 2006.

[111] "Much Ado About Money," *IRIN,* August 18, 2006.

[112] "Bag of Bricks: Hyperinflation in Zimbabwe," *The Economist*, August 26, 2006, and "Zimbabwe: Millions no Longer Millionaires," *African Business,* October 2006.

[113] See, for example, "A Zimbabwean Businessman, His Farms Seized, Takes on Mugabe," *Washington Post,* February 24, 2006.

[114] "Mugabe's 82nd Birthday Blast at Zimbabwe," *Business Day*, February 21, 2006.

[115] IMF, Statement by IMF Managing Director Strauss-Kahn on Zimbabwe, Press Release No. 08/207, September 15, 2008.

[116] Tony Hawkins, "IMF Dampens Hopes of Aid to Zimbabwe," *Financial Times*, March 25, 2009.

[117] "In Reversal, Mugabe Seeks White Farmers," *UPI,* December 17, 2006.

[118]"Zimbabwe to Ration Electricity for Homes to Four Hours a Day," *Reuters*, May 10, 2007.

[119] "Power Cuts Halt Harare Factories," *Business Day*, October 29, 2007.

[120] "Mudzuri Says $1 Billion Needed to Revamp Energy Sector," SW Radio Africa, February 25, 2009.

[121] The largest mining operations in the country are controlled by Impala Platinum and Anglo Platinum, respectively. These South African-owned companies are the world's largest platinum producers.

[122] "Zimbabwe Clarifies Nationalization Legislation," *Financial Times*, March 11, 2008.

[123] World Diamond Council Press Release, "WDC Calls for Concerted International Action to Halt Theft of Natural Resources in Zimbabwe," December 10, 2008; "Soldiers are the New Illegal Diamond Miners," IRIN, January 20, 2009.

[124] Kimberly Process Certification Scheme Secretariat, "Public Statement on the Situation in the Marange Diamond Fields, Zimbabwe," March 2009.

[125] Zimbabwe is a signatory of the Kimberly Process. For more information, see CRS Report RL30751, *Diamonds and Conflict: Background, Policy, and Legislation*, by Nicolas Cook.

[126] "Zimbabwe: Parliamentary Body Urges State to 'Normalize' Trade Ties with West," *BBC Monitoring Africa*, December 8, 2006.

[127] "Militarization of State Firms Cause for Worry," *Zimbabwe Independent*, May 26, 2006.

[128] "Soldiers Go Hungry," *Financial Gazette*, May 23, 2007.

[129] "Army Investigates Reports of Coup Plot," *SW Radio Africa*, June 14, 2007.

[130] Remarks by the German Ambassador to Zimbabwe, Dr. Albrecht Conze, as referenced in "Getting Zimbabwe to Work Again," The *Zimbabwe Times,* March 29, 2009.

[131] "Rice Targets 6 'Outposts of Tyranny,'" *Washington Times*, January 19, 2005. The others were Cuba, Burma, North Korea, Iran, and Belarus.

[132] "Zimbabwe's Mugabe Lashes Out at Rice, Blair at Campaign Launch," *AFP*, February 11, 2005.

[133] Statement by Deputy Assistant Secretary of State for African Affairs Thomas Woods, "Zimbabwe a Textbook Case of Bad Governance, U.S. Official Says," February 28, 2005.

[134] Daily Press Briefing by State Department Spokesman Robert Wood, February 11, 2009.

[135] In 2006, Zimbabwe was found to bc in violation of crimes related to human trafficking and was subject to sanction under the Trafficking Victims Protection Act of 2000 (P.L. 106-386) for FY2007. In 2007, the State Department found that Zimbabwe was "making significant efforts" to combat trafficking, and Zimbabwe was moved from a "Tier 3" to a "Tier 2" designation. The "Tier 2" designation remained in 2008. A Tier 2 rating means that the government still does not meet the minimum standards for the elimination of trafficking, but is making significant efforts to do so. For more information, see U.S. Department of State, *Trafficking in Persons Report,* available at http://www.state.gov/g/tip.

[136] Seventy-seven individuals were named in the executive order (EO 13288), but one of these had died.

[137] The text of this annex to EO 13288 can be found at http://www.whitehouse.gov

[138] "Bush Backs Mbeki on Zimbabwe," *The Guardian* (London) July 10, 2003.

[139] "US Seeks 'Coalition' to Force Zimbabwe Regime Change," *The Independent* (UK), August 25, 2004.

[140] Department of State, FY2008 Foreign Operations Congressional Budget Justification.

[141] DOS's *Consular Information Sheet* for Zimbabwe is available at http://travel.state.gov/.

[142] "EU Demands Probe into Congress of Trade Union Attacks," *Zimbabwe Standard,* September 24, 2006.

[143] "Zimbabwe's Mugabe Marks 81st B*irthday With Attack on Opposition, Blair," AFP, February* 26, 2005.

[144] "Commonwealth Observer Group's Preliminary Report on Zimbabwean Presidential Elections," March 14, 2002. Available at http://www.afrol.com.

[145] "Mugabe Rules Out Zimbabwe's Return to the Commonwealth," *AFP*, December 16, 2003.

[146] "Beijing Quietly Cools Relations With Mugabe," *Financial Times*, June 5, 2007.

[147] Defense analysts describe the K-8 as a trainer jet with light ground attack capabilities. Zambia and Namibia have likewise purchased K-8s from China

[148] EIU, "The Government is to Buy More Jets from China," September 15, 2006.

[149] Excerpt from South Africa-based website ZimOnline in "Zimbabwe Leader 'Frantically' Seeking Allies," *BBC Monitoring Africa*, November 23, 2006.

[150] "China Aid 'Snub' to Enable South Africa to Extract Concessions from Zimbabwe," *BBC Monitoring Africa,* August 1, 2005.

[151] "Zimbabwe, China to Negotiate $2 Billion Dollar Loan Deal," AFP, December 22, 2006 and China and "Beijing Cools on Mugabe China in Africa," *International Herald Tribune*, May 4, 2007.

[152] "Chinese Envoy Supports Zimbabwe's Land Reforms," *AFP*, November 2, 2004.

[153] "Iran Slams Sactions Against Zim," *AllAfrica,* November 22, 2006.

[154] See CRS Report RS21353, *New Partnership for Africa's Development (NEPAD)*, by Nicolas Cook.

[155] September "Nigeria Rolls Out Red Carpet for Tsvangirai," *Zimbabwe Standard*, November 15, 2004.

[156] "The SA, Nigeria, and MDC Connection," *The Herald,* November 6, 2005.

[157] "Hotfoot from Harare," *Africa Confidential*, Vol. 48, No. 24, November 30, 2007.

[158] Michael Wines, "Influx from Zimbabwe to South Africa Tests Both," *New York Times*, June 22, 2007.

[159] "Zimbabwe Pays Part of IMF Debt," *Washington Post,* September 2, 2005.

[160] "We Are Not Quiet Diplomats," *Daily Mail and Guardian* (Johannesburg), November 5, 2004.

[161] "South Africa Ends 's 'Silence' on Zimbabwe, Urges Harare 'to Respect Rule of Law,'" *BBC Monitoring Africa*, March 14, 2007.

[162] ICG, *Zimbabwe: Another Election Chance*, 14.

[163] "Tsvangirai Changes Tune on Mbeki's Quiet Diplomacy," *Business Day*, October 29, 2004.

[164]"Mbeki Pays Tribute to Zimbabwe, Says Polls Will Be Free and Fair," *AFP*, March 2, 2005.

[165] "Mbeki Criticizes U.S Over Zimbabwe," *BBC*, February 22, 2005.

[166] For more information on challenges to a possible Zuma presidency, see CRS Report RL3 1697, *South Africa: Current Issues and U.S. Relations*, by Lauren Ploch.

[167] "I'm No Mugabe, but I Have Sympathy for What He Has Done," *The Sunday Telegraph* (London), November 26, 2006; "Africa Shows Impatience on Zimbabwe Crisis," Reuters, April 22, 2008. "Zuma Ratchets Up Rhetoric Over Zimbabwe," *Financial Times*, April 22, 2008.

[168]"More Pressure Builds on Mugabe to Step Down," SW Radio Africa, December 23, 2008.

[169] "AU Report Slams Erosion of Rule of Law," *Zimbabwe Independent*, July 16, 2004.

[170] "It's the Very Leaders Who Are Denying the People Their Justice," *Financial Gazette,* July 20, 2006.

[171] "African Union Slams Human Rights Record," *IRIN,* January 3, 2006.

[172] International Press Institute, "IPI Disappointed By African Union's Slow Progress in Criticizing Zimbabwe's Record on Human Rights, Press Freedom," April 4, 2006. IPI is a global network of editors, media executives and leading journalists in over 110 countries that promotes press freedoms and journalistic standards.

[173] "Mkapa Has a Long Shot at Moving 'Bad Boy' Mugabe," *AllAfrica*, August 25, 2006.

[174] For further information on the APRM and NEPAD, see CRS Report RS21353, *New Partnership for Africa's Development (NEPAD)*, by Nicolas Cook.

[175] "Harare Raps African Union Human Rights Body," *U.S. Fed News*, July 6, 2005.

[176] *SADC Principles and Guidelines Governing Democratic Elections* (Adopted by the SADC Summit, Mauritius, August 2004). Available at http://www.iss.co.za.

[177] ICG, *Zimbabwe: Another Election Chance*, 13.

[178] Preliminary Statement Presented by the Hon. Jose Marcos Barrica of the SADC Observer Mission, issued on June 30, 2008.

[179] Teddy Brett and Simon Winter, "Origins of the Zimbabwe Crisis," Focus (Helen Suzman Foundation), June 2003.

In: Economic, Political and Social Issues of Africa
Editor: Jeremy S. McQueen

ISBN 978-1-61209-957-6

Chapter 9

PIRACY OFF THE HORN OF AFRICA*

Lauren Ploch, Christopher M. Blanchard, Ronald O'Rourke, R. Chuck Mason and Rawle O. King

ABSTRACT

Recent attacks, including those on U.S.-flagged vessels, in the waters off the Horn of Africa have brought new U.S. and international attention to the long-standing problem of piracy in the region. The International Maritime Bureau recorded 111 attacks in the waters off the Horn of Africa in 2008, almost double the number in 2007. As of April 20, 2009, The International Maritime Bureau had counted 84 attacks since January: approximately 300 non-U.S. crew members on 18 hijacked vessels remain in Somali captivity. Previously concentrated in the Gulf of Aden between Yemen and the northern coast of Somalia and along the country's eastern coastline, attacks on merchant ships are now taking place over an area of more than 1 million sq. miles in the Gulf and the west Indian Ocean, posing a significant threat to commercial shipping. Pirate attacks also have threatened relief shipments bound for East Africa and the countries of the Horn, amid a humanitarian crisis in the region that experts are calling the worst since 1984.

The increase in pirate attacks off the Horn of Africa is directly linked to continuing insecurity and the absence of the rule of law in war-torn Somalia. The absence of a functioning government in Somalia remains the single greatest challenge to regional security and provides freedom of action for those engaged in piracy along the Somali coast. Some observers also have alleged that the absence of coastal security authorities in Somalia has allowed illegal international fishing and maritime dumping to occur in Somali waters, which in turn has undermined the economic prospects of some Somalis and may be providing economic or political motivation to some groups engaged in piracy. The apparent motive of many active Somali pirate groups is profit, and piracy has proven to be a lucrative activity for many thus far. Ransoms paid to Somali pirates and their supporters, estimated at over $30 million in 2008, may exacerbate ongoing fighting and further undermine security in the region.

---

* This is an edited, reformatted and augmented version of CRS Report R40528, dated April 21, 2009.

The U.N. Security Council issued four resolutions (1816, 1838, 1846, and 1851) in 2008 to facilitate an international response to piracy off the Horn of Africa. At present, Resolution 1851 has authorized international naval forces to carry out anti-piracy operations in Somali territorial waters and ashore, with the consent of Somalia's Transitional Federal Government (TFG). In January 2009, a multilateral Contact Group on Piracy off the Coast of Somalia (CGPCS) was established to coordinate antipiracy efforts. U.S., NATO, European Union, regional, and other naval forces are currently patrolling waters near Somalia in coordination with a U.S.-led Task Force.

Some members of the 111th Congress have expressed concern about the threat posed by piracy, and President Obama has stated that his Administration is resolved to halt the rise of piracy in the Horn of Africa region. On April 15, the Obama Administration outlined preliminary plans for a more robust policy response to the threat of piracy and pledged to continue working through multilateral coordination and enforcement mechanisms established during the Bush Administration. Most experts believe that the reestablishment of government authority in Somalia is the only guarantee that piracy will not persist or reemerge as a threat. Congress may seek to influence U.S. policy through oversight of U.S. military operations and diplomacy and through foreign assistance appropriations and authorizations. Also see CRS Report RL339 11, Somalia: Current Conditions and Prospects for a Lasting Peace, by Ted Dagne and CRS Report R4008 1, *Ocean Piracy and Its Impact on Insurance,* by Rawle O. King.

RECENT DEVELOPMENTS

On April 8, 2009, Somali pirates seized the U.S.-flagged commercial shipping vessel MV Maersk Alabama approximately 250 nautical miles south east of the Somali town of Eyl. Press reports suggest that the 20-member crew of U.S. citizens overtook their Somali captors some time after the ship was seized and attempted unsuccessfully to free the ship's captain, Vermont resident Richard Phillips. In response, the United States Navy dispatched the U.S.S. Bainbridge, [1] an Arleigh Burke-class destroyer, and reconnaissance aircraft to the area in order to monitor the small craft where Captain Phillips was being held. Federal Bureau of Investigation personnel worked with naval personnel to conduct hostage negotiations for the captain's release. On April 11, after officials determined that Phillips' life was in immediate danger, U.S. Special Forces mounted a successful rescue operation with the authorization of President Barack Obama. According to the International Maritime Bureau (IMB), as of April 15, approximately 300 nonU.S. crew members on 18 hijacked vessels remain in Somali captivity.

Three pirates were killed by snipers in the U.S. rescue operation; a fourth is now in U.S. custody and will face trial in the United States [2]. Since the beginning of 2009, over 130 pirates have been delivered to Kenyan judicial authorities for trial. Some analysts have expressed concern that the rescue operation could trigger the use of increasingly violent tactics in future pirate attacks.

A leader of the pirate group based in the town of Eyl who held Phillips reportedly vowed revenge, telling reporters that, "this matter will lead to retaliation and we will hunt down particularly American citizens travelling our waters. Next time we get American citizens... they [should] expect no mercy from us." An attack on a second U.S.-flagged vessel, the MV

Liberty Sun, on April 14 appeared to be an attempt by pirates to make good on that threat. A pirate leader told reporters after the Liberty Sun attack that, "We were not after a ransom. We also assigned a team with special equipment to chase and destroy any ship flying the American flag in retaliation for the brutal killing of our friends" [3].

The attack on the Alabama was one of several to occur during a recent resurgence in pirate activity in the west Indian Ocean, where Somali pirates have relocated some of their operations to avoid more robust international naval patrols to the north in the Gulf of Aden. Experts suggested that the higher volume of foreign patrols, bad seasonal weather, and a series of sizeable ransom payments in recent months contributed to a downward trend in pirate attacks in the region from December 2008 through early March 2009. However, a number of recent pirate attacks, including operations conducted hundreds of nautical miles from the Somali coast in the Indian Ocean, have underscored the persistent threat of piracy to international ships transiting the region's waters.

In response, on April 15, 2009, U.S. Secretary of State Hillary Clinton outlined the Administration's preliminary plans for developing a more robust anti-piracy policy. According to Secretary Clinton, U.S. diplomats will engage with Somali Transitional Federal Government (TFG) officials and leaders from the semi-autonomous region of Puntland in the Eyl district to "press these leaders to take action against pirates operating from bases within their territories." The Administration plans to send an envoy to attend an April 23 policy and donors conference on Somalia in Brussels and has called for immediate meetings of the international Contact Group on Piracy off the Coast of Somalia (see "Contact Group on Piracy off the Coast of Somalia" below). Lastly, U.S. officials plan to redouble efforts to work with the shipping and insurance industries "to address gaps in their self-defense measures." U.S. naval personnel have suggested that international security efforts will not be able to guarantee safe passage across the entire vast area of ocean in which the pirates are now operating and have emphasized the importance of finding a solution to the problem ashore.

To that end, the African Union voted in March 2009 to extend the mandate of their peacekeeping force in the country, known as the African Union Mission to Somalia (AMISOM), for three months while the United Nations Security Council continues to review a proposal to send a U.N. peacekeeping force to Somalia to replace AMISOM. AMISOM forces have come under attack in recent months from Islamist groups opposed to the presence of foreign troops in Somalia, including the Al Qaeda influenced group known as Al Shabaab. Meanwhile, a nascent unity government formed between the TFG and the Alliance for the Reliberation of Somalia (ARS) has returned to Mogadishu, and has elected ARS leader Sharif Sheikh Ahmed as its president.

Negotiations continue among the unity government participants and with opposition groups to determine the makeup of an expanded parliament. Elements of the ARS based abroad, as well as groups and factions in Somalia, have vowed to continue fighting against the new government, and violence has surged. The international Contact Group on Somalia continues to work on a multilateral basis to support Somali efforts to reach reconciliation agreements and implement the country's Transitional Federal Charter. The Obama Administration has requested $40 million in 2009 supplemental Peacekeeping Operations (PKO) funding to provide "non-lethal equipment, logistical support, and basing facilities for the African Union Mission to Somalia and to support Somali security sector reform." The Administration also is seeking authority to transfer up to $50 million in supplemental

Contributions for International Peacekeeping Activities (CIPA) funding to the PKO account for Somalia, if necessary. For more information about political developments in Somalia and U.S. policy, see CRS Report RL33911, Somalia: Current Conditions and Prospects for a Lasting Peace, by Ted Dagne.

On March 16, United Nations Secretary General Ban Ki-moon released his report to the Security Council required by Resolution 1846 on the security of international navigation off the coast of Somalia (S/2009/146). In January, the International Maritime Organization convened a meeting of 17 regional States, which adopted the Djibouti Code of Conduct concerning the Repression of Piracy and Armed Robbery against Ships in the Western Indian Ocean and the Gulf of Aden (see "International Maritime Organization and the Djibouti Code of Conduct" below).

BACKGROUND

Piracy has reemerged as a global security threat, most recently in the waters off the Horn of Africa, but also in West Africa, the waters off India, the South China Sea and the Strait of Malacca, and the Caribbean. Pirates tend to operate in regions with large coastal areas, high levels of commercial activity, small national naval forces, and weak regional security cooperation mechanisms. These characteristics facilitate other maritime security threats, including maritime terrorism, weapons and narcotics trafficking, illegal fishing and dumping, and human smuggling operations.

Worldwide rates of piracy began to increase in the early 1990s, peaked at roughly 350 to 450 reported attacks per year during the period 2000-2004, and then declined by almost half by 2005. In 2007, almost half of the world's reported pirate attacks took place in African waters, mainly near Nigeria and Somalia. The number of attacks in Somali waters doubled in 2008, accounting for an estimated 40 percent of the 293 pirate attacks reported worldwide [4]. The recent increase in pirate attacks off Somalia will cause the total number of worldwide pirate attacks to increase, but not necessarily back to the levels of 2000-2004. Nevertheless, recent high profile attacks in the Gulf of Aden and the west Indian Ocean have brought renewed international attention to the problem of piracy in waters off the Horn of Africa.

The U.S. National Maritime Security Strategy, issued in 2005, stated that the "safety and economic security of the United States depends upon the secure use of the world's oceans," and identified "well organized and well equipped" pirates and criminals as threats to international maritime security. The bombing of the U.S.S. Cole in 2000 in the Yemeni harbor of Aden and the bombing of the French oil tanker MV Limburg in 2002 illustrated the threat of potential maritime terrorism in the region, and the United States, working with its international partners, established a combined naval task force (Combined Task Force 1 50) [5] in addition to increasing bilateral military and security assistance to regional navies. However, until the establishment of Combined Task Force 151 (see "Combined Task Force 151") in 2008, the United States did not assign any naval forces the sole task of performing anti-piracy operations in the Horn of Africa region.

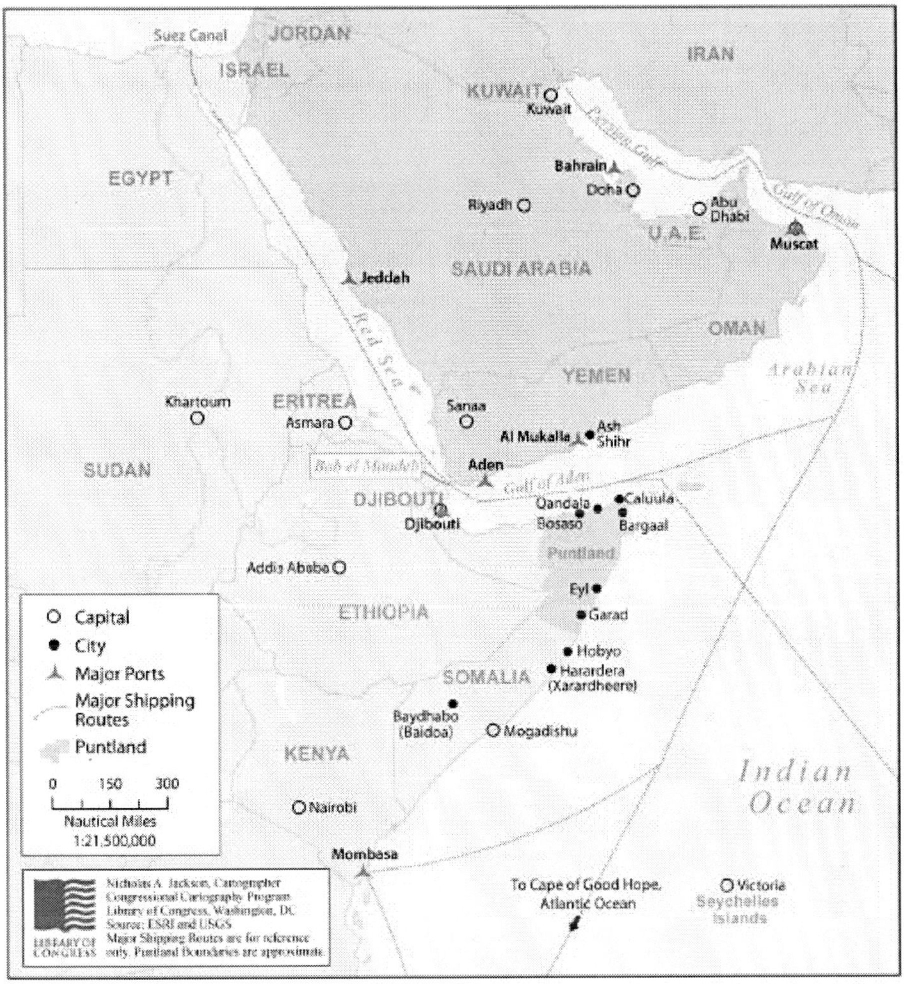

Source: Congressional Cartography Program, Library of Congress, adapted by CRS Graphics.

Figure 1. The Horn of Africa, Surrounding Waters, and Key Locations.

Similarly, until 2008, the international community did not respond to the threat of piracy in the waters off of Somalia in a coordinated, dedicated manner. In December 2008, the European Union launched EU NAVFOR Operation ATALANTA, representing the first naval operation under the framework of the European Security and Defence Policy (ESDP). The development of a collaborative regional response in East Africa in recent months has mirrored regional reactions to the threat of piracy in the Strait of Malacca between Malaysia, Singapore and Indonesia, which are credited with having drastically reduced the instance of piracy in Southeast Asia since 2005 (see "International Maritime Organization and the Djibouti Code of Conduct" below). Eradicating piracy in the Horn of Africa region may prove to be a more daunting task. The vast areas of the western Indian Ocean and the Gulf of Aden where the pirates operate are remote, Somalia remains largely ungoverned, and regional states have relatively weak naval capabilities.

Source: Congressional Cartography Program, Library of Congress, adapted by CRS Graphics.

Figure 2. Somalia Map.

Piracy off the Horn of Africa: Profile

The Pirates

Several groups of pirates currently operate in Somali waters, according to reports from the United Nations Secretary General and the experts group convened by the Secretary General's Special Representative for Somalia [6]. Organized predominantly along clan lines and based in distinct, remote port towns, the groups have varying capabilities and patterns of operation, making generalized responses more difficult. The two primary groups identified by the Secretary General in his March 2009 report were a pirate network based in the Puntland region district of Eyl and a pirate network based in the Mudug region district of Harardera (Xarardheere). The Secretary General and the Special Representative's experts group also report that smaller pirate groups also operate from the Somali ports of Bosaso, Qandala, Caluula, Bargaal, Hobyo, Mogadishu, and Garad [7]. The Secretary General has warned that some of the pirate groups "now rival established Somali authorities in terms of their military capabilities and resource bases."

The northern semi-autonomous region of Puntland appears to be home to the most active and capable pirate networks, and some regional and local government officials there are alleged to have facilitated and profited from piracy prior to recent efforts by regional leaders to crack down on piracy-related corruption. Puntland's regional authorities have developed a basic coast guard, but accounts suggest that the equipment and capabilities of this small force remain very limited. Several of the pirate groups have adopted names to suggest that they are acting in a maritime security capacity. Piracy also appears to have become an attractive pursuit for young men, creating potential legal complexities for regional and international governments seeking to try young pirate suspects for alleged crimes.

Motives

According to the final report of the experts group convened in November 2008 by U.N. Special Representative to Somalia Ahmedou Ould-Abdallah, "poverty, lack of employment, environmental hardship, pitifully low incomes, reduction of pastoralist and maritime resources due to drought and illegal fishing and a volatile security and political situation all contribute to the rise and continuance of piracy in Somalia." While the profitability of piracy appears to be the primary motivating factor for most pirates, other observers argue that since conditions in Somalia make survival difficult for many and prosperity elusive for most, the relative risk of engagement in piracy appears to have been lowered in many areas [8].

Somali pirates interviewed by international media sources frequently link their piracy activities to trends such as illegal fishing and dumping in Somali waters that have emerged as the country has lost its ability to patrol its waters over time.9 While these explanations may mask the opportunistic piracy of some, reports suggest that illegal fishing and dumping have disrupted Somalia's coastal economy. For example, a July 2005 report from the United Kingdom Department for International Development (DFID) estimated that Somalis lost $100 million to illegal tuna and shrimp fishing in the country's exclusive economic zone in 2003-2004 [10].

The international Contact Group on Piracy off the Coast of Somalia (CGPCS) (see "Contact Group on Piracy off the Coast of Somalia") stated at its inaugural meeting that "piracy is symptomatic of the overall situation in Somalia including the prevalence of illegal fishing and toxic waste dumping off the coast of Somalia, which adversely affects the Somali economy and marine environment" [11]. The CGPCS also reaffirmed "its respect for Somalia's sovereignty, territorial integrity, and sovereign rights over natural resources" and underscored that the group's participants "ensure that their flagged vessels respect these rights."

Paradoxically, the regional fishing industry reportedly has been damaged significantly by the threat of piracy. According to some reports, tuna catches in the Indian Ocean fell 30 percent in 2008, in part because of fishing vessels' fears of piracy. This has had a major impact on countries like the Seychelles, who rely on the fishing industry for up to 40 percent of their earnings [12].

The use of force by international naval patrols to apprehend or kill pirate suspects has raised the prospect that revenge may become a motivating factor for pirates whose associates are killed or captured. The April 14 attack on the U.S.-flagged MV Liberty Sun allegedly was carried out with the intention of damaging or sinking the ship and injuring or killing its crew in retaliation for the deaths of three Somali pirates during U.S. military efforts to secure the release of the detained captain of the MV Maersk Alabama days earlier [13]

Tactics and Demands [14]

As noted above, some Somali pirate groups have developed sophisticated operational capabilities and have acquired weaponry, equipment, and funds that place them on par with or more effective than the local forces arrayed against them. The typical Somali pirate team is equipped with a variety of small arms, including AK-47 rifles and rocket propelled grenade (RPG) launchers. Many pirate teams use fishing skiffs powered with large outboard motors to give chase to larger, but slower moving tankers, cargo ships, yachts, cruise ships, barges, and tug boats. Local Somali fisherman reportedly are forced to support pirate activities in some cases, while in other cases, coastal Somalis lend their fishing boats, equipment, and navigational expertise to teams of would- be pirates from inland communities.

Somali pirates initially focused on attacking ships in the western Indian Ocean, off Somalia's eastern coast. When ships operating on that route shifted further out to sea, Somali pirates shifted their focus to the Gulf of Aden, where there is a concentration of merchant ships (about 20,000 per year) operating in a more constrained waterway that is relatively close to Somalia's northern shore. Most recently, now that international naval forces are patrolling the Gulf of Aden with some effectiveness, Somali pirates have shifted some of their focus back to the Indian Ocean, and are now able to operate hundreds of nautical miles from the Somali coastline, often with the support of so-called 'mother ships.' These 'mother ships' are larger fishing vessels often acquired or commandeered by acts of piracy, and tend to operate out of the Somali ports of Bosaso and Mogadishu and the Yemeni ports of Al Mukalla and Ash Shihr.

U.S. and international officials suspect that in some cases, Somali businessmen and international support networks provide pirate groups with financing, supplies, and intelligence on the movements of ships in regional ports in return for shares of ransom payments. The pirates refuel and purchase logistical supplies like fuel and engine parts in Yemen, according to U.S. naval officials [15]. According to the NATO Shipping Center, Somali pirates returning from raids in the Gulf of Aden often stop at the port of Caluula on the northeast tip of Somalia before proceeding to their safe havens on the Indian Ocean coast [16].

One of the unique characteristics of Somali piracy has been the taking of hostages for ransom. In this sense, piracy off Somalia can be viewed as a form of maritime kidnapping. Unlike pirate attacks in Strait of Malacca or Nigeria, where ships are boarded either to take the vessel or its contents, pirates off the Horn of Africa routinely take the target vessel's crew hostage in return for ransom payments. This approach to piracy is possible because the pirates have a sanctuary on land in Somalia and in its territorial waters from which they can launch pirate attacks and conduct ransom negotiations. Pirates in other parts of the world are less likely to have such sanctuaries. This has presented maritime security forces with significant challenges to traditional engagement strategies and tactics.

According to reports, most vessels under attack have less than 15 to 30 minutes between the first sighting of the pirates and their boarding of the ship and taking of hostages. If a naval ship cannot arrive on scene within those 15 to 30 minutes, it will likely arrive too late to prevent the ship's capture. Naval combatant ships generally can steam at speeds of up to 30 knots (speeds of 20+ knots might be more likely), so unless a naval ship happens to be a few miles away when a commercial ship comes under attack, it won't arrive until after (perhaps long after) the 15- to 30- minute window has come and gone. The large area of water to be patrolled and the relatively small number of naval ships available means that the closest naval ship is often far too distant to arrive within that timeframe.

While pirate attacks may involve violence and the use of weaponry, most Somali pirate groups have not shown a willingness to wantonly harm captives taken in the course of their raids. Pirates in other parts of the world who engage in these types of attacks might be more likely to kill or seriously wound merchant ship crew members, since extracting ransom payments is not their objective. Negotiations for ransom involve the use of satellite telephones, third-party intermediaries in Somalia and abroad, and public relations efforts to influence interaction with property owners and foreign officials. Most navies have avoided rescue operations that could endanger the lives of hostages, preferring instead to engage in hostage negotiations or wait for shipping companies to negotiate ransom. According to reports, a recent rescue operation by French naval forces, designed to free a family held hostage onboard a small sailboat off the Somali coast, resulted in the death of the vessel's owner, a French citizen, during an exchange of fire between the pirates and naval personnel [17].

Prior to the U.S. military resolution of the MV Maersk Alabama seizure and other French military operations, the most sensational cases of piracy to date had been resolved through the payment of large sums of money to different pirate syndicates [18]. The Ukrainian ship MV Faina was released for a reported $3.2 million ransom in February 2009 after being held for nearly 6 months by pirates based in Harardera (Xarardheere). The seizure of the ship, carrying T-72 tanks and a significant amount of ammunition and small arms, led several governments, including the United States, to dispatch naval forces to the region to monitor the ship and its cargo. The Saudi oil supertanker MV Sirius Star was released for a reported $3 million ransom to Eyl-based pirates in January 2009 following its seizure in November 2008. The hijacking of the Sirius Star illustrated the threat piracy may pose to international energy supplies as well as the capabilities of some Somali pirates to operate far out to sea against large vessels. Ransom payments are considered to be problematic by some observers because they encourage pirates to continue their attacks with the expectation that insurance and shipping companies will decide that ransoms are cost effective relative to the insured values of personnel and cargo (see "Threats to Commercial Shipping and Global Trade" below).

The use of force by international naval forces to apprehend pirates and to free hostages in recent months has raised the prospect of an escalation in the pirates' use of force. As noted above, pirate leaders have vowed to retaliate for the recent deaths of some of their operatives at the hands of U.S. and other international naval forces. The use of force against suspected pirate vessels also may be problematic because of the difficulty inherent in distinguishing a pirate mother ship from a legitimate commercial ship. According to reports, in November 2008, a ship from the Indian navy attacked what it thought was a pirate mother ship, only to discover, after the attack was conducted, that the targeted ship was an innocent Thai commercial trawler. The effective use of force against pirate strongholds in coastal towns would likely require significant military planning and the investment of considerable resources in order to avoid or minimize civilian casualties.

The number of naval ships that would be needed to completely halt piracy in the Gulf of Aden and the waters of Somalia's Eastern Coast is probably much larger than the 12 to 20 that have been operating there in recent months. As many as 60, for example, might be required to suppress piracy in the Gulf of Aden. The adjoining area of concern in the Indian Ocean off Somalia's eastern coast, which has been measured at more than 1 million square miles, is much larger than the Gulf of Aden, so completely halting piracy in that area would likely also require a large number of ships.

Reports suggest that some pirates have invested ransom earnings in sophisticated weaponry and have fortified their operating bases against local authorities and potential international intervention. Some observers warn that international military operations to combat pirates ashore with force could undermine political reconciliation efforts aimed at reestablishing national governance in Somalia. (See "Oversight of U.S. Military Forces and U.S. Foreign Assistance" below.)

Piracy off the Horn of Africa: Impact

The strategic location of the Horn of Africa increases its importance for international security and commerce. The northern coastline of Somalia lies to the south of the Gulf of Aden, a key transit zone for ships passing to and from the Red Sea and the increasingly active port of Djibouti. The U.S Department of Energy estimated that, as of 2006, as many as 3.3 million barrels of oil per day were transiting the Bab el Mandeb strait between the Gulf of Aden and the Red Sea. The Indian Ocean waters off the southeast coast of Somalia are home to busy shipping lanes for trade between Asia and East Africa, as well as for ships making longer voyages around South Africa's Cape of Good Hope. Ship traffic to and from the Kenyan port of Mombasa is particularly vulnerable to security disruptions in the west Indian Ocean.

Threats to Commercial Shipping and Global Trade [19]

Somali piracy incurs economic costs in a number of ways, including ransom payments, damage to ships and cargoes, delays in delivering cargoes, increased maritime insurance rates, the costs of steps to harden merchant ships against attack, and costs for using naval forces for anti-piracy operations. The total economic costs of piracy, though significant in an absolute sense, are thought to be equivalent to only a very small fraction of the total value of worldwide shipborne commerce. In testimony on February 4, 2009, before the House Committee on Transportation and Infrastructure, Subcommittee on Coast Guard and Maritime Transportation, Peter Chalk, senior policy analyst at the Rand Corporation, stated that the overall annual cost of piracy to the maritime industry is estimated to be between $1 billion and $16 billion. Some of these costs are ultimately paid by the consumer.

In May 2008, insurance underwriters at Lloyds of London designated the Gulf of Aden a "war- risk" zone subject to a special insurance premium. London-based ocean marine insurers have raised rates for ships making the voyage through the Gulf of Aden and the Suez Canal. These levels of increase can only be estimated because of the competitive nature of the ocean marine insurance business. One group of London insurance brokers and underwriters estimates extra premiums at $10,000 to $20,000 per trip through the Gulf [20]. U.S. rates, however, apparently have not changed. According to representatives of the American Institute of Marine Underwriters (AIMU), U.S. ocean marine insurers have not had to pay ransom for any act of piracy; therefore, they say, hull and cargo insurance rates for vessels leaving the United States remain the same.

London-based shipping firms are usually prepared to pay ransom when the demanded sums are considered low, ranging from $500,000 to $2 million, compared with the value of the ships and cargo. Such payments are reimbursed because the hull insurance policies issued in London explicitly cover the peril of piracy [21]. (Hull insurance forms used by American insurers generally exclude coverage for the peril of piracy.) However, when the ransom demanded exceeds the value of the cargo, the shippers typically do not pay the ransom.

Ship operators (and their governments) might judge that the costs of paying occasional ransoms are less than the costs of taking steps to prevent occasional hijackings such as rerouting or arming merchant ships. Some assert that payment of ransoms has tended to keep the level of violence associated with piracy off Somalia relatively low, and while individual ransom payments can be significant, the small percentage of ships operating in the area successfully attacked and captured lowers the overall risk in the eyes of some commercial entities. As such, the payment of occasional ransoms might be viewed by ship operators (and their governments) as a regrettable but tolerable cost of doing business, even if it encourages more piracy.

The increase in pirate attacks is occurring at a time when the shipping industry is expressing concerns about its financial health. One development is that the frequency of hiring dry bulk carriers, a key industry component, has decreased; the "hire" rates have dropped over 90% in the last six months [22] (In some cases, the hire rate has dropped because the financial industry has stopped financing trade due to the global economic crisis.) [23]. In addition, many ship owners and other key industry participants apparently face severe losses from the global financial market crisis. Some major dry bulk shippers lost money speculating on the market in shipping derivatives that offered potential for strong investment returns [24]. Shipping derivatives were developed to manage risk stemming from fluctuations in freight rates, vessel prices, interest rates, and foreign exchange rates, more effectively, in a cheaper and more flexible manner. Many shippers made derivative bets mistakenly on the direction of dry bulk rates during 2008.

In addition to the generalized threat that piracy poses to the security of the shipping lanes described above, the incidence of piracy has important second order effects on the costs, patterns, and benefits of regional and international shipping and trade. Egypt's Suez Canal serves as a vital shipping link between the Mediterranean Sea and Red Sea, and the revenue derived from ships transiting the Canal is an important source of funding for Egypt's government. Canal authorities report that shipping traffic and resulting revenue have declined in recent months, due both to decreased economic activity and the piracy threat to the Canal's approaches in the Gulf of Aden. Rerouting vessels to avoid the Gulf of Aden and other waters near the Horn of Africa adds additional transit days and fuel costs to shipping companies. The costs vary by type of ship and frequency of voyage, according to the U.S. Department of Transportation [25]

Threats to Humanitarian Aid Deliveries

Piracy threatens the delivery of vital humanitarian assistance to the Horn of Africa, much of which arrives by sea [26]. In addition to the 7.2 million Ethiopians currently receiving emergency humanitarian assistance, the U.S. Agency for International Development (USAID) estimates that an additional 4.9 million will require food aid in the first half or 2009. As of April 2009, The United States provided over $600 million in humanitarian assistance to the country in FY2008, and has provided over $111 million to date in FY2009 [27]. In neighboring Somalia, an estimated 3.2 million Somalians, approximately 43 percent of the population, required food aid in the latter half of 2008. U.S. humanitarian assistance to Somalia totaled $270 million in 2008 and over $157 million to date in FY2009 [28]. The Obama Administration has requested $200 million in FY2009 supplemental International

Disaster Assistance (IDA) funding and $300 million in FY2009 supplemental P.L. 480, Title II humanitarian assistance, in part to address food and water shortages in Somalia, Ethiopia, and Sudan.

Food insecurity in the region, caused by drought and instability, has been heightened by high food and fuel prices in the region. Officials from the World Food Program (WFP), which ships tens of thousands of metric tons of food monthly to the Horn of Africa region, reports that it has become more expensive to ship assistance to Mogadishu, and that their ability to deliver relief is significantly hampered. Canada, NATO, and European Union forces have assumed WFP escort responsibilities since late 2008 (see "NATO: Operation Allied Provider and Operation Allied Protector" and "European Union: Operation ATALANTA" below) [29].

The continuing threat of piracy to ongoing relief efforts was illustrated clearly in April 2009, when pirates hijacked the MV Maersk Alabama and attacked the MV Liberty Sun, both U.S.- flagged and crewed cargo vessels contracted by the WFP to deliver USAID food assistance off the southeast coast of Somalia. The Maersk had delivered food aid to the port of Djibouti and was en route to the port of Mombasa, Kenya when it was seized by Somali pirates.

Potential Financing of Regional Conflict and Terrorism Concerns

The volatile Horn of Africa is home to several ongoing armed conflicts, and armed banditry is a common threat in much of the region. The small arms trade in the Horn and its potential to fuel instability remains a major concern to the international community. In spite of the longstanding United Nations arms embargo on Somalia established by Security Council Resolution 733 (1992), U.N. observers have reported "persistent violations" in recent years amid calls from the African Union and others for the lifting of the embargo to allow the armament of transitional government forces battling Islamist insurgents (see "United Nations Security Council" below). According to the Security Council Resolution 1851, "the lack of enforcement of the arms embargo... has permitted ready access to the arms and ammunition used by the pirates and driven in part the phenomenal growth in piracy."

Observers have expressed apprehension that some of the revenue from ransoms paid for the release of ships and hostages may be used to finance an influx of more weapons to the area for pirates or others. U.S. Navy officials have not found that fighters associated with Al Shabaab have financial ties to piracy at present, but the potential for potential personnel linkages may remain [30].

To the extent that ransom payments and new arms further empower criminal pirate groups, the challenge that such groups pose to local authorities at present and to potentially reconstituted national authorities in the future could grow.

U.S. and International Policy Responses

Piracy in the waters off the Horn of Africa is a symptom of the wider instability that has plagued Somalia and the region since the early 1990s. At present, the internationally recognized Transitional Federal Government (TFG) is working with the Alliance for the Reliberation of Somalia (ARS) on efforts to form a unity government and reconstitute national security and law enforcement entities. The Bush and Obama Administrations have supported reconciliation efforts in Somalia and have taken a leadership role in coordinating diplomatic and military responses to the threat of piracy in the region, in coordination with the United Nations Security Council.

To date, U.S. and international efforts to respond to the threat of piracy have taken on a multifaceted approach. In order to provide a short term response to the immediate threat to international navigation in the region's waters, the United Nations Security Council has authorized third party governments to conduct anti-piracy operations in Somali territorial waters and ashore, but only with authorization from and in coordination with the TFG. Regional bodies such as the African Union, the Arab League, and ad hoc groupings such as the participants in the December 2008 International Conference on Piracy in Nairobi, Kenya, have held consultative meetings and issued policy statements condemning piracy in the region and providing guidance for the development of coordinated, collaborative regional responses. Recent pirate attacks such as the seizure of the MV Maersk Alabama also may precipitate changes in U.S. policy and priorities among Administration officials and Members of Congress.

U.S. Policy

The U.S. National Maritime Security Strategy, issued in 2005, stated that the "safety and economic security of the United States depends upon the secure use of the world's oceans," and identified "well organized and well equipped" pirates and criminals as threats to international maritime security. In June 2007, the Bush Administration adopted a Policy for the Repression of Piracy and other Criminal Acts of Violence at Sea that stated that it is the policy of the United States to "[c]ontinue to lead and support international efforts to repress piracy and other acts of violence against maritime navigation and urge other states to take decisive action both individually and through international efforts." In December 2008, the Bush Administration issued an implementation plan based on that policy to address piracy threats in the Horn of Africa region. The U.S. National Security Council (NSC) "*Countering Piracy off the Horn of Africa: Partnership and Action Plan*" set out the objective "to repress this piracy as effectively as possible in the interests of the global economy, freedom of navigation, Somalia, and the regional states" [31]. In pursuit of that objective, the plan outlined three "lines of action" for U.S. policy:

> "1) prevent pirate attacks by reducing the vulnerability of the maritime domain to piracy; 2) disrupt acts of piracy consistent with international law and the rights and responsibilities of coastal and flag States; and 3) ensure that those who commit acts of piracy are held accountable for their actions by facilitating the prosecution of suspected pirates by flag, victim and coastal States, and, in appropriate cases, the United States."

In support of the 2007 policy and 2008 plan, the Bush Administration formed an interagency counter-piracy task force that "addresses the full spectrum of anti- and counter-piracy efforts, from piracy prevention to interruption and termination of acts of piracy, to ensure the accountability of pirates." The State Department and Defense Department are the principal members of the task force and work with other U.S. government agencies to coordinate U.S. policies and engagement in the multilateral initiatives that have been developed since mid-2008. To date, the task force has overseen efforts to implement elements of the December 2008 NSC Action Plan pledges U.S. support for the establishment of an international Contact Group on piracy (established January 2009, see "Contact Group on Piracy off the Coast of Somalia") and a regional counter-piracy coordination center (under development, see "International Maritime Organization and the Djibouti Code of Conduct").

The Obama Administration has not announced new overarching strategic priorities with regard to the piracy threat, although Secretary of State Hillary Clinton has outlined preliminary plans for a more robust policy response. According to Secretary Clinton, U.S. diplomats will engage with Somali Transitional Federal Government (TFG) officials and leaders from the semi-autonomous region of Puntland in the Eyl district to "press these leaders to take action against pirates operating from bases within their territories." The Administration plans to send an envoy to attend an April 23 policy and donors conference on Somalia in Brussels and has called for immediate meetings of the international Contact Group on Piracy off the Coast of Somalia. Lastly, U.S. officials plan to redouble efforts to work with the shipping and insurance industries "to address gaps in their self-defense measures."

The Obama Administration's FY2009 supplemental request appears to anticipate the delivery of some security assistance to the region, contingent upon continued progress in Somali reconciliation negotiations. The December 2008 Plan called for U.S. "bilateral assistance programs for judicial capacity building efforts" for regional states. Comments from Obama Administration officials suggest that their Administration shares the view expressed in the Bush Administration Action Plan that U.S. anti-piracy efforts are intended "to be mutually supportive of longer-term initiatives aimed at establishing governance, rule of law, security, and economic development in Somalia."

United Nations Security Council

Resolution 1816 (June 2008) authorized states acting in cooperation with and with prior notification of the TFG to "enter the territorial waters of Somalia for the purpose of repressing acts of piracy and armed robbery at sea" and to "use, within the territorial waters of Somalia, in a manner consistent with action permitted on the high seas with respect to piracy under relevant international law, all necessary means to repress acts of piracy and armed robbery." The initial authorization lasted for six months from June 2008. Resolution 1838, adopted in October 2008, called on states with military capabilities in the region to contribute to anti-piracy efforts and clarified the standing of the authorization contained in Resolution 1816 with respect to international law.

At the request of the TFG, the mandate established in Resolution 1816 was extended for 12 months in December 2008 in Resolution 1846. In December 2008, Resolution 1851 expanded the mandate by authorizing states and regional organizations that are acting at the TFG's request to "undertake all necessary measures that are appropriate in Somalia [italics added] for the purpose of suppressing acts of piracy and armed robbery at sea." Both resolutions require any authorized international measures to be undertaken in accordance with humanitarian and human rights laws. Other provisions of Resolution 1851 have guided developments since December 2008 and may inform future U.S or international initiatives (see "Contact Group on Piracy off the Coast of Somalia", "United Nations Office on Drugs and Crime", and "Oversight of U.S. Military Forces and U.S. Foreign Assistance" below).

Resolution 1846 authorized the provision of technical assistance to TFG personnel and forces "to enhance the capacity of these States to ensure coastal and maritime security" in accordance with procedures outlined in Resolution 1722. Under paragraphs 11 and 12 of Resolution 1722, the supply of technical assistance to Somali "security sector institutions" is authorized provided that prior case-by-case notification is made to the U.N. arms embargo Committee for Somalia [32]. Resolution 1851 provides similar authorization to weapons and military equipment destined for the sole use of Member States and regional organizations undertaking authorized anti-piracy operations in Somali waters. The transfer of weaponry to Somali maritime security forces would require separate authorization from the Security Council. The African Union's Peace and Security Council and the TFG have requested that the broader U.N. arms embargo be amended or lifted in order to improve the capabilities of forces fighting Islamist insurgents.

Contact Group on Piracy off the Coast of Somalia

Based on Resolution 1851, the Bush Administration led the formation of a multilateral Contact Group on Piracy off the Coast of Somalia (CGPCS) made up of 24 member governments and 5 regional and international organizations [33]. The Contact group held its first meeting in January 2009 and identified six tasks for itself: 1) improving operational and information support to counter-piracy operations, 2) establishing a counter-piracy coordination mechanism, 3) strengthening judicial frameworks for arrest, prosecution and detention of pirates, 4) strengthening commercial shipping self-awareness and other capabilities, 5) pursuing improved diplomatic and public information efforts, and 6) tracking financial flows related to piracy [34]. In support of these goals, four working groups are to make recommendations to the Contact Group secretariat on relevant military/operational, judicial, diplomatic, and public information aspects of regional and international anti-piracy efforts. The goals of the working groups' efforts are to improve operational coordination, information sharing, and the effectiveness of legal enforcement activities among all regional and international actors combating piracy in the region. The latest meeting of the CGPCS was held in Cairo in March 2009.

Combined Task Force 151 and Other Naval Forces

United States Naval Forces Central Command (NAVCENT) commands the Combined Maritime Forces operating in the Arabian/Persian Gulf, Gulf of Oman, Gulf of Aden, Red Sea, Arabian Sea, and Indian Ocean. In January 2009, the command established Combined Task Force 151 (CTF-151), with the sole mission of conducting anti-piracy operations in the Gulf of Aden and the waters off the Somali coast in the Indian Ocean. That role had previously been filled by CTF- 150, which continues to perform counterterrorism and other maritime security operations as it has since 2001-2002. In August 2008, CTF 150 and partner forces agreed to the establishment of a Maritime Security Patrol Area (MSPA) in the Gulf of Aden to serve as a dedicated, more secure transit zone for merchant vessels. The MSPA has been credited in part with lowering the success rate of Somali pirates in the Gulf of Aden transit zone.

As of March 2009, CTF- 151 consisted of personnel and nearly two dozen ships from the United States, the United Kingdom, Canada, Denmark, France, Germany, Greece, Italy, Malaysia, Netherlands, Saudi Arabia, Spain, Turkey and Yemen [35]. U.S. naval commanders expect that Bahrain, Jordan, Japan, Singapore, the Republic of Korea, Sweden, Belgium and Poland also will participate in CTF- 151 operations in the near future. Task force operations are coordinated from the NAVCENT command center in Bahrain. NAVCENT commanders told Congress in early March that CTF- 151 and other cooperating naval forces had disarmed and released 121 pirates, disarmed and turned over for prosecution 117 pirates, and were holding nine pirates pending final disposition [36].

Other countries, most notably Russia, China, and India have deployed naval forces to the region to participate in monitoring and anti-piracy escort operations. From an operational perspective, while these countries do not formally and fully coordinate their policies with CTF- 151, there are ongoing communication efforts. Naval observers and officials in the United States have noted the engagement of China with particular interest, as Chinese naval operations in the Horn of Africa region demonstrate the Chinese government's desire and ability to protect international shipping lanes far from China's shores. As of April 2009, a Chinese destroyer and frigate were departing to replace two Chinese navy destroyers that have been deployed for anti-piracy operations since late December 2008 [37]. A supply ship that is currently deployed is reportedly scheduled to stay on scene with the new task force, which will have the same helicopter and naval special forces team capabilities as its predecessor.

NATO: Operation Allied Provider and Operation Allied Protector

The North Atlantic Treaty Organization (NATO) has deployed two Standing NATO Maritime Groups to conduct anti-piracy operations in the Horn of Africa region since October 2008. The first deployment, named Operation Allied Provider, served as a temporary protection force for World Food Program assistance shipments in the region. In December 2008, NATO ended Operation Allied Provider and transitioned WFP protection responsibilities to the European Union's new naval operation (see "European Union: Operation ATALANTA" below).

In March 2009, NATO launched its second anti-piracy mission, Operation Allied Protector, which will be carried out by Standing NATO Maritime Group 1 (SNMG1) as it transits the Horn region en route to South East Asia and as it returns in June 2009 [38]. According to NATO, the forces participating in Operation Allied Protector will "deter, defend against and disrupt pirate activities" as they transit the region. As of late March 2009, the following ships were participating in SNMG1 and Operation Allied Protector: *NRP Corte Real* (flagship, Portugal), *HMCS Winnipeg* (Canada), *HNLMS de Zeven Provinciën* (The Netherlands), *SPS Blas de Lezo* (Spain), and the *USS Halyburton* (United States).

European Union: Operation ATALANTA

In December 2008, the European Union launched EU NAVFOR Operation ATALANTA, its first naval operation under the framework of the European Security and Defence Policy (ESDP). Forces participating in Operation ATALANTA have been tasked with provide protection for WFP vessels and merchant vessels and are authorized to "employ the necessary measures, including the use of force, to deter, prevent and intervene in order to bring to an end acts of piracy and armed robbery which may be committed in the areas where they are present" [39]. According to the European Union, the force consists of twenty ships and over 1,500 personnel. Greece, France, Spain, Germany and Italy have contributed forces and personnel to the operation for its full term of twelve months. Other EU member states and third party countries are expected to contribute over time. In coordination with the deployment, EU NAVFOR also has established an online center known as Maritime Security Center-Horn of Africa (MSC-HOA) for transiting ships to record their ships' movements voluntarily and to receive updated threat information [40]. Similar voluntary tracking and reporting services are provided by the United Kingdom Maritime Trade Operations office in Dubai and the U.S. Navy's Maritime Liaison Office in Bahrain. Between CTF- 151, Operation ATALANTA and Operation Allied Protector, almost 50 combatant ships are currently patrolling in the region.

International Maritime Organization and the Djibouti Code of Conduct

The International Maritime Organization (IMO) [41] has had an international anti-piracy program since the late 1990s and has successfully engaged on a multilateral basis in other regions to improve anti-piracy cooperation. At present, cooperative mechanisms for managing the security of the waters near the Horn of Africa are being developed as called for by the IMO42 and as encouraged by Resolution 1851 [43]. The IMO began sponsoring consultation meetings on piracy for the Horn of Africa region in 2005, which led to the development of a draft cooperative framework agreement in early 2008.

In January 2009, representatives of 17 regional governments met at an IMO-sponsored meeting in Djibouti and adopted a Code of Conduct concerning the Repression of Piracy and Armed Robbery against Ships in the western Indian Ocean and the Gulf of Aden [44]. As of late January 2009, nine regional governments [45] had signed the Code of Conduct, which remains open for signature by other parties. Three regional facilities---the Maritime Rescue Coordination Centre in Mombasa, Kenya, the Sub-Regional Coordination Centre in Dar es Salaam, Tanzania, and a regional maritime information center that is to be established in Sana'a, Yemen---are to support the information sharing components of the agreement. The parties also agreed to resolutions on technical cooperation and the establishment of a regional training center in Djibouti. The Contact Group on Piracy off the Coast of Somalia (CGPCS) intends to adopt interim measures to facilitate regional coordination until a dedicated coordination center to support the Djibouti Code of Conduct is established.

A similar cooperative framework developed by the IMO, the littoral states of the Strait of Malacca, and other Asian governments has been in force since 2006. Known as the Regional Cooperation Agreement on Combating Piracy and Armed Robbery against ships in Asia (ReCAAP), [46] the agreement established procedures for coordinating responses to piracy and sharing best practices among law enforcement and security personnel. The ReCAAP Information Sharing Center (ISC) in Singapore now serves as the principal clearinghouse for piracy reporting and response coordination [47].

These steps, taken in conjunction with other regional agreements between Malaysia, Indonesia and Singapore to coordinate anti-piracy patrols in the Straits of Malacca and surrounding waters have been successful in reducing piracy in that region. The negotiation of the bilateral and multilateral initiatives in the Straits of Malacca region highlighted several issues that may be of interest to parties seeking to establish similar programs in the Horn of Africa region, namely the importance of addressing local concerns over sovereignty, territorial water rights, and the presence of foreign military forces in regional waters.

United Nations Office on Drugs and Crime: "Shipriders" and Capacity Building

Under the auspices of Resolution 1851 and in conjunction with the judicial working group of the (CGPCS), the United Nations Office on Drugs and Crime has launched a project to facilitate regional law enforcement participation in anti-piracy enforcement efforts off the coast of Somalia [48].

The program was encouraged in language included in Resolution 1851 and focuses on providing judicial capacity building assistance to regional states and facilitating so-called "shiprider" arrangements in which regional law enforcement personnel are seconded to international vessels to perform anti-piracy arrest and investigation functions. The United States has shiprider agreements with a number of Western Hemisphere governments to facilitate maritime security operations in waters of shared concern.

In general, shiprider arrangements are designed to address the logistical and legal challenges inherent in multilateral naval enforcement efforts in remote areas or where the capacity of regional governments does not allow for the provision of sufficient security. With regard to current operations in the Horn of Africa region, long transport times, limited military resources, legal limitations on the operations of military personnel, and complex differences in jurisdictional standards and requirements would complicate the arrest and prosecution by the varied non- regional forces operating under Resolution 1851. In order to help regional governments meet the added resource requirements that the arrest, detention, and prosecution of Somali pirate suspects would create, the UNODC plans to provide judicial capacity building assistance, in coordination with other donors.

Private Sector and Shipping Industry Responses

Private sector and shipping industry responses to the threat of piracy in the waters off the Horn of Africa have varied. In addition to altering financial decisions based on higher insurance costs, some accounts suggest that shipment navigation patterns have changed in response to the threat of piracy, with some vessels preferring to circumnavigate the southern Cape of Good Hope rather than risk attack in the Gulf of Aden. Crews also have developed a number of unique countermeasures and best practices in their attempts to ward off and resist pirate attacks.

The use of water cannons, fire hoses, and passive sonic defenses has become more widespread, and industry surveys suggest that ships that operate at speeds above 15 knots [49] and that have higher freeboards [50] have proven less susceptible to pirate attack, thus far. Debates about the use of armed guards continue among shipping industry representatives, government officials, and observers worldwide (see "Options for Improving the Immediate Security of Merchant Ships").

The IMO and other bodies such as the International Chamber of Commerce International Maritime Bureau (ICC-IMB) have developed detailed guidance and recommendations for governments and commercial vessels seeking to prevent, deter, and respond to pirate attacks. The IMB also has established a 24-hour piracy reporting center in Kuala Lumpur, Malaysia, which seeks to serve as the global, one-stop shop for piracy reporting and piracy threat information distribution for commercial vessels.

The IMB also works with other regional information centers to collect and disseminate threat and situation reporting. For the Horn of Africa region, the IMB and European Union Maritime Security Center-Horn of Africa (MSC-HOA) issue periodic 'Industry Updates' detailing recent trends in pirate attacks and making recommendations to vessels transiting regional waters [51]

ISSUES FOR CONGRESS AND POLICY OPTIONS

The risk of pirate attacks in the waters off the Horn of Africa is unlikely to disappear in the near term, and the United States government has identified piracy as a direct threat to U.S. national security concerns. U.S. policies developed by the Bush Administration to address Somali piracy are now being revisited and enhanced by the Obama Administration in light of high profile attacks on U.S.-flagged vessels and crew members in April 2009.

Most defense analysts acknowledge that while the unprecedented level of naval patrols in the area -- conducted by more than fifteen nations -- has deterred some attacks, the area is simply too vast to prevent all incidents. When the MV Maersk Alabama was attacked on April 8, 2009, the closest naval vessel, the U.S.S. Bainbridge, was approximately 300 nautical miles away. Similarly, the U. S.S. Bainbridge was only able to arrive on the scene of an aborted April 14 attack on the MV Liberty Sun a reported 6 hours after the attack ended. The continuing anti-piracy operations of international navies also comes at significant cost, as governments around the world weigh the budgetary impact of the current economic downturn and military requirements in other theaters of operation.

Like terrorism, acts of piracy in African waters pose a transnational security threat that emanates from areas plagued by conflict, weak governance, and economic insecurity. Regional security forces currently have limited maritime capability, and many governments have prioritized the development of their armies at the expense of navies or coast guards. That has changed to some extent in recent years, as international studies have highlighted the threat to local economies posed by illegal fishing, in addition to more traditional maritime security threats. Regional coordination and intelligence sharing also is weak.

The United States and its international partners have policy tools that have been used to address similarly complex security circumstances in other regions. However, ongoing U.S. and international security operations in environments such as Afghanistan, Pakistan, Iraq, and Colombia suggest that military intervention and foreign assistance require political consensus, political will, and significant coordination in order to be successful. Maritime security efforts in the Persian Gulf, the Caribbean, the waters of West Africa, and the Strait of Malacca have had the same requirements. While short term results in containing other transnational threats have proven to be achievable, the long-term ability of international intervention to eliminate these threats is less certain in the absence of committed and capable regional and local actors.

Oversight of U.S. Military Forces and U.S. Foreign Assistance

U.S. military engagement in the region is divided among two geographic combatant Commands. U.S. Central Command's area of responsibility (AOR) includes the waters of the Gulf of Aden and those off the eastern Somali coast, while the AOR of the new U.S. Africa Command (AFRICOM), which became fully operational in October 2008, encompasses the African continent [52]. To date, much of the U.S. military's anti-piracy response has been conducted at sea, by Central Command (CENTCOM). On land, AFRICOM provides security assistance to several regional maritime security forces, few of which have "blue water capacity." CENTCOM provides similar assistance to the Yemeni coast guard.

Oversight of U.S. Navy anti-piracy operations focuses on forces associated with CTF-151 and with NATO's Operation Allied Protector. Several U.S.-homeported Navy ships support the deployment of U.S. Navy ships operating on a continuous basis in the areas where Somali pirates are active. As such, the commitment of a single additional U.S. Navy ship to the area can have a notable effect on the Navy's ability to perform missions in other parts of the world.

U.S. military operations in the region are not limited to anti-piracy efforts. The United States has conducted anti-terrorism activities in the Horn of Africa and in Yemen for over a decade, including the naval Combined Task Forces established as part of Operation Enduring Freedom. Djibouti has hosted a semi-permanent Forward Operating Site, known as the Combined Joint Task Force – Horn of Africa (CJTF-HOA) since 2003, with over 1,500 U.S. military personnel in residence. The command authority for CJTF-HOA, formerly under CENTCOM, was recently transferred to AFRICOM. Its efforts initially focused primarily on countering violent extremism in the region, but the Task Force's activities have expanded in recent years to include a wide variety of activities aimed at building the capacity of regional militaries to respond to more general threats, such as natural disasters and armed conflict. CJTF-HOA personnel provide training to the region's security forces on counter-terrorism, maritime security, and peacekeeping.

As mentioned above, the United States conducts an array of maritime security assistance programs in East Africa and Yemen. In Kenya, for example, the United States provides maritime security assistance to both the Kenyan Navy and an array of agencies, including the Kenya Wildlife Service, revenue authority, and police, to address an array of threats, from smuggling and illegal fishing to terrorism. The U.S. also began support for a regional Maritime Center of Excellence in Mombasa in early 2009; courses at the Center are attended by participants from throughout East Africa. Several African countries, including Djibouti, Kenya, Tanzania, and Yemen, have received U.S. support for the installation of radar systems that provide enhanced maritime domain awareness. Congress expanded the Department of Defense's Section 1206 "train and equip" authority in FY2009 to include assistance for maritime security forces.

U.N. Security Council Resolution 1851 "calls on Member States to assist the TFG, at its request and with notification to the Secretary-General, to strengthen its operational capacity to bring to justice those who are using Somali territory to plan, facilitate or undertake criminal acts of piracy and armed robbery at sea." The Obama Administration may seek to expand current assistance programs for regional and Somali actors subject to congressional appropriations and authorization and in accordance with United Nations Security Council resolutions. As noted above, the Obama Administration has requested $40 million in 2009 supplemental Peacekeeping Operations (PKO) funding to provide "non-lethal equipment, logistical support, and basing facilities for the African Union Mission to Somalia and to support Somali security sector reform" [53]. While those funds are likely to be directed toward improving Somali capacity to counter threats from insurgents and terrorists, to the extent that assistance improves the overall ability of government forces to operate effectively and assert security control, it may have positive implications for anti-piracy operations in the future.

Although some press reports in April 2009 quoted unnamed U.S. officials as stating that the U.S. military may consider launching military attacks against pirate strongholds, in testimony before the House Armed Services Committee in March 2009, Stephen Mull, Acting

Undersecretary of State for International Security and Arms Control stated that although the United States supported the inclusion in Security Council Resolution 1851 of authorization for anti-piracy operations on land, there were, at that time "no plans to conduct counter-piracy operations on land."

In April, Secretary of State Hillary Clinton appeared to imply that the United States would encourage Somali figures in the Transitional Federal Government or in the region of Puntland to take action against pirate safe havens ashore. The December 2008 National Security Council Partnership and Action Plan stated that the United States "will work with concerned governments and international organizations to disrupt and dismantle pirate bases to the fullest extent permitted by national law."

Piracy, Law Enforcement, and International Cooperation

Several United Nations instruments address the problem of piracy, including the Convention on the High Seas, [54] the Convention on the Law of the Sea (UNCLOS), [55] and the Convention for the Suppression of Unlawful Acts Against the Safety of Maritime Navigation (SUA Convention) [56]. The United States is a signatory to the Convention on the High Seas and the SUA Convention, but not to UNCLOS. A "global diplomatic effort to regulate and write rules for all ocean areas, all uses of the seas and all of its resources" resulted in the convening of The Third United Nations Conference on the Sea in 1973 and the adoption of UNCLOS in 1982 [57]. UNCLOS generally incorporates the rules of international law codified in the Convention on the High Seas, but also comprehensively addresses the use of other areas of the sea including, for example, the territorial seas, natural resources, and the seabed.

The Convention on the High Seas, to which the United States is a party, and UNCLOS both address piracy by stating that "[a]ll states shall cooperate to the fullest possible extent in the repression of piracy on the high seas or in any other place outside the jurisdiction of any State" [58]. The term "piracy" is defined in UNCLOS (Article 101) as:

(a) any illegal acts of violence or detention, or any act of depredation, committed for private ends by the crew or the passengers of a private ship or a private aircraft, and directed-on the high seas, against another ship or aircraft, or against persons or property on board such ship or aircraft; against a ship, aircraft, persons or property in a place outside the jurisdiction of any State;
(b) any act of voluntary participation in the operation of a ship or of an aircraft with knowledge of facts making it a pirate ship or aircraft;
(c) any act of inciting or of intentionally facilitating an act described in subparagraph (a) or (b) [59]

Article 110 of UNCLOS authorizes warships to visit and/or inspect ships on the high seas that are suspected of engagement in piracy. Although the United States is not party to UNCLOS, the Convention on the High Seas also authorizes the right of visitation/inspection of vessels suspected of being engaged in piracy [60]. States, under both the Convention on the High Seas and UNCLOS, are authorized to seize a pirate ship, or a ship taken by piracy and under the control of the pirates, and arrest the persons and seize the property on board [61].

The courts of the State whose forces carry out a seizure may decide the penalties to be imposed on the pirates [62].

The SUA Convention further expands on the judicial treatment of pirates. Its main purpose is "to ensure that appropriate action is taken against persons committing unlawful acts against ships" [63]. Unlawful acts include, but are not limited to, the seizure of ships; acts of violence against persons on board ships; and the placing of devices on board a ship which are likely to destroy or damage it [64]. The SUA Convention calls on parties to the agreement to make its enumerated offenses "punishable by appropriate penalties which take into account the grave nature of those offenses" [65] The United States criminalizes acts of piracy66 and foreigners or U.S. citizens that commit acts of piracy are subject to imprisonment for life [67]. While it appears that U.S. law is sufficient to address the criminality of piracy, this may not be the case in other countries. Additionally, even with comprehensive criminal laws, the logistics related to the enforcement of the laws may be an impediment to their utilization.

Questions regarding legal jurisdiction, due process for detained pirate suspects, and the role of foreign military forces in anti-piracy law enforcement activities may complicate current U.S. and international operations against pirates in the Horn of Africa region. The most immediate legal concern associated with anti-piracy operations are jurisdictional questions that arise based on the location of pirate attacks and/or international naval interventions, the nationalities of crew members, and the countries of registry and/or ownership of any seized vessels [68]. Multiple governments may be able to assert legal jurisdiction depending on the specifics of the incident. But many governments lack sufficient laws and judicial capacity to effectively prosecute suspected pirates. The disposition of property and insurance claims for vessels involved in piracy also raises complex legal questions. A developing legal issue concerns the prosecution of juveniles participating in acts of piracy. Recent reports suggest that some of the Somali pirates are teenage minors, [69] and therefore could have a defense of infancy in certain jurisdictions that may assert jurisdiction over the offense [70]

To date, some of these legal and law enforcement challenges have been addressed through the establishment of bilateral agreements by the United States, the United Kingdom, the European Union and others with governments in the Horn of Africa region, and particularly with Kenya. Some agreements concluded to date define procedures for the detention, transfer, and prosecution of captured pirate suspects. For example, suspected pirates captured by U.S. military forces now may be transferred to Kenyan custody for prosecution according to the terms of a bilateral memorandum of understanding signed in January 2009. As noted above (see "United Nations Office on Drugs and Crime: "Shipriders" and Capacity Building"), efforts also are underway to establish mechanisms for regional law enforcement personnel to serve as shipriders on coalition vessels and to expand the anti-piracy law enforcement and judicial capacities of neighboring states.

Options for Improving the Immediate Security of Merchant Ships

Risk Reduction and Best Practices

The U.S. Department of Transportation Maritime Administration issues detailed guidance to U.S. mariners transiting the waters off the Horn of Africa region to help ensure their safety and security [71]. Its latest guidance, issued April 20, 2009, includes instructions for U.S. flagged vessels seeking escort support from the U.S. Navy and Combined Maritime Forces participating in coalition naval security operations in the region [72].

As noted above, international bodies such as the International Maritime Organization [73] and the International Maritime Bureau [74] also have outlined several actions that merchant ships and their crews can take to reduce their risk of being attacked and captured.

These include measures that can be taken before and during pirate attacks. For example, rerouting ships, if possible, allows ships to avoid waters where Somali pirates are known to operate. This option can lengthen operating routes and increase shipping costs, but perhaps not as much as paying an occasional ransom.

Recommendations suggest that transit of high-risk areas is not recommended at times of day when Somali pirates historically have been more likely to stage attacks, namely in early morning or dusk hours. In transit, effective watch procedures are recommended, since early detection of impending attacks increases the likelihood that avoidance and suppression measures will succeed. Higher ship operating speeds and evasive maneuvers have proven effective in many cases, as have denial systems such as barbed and razor wire and specialized electrical fences for ships. Crew preparation, training, and responses also are credited with reducing risks of successful pirate attacks [75].

Arming Merchant Ships [76]

Arming merchant ships can be done by either giving arms to the ship's crew, or by hiring armed security teams to ride on the ships. U.S. government officials traditionally have expressed concern that merchant ships with armed crew members could pose security or terrorism risks visiting U.S. ports. Many merchant ship owners and operators are strongly averse to arming merchant ships, for practical and financial reasons.

As noted above, private or military gun battles with pirates can raise the overall level of violence associated with piracy off Somalia, which may increase risks to all merchant mariners on ships operating in that area. Since merchant ship crews are often not trained in the use of weapons, they might not be able to use them very effectively in fighting pirates. If ship crews try to defend themselves with firearms and fail, the pirates might be more likely to kill some of the crew members.

Even if used properly, lighter firearms might not be effective in countering pirates armed with heavier weapons, such as rocket-propelled grenades. Pirates with access to large amounts of money from prior ransom payments can acquire heavier weapons, so as to out-gun the merchant ships. In all cases, fire is a major safety concern, particularly on tanker ships, and gunfire could ignite vapors from the ship's cargo, or the cargo itself.

Financial concerns may also mitigate against arming merchant ships. Hiring armed security teams might be more expensive than paying occasional ransoms. Liability for fatal shootings aboard a ship can be a complex legal matter that can lead to expensive lawsuits. Since many ports restrict vessels from having weapons on board, commercial ships that often make calls at multiple ports along their operating routes could find it difficult to operate along certain routes.

Convoys

Convoys escorted by naval ships are an option, though merchant ship operators may be reluctant to use them because it can require merchant ships to wait in a certain location for the next scheduled convoy to begin. The delays associated with this waiting can impose costs on ship operators that could be greater than the cost of paying an occasional ransom. The establishment and maintenance of a convoy system over the long term, in the absence of broader efforts to address the root causes of the piracy problem, could pose unacceptable costs for international navies.

Maritime War Risk Insurance

Federal law (Title XII of the Merchant Marine Act of 1936, as amended) authorizes the federal government to administer a maritime war risk insurance program that insures or reinsures, as a last resort, ocean-going commerce should private ocean marine insurance markets prove insufficient. Available statistics suggest that industry resources are adequate, given the property and casualty insurance industry surplus and the relatively low cost of insurance premiums [77]. As a result, despite the increased activity of pirates, some may contend that Congress does not need to amend the existing federal insurance statutory construct. Others, however, may urge increased levels of oversight and investigation into the situation in an effort to ensure that international commerce remains stabilized, particularly at a time of global economic crisis.

Toward a Long-Term Solution: "Piracy is a Problem that Starts Ashore" [78]

In the short term, the international community has responded to the threat of piracy in the waters off the Horn of Africa with multinational naval patrols, nascent diplomatic coordination efforts, and enhanced private security efforts by members of the commercial shipping industry. In the longer term, U.S. officials and international experts believe that addressing the threat of piracy will require the strengthening of regional security capabilities, improved intelligence gathering and sharing, more effective and capable law enforcement, and enhanced multilateral coordination, both at sea and on land. By all accounts, pirates will likely continue to find sanctuary in Somalia until basic governance and security conditions there change.

Some Members of Congress have called on the Administration to develop a "comprehensive approach" to Somalia that responds to the threat of piracy in the context of a broader initiative to stabilize the country and support transitional government institutions. Some U.S. officials recently have supported a similar approach. In January 2009, Dr. Jun Bando, Maritime Security Coordinator and U.S. AFRICOM Liaison for the U.S. Department of State Bureau of African Affairs argued that "a durable solution for ending piracy in the Horn of Africa will require improving security, stability, rule of law, and economic opportunity in Somalia, as well as solidifying political progress by forming a unity government and advancing the peace process." [79].

Beginning in January, the Obama Administration signaled its intention to continue working with U.S. partners in the Contact Group on Somalia80 and the Contact Group on Piracy off the Coast of Somalia toward those goals. In response to recent attacks on U.S.-flagged and -crewed vessels, U.S. Secretary of State Clinton indicated on April 15, 2009 that a more robust anti-piracy policy is now being developed. The Administration's interagency steering group on piracy was scheduled to convene on April 17 to discuss changes to U.S. strategy. Enhanced diplomatic engagement with Somali Transitional Federal Government officials and leaders from the semi-autonomous region of Puntland also will be launched with the aim of encouraging local Somalis to take steps to secure regions where pirates currently enjoy safe havens.

REFERENCES

[1] The *U.S.S. Bainbridge* is named for Captain William Bainbridge, the commander of the *U.S.S. Philadelphia* who was held in captivity in the Barbary state of Tripoli from 1803 to 1805 after the Philadelphia ran aground in Tripoli harbor during anti-piracy operations. The captivity of Bainbridge and his crew significantly escalated the military confrontation between the United States and the Barbary pirates, whose threats to U.S. vessels in the Mediterranean were a key factor in the early development of the United States Navy. For more information, see http://www.bainbridge.navy.mil/sitepages/history.aspx.

[2] Devlin Barrett, "Captured Somali pirate to face trial in NY," *Associated Press*, April 16, 2009.

[3] *Agence France Presse*, "Pirates stage rocket attack on US freighter," April 14, 2009.

[4] Much of the statistical information on pirate attacks found in this report has been provided by the International Maritime Bureau, a division of the International Chamber of Commerce.

[5] See the U.S. Navy's website for CTF 150, available at: http://www.cusnc.navy.mil/command/ctf150.html.

[6] Report of the Secretary-General pursuant to Security Council Resolution 1846 (2008), S/2009/146, March 16, 2009; and, International Expert Group on Piracy off the Somali Coast, Final Report: Workshop commissioned by the Special Representative of the Secretary General of the UN to Somalia Ambassador Ahmedou Ould-Abdallah, November 10-12, 2008, Nairobi, Kenya.

[7] The Special Representative's experts group report identified the following specific pirate group leaders (clan, location in parentheses): Issc Mahmuud and Leelkase (Darood, Eyl), Omar Mahmuud (Darood, Garad), and the Habargedir (Hawiye, Hobiya, Harardera, and Mogadishu).

[8] The dire economic and security situation in Somalia is illustrated by the continuing outflow of refugees and migrants to neighboring countries. The U.N. High Commissioner for Refugees estimates that as many as 50,000 people, predominantly Somalis, crossed the Gulf of Aden to Yemen in 2008. The deaths of hundreds of migrants in a boat accident off the northern Somali coast in April 2009 were the latest instances in a pattern of similar accidents. "More Somali Migrants Drown off Yemeni Coast," UN IRIN, March 1, 2009.

[9] The U.N. experts group noted the tendency of pirates to characterize their actions as an alternative livelihood or as retribution for illegal international activities in Somali waters: "The pirates also firmly believe that they have every right and entitlement to attack illegal fishing vessels operating in their territorial waters as their fishing

resources are being pillaged daily by international shipping vessels from Asia and Europe." International Expert Group on Piracy off the Somali Coast, Final Report, p.15

[10] DFID, "Review of Impacts of Illegal, Unreported and Unregulated Fishing on Developing Countries," July 2005.

[11] Statement of the Contact Group on Piracy off the Coast of Somalia, New York, January 14, 2009.

[12] "Somali Piracy 'Reduces Tuna Haul,'" *BBC*, January 22, 2009.

[13] An alleged pirate commander named Abdi Garad told reporters, "This attack was the first against our prime target. We intended to destroy this American-flagged ship and the crew on board but unfortunately they narrowly escaped us. The aim of this attack was totally different. We were not after a ransom. We also assigned a team with special equipment to chase and destroy any ship flying the American flag in retaliation for the brutal killing of our friends." *Agence France Presse*, "Pirates stage rocket attack on US freighter," April 14, 2009.

[14] The U.S. government has provided mariners with descriptions of common pirate tactics and instructions for response. See, for example, U.S. Department of Transportation Maritime Administration, "Somali Pirate Tactics," December 2008. Available at http://www.marad.dot.gov/ documents/HOA_Somali%20Pirate%20Tactics_15DEC2008.pdf

[15] Comments by Admiral Mark Fitzgerald in "Work with Yemen Government on Somali Piracy: U.S. Admiral," *Reuters*, March 9, 2009.

[16] Report of the UN Secretary General, S/2009/146, paragraph 6, page 2.

[17] Others onboard were rescued safely.

[18] The French military also has reportedly undertaken a number of raid and rescue operations since April 2008 to free its citizens held aboard seized ships.

[19] For more information about the commercial impact of piracy, see CRS Report R40081, *Ocean Piracy and Its Impact on Insurance*, by Rawle O. King.

[20] *Piracy Threat Hikes Insurance Premiums: Insurers to Raise Rates in High-Risk Areas After Piracy Heists Off Somali Coas*t, November 20, 2008, located at http://www.msnbc.msn.com/id/278262.

[21] Robert F. Worth, "Pirates Seize Saudi Tanker off Kenya: Ship Called the Largest Ever Hijacked," *New York Times*, November 18, 2008, p. A. 6.

[22] Robert Wright, "Shipping in Crisis: Sector Must Navigate Rates Challenge," *Financial Times*, November 19, 2008, p. 18.

[23] Ibid.

[24] A derivative is a financial instrument whose price is dependent upon or derived from one or more underlying assets. The derivative itself is a contract between two or more parties. Its value is determined by fluctuations in the underlying asset. The most common underlying assets include stocks, bonds, commodities, currencies, interest rates, and market indexes.

[25] For example, circumnavigation rather than transiting the Gulf of Aden/Suez Canal increases the annual operating cost of an oil tanker "by reducing the delivery capacity for the ship from about six round-trip voyages to five voyages, or a drop of about 26 percent. The additional fuel cost of traveling via the Cape of Good Hope is about $3.5 million annually." U.S. Department of Transportation Maritime Administration, Economic Impact of Piracy in the Gulf of Aden on Global Trade, December 2008.

[26] Food insecurity in the region is also exacerbated by banditry, roadblocks, inter-clan fighting, and attacks on aid workers.

[27] USAID, Complex Emergency – Ethiopia, Situation Report #6, April 9, 2009.

[28] USAID, Complex Emergency – Somalia, Situation Report #4, January 15, 2009.

[29] Christian Fraser, "On Patrol with the Pirate Hunters," BBC, November 21, 2008.

[30] Vice Admiral William Gortney, the commander of U.S. Naval Forces Central Command told the House Armed Services Committee on March 5, 2009, that "We look very, very carefully for a linkage between piracy and terrorism or any kind of ideology and we do not see it. It would be a significant game changer should that linkage occur. But we have not seen it. We watch very carefully for it."

[31] U.S. National Security Council, "Countering Piracy off the Horn of Africa: Partnership and Action Plan," December 2008. Available at: http://www.marad.dot.gov/documents/Countering_Piracy_Off_The_Horn_of_Africa_-_Partnership__Action_Plan.pdf.

[32] For more information, see the Committee web page at: http://www.un.org/sc/committees/751/.

[33] Resolution 1851 "encourages all States and regional organizations fighting piracy and armed robbery at sea off the coast of Somalia to establish an international cooperation mechanism to act as a common point of contact between and among states, regional and international organizations on all aspects of combating piracy and armed robbery at sea off Somalia's coast."

[34] Statement of Contact Group on Piracy off the Coast of Somalia, New York, January 14, 2009.

[35] Vice Admiral William Gortney, Commander, U.S. Naval Forces Central Command, Testimony before the House Armed Services Committee, March 5, 2009.

[36] Ibid.

[37] Cui Xiaohuo, "New fleet sails to fight Somali pirates," *China Daily*, April 2, 2009.

[38] The task force is scheduled to visit Karachi, Pakistan, Singapore, and Perth, Australia, before returning to the Horn of Africa Region.

[39] European Union Council Secretariat, "Fact Sheet: EU naval operation against piracy (EU NAVFOR Somalia - Operation ATALANTA)," EU NAVFOR/04, March 2009.

[40] Information on the Maritime Security Center-Horn of Africa (MSC-HOA) is available at: http://www.mschoa.eu/Default.aspx.

[41] The International Maritime Organization is a United Nations agency with over 168 member governments. Based in the United Kingdom, its members develop regulations for international shipping related to safety, the environment, and maritime security. It also serves as a global coordinating body for legal issues, technical co-operation, and maritime security including anti-piracy efforts. For more information, see: http://www.imo.org/.

[42] IMO Resolution A. 1002(25) "calls Upon Governments in the region to conclude, in co-operation with the Organization, and implement, as soon as possible, a regional agreement to prevent, deter and suppress piracy and armed robbery against ships."

[43] Resolution 1851 "encourages all states and regional organizations fighting piracy and armed robbery at sea off the coast of Somalia to consider creating a center in the region to coordinate information relevant to piracy and armed robbery at sea off the coast of Somalia."

[44] International Maritime Organization, "High-level meeting in Djibouti adopts a Code of Conduct to repress acts of piracy and armed robbery against ships,"

[45] Djibouti, Ethiopia, Kenya, Madagascar, Maldives, Seychelles, Somalia, the United Republic of Tanzania, and Yemen signed the code of conduct in January.

[46] Text available at: http://www.recaap.org/about/pdf/ReCAAP%20Agreement.pdf. Sixteen signatories include the People's Republic of Bangladesh, Brunei Darussalam, the Kingdom of Cambodia, the People's Republic of China, the Republic of India, the Republic of Indonesia, Japan, the Republic of Korea, the Lao People's Democratic Republic, Malaysia, the Union of Myanmar, the Republic of the Philippines, the Republic of Singapore, the Democratic Socialist Republic of Sri Lanka, the Kingdom of Thailand, and the Socialist Republic of Viet Nam

[47] A diagram of ReCAAP-ISC reporting and response procedures is available at: http://www.recaap.org/about/pdf/Information_Flow_ Response_chart.pdf.

[48] Resolution 1851 "invites" states and regional organizations "to conclude special agreements or arrangements with countries willing to take custody of pirates in order to embark law enforcement officials ("shipriders") from the latter countries, in particular countries in the region, to facilitate the investigation and prosecution of persons detained as a result of operations conducted under [the] resolution."

[49] One knot is unit of measurement equivalent to one nautical mile per hour or 1.15 miles per hour.

[50] The term 'freeboard' refers to the distance between the waterline and the main deck of the ship.

[51] Available at: http://www.icc-ccs.org/index.php?option=com_content&view=article&id=344&Itemid=233.

[52] AFRICOM's AOR includes all African countries except Egypt, which remained in the AOR of CENTCOM after that command transferred responsibilities for the Horn of Africa countries to AFRICOM in 2008. For more information see CRS Report RL 34003, *U.S. Africa Command: U.S. Strategic Interests and the Role of the U.S. Military in Africa*, by Lauren Ploch.

[53] According to the Administration justification for the supplemental request, "funding may also be directed towards Security Sector Reform (SSR) efforts. Some funding will pay for equipment and logistical support for training efforts for Somali troops by Tanzania, Uganda, Rwanda, and other nations in the region that will implement the training activities." The Administration also is seeking authority to transfer up to $50 million in supplemental Contributions for International Peacekeeping Activities (CIPA) funding to the PKO account for Somalia, if necessary.

[54] Convention on the High Seas, 13 U.S.T. 2312; T.I.A.S. 5200; 450 U.N.T.S. 82. Signed at Geneva, April 29, 1958. Entered into force September 30, 1962.

[55] United Nations Convention on the Law of the Seas (UNCLOS), 21 I.L.M. 1261. Convention adopted December 10, 1982. Entered into force November 16, 1994 (the United States is not a party to the Agreement).

[56] Convention for the Suppression of Unlawful Acts Against the Safety of Maritime Navigation, T.I.A.S. Signed at Rome, March 10, 1988. Entered into force March 1, 1992 (for the United States March 6, 1995).

[57] The United Nations Convention on the Law of the Sea (A historical perspective), available at http://www.un.org/Depts/los/convention_agreements/convention_historical_perspective.htm.

[58] Convention on the High Seas at Article 14; UNCLOS at Article 100.

[59] UNCLOS at Article 101. (The definition is, with a minor grammatical change, the same definition found in the Convention on the High Seas (Article 14).

[60] Convention on the High Seas at Article 22.

[61] Convention on the High Seas at Article 19; UNCLOS at Article 105.

[62] *Id.*

[63] International Maritime Organization statement on aims for the Convention for the Suppression of Unlawful Acts Against the Safety of Maritime Navigation. Available at http://www.imo.org/.

[64] *Id.*

[65] Convention for the Suppression of Unlawful Acts Against the Safety of Maritime Navigation at Article 5.

[66] 18 U.S.C. § 1651 *et seq.*

[67] 18 U.S.C. §§ 1651 and 1652.

[68] For one review and discussion of these legal questions from a U.S. military point of view, see Cmdr. James Kraska and Capt. Brian Wilson, "Fighting Piracy," *Armed Forces Journal*, February 1, 2009 (expressing view that international and regional cooperation, not armed force, is the long-term solution to piracy).

[69] See http://www.smh.com.au/world/fate-of-teen-pirate-uncertain-200904 14-a5ih.html.

[70] For example, under common law, children under the age of seven are conclusively presumed to be without criminal capacity, those who have reached the age of fourteen are treated as fully responsible, while as to those between the ages of seven and fourteen there is a rebuttable presumption of criminal incapacity. In addition jurisdictions have adopted juvenile court legislation providing that some or all criminal conduct by those persons under a certain age (usually eighteen) must or may be adjudicated in the juvenile court rather than in a criminal proceeding. LaFave & Scott, Criminal Law §4.11 (2d ed. 1986).

[71] U.S. Department of Transportation Maritime Administration Advisories are available at: http://www.marad.dot.gov/news_room_landing_page/maritime_advisories/advisory_summary.htm.

[72] Advisory #: 2009-05, East Coast Of Somalia And Gulf Of Aden Transits, April 20, 2009.

[73] International Maritime Organization, "Guidance to shipowners and ship operators, shipmasters and crews on preventing and suppressing acts of piracy and armed robbery against ships," MSC/Circ.623/Rev.3, May 29, 2002. Available at: http://www.imo.org/includes/blast_bindoc.asp?
doc_id=941&format=PDF.

[74] International Maritime Bureau-Piracy Reporting Center, Advice to Masters, April 2009. Available at: http://www.icc-ccs.org/index.php?option=com_content&view=article&id=309&Itemid=97.

[75] International Maritime Organization, "Guidance to shipowners and ship operators, shipmasters and crews on preventing and suppressing acts of piracy and armed robbery

against ships," MSC/Circ.623/Rev.3, May 29, 2002. Available at: http://www.imo.org/includes/blast_bindoc.asp?doc_id=941&format=PDF. See also: International Maritime Bureau-Piracy Reporting Center, Advice to Masters, April 2009. Available at: http://www.icccs.org/index.php?option=com_content&view=article&id=309&Itemid=97.

[76] Most of the concerns listed here are discussed in John W. Miller and Paulo Prada, "Attack Raises Debate On Guns For Sailors," *Wall Street Journal*, April 11, 2009; and Keith Bradsher, "Rescue Fuels Debate Over Arming Crews," *New York Times*, April 13, 2009.

[77] According to the A.M. Best Company, the U.S. property/casualty insurance industry's reported surplus, a measure of claims-paying capacity or capital, declined by about $62.3 billion or 12%, at year-end in 2008 to $455.6 billion from $517.9 billion at year-end 2007. While not all of the $455.6 billion is allocated to ocean marine insurance, the level of industry-wide surplus suggests U.S. private insurers have the overall financial resources to cover potential losses from incidences of ocean piracy.

[78] United States Navy, Commander, Combined Maritime Forces Public Affairs, "Combined Maritime Forces Issues New Alert to Mariners," April 7, 2009.

[79] Dr. Jun Bando, Maritime Security Coordinator/U.S. Africa Command Liaison, U.S. Department of State Bureau of African Affairs, "International Response to Piracy Expanded, Unified," *DipNote*, January 30, 2009.

[80] The Contact Group participants are as follows: Italy, Kenya, Norway, Sweden, Tanzania, the United Kingdom, the United States, and representatives of the African Union, the European Union Council President and Commission, the Inter-governmental Authority on Development, the Arab League, and the United Nations.

In: Economic, Political and Social Issues of Africa
Editor: Jeremy S. McQueen

ISBN 978-1-61209-957-6

Chapter 10

INTERNATIONAL CRIMINAL COURT CASES IN AFRICA: STATUS AND POLICY ISSUES*

Alexis Arieff, Rhoda Margesson and Marjorie Ann Browne

ABSTRACT

The International Criminal Court (ICC), established in 2002, has to-date initiated investigations exclusively in Sub-Saharan Africa. The ICC Prosecutor has opened cases against 16 individuals for alleged crimes in northern Uganda, the Democratic Republic of Congo, the Central African Republic, and the Darfur region of Sudan. In addition, the Prosecutor is analyzing situations—a preliminary step toward initiating a full investigation—in Kenya, Côte d'Ivoire, and Chad, as well as in Colombia, Afghanistan, and Georgia. Recent congressional interest in the work of the ICC in Africa has arisen from concern over gross human rights violations on the African continent and beyond.

On March 4, 2009, ICC judges issued an arrest warrant for Sudanese President Omar Hassan alBashir for war crimes and crimes against humanity. The case against Bashir represents the first attempt by the ICC to prosecute a sitting head of state. The prosecution has drawn praise from human rights advocates as a step toward ending impunity for serious human rights abuses in Africa. However, it also has raised concerns that ICC actions could endanger peace processes in Darfur and southern Sudan. Additional fears that the ICC could imperil international humanitarian operations in Sudan were heightened when the Sudanese government responded to the warrant by expelling international relief agencies.

Unlike the three other African countries under ICC investigation, Sudan is not a party to the ICC; instead, the ICC was granted jurisdiction over Darfur through a United Nations Security Council resolution in March 2005. The United States, as a member of the Security Council, may influence the ICC's actions. Obama Administration officials have expressed support for the prosecution of perpetrators of atrocities in Darfur and have suggested that Bashir should face the accusations

* This is an adited, reformatted and augmented version of CRS Report RL34665, dated July 14, 2009.

against him. Legislation before the 111th Congress references the ICC warrant against Bashir and, more broadly, U.S. government support for ICC prosecutions.

Four suspects in other ICC investigations are currently in ICC custody, pending trial. Three are alleged leaders of Congolese militias, and the fourth is a former Congolese rebel leader, transitional vice president, and senator and who is accused of overseeing war crimes in neighboring Central African Republic. Additionally, a Darfur rebel leader summoned by ICC judges voluntarily appeared before the Court in May.

This report provides background on ICC investigations in Africa and gives an overview of cases currently before the Court. The report also examines issues raised by the ICC's actions in Africa, including the ICC's possible role in deterring future abuses and the potential impact of international criminal prosecutions on peace processes, ongoing in many countries on the continent. In-depth background on U.S. policy toward the ICC can be found in CRS Report RL31495, *U.S. Policy Regarding the International Criminal Court (ICC),* by Jennifer K. Elsea.

RECENT DEVELOPMENTS

On March 4, 2009, a panel of judges of the International Criminal Court (ICC) issued an arrest warrant for Sudanese President Omar Hassan al-Bashir for war crimes and crimes against humanity in the Darfur region of Sudan. This represents the first attempt by the ICC to prosecute a sitting head of state. While the decision to seek Bashir 's arrest has drawn praise from human rights advocates, it also has raised concerns that ICC actions could endanger peace processes in Darfur and southern Sudan. Additional fears that the ICC could imperil humanitarian operations in Sudan were heightened when the Sudanese government responded to the warrant by expelling over a dozen international relief agencies. While the ICC judges approved the Prosecutor's request for a warrant for Bashir, they dismissed the Prosecutor's attempt to prosecute Bashir for the crime of genocide. The Prosecutor has appealed the dismissal.

The decision to prosecute an African head of state has sparked a backlash among African countries, 30 of which are parties to the Court. The African Union (AU) has repeatedly called for a deferral of the prosecution. In July 2009, AU members resolved not to cooperate with the ICC on carrying out the Bashir arrest warrant [1]. At the same time, African parties to the ICC suggested they would refrain from withdrawing from the Court altogether [2] International human rights groups criticized the move by the AU, and the government of Botswana, a party to the ICC, said in a statement that Botswana "does not agree with this decision and wishes to reaffirm its position that as a state party... it has treaty obligations to fully cooperate with the ICC in the arrest and transfer of the president of Sudan to the ICC." [3] An AU panel on Darfur, headed by former South African President Thabo Mbeki, said it had not taken a stance with regard to the Bashir warrant. [4]

The Obama Administration has expressed support for the ICC investigation and prosecution of war crimes in Sudan, and an Administration spokesman stated that "those that have committed atrocities [in Darfur] should be held accountable" [5] Secretary of State Hillary Clinton, speaking to reporters, said "President Bashir would have a chance to have his day in court if he believes that the indictment is wrongly charged. He can certainly contest it" [6] In late March 2009, then acting State Department spokesman Robert Wood said, "We have said over and again that those who commit atrocities need to be held accountable... We are under no obligation to the ICC to arrest President Bashir. We're not a party to the Rome Statute. And let's leave it at that" [7] In July, the Obama Administration's Special Envoy on Sudan, Gen. Scott Gration, stated that the United States would engage with Sudan's president, "but that does not mean that [Bashir] does not need to do what's right in terms of facing the International Criminal Court and those charges." [8]

In July 2009, President Obama referred to the conflict in Darfur as a "genocide," and averred that it was a "millstone around Africa's neck."[9] At the same time, Special Envoy Gration suggested at a press briefing in June that the Sudanese government was no longer engaged in a "coordinated" genocidal campaign in Darfur, contending that ongoing violence represented "the remnants of genocide" and fighting "primarily between rebel groups, the Sudanese government, and... some violence between Chad and Sudan."[10]

Members of Congress have expressed a range of positions with regard to the warrant for Bashir. Senator Russell Feingold has urged the Administration not to defer the ICC prosecution, stating, "If there is significant progress made toward ending violence on the ground in Darfur, it may be appropriate to consider a suspension at that time." [11] Senator John Kerry has said the warrant "complicates matters," but should not stop U.S. efforts to resolve the conflict in Darfur [12]. Legislation before the 111th Congress references the ICC warrant against Bashir and, more broadly, U.S. government support for ICC prosecutions.

BACKGROUND

Overview of the International Criminal Court

The Statute of the ICC, also known as the Rome Statute, entered into force on July 1, 2002, and established a permanent, independent Court to investigate and bring to justice individuals who commit the most heinous violations of international law and human rights, namely war crimes, crimes against humanity, and genocide [13] The ICC's jurisdiction extends only over crimes committed since the entry into force of the Statute. The ICC is headquartered in The Hague, Netherlands. As of January 2009, 108 countries were parties to the Statute [14]. The United States is not a party to the ICC. The Assembly of States Parties (the body made up of the 108 parties) provides administrative oversight and other support for the Court, including adoption of the budget and election of 18 judges, a Prosecutor (currently Luis Moreno Ocampo from Argentina), and a Registrar (currently Bruno Cathala from France). [15]

Situations [16] may be referred to the ICC in one of three ways as outlined in the articles of the Statute: by a state party to the Statute, the ICC Prosecutor, or the United Nations (U.N.) Security Council. Currently, four situations have been publicly referred to the Prosecutor. The governments of three countries (all parties to the ICC)—Uganda, the Democratic Republic of Congo, and the Central African Republic—each have referred situations to the Prosecutor. The U.N. Security Council has referred one situation (Darfur, Sudan) to the Prosecutor [17]. At least two potential situations were dismissed following preliminary analysis, and at least six others remain under consideration. [18]

The ICC is considered a court of last resort—it will only investigate or prosecute cases of the most serious crimes perpetrated by individuals (not organizations or governments), and then, only when national judicial systems are unwilling or unable to handle them. This principle of admissibility before the Court is known as "complementarity" [19]. Although many domestic legal systems grant sitting heads of state immunity from criminal prosecution, the Rome Statute grants the ICC jurisdiction over any individual, regardless of official capacity. [20]

The U.S. Position on the ICC

The United States is not a party to the Rome Statute. The Bush Administration opposed the Court and renounced any U.S. obligations under the treaty [21] It objected to the Court on a number of grounds, including:

- the Court's assertion of jurisdiction (in certain circumstances) over citizens, including military personnel, of countries that are not parties to the treaty [22];
- the perceived lack of adequate checks and balances on the powers of the ICC prosecutors and judges;
- the perceived dilution of the role of the U.N. Security Council in maintaining peace and security; and
- the ICC's potentially chilling effect on America's willingness to project power in the defense of its interests.

The Bush Administration sought to conclude bilateral immunity agreements (BIAs), known as "Article 98 agreements," with most states parties to exempt U.S. citizens from possible surrender to the ICC [23]. These agreements are named for Article 98(2) of the Statute, which bars the ICC from asking for surrender of persons from a state party that would require it to act contrary to its international obligations.

The U.S. government is prohibited by law from assisting the ICC in its investigations, arrests, detentions, extraditions, or prosecutions of war crimes, under the American Servicemembers' Protection Act of 2002, or ASPA (P.L. 107-206, Title II). The prohibition is extensive, covering, among other things, the obligation of appropriated funds, assistance in investigations on U.S. territory, participation in U.N. peacekeeping operations unless certain protections from ICC actions are provided to specific categories of people, and the sharing of classified and law enforcement information. [24]

The Obama Administration is conducting a high-level review of its policy toward the ICC. In her confirmation hearing before the Senate Foreign Relations Committee in January 2009, Secretary of State Hillary Clinton said, "Whether we work toward joining or not, we will end hostility toward the ICC and look for opportunities to encourage effective ICC action in ways that promote U.S. interests by bringing war criminals to justice" [25]. In March 2009, then-acting Assistant Secretary for International Organizations James B. Warlick said, in response to a question on the Administration's position on joining the ICC, "There will be a policy process that will address this Administration's position on the International Criminal Court, so it's too early to say." [26]

The ICC and Other International Courts and Tribunals

The post-World War II Nuremberg and Tokyo tribunals to prosecute Nazi and Japanese leaders for crimes against peace, war crimes, and crimes against humanity established precedent for the ICC. Other international courts and tribunals, such as the International Criminal Tribunals for the former Yugoslavia and for Rwanda, also built on these precedents. However, there are some important distinctions between the work of the ICC and that of courts created with limited jurisdiction. The ICC was established through a multilateral treaty and is a permanent, international criminal tribunal [27]. It is not a U.N. body. By contrast, the tribunals for the former Yugoslavia [28] and Rwanda, [29] which were created under separate U.N. Security Council resolutions to address the allegations of crimes against humanity in those countries, are case specific, limited in jurisdiction, and temporary. The Security Council may establish international criminal tribunals on a case-by-case basis.

Numerous regional and other international courts and tribunals also have been created, some on an *ad hoc* basis, to address particular issues [30]. For example, there are options for mixed courts, which may consist of both international judges and prosecutors as well as judges and prosecutors having the nationality of the state in which the trial takes place. Moreover, a mixed court may draw on domestic as well as international law. The mixed court may be part of the judicial organ of the state, as in Kosovo, Cambodia, or Timor-Leste, or it may be more international in the form of a special court, such as the one established for Sierra Leone [31]. These courts and tribunals are distinct from the ICC.

International Court of Justice

The International Court of Justice (ICJ), also located in The Hague, is the principal judicial organ of the United Nations. The ICJ does not prosecute individuals; its role is to settle, in accordance with international law, legal disputes submitted to it by states. Only states may submit cases for consideration, although the ICJ also will give advisory opinions on legal questions when requested to do so by authorized international organizations [32].

Congressional Interest in the ICC in Africa

Members of Congress have taken a range of positions on the ICC with regard to Africa. Many in Congress are concerned about massive human rights violations on the continent, and some see the ICC as a possible means of redress for these crimes. At the same time, some oppose the Court on jurisdictional grounds. A combination of presidential waivers and changes to the law have effectively nullified restrictions on U.S. assistance to African parties to the ICC. Restrictions on military assistance to ICC members under the American Servicemembers' Protection Act of 2002, or ASPA (P.L. 107-206, Title II), were repealed under the National Defense Authorization Acts for FY2007 and FY2008. Separately, a restriction on Economic Support Fund (ESF) assistance to certain foreign governments that were parties to the ICC was not carried forward in the Omnibus Appropriations Act of 2009 (P.L. 111-8).

The ICC and Human Rights

Recent draft legislation before Congress has referenced the ICC in connection with human rights abuses in conflicts in Uganda and the Democratic Republic of Congo, and in connection with the global use of child soldiers. Additionally, there has been particular congressional interest in the ICC's work related to Darfur. Relevant legislation before the 111th Congress includes:

- H.Con.Res. 97 ("Calling on the President to support United Nations Security Council referrals of situations involving genocide, war crimes, and crimes against humanity to the International Criminal Court, to cooperate with investigations and prosecutions conducted by the International Criminal Court, and participate as an observer at meetings of the Assembly of States Parties to the Rome Statute"), introduced on April 2, 2009 and referred to the House Committee on Foreign Affairs; and
- H.Res. 241 ("Commending the International Criminal Court for issuing a warrant for the arrest of Omar Hassan Ahmad al-Bashir, President of the Republic of the Sudan, for war crimes and crimes against humanity, and expressing the hope that this will be a significant step in the long road towards achieving peace and stability in the Darfur region"), introduced on March 12, 2009 and referred to the House Committee on Foreign Affairs.

Restrictions on U.S. Assistance to African Parties to the ICC

Observers have raised concerns over the possible assertion of ICC jurisdiction over U.S. military personnel in connection with U.S. participation in U.N. peacekeeping missions in Africa, and with respect to the new U.S. Combatant Command for Africa, AFRICOM [33]. Jurisdictional and other concerns led Congress to pass the American Servicemembers' Protection Act of 2002, or ASPA (P.L. 107-206, Title II), which was signed into law on August 2, 2002. Section 2007 of ASPA prohibited U.S. military assistance to ICC member-states, except for NATO countries, major non-NATO allies, and countries subject to various other waiver provisions. Permanent waivers were granted to countries that ratified Article 98 agreements promising not to surrender U.S. nationals to the Court.

In Sub-Saharan Africa, ASPA effectively froze International Military Education and Training (IMET), Foreign Military Financing (FMF), and Excess Defense Articles (EDA) accounts for Kenya, Mali, Namibia, Niger, South Africa, and Tanzania. However, President Bush waived the prohibition on IMET assistance to 21 countries, including these six, on September 29, 2006, due to concerns that the restrictions could preclude valuable military-to-military ties [34] Congress repealed the ASPA restriction on IMET funding in the National Defense Authorization Act for FY2007 (P.L. 109-364), which was signed into law on October 17, 2006. The National Defense Authorization Act for FY2008 (P.L. 110-181), signed into law on January 28, 2008, repealed Section 2007 of ASPA entirely, ending remaining prohibitions on FMF and EDA assistance.

Separately, the Nethercutt Amendment to the FY2005 Consolidated Appropriations Act (P.L. 108- 447) prohibited Economic Support Fund (ESF) assistance to members of the ICC that had not entered into an Article 98 agreement with the United States, with certain waiver provisions. This prohibition was included as part of the FY2006 Consolidated Appropriations Act (P.L. 109-102, Section 574), and subsequently carried over via continuing resolutions on February 15, 2007 (P.L. 110-5) and September 29, 2007 (P.L. 110-92). A substantially identical restriction was included in the Consolidated Appropriations Act of 2008 (P.L. 110-161, Section 671), signed into law December 26, 2007. However, this restriction was not applied to African countries, due to presidential waivers with respect to Kenya, Mali, Namibia, Niger, South Africa, and Tanzania [35]. The Omnibus Appropriations Act of 2009 (P.L. 111-8) did not carry forward Section 671, which contained the restrictions. This ended such limitations on ESF assistance.

THE ICC AND SUDAN

Sudan is a unique case because of the circumstances of ICC involvement, and because of whom the ICC Prosecutor has chosen to pursue. ICC jurisdiction in Sudan was referred by the U.N. Security Council, as Sudan is not a party to the Court. In September 2004, the Security Council established an International Commission of Inquiry on Darfur under Resolution 1564, citing concern that the Sudanese government had not met its obligations under previous Resolutions [36]. In January 2005, the Commission reported that it had compiled a confidential list of potential war crimes suspects, and "strongly recommend[ed]" that the Security Council refer the situation in Darfur to the ICC [37] On March 31, 2005, U.N. Security Council Resolution 1593 referred the situation in Darfur to the ICC Prosecutor. Following the referral, the ICC Prosecutor received the document archive of the Commission of Inquiry. The Prosecutor also received the Commission's sealed list of individuals suspected of committing serious abuses in Darfur, though this list is not binding on the selection of suspects. The Office of the Prosecutor initiated its own investigation in June 2005.

In April 2007, the ICC issued arrest warrants for a former Sudanese Cabinet Minister and an alleged former leader of the Janjaweed militia in Darfur. The Sudanese government has refused to comply with the warrants, and both suspects remain at large. The Prosecutor is also investigating alleged attacks on peacekeepers and aid workers in Darfur, and in December 2008 filed cases against three rebel commanders in connection with an attack in 2008 that killed twelve African Union peacekeeping troops.

On March 4, 2009, ICC judges issued an arrest warrant for Sudanese President Omar Hassan alBashir for crimes against humanity and war crimes in the Darfur region. The warrant, which was issued in response to a request by the ICC Prosecutor in July 2008, represents the first time the ICC has attempted to prosecute a sitting head of state. The judges' decision, welcomed by many as a step toward ending impunity in Darfur, has provoked condemnation in Sudan and controversy in the region. Sudanese government officials have rejected the ICC's jurisdiction, as Sudan is not a party to the Court, [38] while many international legal experts argue that Sudan is obligated as a U.N. member state to cooperate with ICC actions because they stem from a U.N. Security Council resolution.

U.N. Security Council Resolution 1593

On March 31, 2005, the U.N. Security Council, acting under Chapter VII of the U.N. Charter, adopted Resolution 1593 (2005), which refers reports about the situation in Darfur, Sudan (dating back to July 1, 2002) to the ICC Prosecutor [39] The Resolution was adopted by a vote of 11 in favor, none against, and with four abstentions—the United States, China, Algeria, and Brazil [40] While Sudan is not a party to the ICC and has not consented to its jurisdiction, the case can be referred to the ICC by the U.N. Security Council under Chapter VII. The Resolution is binding on all U.N. member states, including Sudan. Under the ICC Statute, the ICC is authorized, but not required, to accept the case. [41]

The U.S. Position on U.N. Security Council Resolution 1593

In statements made in July and September 2004, respectively, Congress and the Bush Administration declared that genocide was taking place in Darfur [42]. The Administration supported the formation of the International Commission of Inquiry for Darfur [43]. However, the Bush Administration preferred a special tribunal in Africa to be the mechanism of accountability for those who committed crimes in Darfur. It objected to the U.N. Security Council referral to the ICC because of its stated objections to the ICC's jurisdiction over nationals of states not party to the Rome Statute [44] However, the United States had at one time supported a version of the Rome Statute that would have allowed the U.N. Security Council to refer cases involving non-states parties to the ICC, but would not have allowed other states or the Prosecutor to refer cases. The United States abstained on Resolution 1593 (which is not equivalent to a veto in the Security Council) because the Resolution included language that dealt with the sovereignty questions of concern and essentially protected U.S. nationals and other persons of non-party States other than Sudan from prosecution [45]. The abstention did not change the fundamental objections of the Bush Administration to the ICC.

At the same time, the Bush Administration supported international cooperation to stop atrocities occurring in Darfur [46]. The Administration and Congress expressed support for bringing to justice those who perpetrate genocide, war crimes, and crimes against humanity in the region. However, U.S. legal restrictions on providing assistance to the ICC presented an obstacle to the use of the ICC for that purpose. As discussed above, the Obama Administration is conducting a review of its policy towards the ICC and it remains to be seen how it will address situations like Darfur.

ICC Warrants Issued in 2007

In April 2007, the ICC issued arrest warrants for Ahmad Muhammad Harun, who had served as Interior Minister from 2003 and 2005, and Ali Muhammad Ali Abd-Al-Rahman (known as Ali Kushayb), who had allegedly acted as leader of the Janjaweed in the Wadi Salih area of Darfur. [47]

They were each accused of over 40 counts of war crimes and crimes against humanity in connection with abuses allegedly committed in Darfur in 2003 and 2004 [48]. While the Sudanese government initially refused to comply with either warrant, news reports suggest that Sudanese authorities arrested Kushayb in October 2008 [49]. However, Sudanese officials stated they would conduct their own investigation into his alleged crimes in Darfur, and did not indicate that they planned to turn him over to the ICC. Harun was promoted to Minister of Humanitarian Affairs and co-president of a committee to investigate human rights violations in Sudan [50]. In May, Harun was reportedly appointed Governor of South Kordofan State. In 2005, following the initiation of the ICC's investigation, the Sudanese government created its own special courts for Darfur in an apparent effort to stave off the ICC's jurisdiction under the principle of complementarity. However, the courts' efforts were widely criticized as insufficient. [51]

Investigation of Rebel Crimes

In December 2007, the ICC Prosecutor announced the opening of a new investigation into the targeting of peacekeepers and aid workers in Darfur. In November 2008, the Prosecutor submitted a sealed case against three alleged rebel commanders in Darfur whom he accused of committing war crimes during an attack on the town of Haskanita on September 29, 2008. According to the office of the Prosecutor, twelve African Union peacekeepers were killed and eight were injured in the attack [52]. In May, ICC pretrial judges issued a summons to one of the three, Bahar Idriss Abu Garda, to appear before the Court on May 18 [53] Abu Garda reported to The Hague voluntarily.

The judges are still deliberating on whether to issue summonses, or warrants, for the two other alleged rebel commanders sought by the Prosecutor, whose names remain undisclosed.

The Case Against Bashir Arrest Warrant

On March 4, 2009, ICC judges issued a warrant for the arrest of Sudanese President Omar Hassan al-Bashir. The warrant holds that there are "reasonable grounds" to believe Bashir is criminally responsible for five counts of crimes against humanity and two counts of war crimes. The accusations refer to alleged attacks by Sudanese security forces and pro-government militia in the Darfur region of Sudan during the government's six-year counter-insurgency campaign. [54]

The ICC warrant states that there are reasonable grounds to believe attacks against civilians in Darfur were a "core component" of the Sudanese government's military strategy, that such attacks were widespread and systematic, and that Bashir acted "as an indirect perpetrator, or as an indirect co-perpetrator." In his application for an arrest warrant, filed in July 2008, the ICC Prosecutor affirmed that while Bashir did not "physically or directly" carry out abuses, "he committed these crimes through members of the state apparatus, the army, and the Militia/Janjaweed" as president and commander-in-chief of the Sudanese armed forces.

Although many domestic legal systems grant sitting heads of state immunity from criminal prosecution, the Rome Statute grants the ICC jurisdiction regardless of official capacity [55] Human rights organizations, including Amnesty International and Human Rights Watch, hailed the arrest warrant, the first issued by the ICC against a sitting head of state, as an important step against impunity. Many Western governments, including France, Germany, Canada, the United Kingdom, and Denmark, and the European Union as an entity, have called on Sudan to cooperate with the warrant. Reactions by African and Middle Eastern governments have been more critical, with many condemning the ICC or calling for its prosecution to be deferred. Additionally, the governments of Russia and China have opposed the prosecution attempt.

The arrest warrant is not an indictment; under ICC procedures, charges must be confirmed at a pre-trial hearing. The decision to issue a warrant is expected to take into account whether there are reasonable grounds to believe that a suspect committed crimes as alleged by the Prosecutor and whether a warrant is necessary to ensure the suspect's appearance in court. The ICC urged "all States, whether party or not to the Rome Statute, as well as international and regional organizations," to "cooperate fully" with the warrant [56]. One analysis noted that while Bashir may risk arrest if he travels overseas, "no one expects Sudan to hand over Bashir, who has been executive ruler of the country for more than 15 years, absent major political changes in the country." [57]

Genocide Accusations [58]

In his request for an arrest warrant in July 2008, the ICC Prosecutor accused Bashir of three counts of genocide, making Bashir the first individual to be accused of genocide before the Court. The Prosecutor alleged that Bashir "intends to destroy in substantial part the Fur, Masalit and Zaghawa ethnic groups as such" through coordinated attacks by government troops and Janjaweed militia [59]. However, the panel of ICC judges who responded to the application for a warrant found, by a ruling of two-to-one, that the Prosecutor had "failed to provide reasonable grounds to believe that the Government of Sudan acted with specific intent" to destroy these groups [60]. The judges added, however, that the arrest warrant could be amended to include accusations of genocide if further evidence was submitted by the Prosecutor. The Prosecutor is appealing the judges' decision to omit the genocide counts from the arrest warrant. [61]

Many human rights advocates had welcomed the attempt to prosecute Bashir for genocide [62] However, the formulation of the Prosecutor's accusation had drawn some criticism. The U.N. Commission of Inquiry concluded in its January 2005 report that the violence in Darfur did not amount to genocide, although "international offences such as the crimes against humanity and war crimes that have been committed in Darfur may be no less serious and heinous than genocide" [63] Many Darfur activists accused the Commission of allowing political considerations to affect its conclusions [64] Other analysts argue that while the Sudanese government is responsible for serious crimes in Darfur, the Prosecutor's justification for genocide charges did not sufficiently establish intent or Bashir's alleged role. [65]

In July 2009, President Obama referred to the conflict in Darfur as a "genocide," and averred that it was a "millstone around Africa's neck." [66].

At the same time, Special Envoy Gration suggested at a press briefing in June that the Sudanese government was no longer engaged in a "coordinated" genocidal campaign in Darfur, contending that ongoing violence represented "the remnants of genocide" and fighting "primarily between rebel groups, the Sudanese government, and... some violence between Chad and Sudan." [67]

Sudanese Reactions

The Bashir Administration has rejected ICC jurisdiction over Darfur as a violation of its sovereignty and accused the Court of being part of a neocolonialist plot against a sovereign African and Muslim state [68] Other Sudanese reactions have focused on the potential impact of an arrest warrant on ongoing peace processes, peacekeeping operations, and humanitarian relief, and on the potential impact on legislative and presidential elections scheduled to take place in 2010.

The Bashir Administration

The Bashir Administration has portrayed the ICC as an instrument of Western pressure for regime change [69]. The Sudanese president has repeatedly denied that genocide or ethnic cleansing is taking place in Darfur and has rejected ICC jurisdiction as an infringement on Sudanese sovereignty. The last mission to Sudan by ICC prosecutorial staff was in January-February 2007, after which the government announced it would no longer allow ICC personnel to speak to Sudanese officials [70] Days before the request for a warrant against Bashir was announced, a presidential spokesman reportedly called the Prosecutor a "terrorist" whose investigation was based on testimony by rebel leaders and spies posing as humanitarian workers. [71]

Government authorities have taken a hardline stance against Sudanese suspected of sympathizing with the ICC prosecution attempt. In November 2008, Sudanese police detained a human rights activist they accused of being in contact with the ICC, while in January 2009, authorities jailed a prominent Islamist opposition leader who had called for Bashir to surrender to the ICC in order to avoid internal strife [72] Also in January, a Sudanese man was reportedly convicted of "spying" for the ICC and sentenced to 17 years in prison [73]. In February, a senior official warned that an arrest warrant for Bashir would derail peace talks with Darfur rebels. [74]

The government responded to the arrest warrant by expelling over a dozen international aid organizations it accused of collaborating with the ICC, including Oxfam and Doctors Without Borders. Bashir reportedly warned that "all the diplomatic missions in Sudan, the NGOs, and the peacekeepers" could face the same punishment, the latest in a series of remarks by Sudanese officials that appeared the threaten the safety of U.N. personnel in Sudan if an arrest warrant were issued [75]. Officials reportedly threatened to retaliate harshly against anyone who "cooperated" with the court, while government supporters organized mass rallies in the president's favor. A New York Times analysis noted that while many advocates hope the arrest warrant will weaken Bashir 's hold in power, "Sudanese resentment of the court's actions could have the reverse effect and rally the nation to his side. After the court's prosecutor first announced that he was seeking a warrant for Mr. Bashir, some of the president's political enemies closed ranks behind him" [76] Similarly, analysts disagree over whether the warrant has intensified Bashir 's international isolation. The Sudanese leader has engaged in aggressive diplomatic outreach to allied states, traveling overseas to multiple friendly countries in the weeks following the warrant's issuance.

Other Sudanese Reactions

Islamist opposition leader Hassan Al-Turabi (and former key Bashir ally) has criticized the Bashir Administration's stance toward the ICC and has called on the president to turn himself over to the international justice system [77] (Turabi was detained for two months in 2009 in apparent connection with statements to this effect.) Other Sudanese opposition members have displayed measured support for Bashir, reportedly due to concerns that ICC actions could derail elections scheduled for early 2010, while privately acknowledging mixed reactions [78]. Spokesmen for three major Darfur rebel factions—the Sudan Liberation Movement (SLM), Sudan Liberation Army (SLA), and Justice and Equality Movement (JEM)—welcomed the prosecution of Bashir, as have many Darfuri refugees, according to news reports [79] The JEM, which in February had signed a deal on confidence-building measures with the government, stated in March that the arrest warrant precluded the continuation of peace talks. [80]

Reports suggest southern Sudanese are ambivalent about the attempt to prosecute Bashir [81] The Sudan People's Liberation Movement (SPLM)—the former southern rebel group and partner in the Government of National Unity under the 2005 Comprehensive Peace Agreement (CPA)— initially called on the Government of National Unity "to forge an understanding with the international community and to cooperate with [the] ICC on the legal processes." [82] However, after the arrest warrant was issued, the SPLM released a statement saying that "Sudan should stand with Bashir at this hard time." [83] The SPLM nevertheless criticized the expulsion of aid organizations. Some SPLM officials are reportedly concerned that ICC actions could endanger the CPA, while others have expressed hope that prosecution could leverage international pressure on Khartoum. [84]

Regional Reactions

The Sudanese government has rallied support among Arab and African leaders, as well as among regional organizations such as the African Union (AU), the Arab League, and the Organization of the Islamic Conference (OIC), [85] all of which have criticized the ICC arrest warrant and called for a deferral of prosecution. Many African and Middle Eastern governments expressed concern over the arrest warrant, including the governments of South Africa, Nigeria, Kenya, Rwanda, Tanzania, Benin, Eritrea, Egypt, Iran, Syria, Libya, Algeria, and Morocco. Some African leaders, notably Botswana's President Ian Khama and Uganda's President Yoweri Museveni, have taken a more supportive stance toward the ICC [86]. Some African and Middle Eastern commentators have praised the ICC decision to pursue Bashir as an important step against impunity in the region, while others expressed concern that the move displayed bias against African countries or a neocolonial attitude [87]

By mid-2009, the decision to prosecute an African head of state appeared to have sparked a backlash among African countries, 30 of which are parties to the Court. In July 2009, AU members resolved not to cooperate with the ICC on carrying out Bashir's arrest [88] At the same time, African states parties suggested they would refrain from withdrawing from the Court altogether [89] International human rights groups criticized the AU resolution, and the government of Botswana, a party to the ICC, said in a statement that Botswana "does not agree with this decision and wishes to reaffirm its position that as a state party... it has treaty obligations to fully cooperate with the ICC in the arrest and transfer of the president of Sudan to the ICC" [90] An AU panel on Darfur, headed by former South African President Thabo Mbeki, said it had not taken a stance with regard to the Bashir warrant. [91]

Security Council Considerations in July 2008: Context and Background

The July 14, 2008, ICC Prosecutor's request for an arrest warrant for Bashir occurred during the time that the U.N. Security Council was considering extension of the Council mandate for the African Union-United Nations Hybrid Operation in Darfur (UNAMID). The Council had before it the report of the U.N. Secretary-General on the deployment of the operation, dated July 7 and covering the period April to June 2008 [92]. It was expected that this mandate, which was to expire July 31, would be extended, albeit with some discussion of UNAMID-related issues.

Council considerations were significantly impacted by the ICC Prosecutor's announcement. In the light of reactions to this request (see previous section) and in view of the fact that the Council had sent the case to the ICC for investigation, protracted consultations within the Council on the content of a resolution extending the UNAMID mandate delayed Council action until nearly the final hour. [93]

Among the issues engaging Council members after the July 14 action was the oft-made suggestion that the Council include in its resolution a request, under Article 16 of the ICC Statute, for a deferral or suspension of further ICC action on the case for up to 12 months for the purpose of, among other things, facilitating efforts toward a peaceful settlement of the situations in Darfur and south Sudan. Some governments also expressed concerns that a positive ICC response to the request for an arrest warrant would exacerbate the situation on the ground in Darfur, making both peacekeepers and humanitarian workers subject to further attacks.

Article 16 of the ICC Statute is entitled Deferral of investigation or prosecution and provides that

> No investigation or prosecution can be commenced or proceeded with under this Statute for a period of 12 months after the Security Council, in a resolution adopted under Chapter VII of the Charter of the United Nations, has requested the Court to that effect; that request may be renewed by the Council under the same conditions.

Thus, if the U.N. Security Council, acting under Chapter VII of the Charter, adopts a resolution requesting the ICC to suspend or defer any further investigation or prosecution of the case against Bashir, the ICC, including the Prosecutor, would be obliged to cease its investigation in that particular situation and the Pre-Trial Chamber, before which the warrant request is pending, would have to suspend its considerations. The Council request would be applicable for 12 months and would be renewable.

David Scheffer, who headed the U.S. delegation to the conference that drafted the ICC Statute, in an August 20, 2008, Op-ed in Jurist, noted that the "negotiating history of Article 16 should be instructive to how the Council currently examines the Darfur situation" [94] Scheffer alleged that Article 16 was drafted and adopted to enable the U.N. Security Council to suspend or defer an ICC investigation or prosecution of a situation "before either is launched if priorities of peace and security compelled a delay of international justice." He stated that "the original intent behind Article 16 was for the Security Council to act pre-emptively to delay the application of international justice for atrocity crimes in a particular situation in order to focus exclusively on performing the Council's mandated responsibilities for international peace and security objectives." This was a tool to be employed by the

Council in instances of "premature State Party or Prosecutor referrals." In addition, Scheffer claimed that if the current proposals for Council suspension of further ICC action on a situation referred to the ICC by the Council had been foreseen, "Article 16 never would have been approved by the.. .majority of governments attending the U.N. talks on the Rome Statute for it would have been viewed as creating rights for the Security Council far beyond the original intent of the Singapore compromise."

Scheffer noted, "Nonetheless, one plausibly may argue that the language of Article 16 of the Rome Statute technically empowers the Security Council to intervene at this late date and block approval of an arrest warrant against President Bashir or even suspend its execution following any approval of it by the judges." [95]

U.N. Security Council Resolution 1828 (2008), adopted on July 31, 2008, by a vote of 14 in favor and with the United States abstaining, extended UNAMID for a further 12 months [96]. In abstaining on the vote rather than voting against it, the United States supported renewal of the UNAMID mandate but noted that the language in preambular paragraph 9 "would send the wrong signal to President Bashir and undermine efforts to bring him and others to justice." [97] In remarks with the press following the vote, U.S. Deputy Permanent Representative Alejandro Wolff stated:

> The reason for our abstention.. .had to do with one paragraph that would send the wrong signal at a very important time when we are trying to eliminate the climate of impunity, to deal with justice, and to address crimes in Darfur, by suggesting that there might be a way out. There is no compromise on the issue of justice. The ... United States felt it was time to stand up on this point of moral clarity and make clear that this Permanent Member of the Security Council will not compromise on the issue of justice [98]

The United States also abstained on Council Resolution 1828 (2008), extending the UNAMID mandate, pointing to the language in a preambular paragraph that referred to the July 14 application by the ICC prosecutor and the possibility of a Council request for deferral of further consideration of ICC consideration of that case as the reason for the abstention. While the Bush Administration would have likely preferred a different venue for consideration of the genocide conditions in Darfur, it did not halt referral to the ICC by vetoing the resolution.

Some observers have suggested that the U.S. position in the past would not have permitted abstention on the two Council resolutions. Thus, they maintain that under the Bush Administration, the United States moved to a policy that recognized that under certain circumstances, the ICC might have a role [99]. Others have pointed out, however, that any perceived moderation in U.S. views toward the Court did not affect its overall position not to become a party to the ICC Statute.

The two U.S. abstentions in the Council appear to have been driven by non-ICC foreign policy issues that were perceived as more important. The need to support the U.S. policy against genocide in Darfur was perceived as more important than overall U.S. opposition to the ICC. (This broader policy drove the U.S. abstention on Council referral of the situation to the ICC in 2005.) Moreover, the need to ensure that the UNAMID mandate, on the brink of expiring, was extended for another 12 months was also perceived as more important and led to the U.S. abstention in July 2008.

OTHER ICC CASES IN AFRICA

The ICC Prosecutor has opened five cases in connetion with northern Uganda, four in connection with the Democratic Republic of Congo (DRC), and one in connection with the Central African Republic (CAR). In contrast to Sudan, which has resisted ICC jurisdiction, these three countries are states parties to the ICC; all three and referred situations in their countries to the Prosecutor. Four suspects are currently in ICC custody, all Africans: Jean-Pierre Bemba, Thomas Lubanga, Germain Katanga, and Mathieu Ngudj olo. No one has yet been convicted by the ICC.

In addition, the ICC Prosecutor is analyzing situations in Kenya, Côte d'Ivoire, and Chad, a preliminary step toward opening a full investigation. In Kenya, an official inquiry into abuses committed in the aftermath of disputed elections in late 2007 has stalled, prompting mediator Koffi Annan to submit information on individuals suspected of orchestrating the violence to the ICC Prosecutor in July 2009 [100].

Additionally, many observers of Zimbabwe, including local human rights activists, Archbishop Desmond Tutu of South Africa, and the organization Physicians for Human Rights, have called for an ICC investigation into human rights abuses reportedly committed by government forces in Zimbabwe. [101]

Uganda

The government of Uganda, a party to the ICC, referred "the situation concerning the Lord's Resistance Army" to the Court in 2003 [102]. The Lord's Resistance Army (LRA) is a rebel group that has fought for over two decades in northern Uganda [103]. In October 2005, the ICC unsealed arrest warrants—the first issued by the Court—for LRA leader Joseph Kony and LRA commanders Vincent Otti, Okot Odhiambo, Dominic Ongwen, and Raska Lukwiya. The Prosecutor accused the LRA of establishing "a pattern of brutalization of civilians," including murder, forced abduction, sexual enslavement, and mutilation, amounting to crimes against humanity and war crimes. [104]

None of the suspects are in custody; Lukwiya and Otti have reportedly been killed since the warrants were issued, while other LRA commanders are reportedly in hiding in neighboring countries. In February 2009, Odhiambo and Ongwen reportedly entered negotiations on surrendering to the ICC, under the auspices of the U.N. peacekeeping force in southern Sudan [105] While Uganda's referral specifically mentioned the Lord's Resistance Army, the Prosecutor also is investigating crimes allegedly committed by the Ugandan military in northern Uganda.

Despite widespread documentation of LRA abuses, the ICC's actions in Uganda have met with some strong domestic and international opposition due to debates over what would constitute justice for the war-torn communities of northern Uganda and whether the ICC has helped or hindered the pursuit of a peace agreement [106]. Some observers argue that ICC arrest warrants were a crucial factor in bringing the LRA to the negotiating table in 2006 for peace talks brokered by the Government of South Sudan. In August 2006, rebel and government representatives signed a landmark cessation of hostilities agreement; in February 2008, the government and the LRA reached several significant further agreements, including a permanent cease-fire. However, threats of ICC prosecution are considered by some to be a stumbling block to achieving an elusive final peace deal. The LRA has reportedly demanded that ICC arrest warrants be annulled as a prerequisite to a final agreement. The Ugandan government has offered a combination of amnesty and domestic prosecutions for lower-and mid-ranking LRA fighters, and is reportedly willing to prosecute LRA leaders in domestic courts if the rebels accept a peace agreement. This could entail challenging the LRA cases' admissibility before the ICC under the principle of complementarity. However, only the ICC's Pre-Trial Chamber has the authority to make a decision on admissibility. The ICC Prosecutor has reportedly stated that he will fight any move to drop the LRA prosecutions. [107]

Democratic Republic of Congo (DRC)

The DRC government referred "the situation of crimes within the jurisdiction of the Court allegedly committed anywhere in the territory of the DRC" to the Prosecutor in April 2004 [108] Despite the end of a five-year nationwide civil war in 2003 and the conduct of national elections in 2006, the DRC has continued to suffer from armed conflict, particularly in the volatile eastern regions bordering Rwanda, Uganda, and Burundi. The ICC has issued four arrest warrants in its first DRC investigation, which focuses on the eastern Congolese district of Ituri, where an inter- ethnic war erupted in June 2003 with reported involvement by neighboring governments [109]. Three suspects are in custody, while a fourth remains at large. The Prosecutor has stated that a second investigation in the DRC will focus on sexual crimes committed in the eastern provinces of North and South Kivu, while a third will look into "the role of those who organized and financed" armed groups throughout the country [110] The latter investigation could potentially target officials from neighboring countries along with members of the Congolese government and military [111]

Thomas Lubanga Dyilo

The ICC issued a sealed arrest warrant in February 2006 for Thomas Lubanga Dyilo, the alleged founder and leader of the Union des Patriotes Congolais (UPC) in Ituri and its military wing, the Forces Patriotiques pour la Libération du Congo (FPLC). At the time, Lubanga was in Congolese custody and had been charged in the domestic justice system [112] After a determination of admissibility by the ICC, Lubanga was transferred to ICC custody in March 2006. The ICC has charged Lubanga with three counts of war crimes related to the recruitment and use of child soldiers [113]. Despite a lengthy delay due to a procedural challenge, Lubanga's trial began in January 2009. Lubanga has pleaded not guilty.

Germain Katanga and Mathieu Ngudjolo Chui

Germain Katanga, the alleged highest-ranking commander of the *Force de Résistance Patriotique en Ituri* (FRPI) and Ngudj olo, the alleged highest-ranking commander of the Front des Nationalistes et Intégrationnistes (FNI), are being prosecuted as co-perpetrators for allegedly having "acted in concert to mount an attack targeted mainly at Hema civilians" in Ituri in 2003 [114]

The ICC issued sealed arrest warrants for Katanga and Ngudjolo in July 2007, and they were transferred by Congolese authorities to ICC custody in October 2007 and February 2008, respectively.

The Prosecutor has accused them jointly of four counts of crimes against humanity and nine counts of war crimes related to murder, "inhumane acts," sexual crimes, the use of child soldiers, rape, and other abuses [115]. The case is in the pre-trial phase.

Bosco Ntaganda

The ICC issued a sealed warrant for the arrest of Bosco Ntaganda, the alleged former Deputy Chief of General Staff for Military Operations in Lubanga's FPLC, in August 2006.

In April 2008, the ICC unsealed the warrant, having determined that public knowledge of ICC proceedings would neither endanger witnesses nor further obstruct attempts to bring Ntaganda into custody [116] The ICC Prosecutor has accused Ntaganda of three counts of war crimes related to the alleged recruitment and use of child soldiers in 2002 and 2003 [117].

Attempts to arrest Ntaganda have been complicated by the fact that he is reportedly currently leading the Congrès National pour la Défense du Peuple (CNDP) in the DRC's North Kivu province. The CNDP was founded by Laurent Nkunda, a dissident military general [118] However, in January 2009, Ntaganda, who was formerly second in command, ousted Nkunda, who was later taken into Rwandan custody. Ntaganda agreed to be integrated into the Congolese military, where he was promoted to the rank of general. [119]

The Congolese government has since refused to pursue Ntaganda on behalf of the ICC, arguing that to do so would jeopardize peace efforts in the Kivu region [120] Congolese human rights advocates have rejected this reasoning [121] Ntaganda remains at large.

Central African Republic (CAR)

The government of CAR, a party to the ICC, referred "the situation of crimes within the jurisdiction of the Court committed anywhere on [CAR] territory" to the ICC Prosecutor in January 2005 [122]. In May 2008, the ICC issued a sealed warrant of arrest for Jean-Pierre Bemba Gombo, a former DRC rebel leader. The warrant alleged that as commander of the Mouvement de Libération du Congo (MLC), one of two main DRC rebel groups during that country's civil war, Bemba had overseen systematic attacks on civilians in CAR territory between October 2002 and March 2003 [123] Bemba's MLC, based in the DRC's north, was reportedly invited into CAR by then-President Ange-Félix Patassé to help quell a rebellion led by François Bozizé. The Prosecutor accused Bemba of five counts of war crimes and three counts of crimes against humanity for alleged rape, torture, pillaging, and other abuses [124] Bemba, in exile in Europe since 2007, was arrested by Belgian authorities in May 2008 and turned over to the ICC in July 2008. Bemba's prosecution is in the pre-trial phase.

Bemba's prosecution by the ICC has been controversial in the DRC, where the MLC is now the largest opposition party [125]. After serving as one of four vice-presidents in the DRC transitional government from 2003 to 2006, Bemba took 42% of the vote in the DRC's 2006 presidential election, second only to the incumbent president, Joseph Kabila; Bemba's supporters accused the president of electoral fraud. Bemba won a Senate seat in January 2007, but he went into exile in April after relations with Kabila continued to deteriorate. Some observers consider Bemba's prosecution by the ICC to be politically expeditious for President Kabila, whose main rival is now in international custody. The Office of the Prosecutor has denied that political considerations played a role in the decision to pursue Bemba, and the government of DRC has denied involvement in the ICC case against him. [126]

ISSUES RAISED BY THE ICC'S ACTIONS IN AFRICA

Some observers have praised the ICC's investigations in Africa as a crucial step against impunity on the continent. Nevertheless, the ICC's actions have provoked debates over the court's potential impact, its perceived prioritization of Africa over other regions, its selection of cases, and the effect of international prosecutions on peace processes. Most persistently, critics have accused the ICC of potentially jeopardizing the settlement of long-running civil wars in the pursuit of an often abstract "justice." Supporters of the Court reject these criticisms, and hope that ICC investigations will build accountability for the world's gravest atrocities and contribute to Africa's long-term peace and stability.

Potential Deterrent Effect

Many hope that the ICC will usher in a new period of international accountability for the gravest human rights abuses by ensuring that perpetrators are brought to justice. The ICC's founders anticipated that by ending impunity, the ICC would deter future atrocities [127] Indeed, some observers have argued that the ICC's success should be evaluated not just based on the punishment of past atrocities, but also in terms of "the effect its investigations have on reducing abysmal conduct in the present and future." [128] (The Office of the Prosecutor maintains that the choice of cases is not based on calculations of deterrent effect, though the Office acknowledges that strategic communications related to ICC prosecutions may play a role in deterrence [129])

The goal of deterrence has been particularly salient in the ICC's investigations in Africa, which have focused to-date on regions where conflict is ongoing or only recently settled [130] However, difficulties in enforcing ICC arrest warrants and the fact that the Court has yet to convict any suspects have led some to question whether the threat of ICC prosecution is credible. Some observers suggest that the Court's failure to apprehend suspects in Darfur in particular has bared tensions between the ICC's universal mandate and its reliance on the enforcement power of states [131]. Others maintain that deterrence is difficult to evaluate and that changes in perpetrators' behavior may be visible only over the long-run. Some argue that the Court's compilation of evidence, including transcribed interviews with witnesses, may serve future prosecutions or reconciliation processes even if they do not immediately lead to convictions.

Accusations of Bias

The ICC's investigations in Sub-Saharan Africa have stirred concerns over African sovereignty and the long history of foreign intervention on the continent. For example, President Paul Kagame of Rwanda, which is not a state party to the Court, has portrayed the ICC as a new form of "imperialism" that seeks to "undermine people from poor and African countries, and other powerless countries in terms of economic development and politics." [132] Other commentators allege that the Prosecutor has limited investigations to Africa because of geopolitical pressures, either out of a desire to avoid confrontation with major powers or as a tool of Western foreign policy [133] The attempt to prosecute Bashir has been particularly controversial, drawing rebuke from African governments and regional organizations. Supporters of the Court respond that investigations to-date have been determined by referrals, either by African states or the Security Council, and that the Prosecutor continues to analyze situations outside of Africa. In addition, observers have pointed out that national legal systems in Africa are particularly weak, which has allowed the ICC to assert its jurisdiction under the principle of complementarity [134] The Office of the Prosecutor maintains that its choice of cases is based on the relative gravity of abuses, and that crimes committed in Sub-Saharan Africa are among the world's most serious. [135]

The Prosecutor's selection of cases also has proven controversial. ICC prosecutions in Sudan had, prior to the request for a warrant against President Bashir, drawn criticism for targeting mid-level officials rather than those with alleged higher-order responsibility for abuses in Darfur. Some have criticized ICC prosecutions in Uganda, the DRC, and CAR for focusing on alleged abuses committed by rebel fighters to the exclusion of those reportedly committed by government troops. In Uganda, some observers suggest that the ICC is locally seen as associated with the administration of President Museveni, as only LRA commanders have been targeted since the Prosecutor's investigation in northern Uganda began despite reported abuses by government troops [136]. The decision to pursue DRC opposition leader Jean-Pierre Bemba Gombo has provoked accusations that the Prosecutor was swayed by political bias, as Bemba was seen as a leading opposition figure in DRC before he entered into exile and was arrested; or excessive pragmatism, since other Congolese political actors accused of similar abuses have not been pursued to date. As one pair of authors has written, "perceptions of the ICC on the ground have at times been damaged by insufficient efforts by the Court to make clear the basis on which individuals have been the subject of warrants and of particular charges, while those of apparently equal culpability have not." [137] ICC supporters have responded that the Prosecutor is mandated to focus on a limited number of particularly serious cases, and that investigations are ongoing and could lead to prosecutions against members of opposing sides in the future.

Justice vs. Peace?

One of the most persistent criticisms of the ICC's actions in Africa has been that by prosecuting active participants in ongoing or recently settled conflicts, the Court risks prolonging violence or endangering fragile peace processes. By removing the bargaining chip of amnesty from the negotiating table, critics allege, the ICC may remove incentives for peace settlements while encouraging perpetrators to remain in power in order to shield themselves from prosecution. Some observe that in such cases, "it is difficult to tell victims of these conflicts that the prosecution of a small number of people should take precedence over a peace deal that may end the appalling conditions they endure and the daily risks they face." [138]

Concerns that the aims of "justice" and "peace" may conflict have been particularly prominent in Uganda and Sudan. In Uganda, some observers argue that ICC arrest warrants against LRA commanders have acted as an impediment to achieving a final peace agreement. However, others counter that the threat of ICC prosecution, on top of other shifts in the conflict, was a decisive factor in bringing the LRA to the negotiating table in 2006. This observation has led some to see the ICC in Uganda as "an important ingredient in a political solution" for the conflict-plagued north [139]. In Sudan, some observers have argued that the attempt to prosecute President Bashir could endanger the Comprehensive Peace Agreement for southern Sudan and the peace process in Darfur, or provide an incentive to the ruling party to cling to power ahead of elections scheduled for 2009. For example, according to former U.S. envoy to Sudan Andrew Natsios, "the regime will now avoid any compromise or anything that would weaken their already weakened position, because if they are forced from office they face trials before the ICC... [An ICC warrant for Bashir] may well shut off the last remaining hope for a peaceful settlement for the country." [140]

These criticisms were reinforced when the Sudanese government responded to the ICC arrest warrant for Bashir by expelling aid agencies and threatening NGOs and peacekeeping troops. In testimony before Congress, when asked about the impact of the ICC warrant on U.N. peacekeeping operations in Darfur, Director of National Intelligence Dennis C. Blair said, "the indictment and President Bashir 's reaction have made him less cooperative than he was—than he was before... I think it will make it harder [for the U.N. to run peacekeeping operations in Darfur]" [141] U.N. Secretary-General Ban Ki-moon, who has maintained a neutral position on the ICC's actions in Sudan, has nonetheless argued that the international community must seek to balance "peace" and "justice" in dealing with the conflict in Darfur and expressed concern that the expulsion of aid organizations was extremely detrimental to relief and peacekeeping operations. [142]

Supporters of the Court argue the ICC request for a warrant against Bashir has opened up new opportunities to secure peace in Darfur, as a credible threat of prosecution may serve as an important lever of pressure on actors in a conflict [143]. For example, Priscilla Hayner of the International Center for Transitional Justice writes, "it would be wrong to suggest that pragmatism always trumps principle in matters of life and death, and thus that one must ease up on justice in order to achieve peace. In some cases, the interest of peace has been well served by strong, forthright efforts to advance justice." [144]. Some argue that "peace deals that sacrifice justice often fail to produce peace" in the long-run [145] Observers have pointed out that discerning the effect of ICC actions on complex processes is extremely difficult.

Appendix A. List of African States Showing Whether They Are Parties to the ICC and Have Ratified an "Article 98 Agreement"

Country	Party to ICC	Ratified Article 98 Agreement
Algeria		X
Angola		X
Benin	X	X
Botswana	X	X
Burkina Faso	X	X
Burundi	X	X
Cameroon		X
Cape Verde		X
Central African Republic	X	X
Chad	X	X
Comoros	X	X
Congo, Republic of	X	X
Congo, Democratic Republic of	X	X
Côte d'Ivoire		X
Djibouti	X	X
Egypt		X
Equatorial Guinea		X
Eritrea		X
Ethiopia		
Gabon	X	X
Gambia, The	X	X
Ghana	X	X
Guinea	X	X
Guinea-Bissau		X
Kenyaa	X	
Lesotho	X	X
Liberia	X	X
Libya		
Madagascar	X	X
Malawi	X	X
Malia	X	
Mauritania		X
Mauritius	X	X
Morocco		X
Mozambique Namibiaa	X	X
NigeraNigeria Rwanda	X X	X X
São Tomé and Príncipe	X	X
Senegal	X	X
Seychelles		X
Sierra Leone	X	X
Somalia		
South Africa[a]	X	
Sudan		
Swaziland		X
Tanzaniaa	X	
Togo		X
Tunisia		X
Uganda	X	X
Zambia	X	X
Zimbabwe		

Sources: International Criminal Court; U.S. Department of State, Treaties in Force 2007.

[a.] Economic Support Fund (ESF) assistance to these countries, which are parties to the ICC but have not signed Article 98 agreements, remains restricted under the Nethercutt Amendment. However, the restriction was waived by President Bush in 2006 and 2008 (see report).

REFERENCES

[1] *Reuters*, "AU Leaders Vote to End Bashir Cooperation with ICC," July 3, 2009.
[2] Barry Malone, "Africa ICC Members Will Not Quit Despite Bashir Move," *Reuters*, June 9, 2009.
[3] *AFP*, "Botswana Says Al-Bashir Must Stand Trial at ICC," July 6, 2009.
[4] *Reuters*, "Mbeki-Led African Panel Says No Stance on ICC," July 11, 2009.
[5] *Agence France-Presse* (*AFP*), "White House Demands 'Accountability' on Darfur After Warrant," March 4, 2009; Colum Lynch, "Sudan Retains Clout While Charges Loom," *The Washington Post*, February 9, 2009.
[6] *Reuters,* "Clinton Says Al-Bashir Can 'Have His Day in Court,' March 4, 2009.
[7] *AFP*, "US Says 'Under No Obligation' to Arrest Beshir," March 24, 2009.
[8] *AFP*, "US Envoy: Must Cooperate With Sudan Even if New Warrant Issued," July 9, 2009.
[9] *AFP*, "Sudan: Obama Comments 'A Step Back,'" July 11, 2009.
[10] Colum Lynch, "Sudan's 'Coordinated' Genocide in Darfur is Over, U.S. Envoy Says," *The Washington Post*, June 18, 2009.
[11] *AFP*, "Obama Must Support Beshir Warrant: US senator," March 4, 2009.
[12] *Reuters*, "INTERVIEW-Kerry says ICC case no bar on Darfur peace drive," April 17, 2009.
[13] The ICC began operating at its inauguration on March 11, 2003. The ICC plans to define and determine its jurisdiction over Crimes of Aggression in 2009. The Statute also established a second independent institution, the Trust Fund for Victims, to help victims of these crimes. The Trust Fund for Victims can only act in situations where the ICC has jurisdiction.
[14] For the current status of signatures, ratifications, and reservations, see the ICC's website, http://www.icc-cpi.int/asp/ statesparties.html.
[15] For background information on the International Criminal Court, see CRS Report RL3 1437, *International Criminal Court: Overview and Selected Legal Issues*, by Jennifer K. Elsea
[16] Articles 13 and 14 (1) of the Rome Statute provide for both States Parties and U.N. Security Council referral of "situations" to the Court. During the negotiations, the question arose of whether individual "cases" or "situations" should be referred to the ICC Prosecutor. According to one author, writing on the jurisdiction of the ICC, "it was suggested that States Parties should not be able to make complaints about individual crimes or cases: it would be more appropriate, and less political, if 'situations' were instead referred to the Court." (Elizabeth Wilmshurst, "Jurisdiction of the Court," Chapter 3, in Roy S. Lee, editor, The International Criminal Court. The *Making of the Rome Statute: Issues, Negotiations, Results* [Boston: Kluwer Law International, 1999], p. 131.) Another author, writing on the role of the Prosecutor, noted that the "powers of the Prosecutor could also be broadened in the context of a State's complaint to the Court, if the complaint referred to 'situations' rather than to individual 'cases.'" A proposal to this effect, introduced by the U.S. delegation in 1996, was "very soon supported by a large majority of States," many of whom had been "uneasy" with allowing a party to "select individual cases of violations and lodge complaints...with

respect to such cases. This could...encourage politicization of the complaint procedure." The Prosecutor, after referral of the situation, could "initiate a case against the individual or individuals concerned." (Silvia A. Fernandez de Gurmendi, "The Role of the International Prosecutor," Chapter 6, in Lee, *The International Criminal Court*, p. 180.)

[17] See press releases on each referral at the ICC's website, http://www.icc-cpi.int.

[18] Reportedly, the ICC has received 1,700 communications about alleged crimes in 139 countries, but 80 percent have been found to be outside the jurisdiction of the court. The Prosecutor has received self referrals only from African countries. See Stephanie Hanson, Global Policy Forum, "Africa and the International Criminal Court," *Council on Foreign Relations*, July 24, 2008.

[19] The bar for proving complementarity has been set very high. In the ICC case against Congolese suspect Thomas Lubanga Dyilo, the Pre-Trial Chamber ruled that in order for a case to be inadmissible, national proceedings must encompass "both the person and the conduct which is the subject of the case before the Court" (ICC Pre-Trial Chamber I, The Prosecutor Vs. Thomas Lubanga Dyilo, *Decision on the Prosecutor's Application for a Warrant of Arrest, Article 38*, February 10, 2006). This language suggests that a domestic prosecution must essentially duplicate the ICC prosecution in order for admissibility to be challenged. Even in such a case, the ICC may retain jurisdiction if domestic proceedings are not conducted impartially or independently (Rome Statute, Article 17).

[20] Article 27 of the Rome Statute.

[21] The United States signed the Rome Statute under the Clinton Administration, on December 31, 2000, but did not submit the agreement to the Senate for its advice and consent to treaty and ratification. In May 2002, the Bush Administration notified the United Nations that it did not intend to become a party to the ICC, and that there were therefore no legal obligations arising from the signature.

[22] The United States had supported a version of the Rome Statute that would have allowed the U.N. Security Council to refer cases involving non-states parties to the ICC, but would not have allowed other states or the Prosecutor to refer cases.

[23] Each state party to an Article 98 agreement promises that it will not surrender citizens of the other state party to international tribunals or the ICC, unless both parties agree in advance. An Article 98 agreement would prevent the surrender of certain persons to the ICC by parties to the agreement, but would not bind the ICC if it were to obtain custody of the accused through other means. See the Appendix A for a list of states parties to the ICC and Article 98 agreements in Africa.

[24] These prohibitions do not apply to cooperation with an *ad hoc* international criminal tribunal established by the U.N. Security Council such as the International Criminal Tribunal for the Former Yugoslavia (ICTY) or the International Criminal Tribunal for Rwanda (ICTR). See 22 U.S.C. 7423(a)(1). In the case of Darfur, the *Darfur Accountability and Divestment Act of 2007* (H.R. 180), passed by the House on August 3, 2007, would have offered U.S. support to the ICC's efforts to prosecute those responsible for acts of genocide in Darfur, but was not enacted into law.

[25] Walter Pincus, "Clinton's Goals Detailed," *The Washington Post*, January 19, 2009.

[26] U.S. State Department, "U.S. Reengagement with the U.N." March 20, 2009, Foreign Press Center briefing transcript.

[27] The creation of the ICC is the culmination of a decades-long effort to establish an international court with the jurisdiction to try individuals for the commission of crimes against humanity. For a general background and discussion of the ICC, see CRS Report RL30020, *The International Criminal Court Treaty: Description, Policy Issues, and Congressional Concerns*, by Ellen Grigorian; CRS Report RL3 1437, *International Criminal Court: Overview and Selected Legal Issues*, by Jennifer K. Elsea; and CRS Report RL32605, *Genocide: Legal Precedent Surrounding the Definition of the Crime*, by Judith Derenzo and Michael John Garcia.

[28] On May 25, 1993, U.N. Security Council Resolution 827 (1993) established the International Criminal Tribunal for the former Yugoslavia (ICTY). It had its precursors in U.N. Security Council Resolution 752, which asked parties to respect humanitarian law; U.N. Security Council Resolution 771, which condemned ethnic cleansing and demanded access by international observers; and U.N. Security Council Resolution 780, which requested the U.N. Secretary- General to establish a Commission of Experts to investigate alleged violations of humanitarian law.

[29] U.N. Security Council Resolution 935 (2004) asked the Secretary-General to establish a Commission of Experts to examine the allegations of genocide and grave violations of international humanitarian law in Rwanda. After its investigation, the Commission recommended that an international tribunal be established to address the crimes. On November 8, 2004, the Security Council, in Resolution 955, established the International Criminal Tribunal for Rwanda (ICTR).

[30] See, for example, "African International Courts and Tribunals" website, at http://www.aict-cita.org.

[31] The Special Court for Sierra Leone (SCSL), a hybrid international-domestic court based in Sierra Leone's capital, Freetown, was set up jointly by the Government of Sierra Leone and the United Nations under Security Council Resolution 1315 (2000). It is mandated to try those who bear the greatest responsibility for serious violations of international humanitarian law and Sierra Leonean law committed in the territory of Sierra Leone after November 30, 1996. While most suspects have been tried in Freetown, former President Charles Taylor of Liberia is in custody in the Hague, where he is being tried by the SCSL for crimes against humanity and other violations of international humanitarian law.

[32] See U.S. Department of State, United States Participation in the United Nations—2006, p. 130.

[33] See CRS Report RL34003, *Africa Command: U.S. Strategic Interests and the Role of the U.S. Military in Africa*, by Lauren Ploch. The Defense Department has signaled its intention to locate an AFRICOM staff presence on the continent, either in the form of a headquarters or regional offices. Depending on the country, the United States may or may not have a Status of Forces Agreement (SOFA) that appropriately covers military personnel not detailed to the Embassy. The United States also has a semi-permanent troop presence known as Combined Joint Task Force-Horn of Africa (CJTF-HOA), in Djibouti. Personnel associated with CJTF-HOA conduct activities throughout the region. The command authority for CJTF-HOA, previously under Central Command (CENTCOM), was transferred to AFRICOM in 2008.

[34] Presidential Determination No. 2006-27 of September 29, 2006; CRS interview with State Department official, September 4, 2008.
[35] Presidential Determination No. 2007-5 of November 27, 2006, waives restrictions on FY2006 ESF assistance; Presidential Determination No. 2008-21 of June 20, 2008, does not specify a fiscal year.
[36] S/RES/1564 (2004), September 18, 2004.
[37] Report of the International Commission of Inquiry on Darfur to the United Nations Secretary-General, S/2005/60, January 25, 2005.
[38] The Sudanese government signed the Rome Statute on September 8, 2000, but did not ratify it. On August 26, 2008, Sudan notified the Secretary-General of the United Nations, as depositary of Rome Statute of the International Criminal Court, that Sudan "does not intend to become a party to the Rome Statute. Accordingly, Sudan has no legal obligation arising from its signature on 8 September 2000." (Reference: C.N.612.2008.TREATIES-6 [Depositary Notification], Rome Statute of the International Criminal Court, "Sudan: Notification.")
[39] See U.N. Press Release, "Security Council Refers Situation in Darfur, Sudan, to Prosecutor of International Criminal Court," SC/835 1; and U.N. Press Release, "Secretary-General Welcomes Adoption of Security Council Resolution Referring Situation in Darfur, Sudan to International Criminal Court Prosecutor," March 31, 2005, SG/SM/9797- AFR/1 132.
[40] U.N. Security Council Resolution 1593 (2005), March 31, 2005.
[41] Frederic L. Kirgis, "U.N. Commission's Report on Violations of International Humanitarian Law in Darfur: Security Council Referral to the International Criminal Court," *American Society of International Law Insight Addendum*, April 5, 2005.
[42] Concurrent Resolution Declaring Genocide in Darfur, Sudan (H.Con.Res. 467 [108th], July 22, 2004; Congressional Testimony by then-Secretary of State Colin Powell, September 9, 2004.
[43] U.N. Press Release, "Security Council Declares Intention to Consider Sanctions to Obtain Sudan's Full Compliance with Security, Disarmament Obligations on Darfur," SC/8191, September 18, 2004.
[44] U.S. Mission to the United Nations (USUN) Press Release #055, "Explanation of Vote on the Sudan Accountability Resolution," Ambassador Ann W. Patterson, March 31, 2005.
[45] See Paragraph 6 of Security Council Resolution 1593; also see Kirgis, Op. Cit.
[46] USUN Press Release #055, Op. Cit.; USUN Press Release #229, "Statement on the Report of the International Criminal Court," Carolyn Willson, Minister Counselor for International Legal Affairs, November 23, 2005.
[47] The Sudanese government has denied having control over the Janjaweed, a term for ethnic Arab militias accused of perpetrating human rights abuses in Darfur. However, consensus exists among human rights researchers, journalists, and others who have visited Darfur that the Janjaweed have received arms and support from the government. The warrants were made public in early May 2007.
[48] ICC Press Release, "Warrants of Arrest for the Minister of State for Humanitarian Affairs of Sudan, and a Leader of the Militia/Janjaweed," May 2, 2007.

[49] Jeffrey Gettleman, "Sudan Arrests Militia Chief Facing Trial," *The New York Times*, October 14, 2008.
[50] International Federation of Human Rights, "The International Criminal Court and Darfur: Questions and Answers," available online at http://www.iccnow.org/documents/FIDH_QA_Darfur_ENG.pdf.
[51] See e.g. Human Rights Watch, *Lack of Conviction: The Special Criminal Court on the Events in Darfur*, June 2006; U.N. News, "Sudan's Special Court On Darfur Crimes Not Satisfactory, UN Genocide Expert Says," December 16, 2005.
[52] ICC Office of the Prosecutor, "Attacks on Peacekeepers Will Not Be Tolerated; ICC Prosecutor presents evidence in third case in Darfur," November 20, 2008. The peacekeepers were serving under the African Union Mission in Sudan (AMIS).
[53] The ICC judges issued a summons for Abu Garda, having decided that an arrest warrant was not necessary to ensure the suspect's appearance before the Court. ICC, "Questions and Answers on the Summons to Appear Issued for Bahr Idriss Abu Garda," May 18, 2009.
[54] ICC Pre-Trial Chamber I, Warrant of Arrest for Omar Hassan Ahmad Al Bashir, March 4, 2009.
[55] Rome Statute, Art. 27. International legal experts are, however, divided as to whether the Rome Statute waives "procedural" immunity for sitting heads of state – i.e., protection from arrest while traveling in official capacity – under customary international law.
[56] ICC press release, "ICC Issues a Warrant of Arrest for Omar Al Bashir, President of Sudan," March 4, 2009.
[57] Patrick Worsnip, "No Quick Way to Enforce ICC Warrant for Bashir," *Reuters*, March 5, 2009.
[58] See CRS Report RL32605, *Genocide: Legal Precedent Surrounding the Definition of the Crime*, by Judith Derenzo and Michael John Garcia, for a discussion of the legal elements of genocide under the Rome Statute and under the 1948 Convention on the Prevention and Punishment of the Crime of Genocide.
[59] Darfur's main rebel groups are associated with these ethnicities; the Prosecutor's case against Bashir alleges that military and militia attacks specifically targeted civilians even where rebel locations were spatially separate and well- known. The Prosecutor's application for a warrant referenced additional attacks against other ethnic groups in connection with alleged war crimes and crimes against humanity.
[60] ICC press release, "ICC Issues a Warrant of Arrest for Omar Al Bashir, President of Sudan," March 4, 2009.
[61] ICC Office of the Prosecutor, "Prosecution's Application for Leave to Appeal the "Decision on the Prosecution's Application for a Warrant of Arrest against Omar Hassan Ahmad Al Bashir," March 10, 2009.
[62] See e.g. Human Rights Watch, "Darfur: ICC Moves Against Sudan's Leader; Charges Against al-Bashir a Major Step to Ending Impunity," July 14, 2008; Amnesty International, "President Of Sudan Could Face Arrest Over Darfur War Crimes," July 18, 2008.
[63] Report of the International Commission of Inquiry on Darfur to the United Nations Secretary-General Pursuant to Security Council Resolution 1564 of 18 September 2004, January 25, 2005.

[64] E.g., Eric Reeves, "Report of the International Commission of Inquiry on Darfur: A critical analysis (Part II)," Sudanreeves.org, February 6, 2005.

[65] See e.g. Alex de Waal, "Darfur, the Court and Khartoum: The Politics of State Non-Cooperation," in Nicholas Waddell and Phil Clark, eds., *Courting Conflict? Justice, Peace and the ICC in Africa* (London: The Royal Africa Society, March 2008); Andrew Heavens, "ICC Case Against Bashir Has Holes – Sudan Expert," *Reuters*, January 27, 2009; Rony Brauman, "The ICC's Bashir Indictment: Law Against Peace," *World Politics Review*, July 23, 2008. For further background, see Human Rights Watch, *Entrenching Impunity: Government Responsibility for International Crimes in Darfur*, December 2005.

[66] *AFP*, "Sudan: Obama Comments 'A Step Back,'" July 11, 2009.

[67] Colum Lynch, "Sudan's 'Coordinated' Genocide in Darfur is Over, U.S. Envoy Says," *The Washington Post*, June 18, 2009

[68] E.g., BBC Monitoring, "Sudanese Leader Calls International Court 'Tool of Imperialist Forces,'" [State-owned] Suna News Agency, August 20, 2008; Marlise Simons and Neil MacFarquhar, "Bashir Defies Arrest Order on War Crime Charges," *The New York Times*, March 6, 2009.

[69] See e.g. *Al-Sahafah* [Khartoum], "Sudanese Aide Accuses West of Striving to Replace Al-Bashir," via BBC Monitoring, August 21, 2008; *Sudan Tribune*, "Sudan Warns UN Chief Over ICC," via BBC Monitoring, August 18, 2008; and de Waal, Op. Cit.

[70] CRS interview with ICC Office of the Prosecutor official, September 3, 2008. ICC prosecutorial staff have conducted extensive interviews with witnesses outside of Sudan, including in neighboring countries.

[71] *The Associated Press* (hereafter, *AP*), "Sudan Dismisses ICC Proceedings on Darfur, Reiterates Refusal to Hand Over Any Suspects," July 11, 2008.

[72] *AFP*, "Sudan Police Detain Rights Activist for Contact with the ICC," November 26, 2008; Mohamed Osman, "Sudan Detains Opposition Leader Who Urged President to Face Darfur Genocide Charges," *AP*, January 15, 2009.

[73] BBC News Online, "Sudanese 'War Crimes Spy' Jailed," January 28, 2009.

[74] Andrew Heavens, "Darfur War Crimes Warrant Will Ruin Talks – Official," *Reuters*, February 16, 2009.

[75] Abdelmoniem Abu Edries Ali, "Defiant Beshir in Darfur, Warns Foreigners," *AFP*, March 8, 2009; *AFP*, "ICC Action Against Sudan's Beshir Could Hurt UN: Ban," February 4, 2009.

[76] Marlise Simons, "Court Issues Warrant for Arrest of Sudan President," *The New York Times*, March 5, 2009.

[77] Guillaume Lavallee, "Freed Opposition Leader Slams Sudan Response to Warrant," *AFP*, March 9, 2009.

[78] Lydia Polgreen and Jeffrey Gettleman, "Sudan Rallies Behind Leader Reviled Abroad," *The New York Times*, July 28, 2008; Sarah El Deeb, "Indicted Sudanese President Seeks Help From Rivals," *AP*, August 6, 2008.

[79] *Reuters*, "Reaction to Warrant for Bashir's Arrest," March 4, 2009; Sarah El Deeb, "Darfur Refugees Say Genocide Trial for Sudan President is Only Path to Real Peace," *AP*, November 15, 2008.

[80] Samer al-Atrush, "Darfur Rebel Group Says Peace Talks Not Possible," *AFP*, March 4, 2009.

[81] See e.g. "Sudan: Saving Omer," *Africa Confidential*, August 1, 2008; and Naseem Badiey, "Ocampo v Bashir: The Perspective from Juba," *Oxford Transitional Justice Research Working Paper Series*, July 18, 2008.

[82] SPLM Press Release, "SPLM Position On ICC Indictment," July 21, 2008; see also Wasil Ali, "SPLM Official Calls on Sudan to 'Deal Legally' With ICC," *Sudan Tribune*, August 15, 2008.

[83] *Reuters*, "Reaction to Warrant for Bashir's Arrest," March 4, 2009.

[84] Opheera McDoom, "Analysis-Justice Clashes With Peace on Darfur Bashir Warrant," *Reuters*, July 14, 2008; Mushtaq, Op. Cit

[85] The OIC is an inter-governmental organization of 57 states that aims to "project the interests of the Muslim world" (OIC website, at http://www.oic-oci.org/oicnew/page_detail.asp?p_id=52).

[86] Rodney Muhumuza, "We Can't Condemn ICC Over Bashir—Museveni," *The Monitor* [Kampala], August 4, 2008; *BBC Monitoring Africa*, "AU differs with Botswana leader over ICC warrant against Sudan's Bashir" (via Factiva), May 6, 2009.

[87] See e.g., *The Daily Champion* [Lagos, Nigeria], "Al-Bashir's Indictment," August 6, 2008; Paul Ejime, "Before AlBashir Goes on Trial," The Guardian [Lagos], July 28, 2008; Al-Jazeera, "The Opposite Direction," presented by Faysal al-Qasim, August 12, 2008, via the Open Source Center; *AFP*, "Praise and Criticism for ICC From African Rights Organizations," July 16, 2008. Archbishop Desmond Tutu of South Africa, who serves on the board of directors of the ICC's Trust Fund for Victims, has criticized African governments for supporting Bashir, writing, "I regret that the charges against President Bashir are being used to stir up the sentiment that the justice system—and in particular, the international court—is biased against Africa. Justice is in the interest of victims, and the victims of these crimes are African. To imply that the prosecution is a plot by the West is demeaning to Africans and understates the commitment to justice we have seen across the continent."

[88] *Reuters*, "AU Leaders Vote to End Bashir Cooperation with ICC," July 3, 2009.

[89] Barry Malone, "Africa ICC Members Will Not Quit Despite Bashir Move," *Reuters*, June 9, 2009.

[90] *AFP*, "Botswana Says Al-Bashir Must Stand Trial at ICC," July 6, 2009.

[91] *Reuters*, "Mbeki-Led African Panel Says No Stance on ICC," July 11, 2009.

[92] The U.N. Security Council requested that the Secretary-General report every 90 days on progress made in implementation of UNAMID and the status of the political process.

[93] Security Council Report, "Update Report, Sudan," July 28, 2008, available at http://www.securitycouncilreport.org.

[94] David Scheffer, "The Security Council's Struggle over Darfur and International Justice," Jurist—Forum (Jurist, University of Pittsburgh School of Law), online at http ://jurist. law.pitt/forumy/2008/08/security-councils-struggle-overdarfur.php.

[95] Scheffer, Op. Cit. A more academic commentary on Article 16 may be found in Luigi Condorelli and Santiago Villalpando, *Referral and Deferral by the Security Council,* Chapter 17.2, in *The International Criminal Court: A Commentary*, edited by Antonio Cassese, Paola Gaeta, and John R.W.D. Jones (New York: Oxford University Press, 2002), vol. I, pp. 644-654.

[96] See S/PV.5947 for verbatim record of the meeting and U.N. Press Release S/94 12 for an unofficial summary of the statements made and the text of the adopted resolution. For links to both items, see under July 31 at http://www.un.org/Depts/dhl/resguide/scact2008.htm. A U.S. vote against the resolution would have defeated the resolution since that "no" vote would have been a veto.

[97] Explanation of vote by Ambassador Alejandro Wolff, U.S. Deputy Permanent Representative, USUN Press Release # 209 (08), July 31, 2008. The text of preambular paragraph 9 follows: "Taking note of the African Union (AU) communiqué of the 142nd [AU] Peace and Security Council (PSC) Meeting dated 21 July (S/2008/48 1, annex), having in mind concerns raised by members of the Council regarding potential developments subsequent to the application by the Prosecutor of the International Criminal Court of 14 July 2008, and taking note of their intention to consider these matters further."

[98] Remarks by Ambassador Alejandro Wolff, U.S. Deputy Permanent Representative, at the Security Council Stakeout [with the press], USUN Press Release #210 (08), July 31, 2008.

[99] See, for example, Council on Foreign Relations, "Bellinger Says International Court Flawed But Deserving of Help in Some Cases," Interview, July 10, 2007; AP, "U.S. Ambivalent on Genocide Charge Against Sudan's President," *International Herald Tribune*, July 15, 2008; Hanson, Op. Cit.; and *Council on Foreign Relations*, "The Dilemma of International Justice," Interview, July 28, 2008.

[100] United Nations via States News Service, "International Criminal Court Receives Materials on Kenyan Post-Election Violence," July 9, 2009.

[101] *AFP*, "Rape in Zimbabwe: Human rights lawyers build prosecution case," August 7, 2008; Angus Shaw, "Nobel Peace Prize Winner Tutu Says Time Has Come for Threat of Force Against Zimbabwe's Leader," AP, December 24, 2008; Michelle Faul, "Physicians: Corruption killing people in Zimbabwe," *AP*, January 13, 2009. Zimbabwe is not a party to the ICC, but ICC jurisdiction could be referred through a U.N. Security Council resolution, as with Sudan.

[102] ICC Office of the Prosecutor Press Release, "President of Uganda Refers Situation Concerning the Lord's Resistance Army (LRA) to the ICC," January 29, 2004. According to an Office of the Prosecutor official, referrals by the governments of Uganda and DRC followed moves by the Office of the Prosecutor to open investigations under its discretionary power (CRS interview, September 3, 2008); see also Payam Akhavan, "The Lord's Resistance Army Case: Uganda's Submission of the First State Referral to the International Criminal Court," *The American Journal of International Law*, 99, 2 (April 2005), pp. 405-406.

[103] See CRS Report RL33701, *Uganda: Current Conditions and the Crisis in North Uganda*, by Ted Dagne.

[104] ICC Press Release, "Warrant of Arrest Unsealed Against Five LRA Commanders," October 14, 2005. Kony is wanted for 12 counts of crimes against humanity, including murder, enslavement, sexual enslavement, rape, and "inhumane acts," and 21 counts of war crimes, including murder, cruel treatment of civilians, directing an attack against a civilian population, pillaging, inducing rape, and the forced enlistment of children; the other LRA commanders are accused of crimes against humanity and war crimes, ranging from four to 32 counts.

[105] *AFP*, "Two Ugandan Rebel Chiefs Want to Surrender," February 6, 2009; *AFP*, "LRA Fighters Trapped: Congo spokesman," February 14, 2009.

[106] See Tim Allen, Trial Justice: The International Criminal Court and the Lord's Resistance Army (London: Zed Books, 2006).

[107] CRS interview with ICC Office of the Prosecutor official, September 3, 2008. According to the official, the Ugandan government has expressed continued commitment to arresting the LRA leaders in discussions with the ICC.

[108] ICC Office of the Prosecutor Press Release, "Prosecutor Receives Referral of the Situation in the Democratic Republic of Congo," April 19, 2004.

[109] Ituri's armed groups did not participate in the peace process between DRC's major rebel movements that brought the country's nationwide civil war to an end in 2003. While U.N. peacekeepers and DRC government troops have succeeded in staunching much of the violence in Ituri, many of the groups have not disarmed, and the area is still considered unstable. See International Crisis Group, *Congo: Four Priorities for Sustainable Peace in Ituri*, Africa Report No. 140, May 13, 2008.

[110] ICC Press Release, "DRC: ICC Warrant of Arrest Unsealed Against Bosco Ntaganda," April 29, 2008.

[111] CRS interview with Office of the Prosecutor official, September 3, 2008. Nationals of non-member states are subject to ICC jurisdiction for crimes committed on the territory of a member state.

[112] According to Human Rights Watch, Lubanga was arrested by Congolese authorities after the killing of nine U.N. peacekeepers in Ituri in February 2005. He and other Ituri militia members had been charged with genocide, war crimes, and crimes against humanity, but had not been brought to trial when the ICC warrant was issued. (Human Rights Watch, "D.R. Congo: ICC Arrest First Step to Justice," March 17, 2006.)

[113] ICC, The Prosecutor Vs. Thomas Lubanga Dyilo, Document Containing the Charges, Article 61(3)(a) (Public Redacted Version), August 28, 2006.

[114] ICC, Combined Factsheet: Situation in the Democratic Republic of the Congo, Germain Katanga and Mathieu Ngudjolo Chui, June 27, 2008. Their cases were joined in March 2008.

[115] ICC, Combined Factsheet, Op. Cit.

[116] ICC Press Release, "Warrant of Arrest Against Bosco Ntaganda Unsealed," April 29, 2008.

[117] ICC Pre-Trial Chamber, The Prosecutor vs. Bosco Ntaganda, Warrant of Arrest, August 22, 2006. The warrant states that Ntaganda is "believed to be" a Rwandan national.

[118] For background on the conflict, see International Crisis Group, *Congo: Bringing Peace to North Kivu*, Africa Report No. 133, October 31, 2007.

[119] *HRW*, "DR Congo: Brutal Rapes by Rebels and Army," press release, April 8, 2009.

[120] *AFP*, "Peace Before Justice, Congo Minister Tells ICC," February 12, 2009.
[121] *AFP*, "Hand Over Rebel Leader Ntaganda to ICC, Say DR Congo NGOs," February 19, 2009.
[122] ICC Office of the Prosecutor Press Release, "Prosecutor Receives Referral Concerning Central African Republic," January 7, 2005.
[123] Bozizé took power in a coup in 2003 and is the current president of CAR.
[124] ICC Press Release, "Surrender of Jean-Pierre Bemba to the International Criminal Court," July 3, 2008. The counts as listed in this document appear to have changed slightly from those listed in the original arrest warrant.
[125] The MLC converted itself into a political party following the end of the DRC civil war in 2003.
[126] CRS interview with Office of the Prosecutor official, September 3, 2008; Voice of America, "Congo Denies Instigating ICC Charges Against Former VP Bemba," June 16, 2009.
[127] Preamble of the Rome Statute; see also International Criminal Court Assembly of States Parties, "Court Adopts Agreements to Launch Court's Operation," United Nations Press Release L/3013, September 9, 2002.
[128] Waddell and Clark, "Introduction," in *Courting Conflict?*
[129] CRS interview, September 3, 2008.
[130] The ICC's temporal jurisdiction, which limits prosecution to crimes committed after the entry into force of the Rome Statute, has contributed to this phenomenon.
[131] See e.g. Kenneth A. Rodman, "Darfur and the Limits of Legal Deterrence," *Human Rights Quarterly*, 30, 3, August 2008.
[132] *AFP*, "Rwanda's Kagame says ICC Targeting Poor, African Countries," July 31, 2008; Rwanda Radio via BBC Monitoring, "Rwandan President Dismisses ICC as Court Meant to 'Undermine' Africa," August 1, 2008.
[133] See e.g. Oraib Al Rantawi, "A Step Forward or Backward?" *Bitter Lemons*, 32, 6, August 14, 2008.
[134] See e.g. Stephanie Hanson, "Africa and the International Criminal Court," *Council on Foreign Relations*, July 24, 2008.
[135] CRS interview with Office of the Prosecutor official, September 3, 2008.
[136] Michael Otim and Marieke Wierda, "Justice at Juba: International Obligations and Local Demands in Northern Uganda," in *Courting Conflict?* See also Tim Allen, Op. Cit. The Prosecutor is investigating alleged abuses by the Ugandan military. Observers agree, however, that alleged abuses by government troops are not equal in gravity to those reportedly committed by the LRA.
[137] Waddell and Clark, Op. Cit.
[138] Nick Grono and Adam O'Brien, "Justice in Conflict? The ICC and Peace Processes," in *Courting Conflict?*
[139] Akhavan, "The Lord's Resistance Army Case," Op. Cit.
[140] Quoted in Opheera McDoom, "Analysis: Justice Clashes With Peace on Darfur Bashir Warrant," *Reuters*, July 14, 2008.
[141] Transcript of Senate Committee on Armed Services hearing on "Current and Future Worldwide Threats to the National Security of the United States, provided by *CQ Transcriptions*, via Factiva, March 10, 2009.

[142] U.N. Security Council, Report of the Secretary-General on the deployment of the African Union-United Nations Hybrid Operation in Darfur, S/2008/558, August 18, 2008; UN News Service, "Ban-Aid Workers' Expulsion Impeding Peacekeeping, Relief Efforts," April 22, 2009.

[143] E.g., Caroline Flintoft [International Crisis Group], "Our Silence on Sudan Shames Us," *The Globe and Mail*, June 16, 2008; Sara Darehshori [Human Rights Watch], "Doing the Right Thing for Darfur: An ICC indictment of Sudan's president serves peace and justice," *The Los Angeles Times*, July 15, 2008.

[144] Priscilla Hayner, "Seeking Justice as War Crimes Rage On," *The Chicago Tribune*, July 16, 2008.

[145] Grono and O'Brien, Op. Cit.

INDEX

A

B

C

D

E

G

J

K

L

N

O

P

S

T

U

V

W

Y

Z